Building Jewish in the Roman East

Supplements
to the
Journal for the Study
of Judaism

Editor

John J. Collins

The Divinity School, Yale University

Associate Editor

Florentino García Martínez

Qumran Institute, University of Groningen

Advisory Board

J. DUHAIME — A. HILHORST — P.W. VAN DER HORST
A. KLOSTERGAARD PETERSEN — M.A. KNIBB — J.T.A.G.M. VAN RUITEN
J. SIEVERS — G. STEMBERGER — E.J.C. TIGCHELAAR — J. TROMP

VOLUME 92

Building Jewish
in the Roman East

PETER RICHARDSON

Baylor University Press
Waco, Texas 76798

Cover Design: Pam Poll
Book Design: Diane Smith

All photographs and drawings are by Peter Richardson, unless otherwise
credited. They may not be reproduced without permission.

The hardback version of this book is published by Brill as volume 92 of
Supplements to the Journal for the Study of Judaism. ISBN: 90 04 14131 6

Library of Congress Cataloging-in-Publication Data

Richardson, Peter, 1935-
  Building Jewish in the Roman East / Peter Richardson.
    p. cm.
  Includes bibliographical references and indexes.
  ISBN 90-04-14131-6 -- ISBN 1-932792-01-5 (pbk. : alk. paper)
  1. Synagogue architecture--Israel. 2. Synagogues--Israel. 3. Israel--
Antiquities. 4. Architecture and religion. 5. Rome--History--Empire, 30
B.C.-284 A.D. I. Title.

  NA4690.R53 2004
  722'.7'0933--dc22
                                        2004012382

Printed in the United States of America on acid-free paper

Mary Rebekah

Susan Elizabeth

Jonathan Peter

Ruth Anne

who have enriched our lives
and shared their children
so generously with us

CONTENTS

ACKNOWLEDGMENTS

The following publishers have graciously permitted use of previously published materials. There are deletions, a few additions, and changes in almost every sentence, but the arguments remain unchanged. Only rarely have I brought them up-to-date or indicated how my mind has changed.

Almqvist and Wiksell
"An Architectural Case for Synagogues as Associations," chapter 5 in *The Ancient Synagogue from Its Origins until 200 C.E.: Papers Presented at an International Conference at Lund University,* October 14–17, 2001. Edited by Birger Olsson and Magnus Zetterholm. Coniectanea Biblica NT series 39; Stockholm: Almqvist and Wiksell, 2003.

Altamira
"Jesus and Palestinian Social Protest: Archaeological and Literary Perspectives" (with Douglas Edwards), pp. 247–66 in *Handbook of Early Christianity: Social Science Approaches.* Edited by Anthony J. Blasi, Jean Duhaime and Paul-André Turcotte. Walnut Creek, Calif.: Altamira, 2002.

Archaeopress (BAR International)
"3 D Visualizations of a First-Century Galilean Town" (with Charles Hixon and Ann Spurling), pp. 195–204 in *Virtual Reality in Archaeology.* Edited by Juan Barceló, Maurizio Forte and Donald H. Sanders. BAR International Series 843; Oxford: Archaeopress, 2000.

E. J. Brill
"First-Century Houses and Q's Setting," pp. 63–83 in *Christology, Controversy and Community: New Testament Essays in Honour of David Catchpole.* Edited by David G. Horrell and Christopher M. Tuckett. Leiden: Brill, 2000.

Canadian Society of Biblical Studies
"Religion and Architecture: A Study of Herod's Piety, Power, Pomp and Pleasure," pp. 3–29 in *Bulletin of the Canadian Society of Biblical Studies* 45. Edited by David J. Hawkin, 1985.

Wm. B. Eerdmans
"Khirbet Cana (and Other Villages) as a Context for Jesus," in *Jesus and Archaeology*. Edited by James Charlesworth. Grand Rapids: Wm. B. Eerdmans, forthcoming.
and
"Augustan-era Synagogues in Rome?," pp. 17–29 in *Judaism and Christianity in First-Century Rome*. Edited by Karl P. Donfried and Peter Richardson. Grand Rapids: Wm. B. Eerdmans, 1998.

Hendrickson
"Building a *Synodos* . . . and a Place of Their Own," pp. 36–56 in *Models of Ministry: Community Formation in the New Testament, the Ante-Nicene Fathers, and the Church Today*. Edited by Richard N. Longenecker. Peabody: Hendrickson, 2002.

Routledge
"Jewish Voluntary Associations in Egypt and the Roles of Women" (with Valerie Heuchan), pp. 226–51, and "Early Synagogues as *Collegia* in the Diaspora and Palestine," pp. 90–109 in *Voluntary Associations in the Ancient World*. Edited by John S. Kloppenborg and Stephen G. Wilson. London: Routledge, 1996.

Sheffield Academic Press
"Philo and Eusebius on Monasteries and Monasticism: The Therapeutae and Kellia," pp. 334–59 in *Origins and Method: New Understandings of Judaism and Early Christianity. Essays in Honour of John C. Hurd, Jr.* Edited by Bradley McLean. Sheffield: Sheffield Academic Press, 1993.

Society for New Testament Studies
"What has Cana to do with Capernaum?," *New Testament Studies* 48 (2002): 314–31.

Society of Biblical Literature
"Why Turn the Tables? Jesus' Protest in the Temple Precincts," *SBL Seminar Paper*s 1992 (Atlanta: Scholars Press, 1992): 507–23.

Trinity Press International
"Architectural Transitions from Synagogues and House Churches to Purpose-Built Churches," pp. 373–89, in *Common Life in the Early Church: Essays in Honor of Graydon F. Snyder*. Edited by Julian V. Hills, in collaboration with Richard B. Gardner, Robert Jewett, Robert Neff, Peter Richardson, David M. Scholer, and Virginia Wiles. Valley Forge: Trinity Press International, 1998.

Wilfrid Laurier University Press (Waterloo)/Canadian Corporation for Studies in Religion
"Law and Piety in Herod's Architecture," pp. 347–60 in a special issue titled "Torah-Nomos," *Studies in Religion* 15.3 (1986).

ABBREVIATIONS

The conventions and abbreviations adopted throughout follow The *SBL Handbook of Style* (Peabody: Hendrickson, 1999), with the exception of citations of Josephus, for which I have used the more common abbreviations: *War*, *Antiquities* (*Ant.*), *Apion*, and *Life*. I repeat only a few of the more important abbreviations here and introduce a few new abbreviations for frequently cited works.

ABD	D. N. Freedman, gen. ed., *The Anchor Bible Dictionary*. New York: Doubleday, 1962.
ANRW	Hilda Temporini, et al., eds., *Aufstieg und Niedergang der römischen Welt*. Berlin: de Gruyter, 1972–.
Antiquities (*Ant.*)	Josephus, *Jewish Antiquities* (*Antiquitates Judaicae*). In Josephus, Loeb Classical Library; Cambridge, Mass.: Harvard University Press, 1930–1965.
Apion	Josephus, *Against Apion* (*Contra Apionem*). In Josephus, Loeb Classical Library; Cambridge, Mass.: Harvard University Press, 1926.
Aviam & Richardson, *Galilee*	Mordechai Aviam and Peter Richardson, "Josephus's Galilee in Archaeological Perspective." Pages 177–209, in *Josephus, Translation and Commentary*. Edited by Steve N. Mason; vol. 9, Appendix A; Leiden: Brill, 2001.
CH	Eusebius, *History of the Church*
CIJ	J.-B. Frey, *Corpus Inscriptionum Judaicarum* (1936–1952)
CIL	*Corpus Inscriptionum Latinarum* (Berlin, 1962–)
CPJ	Victor A. Tcherikover, ed., *Corpus Papyrorum Judaicarum*. 3 vols.; Cambridge, Mass.: Harvard University Press, 1957–1964.
City and Sanctuary	Peter Richardson, *City and Sanctuary: Religion and Architecture in the Roman Near East*. London: SCM, 2002.
Donfried & Richardson, *Rome*	Karl Donfried and Peter Richardson, editors, *Judaism and Christiantity in Rome*. Grand Rapids: Wm. B. Eerdmans, 1998.

EncJud	*Encyclopedia Judaica* (Jerusalem: Keter, 1972)
Eusebius	Eusebius, *History of the Church*. Harmondsworth: Penguin, 1965; K. Lake and J. E. L. Oulton, *Eusebius Ecclesiastical History*. Loeb Classical Library, 2 vols.; Cambridge, Mass: Harvard University Press, 1932 [1926].
Finegan, *Archeology*	Jack Finegan, *Archeology of the New Testament*. Princeton: Princeton University Press, rev. 1992.
Herod	Peter Richardson, *Herod, King of the Jews and Friend of the Romans*. Columbia: University of South Carolina Press, 1996; Minneapolis: Fortress Press, 1999; Edinburgh: T&T Clark, 1999.
IAA	Israel Antiquities Authority
ILS	Dessau, H. *Inscriptiones Latinae Selectae*, Dublin: Apud Weidmannos, 1974 [1892].
Life	Josephus, *Life* (*Vita*). In Josephus, Loeb Classical Library; Cambridge, Mass.: Harvard University Press, 1926.
LSJ	H. G. Liddell, R. Scott, and H. S. Jones, *A Greek-English Lexicon: A New Edition*. Oxford: Clarendon, 1940.
McCane, *Roll Back the Stone*	Byron R. McCane, *Roll Back the Stone: Death and Burial in the World of Jesus*. Harrisburg: Trinity Press International, 2003.
NEAEHL	E. Stern, ed., *New Encyclopedia of Archaeological Excavations of the Holy Land*. Jerusalem: Israel Exploration Society, 1993.
OGIS	W. Dittenberger, *Orientis Graeci Inscriptiones Selectae*. Leipzig: Hirzel, 1903–1905.
Rahmani, *Catalogue*	L. Y. Rahmani, *A Catalogue of Jewish Ossuaries in the Collections of the State of Israel*. Jerusalem: Israel Antiquities Authority/Israel Academy of Sciences and Humanities, 1994.
Sanders, *Judaism*	E. P. Sanders, *Judaism: Practice and Belief: 63 B.C.E.-66 C.E.* Philadelphia: Trinity Press International, 1992.
Schürer	Emil Schürer et al., *The History of the Jewish People in the Age of Jesus Christ (175 B.C.–A.D. 135)*. 3 vols. Edinburgh: T&T Clark, 1973–1987.
SEG	*Supplementum Epigraphicum Graecum*. 1923–.
Text and Artifact	Stephen G. Wilson and Michel Desjardins, eds., *Text and Artifact in the Religions of Mediterranean Antiquity: Essays in Honour of Peter Richardson*. Waterloo: Wilfrid Laurier University Press, 2000.

Urman & Flesher, *Synagogues*	Dan Urman and Paul V. M. Flesher, *Ancient Synagogues: Historical Analysis and Archaeological Discovery*. 2 vols. SPB 47; Leiden: Brill, 1995.
Voluntary Associations	John Kloppenborg and Stephen G. Wilson, eds., *Voluntary Associations in the Graeco-Roman World*. London: Routledge, 1996.
War	Josephus, *Jewish War* (*Bellum Judaicum*). In Josephus, Loeb Classical Library; Cambridge, Mass.: Harvard University Press, 1927–1928.
White, *Social Origins*	L. Michael White, *The Social Origins of Christian Architecture*. 2 vols. Valley Forge: Trinity Press International, 1996, 1997.

LIST OF TABLES AND ILLUSTRATIONS

TABLES

FIGURES

PLATES

PREFACE

This book derives from a growing familiarity with the archaeology of the Middle East, my early training in architecture, convictions about the importance of religion and architecture to the study of antiquity, and an interest in linking archaeological and literary data. The studies in this volume, some previously published and some unpublished, cover wide geographical and chronological ranges. They are, however, united by several convictions: (a) religion and architecture are symbiotically related and mutually informative; (b) archaeology and literature offer complementary insights into antiquity; (c) archaeology can pose questions and prompt answers that the literature sometimes cannot; (d) literary texts can sometimes answer questions that the uncertainties of archaeological practice cannot. The book shows the strains of listening to both voices.

Part I derives from archaeological work as site architect in the Galilee, where I have worked with two splendid teams of archaeologists: at Yodefat, with Mordechai Aviam, Dina Avshalom-Gorni, Donald Ariel, and William Scott Green; at Khirbet Qana, with Douglas Edwards, Alysia Fischer, Douglas Oakman, and Jack Olive. Part II centers on my interest in synagogue origins and architecture. I am especially grateful to Birger Olsson, Dieter Mitternacht, Anders Runesson, and Magnus Zetterholm, who directed a symposium at Lund, Sweden, in the fall of 2001, and to Lee I. Levine, who was the center of the discussion. Part III has benefited from many friendships, among them my shared interests with Aaro Söderlund deserve pride of place, but the thanks includes Hanan Eshel, Steve Mason, Byron McCane, Jerome Murphy-O'Connor, and Ehud Netzer.

I have dispensed with a full bibliography, since the literature cited is extensive and diverse. Specific debts are acknowledged in full footnote citations, and indexes provide access to that information. I have provided suggestions for further reading, organized under the three main subdivisions of the book with appropriate subdivisions, which provide references to recent literature. I have also included a glossary to assist with some technical terms that are difficult to avoid. The list of abbreviations presupposes familiarity with the usual conventions of biblical scholarship, as outlined in *The SBL Handbook of Style* (Peabody: Hendrickson, 1999).

I owe special thanks to some graduate and undergraduate students at the University of Toronto who have participated in a work-study program (funded jointly by the Government of Ontario and the University of Toronto), aimed at increasing their skills in the job market. They were to learn editorial and research skills by assisting me in integrating diverse materials—in format, conventions, and style—into a coherent whole. They eliminated redundancies and overlaps, removed inconsistencies, and stripped away a good bit of extraneous notation. They helped order the essays logically and make transitions from one to the other. I am indebted especially to Jennifer Cianca, Maureen Conley, Tymen deVries (who also prepared the indexes), Debby Donnelly, Jonathan Ferguson, Alana Foley, Scott Halse, Mona Tokarek LaFosse, Geocelyne Meyers, Eileen Morrison, and Melissa Prado.

I am grateful to Baylor University Press and especially to its director, Carey Newman, for enthusiasm for the book and for very helpful advice on improvements to it; I am equally indebted to Diane Smith for ongoing assistance in the production stages.

Nancy has been my constant companion in travels associated with this work; she takes the same pleasure as I in the riches of the Middle East. Her patience exerts a calming influence. She has a defter touch than I in dealing with children, shopkeepers, hotel owners, bus drivers, and tourist guides; and she keeps in constant touch with children and grandchildren at home when we are away, reducing the sense of absentee parents. The book is as much a tribute to Nancy as to our children, Mary, Susan, Jonathan, and Ruth, to whom it is gratefully dedicated.

Peter Richardson
Toronto, November 2003

PART ONE

INTRODUCTION

CHAPTER ONE

RELIGION AND ARCHITECTURE
IN THE EASTERN MEDITERRANEAN

While the connections between religion and architecture are often noted, much of the interest in the two together has been either in the aesthetics or in the history of the development of religious buildings. Interest in buildings within specific religious contexts, particularly buildings within a Jewish context, is less common. This book juxtaposes the study of religion and of architecture to examine the ways architecture impinges on the practice of religion and religion on the practice of architecture. Since I deal with material two millennia before the present, such a study must be either theoretical, something I have little interest in pursuing, or deeply rooted in archaeological excavations of the ancient world.

The modern discipline of archaeology informs this book directly, though I do not write as an archaeologist, but as a scholar of religion. To my longstanding interest in texts I add an even longer-standing interest in architecture, having practiced architecture before turning to religious studies. So this book is concerned with the intersection between religion and architecture and the intersection between archaeology and texts.[1] I weave into this my interests in late Hellenism, Roman Imperialism, Second Temple Judaism, and early Christianity.

LATE HELLENISM, ROMAN IMPERIALISM, SECOND TEMPLE JUDAISM, AND EARLY CHRISTIANITY

It is almost impossible to exaggerate the complexity of the late Hellenistic world in the eastern end of the Mediterranean in the first centuries B.C.E. and C.E., the period on which this book focuses. On the one hand, Greek culture, religion, and institutions, as those were refracted by the conquests of Alexander the Great and his successors,

3

had deeply influenced the cultural norms of the region, especially among the elites. At the same time as these influences continued to be felt, Rome continued its almost inexorable progress eastwards to assume political control of all the lands bordering the Mediterranean, encouraging the adoption of that curious blend of Roman and Greek religion and culture, especially the form developed from 27 B.C.E. onwards that we think of as Roman Imperialism.[2] Both late Hellenism and Roman Imperialism encouraged a more unified view of the Mediterranean world than had generally characterized other cultures and periods, with more trade, travel, and international contacts. One result of the increased opportunities for contacts across previous boundaries was the establishment of numerous "Diaspora" communities of more or less ethnically coherent groups of dislocated peoples— dislocated mainly by choice—in large metropolises. No Diaspora group was more visible than the groups of Jews who by circumstance or choice had settled in various places around the Mediterranean.

Homelands were of abiding significance for Diasporas. Most Jews continued to feel a strong attachment to Judea, Judaism's center and the place where its major institutions dominated the landscape until the time of the First Jewish Revolt (66–74 C.E.), which resulted in the destruction of the Second Temple in 70 C.E. The vibrancy of Judaism continued to be felt even after the consequences of this revolt and a Second Revolt (132–135 C.E.), together with a series of Diaspora Revolts (115–117 C.E.) in such places as Mesopotamia, Cyprus, Egypt, and Cyrenaica. The homelands of other ethnic groups were also affected by similar feelings of nationalistic fervor, which resulted in other revolts against Rome at about the same time as the Jewish Revolts: Germans, Illyrians, Pannonians, Thracians, Batavians, and Britons. Commitment to indigenous religions continued to be strong, even though indigenous religions lived alongside imported Greek and Roman religious influences and commitments. Palmyrene, Nabatean, Samaritan, and Egyptian religions, like Jewish religion, continued vigorously at the very same time as Greek and Roman religions were being encouraged and voluntarily adopted. To make matters more complex, within this matrix and during this period, new religions or new articulations of old religions developed that began to attract considerable attention. The worship of Jesus the Messiah (Christ) from Galilee, Mithra from Persia, Isis from Egypt, and Cybele from Phrygia, became prominent and gained numerous adherents, altering the ways in which both indigenous and imported religions were viewed and supported.

One of the legacies of the late Hellenistic period in the Levant, as elsewhere in the eastern Mediterranean, was a widespread distribution of impressive and architecturally sophisticated structures that expressed clearly the dynamic architectural, urban, and spatial program of the period. This legacy continued even after Roman influence began to be felt, and it is impossible to draw a sharp line between the two, since, of course, Rome drew extensively on Greek and Hellenistic influences in its own architectural developments. To appreciate the general point, it is sufficient to refer to cities such as Gerasa, Palmyra, Baalbek, Antioch, Damascus, and Petra in the Levant, or to cities such as Rhodes, Lindos, Ephesus, Miletus, Priene, and Pergamon in the Greek East. There is an almost seamless architectural transition from late Hellenism to Roman Imperialism; in some cases, late Hellenistic styles of building continue into the early Roman period. Individual monuments still startle: the Khasneh in Petra, Zeus in Gerasa, Bel in Palmyra, Athena in Lindos, Apollo in Didyma, and the Asklepieion at Pergamon are representative of a much longer list.

Late Hellenistic works led the way in a program of urban development and renewal that continued in the early Roman period in many of the same cities, resulting in structures bent more deliberately to promote a Roman program of urban sophistication and excitement. Roman ideals and standards for the articulation of space show up in the widespread adoption of a colonnaded main street (*cardo maximus*) in Petra, Gerasa, Apamea, Palmyra, Damascus, and Antioch—where the development began—and such a feature illustrates well the merging of eastern and Roman aesthetics and functions. But Roman approaches showed even more directly in the widespread distribution of baths, nymphaea (public fountains), hippodromes, amphitheaters, and theaters. It showed especially in structures for the Imperial cult, a distinctive form of the Roman Imperial period. Not all of these building types were uniformly widespread; for example, the Near East was more restrained in promoting the Imperial cult than the Greek East in Ionia. There were important temples to Roma and Augustus in Caesarea Maritima, Sebaste, and Panias (all built by the Romanophile, Herod the Great), but none of any substance in the cities of the Decapolis, Petra, Palmyra (where there was a modest Caesareum), or Damascus.[3] The liveliness of indigenous religion seems to have acted as a brake on the spread and distribution of the worship of the emperor, so Herod's promotion of the Imperial cult makes his building program distinctive in the eastern Mediterranean, more like the province of Asia than the surrounding provinces.

Mention of Herod introduces Part 4. Herod was a Jew who, though observant, practiced his Judaism in a relatively liberal way.[4] Spanning late Hellenism and early Roman Imperialism, Herod was a major architectural patron whose benefactions and building projects decisively altered the region, not just Judea but the surrounding areas, as well as parts of Asia, the Aegean Islands, and Greece. His role was seminal. In his projects we find an intricate blending of late Hellenistic aesthetic ideals with Roman building programs and Roman technology. Nowhere else in the Mediterranean world outside Rome was there such a powerful and important patron with such a longstanding and influential interest in building. He was among the most significant architectural patrons of his immediate period and perhaps the most exciting architectural patron of the ancient world. To mention a few examples: he built the first colonnaded main street in Antioch-on-Orontes; he built three Temples to Roma and Augustus in his own territories, he donated theaters, gymnasia, baths, and marketplaces to nearby cities; he was responsible for public buildings in the new city of Nicopolis; he created whole new cities, such as Caesarea Maritima; and he thoroughly reconstituted the center of Judaism in Jerusalem.

Herod's projects were mainly buildings for Jewish elites. Alongside elite buildings there were other forms of Jewish building, however. This book concentrates on two of these, buildings of ordinary Jewish villages and buildings for Jewish worship. Knowledge of villages and small towns in the Galilee has been increasing exponentially because archaeological projects have focused on the ordinary life of rural and agrarian peasants. This move beyond a "great monuments" approach to antiquity has exposed the structures, activities, and life of ordinary Jews.[5] The two major test cases in Part 2 of this book are Yodefat (Jotapata) (Plate 3), a small fortified town that was destroyed in 67 C.E. because of its resistance to Roman reconquest of Judea, and Cana (Khirbet Qana) (Plate 4), a small unfortified village about two kilometers away, that became an important stop on the itinerary of Christian pilgrims in the Byzantine period because of its association with Jesus. Alongside these, towns such as Gamla (Plate 1) and Capernaum figure in the discussion, because they situate first-century Jews (and Jesus) within their natural Jewish context.

Interest in Jewish synagogues—both in the homeland and the Diaspora—has also increased exponentially. Strong contrasting positions have developed, with little consensus on major scholarly issues. My interest in Part 3 is primarily in the origins of synagogue buildings; my position is one among several competitors, though I should like to think it is an opinion that has been gathering strength.[6] I am convinced that synagogue buildings developed first in the Diaspora, probably in Egypt; the model for its development was the association (*collegium, thiasos, koinon*). A secondary interest has been the connection between the architectural development of buildings for Jewish and for Christian communities, which has drawn me into a discussion of early churches and early monasteries in a preliminary way. My continuing interest in Christian origins thus finds expression tangentially in this book. Christianity initially developed within a Jewish matrix, so its setting in Jewish villages was a fundamental aspect of its practices and institutions. When churches began to be built, they adopted and adapted Jewish models—and more broadly other models from the surrounding Roman world—seen most clearly in the use of "house churches" in the earliest phase, parallel to the early adoption of "house synagogues" among a number of Diaspora communities of Jews.[7] Even the development of the basilican-style church and the creation of monastic communities had earlier Jewish parallels or analogies. So the fruits of Jewish building practices continued to be garnered among Christian communities from the second century onward.

In the following three parts of this book, the self-conscious expression of Judaism in material forms—through synagogues, the activity of Herod the Great, and the natural expression of Jewish social organization and religious activities in small towns and villages—represents the primary data. I include a wide range of Jewish building activities, for religion informs all these diverse activities. When looking at the material products of Judaism, various *realia* need to be included: stoneware, pottery, ossuaries, and tombs from daily life; the various forms that expressed Judaism's communal life in Diaspora synagogues; villages, towns, and new suburbs in major cities; and the massive rebuilding projects of important patrons such as Herod the Great.

Texts and Artifacts

The study of antiquity relies fundamentally on two kinds of evidence, texts and archaeological investigations. Each supplements the other; neither suffices alone. Reconstruction of the past is most secure when the evidence from both coheres; historical reconstructions are most debatable when one or other kind of evidence is absent or ignored.[8] A simple illustration makes the point. One of the most suggestive bits of literary information about Herod the Great is the comment, put in Augustus's mouth at a dinner party, that he would rather be Herod's pig than his son.[9] This is from a fourth-century report that is so late that on ordinary grounds it would have little claim to reliability. It makes a point about Herod—that he observed Jewish prohibitions against pork—that might hardly be thought current in Rome. The report is widely doubted and could be wrong, but it raises an important question: Was Herod religiously observant? Material evidence from Herod's buildings has accumulated to the point where two elements of his observance can be noted with some degree of certainty. On the one hand, none of his private buildings in Judea had decorations that offended against torah. On the other hand, these same buildings had *mikvaoth*, Jewish ritual bathing pools. It is possible to argue convincingly now that Herod was religiously observant, at least in Judea and to a considerable extent in the Diaspora. It is not improbable that Augustus knew of Herod's kosher food observance, for his buildings testify both to cultic and torah observance.

An exciting aspect of keeping both texts and material evidence in the forefront is that it leads to fresh kinds of questions and new approaches to resolving old questions. Several chapters in the following exemplify some of these varied approaches. In Part 2, the cross-fertilization between an analysis of the Q source and the results of investigations into Jewish village life permit approaching a text from relevant excavations. In Part 3, the literary use that Eusebius makes of Philo sheds light on the connections between Jewish and Christian building practices, especially the building of monastic buildings, working from a literary text to an architectural problem. In Part 4, the use of archaeological information bears upon the literary problem of Josephus's sources, particularly his use of Nicolas of Damascus (an important person within Herod's entourage). Though methodology is not prominent in the following pages, substantial methodological questions are at issue.

Many works of ancient authors demonstrate that they shared similar concerns. On the Roman side, Strabo (ca. 58 B.C.E.–25 C.E.), whose interests ran more to the ethnographic and anthropological than to the architectural, helps in reconstructing the character of ancient cultures. His *Geography* often mentions cities and occasionally individual buildings in ways that resonate with the archaeological evidence that has emerged. Pliny the Elder (23–79 C.E.) was mainly interested in natural history, and he is a mine of information about such material developments as glass-making, building materials, decorative elements for sculpture, mosaics, and the like (*Natural History*). On directly architectural topics, none is as important as Vitruvius (late first century B.C.E.), whose *On Architecture* was penned under Augustus's patronage; he describes issues such as climate, site development, and urban design; materials and methods of construction; differentiations among building types; details of acoustics, hydraulics, machines, and even military equipment. And one can hardly ignore Pausanias (fl. about 150 C.E.), whose *Description of Greece* includes detailed descriptions of numerous ancient cities that permit surer identification of buildings and monuments than might otherwise be possible. There are, of course, numerous others who have important asides on material culture, but these suffice to make the point that literary texts and material culture fit together.

In antiquity a distinction between literary texts—for these were all literary works, sometimes of considerable rhetorical force—and material culture was hardly sharp. In developing their accounts of Greek and Roman culture these authors utilized the material world around them as an essential element. On the Jewish side, there is less. Josephus, the most famous Jewish historian of antiquity, had strong interests in his built environment. Some of this interest was no doubt taken over from Nicolas, whose works have survived only in small fragments. But some of it was his own, as in his descriptions in *War* of his construction of village defenses. Regrettably, the *Memoirs* of Herod, which Josephus says he used, have been totally lost; it is unclear how much Josephus drew on them. They would have told us much of what we might wish to know in interpreting the archaeological remains of Herod's buildings, and who his architect was, if he had one. Philo was inclined to philosophy and theology, so his major contribution for our purposes was his description of the Therapeutae and their monastic life. The *Mishnah* is sometimes interested in material things, such as its accounts of baths, sculpture, and images, and no study of first-century Judaism can ignore it. In connection with the Jerusalem temple, we have to fall back on descriptions in Ezekiel, 11QT, Philo, Josephus, and the *Mishnah*.

Most of these points of intersection between material culture and texts are mutually reinforcing. They do not always speak with one voice, one does not necessarily prove the other, but the combination of two kinds of evidence leads to reconstructions that are surer and more confident in knowing how things worked in antiquity. Reliance on one kind of evidence leaves the observer open to the biases or limitations of ancient authors on the one hand, or inadequate and misleading generalizations from the less than complete archaeological evidence on the other.

Religion and Architecture

Religion and architecture are the central points of my intellectual interests. Trips to the American east coast as a university student first exposed me to the profoundly satisfying conjunction of religion and architecture, though that interest may have been piqued as a high school student when I worshiped on an Easter Sunday in the Bruton Parish Church in Williamsburg. Influential in my architectural education were Eero Saarinen's MIT chapel in Cambridge, Mass., the three chapels that formed a single project by Max Abramovitz at Brandeis University in Waltham, Mass., and the synagogue by Philip Johnson in Port Chester, Conn. These were all mid-twentieth century projects with a sense of excitement about the fruitful juxtaposition of religion and architecture. When in 1956–1957 I needed to propose a design thesis that would integrate the work of our fifth and final year in architecture, I borrowed a project for a Presbyterian congregation in a suburb north of Toronto. Thornhill still functioned then as a real town, before being swallowed up in the megalopolis that Toronto has since become. The deepest influence on me that year was Marcel Breuer's imaginative—almost brutalist—project for a monastery church at St. John's College, Collegeville, Minn. I knew it only from photos, and only saw the completed project 45 years later. It was even more dramatic and satisfying than I had visualized it. It had stood the test of time and had been appreciated so much by its users that it was still in nearly pristine condition.

After graduation I traveled widely in Latin America. I now appreciate more fully the juxtaposition of important archaeological sites and
modern architectural projects. Many of the religious buildings have
stuck with me. San Juan Teotihuacán—the vast Aztec center with its
great Pyramid to the Sun, Pyramid to the Moon, and Sacrificial
Court—bowled me over by its immense scale and capacity to evoke
the culture and religious activities of an ancient people. It was the
first true archaeological site that I ever visited. In Mexico City I visited several startling projects of Felix Candela, the creative Mexican
engineer whose deft touch resulted in architectural expressions that
few architects could, at the time, emulate. His hyperbolic paraboloids
created a sense of mystery and exaltation similar to that of Gothic
cathedrals. Their strong visual and emotional effect on me is still
almost palpable.

I visited Machu Picchu, the Inca town of Vilcabamba, rediscovered
in 1911 by Hiram Bingham and subsequently excavated. Its exotic reputation was based on the way it seemed to hang in the clouds above the
Urubamba River. What was most instructive, however, was that it was
not very exotic at all. Machu Picchu was a real town, whose houses
tumbled down the steep slopes within the urban confines, whose aqueducts could be traced, whose main religious site was a rather modest
affair on one of the higher points of the town, clearly understandable
as a cultic area. Public areas, children's play areas, and communal
buildings were all clearly visible even to an unpracticed eye. The
"Hitching Post of the Sun" (Intihuatana) had nothing like the over-
powering scale of San Juan Teotihuacán, yet it spoke just as strongly of
communal worship and even more clearly of piety in the service of
Inca gods. Back in Cuzco, the Spanish colonial town founded on Inca
ruins, the early colonial churches—dark, mysterious, emotional, and
non-rational—struck me as a poor second to the richness of the Inca
religious experience. But I was still very deeply enmeshed in
Presbyterian Puritanism at the time.

On the arid Peruvian coastline, I walked through a largely unexcavated pre-Inca site whose enormous burial ground showed not traces
but hundreds or thousands of burials. Bones, tatters of cloth, and grave
goods lay on the surface. Two large pyramids, the street layout, and the
site's social organization were still visible. I had become interested in
ancient architecture, though on reflection the two most persistent
impacts were the integration of religion into the urban fabric, and

dismay at the depredations of looters. A week later, in Brazil, I saw structures by two other architectural heroes, Oscar Niemeyer and Lúcio Costa. Some of their work was strongly rationalistic in an International Style idiom, which I found enormously attractive. Other work of the same architects had an emotional element, reflecting organic forms and flowing curves, that despite my rationalistic impulses I found satisfying and evocative. While I did not want to reproduce this in my own work, I found it surprisingly attractive.

My professional architectural career began in the design department of Canada's premier expositor of the International Style, John B. Parkin Associates, which meant working in the idiom of Mies van der Rohe. In the interstices between designing schools, factories, an occasional house, and other utilitarian projects, I was involved in two buildings for Christian worship: an addition to a downtown church that included a chapel, gymnasium, bowling alleys, and meeting rooms; and a new sanctuary with related rooms to be added to a suburban church, where the original sanctuary was to be adapted for reuse for Christian education. Both projects required rethinking everything I thought I knew about expressing religious "feeling" and creating a sense of "community" for a group of worshipers. The demands were different from each other and the solutions were also very different. To my surprise, both solutions broke out of the firm's long-standing commitment to Miesian rationalism. Drawing on my Latin American experiences, I found myself more open to emotion in architecture and to the varied ways it might be expressed and served.

When I returned to university to study theology I was unsure if I wanted to be a theologian, but I did want to develop a theological approach to life and to architecture. My enthusiasm for early Christianity, Judaism, and architecture belong to this period in the early 1960s. These new interests led to leaving architecture behind and developing expertise in Christian origins. Consistent with the time and the persons who influenced me, especially my supervisor at Cambridge, C. F. D. Moule, I was text-oriented. This focus gradually but fundamentally altered, beginning with my first visits to Israel and Greece. Prolonged visits to Greece and the Holy Land stunned me, in part because I realized that an architectural background assisted in "reading" sites with more acuity and understanding than many nonarchaeological biblical scholars had. I was working on a commentary on 1 Corinthians and was excited by Corinth's ability to shed light on the text, though I soon gave up the commentary project. I fell in love with the cultural worlds in which early Christianity was set, leading inexorably in the present direction.

It is clearer to me now that religion was deeply entrenched in the architectural realities of the ancient world and that architecture was essential in expressing the religious realities of the ancient world. The two played off each other, both in large and small scale. Religious convictions and expressions were deeply interwoven in the fabric of small villages such as Machu Picchu or Cana, just as they were woven into the urban fabric of large cities such as Mexico City or Corinth. Tracking some of the impact of religion and architecture on each other has dominated the last decade or two of my work.

Since religion and architecture are two significant expressions of culture—ways society expresses itself publicly and visibly, rationally and emotionally—it stands to reason that their intersection may provide a reliable, or at least a helpful, guide to understanding society. There is no one way to appreciate connections between religion and architecture: any number of lenses will do. Here I use three lenses: a major patron expressing his understanding of his religion and his society at an elite level; a building type, the synagogue, exemplifying multivariant expressions in different cultural and historical circumstances; and a form of social expression, the small village, with a more or less coherent population, expressing its convictions about life and values.

There are variations on a theme in *Building Jewish*. Or to shift from a musical to a literary metaphor, it might be considered postmodern (as one reviewer called my biographical study, *Herod*). I explore the diverse streams of Judaism at the root of its complexity: temple and synagogue, homeland and Diaspora, Judea and Galilee, elite and peasant, living and dead, observant and unobservant, male and female, recluse and social butterfly. Jews built wherever they lived. Investigations of their building practices should shed light on the realties of their social situation, their religious convictions, their hopes and aspirations. These investigations begin to show what held Jews together in the period just before and just after the destruction of Jerusalem and its temple. Herod, despite his wealth and power and opportunities, was not as far removed in certain respects from the humble resident of Yodefat as one might expect. And the worshiping Jew in a Diaspora city such as Ostia (Plate 34) or Priene (Plate 31) had much in common with fellow Jews in Gamla (Plate 25) or Capernaum. Homogenization of all these into a single "Jew" of the first century is wrong; Judaism was expressed in multivariant forms that found clear expression in the various Jewish worlds of the early Roman period. Yet at the same time there was commonality in the religious convictions about the nature of God and the place of his people in the world.

PART TWO

TOWNS AND VILLAGES

CHAPTER TWO

JESUS AND PALESTINIAN SOCIAL PROTEST IN ARCHAEOLOGICAL AND LITERARY PRESPECTIVE

INTRODUCTION[1]

Jesus and Palestinian social protest should be viewed, in socio-histori-cal terms, as a subordinate issue to two more general questions: (1) how closely Palestinian social protest corresponded with other protest move-ments within the Mediterranean world; and (2) whether Jesus' move-ment corresponded with protest movements before and after his period of activity. To put the question differently, was Jesus' movement related to an extreme form of social protest—social banditry, as this arose within a Palestinian setting—and was Palestinian banditry consonant with broader Mediterranean banditry? This chapter considers theoret-ical issues, archaeological evidence, the Mediterranean world, Syria-Palestine, and finally the Jesus movement.

SOCIAL PROTEST AS A MODERN CATEGORY AND ITS APPLICATION TO ANCIENT SOCIETIES

Social protest takes many forms in ancient and modern societies, social banditry and outright revolt being the most extreme examples. Resistance might occur against an outside power such as the Romans in Palestine or against local elites who were perceived to be associated with that power (e.g., the Herodians) or even other groups who were ethnically different or who had different religious and cultural perspec-tives. Many discussions of banditry argue that the political-economic environment created social protest and banditry. An ardent proponent of this view, Richard Horsley, acknowledges the role of culture in peo-ple's responses but generally interprets culture by means of a dispro-portionate economic system set up by imperialistic powers and their retainers. Banditry in Galilee and elsewhere was caused by acute economic pressure on villagers resulting in social disintegration.[2] This reductionist approach, while not without merit, misses the complexity of social protest as it existed in first-century Palestine. Current anthropological studies suggest that forms of social protest or resistance used subtle as well as overt acts to convey their point. Often the protest was intended not so much for those in power, who often are kept out of the loop, but rather for those who felt outside the realm of real power decision-making. Patterns found in Palestine were found throughout the Roman Empire during the same period.

Resistance by conquered persons has become central in many modern studies of colonialism,[3] with great variety in forms of protest against foreign control. One common form was the re-creation or reclamation of traditional culture, even when moribund for some time. Other common forms of protest included work slowdowns, poor workmanship, arriving late, and creating stories or songs uncomplimentary to those in power.[4] But forms of protest could extend further: using a language different from those in power, dressing in a manner that stressed allegiance to one's own group, use of particular forms of pottery or artifacts or textiles, and emphasis on one's religion and tradition. Such forms of protest were directed against powers that dictated other important aspects of people's lives.

Archaeologically, there is good evidence that the private worlds of Jews offered an outlook different from the public presentation. These private worlds represented means by which they established their identity and at the same time offered a form of protest to Roman power, even if they were the only ones who acknowledged it. Two examples represent extreme forms of protest or resistance promoting outright revolt. The better known is the siege of Yodefat (Chapter 3); Josephus describes at length the struggle between Romans and Jews in the summer of 67 C.E.[5] The town, according to Josephus and now supported by archaeological evidence, was totally destroyed, most of the inhabitants killed or enslaved, and Josephus captured. Its destruction represented the commitment of many to outright rebellion against the outside power. In the same war, Gamla, another Jewish village, also revolted against Rome. It met the same end. Both sites (with Jerusalem and other places that revolted) also show subtler forms of resistance or protest prior to their revolt. Similar features are present at other sites that were not destroyed, a point discussed below.

The second example is Qumran, where an apocalyptically oriented community believed it was participating in the end times. Recent work has shown that many of the references to the *kittim*, the enemy against which the community and God would battle, referred to the Romans. Qumran provides another example of overt hostility against Roman power, an extreme form of social protest, probably reserved for those in the community or those affiliated with it.

Archaeology has other examples of subtler forms of social protest or resistance. Hellenistic and Roman coins typically had images of gods, temples, or political leaders. This tradition was not part of the Hasmonean expression of authority, as they assiduously avoided images of any sort on their coins (except for the occasional palm tree or stalk of wheat). In the first century C.E., Herod Philip, son of Herod the Great, had little difficulty placing images on his coins in Gaulanitis. But Herod Antipas of Galilee, whose territory was more extensively Jewish, had no images on his coins. This expression of Jewish identity stood in sharp contrast to general practice throughout the Roman Empire. Did this stress Jewish identity? Without question. Understood within the general cultural framework of Roman power, it was a form of resistance against the pressures of Roman power. Archaeology has also shown that in several sites in Galilee (e.g., Yodefat and Khirbet Qana) and Gaulanitis (Gamla), the vast majority of coins found in first-century contexts are Hasmonean (mostly Alexander Jannaeus). If, as some have suggested, Hasmonean coins constituted a major part of the local economy, then we have evidence of the reclamation of a tradition—when Israel was ruled by its own Jewish kings—and of a form of resistance or social protest. (The coin distribution is different in the more Gentile regions just to the north of lower Galilee.)

Mikvaoth were another form of Jewish identity found in archaeological contexts. The usual, probably correct, interpretation is that these were expressly for Jewish ritual bathing purposes, although diverse functions cannot be ruled out. They were found in Judea and Galilee in Jewish contexts, uniquely associated with Jews. Was this resistance or social protest or simply an architectural feature that only Jews and no one else liked? A minimalist view might argue the latter, but the framework of power in which these features are now found needs to be understood. Baths were not normally built this way; for Jews this was the way one washed ritually. Herod had them. Priests' houses in Jerusalem had them. Towns such as Gamla, Yodefat, Khirbet Qana, and Nazareth had them, and cities such as Sepphoris and Jerusalem had them. They appeared as early as the Hasmonean period (e.g., Jericho) and seem to have had the force of tradition behind them. Whether Herod's and the Qumran community's use of *mikvaoth* were attempts to reemphasize Hasmonean traditions is unclear, but it is likely that they were expressions of proper Jewish tradition. Were they forms of social protest? The Qumran example was likely based on the community's attitude towards the Romans, as expressed in their literature; similarly the Galilean examples showed Jewish identity and represented a form of resistance to the general culture. Priests' houses in Jerusalem and Herodian structures suggest that even the elite did not give in completely to prevailing external cultures.

Stone vessels that appear only in Jewish contexts correspond with this interpretation. Many scholars interpret them as having ritual importance, since the *Mishnah* indicates that stoneware does not contract ritual impurity. One form of protest was to have one's own unique vessels, and the many examples of stoneware fit that general tendency. No doubt some would have used these vessels without a thought to their representing a protest against Rome or the general culture; they might even have appreciated Roman rule for many things. Nevertheless, they were participating in an expression of resistance whether they personally acknowledged it or not. Andrea Berlin has shown in a provocative study that at Gamla, as compared with adjacent towns in more thoroughly Gentile territory, there was a marked change in the first-century C.E. use of ceramics.[6] Prior to this period, Gamla's Jewish inhabitants ate off red-slipped plates and bowls, which were imported from Gentile coastal cities. Ceramic trade flowed in both directions and there was no sharp distinction in dining habits. A dramatic change occurred during the reigns of Antipas and Philip. Ceramic trade became one-directional. Kfar Hananiah pottery appeared in Gentile towns (Tel Anafa, Caesarea Philippi) but Gentile ceramics were no longer imported; people now ate from locally or regionally made cooking pots. Gentile sites still received ceramics from Jewish manufacturers in the Galilee, while Jews stopped using Gentile-made material and adopted eating habits that contrasted both with Gentile habits and their own previous practices. Berlin argues that a cultural line in the sand was drawn; when Jews crossed it they entered another world. This is a clear example of subtle social protest, to which we might add the absence of pig bones in Jewish sites. The prohibition against pork was taken seriously, and was viewed as a symbol of one's identity. Circumcision functioned similarly. Together with *mikvaoth*, Hasmonean coins, stone vessels, special ceramic vessels, and lack of pig bones, there were vigorous efforts to establish a special identity against powerful cultural influences.

Another aspect, important for understanding the environment of the Jesus movement, should be mentioned. The Dead Sea Scrolls are replete with examples of community traditions used to address issues of authority, power, and the community's relationship to the current authorities. The communal attitude toward the *kittim* has already been mentioned. Tradition—or better, reclaimed tradition—allowed the community to protest the nature of the powers of this world (especially Roman power but also illegitimate powers in Jerusalem). Their apocalyptic worldview, perhaps the ultimate in social protest (at least literarily), shows where true power lay: not with the Romans or the culture they promoted but with God who worked through his community that adhered to strict laws of righteousness.

The Romans understood some of these forms of resistance; overt ones were obvious, but even some of the less obvious were noted. They understood the power of religion as a form of protest and a real problem if not dealt with properly. They walked a fine line. When a soldier exposed his posterior while Jews celebrated Passover, causing a riot, the Romans executed the soldier, not the rioters. Roman authorities engaged in a tug of war with the priests over control of the High Priest's garments; both sides understood their symbolic importance for the identity and traditions of the Jewish people. Both also understood how garments could become the center of (and represent) a form of social protest.[7] But the most obvious symbol, which could easily turn to social protest, was the temple itself. In the First Jewish Revolt, as coins attest, rebel leaders made it the symbol of outright revolt against Roman power,[8] upping the ante of the less overt forms of resistance mentioned above. Roman portrayals of its destruction emphasized the temple's importance. Titus's arch displayed Roman soldiers carrying the temple's sacred implements in triumph. Even the Romans could not miss which symbol was the focal point of the social revolt, and they emphasized that faith in such symbols was useless. Josephus's account offers a different version but the final result is much the same: while the temple served as the central symbol, the leaders of the revolt—bandits as he calls them—had offended God, who withdrew support and gave it to the Romans. Yet Josephus still seeks to preserve a sense of social protest, for it was God who caused the Jews to lose and allowed the Romans to win (though the Romans may not have agreed). The following discussion summarizes what is known of public social protests: banditry, revolts, and riots.

FURTHER ARCHAEOLOGICAL EVIDENCE OF PALESTINIAN SOCIAL UNREST

Josephus's Accounts and Archaeological Evidence

Despite the fact that social protest movements generally leave few substantial material remains, the evidence from both the First Jewish Revolt (66–74 C.E.) and the Bar Kochba Revolt (132–135 C.E.) is reasonably abundant, though largely outside the scope of this chapter. Prior to 70 C.E., however, a few incidents of overt social unrest have left important remains.

The record of social protest seems to begin with the Hasmonean Revolt, which broke out in 168/167 B.C.E. Its earliest phases, however, have left no marks in the archaeological record, though the following developments left clear archaeological remains everywhere in the Holy Land, records both of destruction and of construction, in addition to the smaller finds noted above. These evidences of the Hasmonean Revolt, broadly understood, may not be evidence of social protest, for they derived not from the initial protests but from periods of consolidation, wars of conquest, and subsequent settlement, as shown clearly, for example, at Yodefat and Gamla. The Hasmonean Revolt succeeded as a protest movement and was transformed.

Other protest movements developed in the late Hasmonean period. They came mainly in the context of struggles between the Hasmoneans and the rising power of the Herodian family (Josephus, *War* 1; *Ant.* 13, 14). No physical evidence of Herod the Great's earliest confrontations with social bandits in ca. 47 B.C.E. has survived, but two subsequent confrontations from about 38 B.C.E. have left marks. Near Arbel, at a gap in the cliff face where natural caves offered a vantage point, bandits preyed on travelers passing by on the road. The surviving caves provide evidence of an incident in which Herod eradicated many of the bandits from the region by lowering troops on platforms from the top. During the First Revolt Josephus had a wall with towers built across Mount Nitai to protect these caves from attack from above as part of strengthening of sites in the Galilee.[9] Herod returned to the Galilee later in 38 B.C.E. to complete the elimination of bandits; some fled to the Huleh swamp and some to a fortress, no doubt the recently excavated fortress at Keren Naftali (Plate 2).[10] The fortress was first occupied in the late Hellenistic period and marked the eastern boundary of Tyrian territory; evidence of Jewish life suggests the Hasmoneans subsequently took it over, but occupation ended abruptly at the transition between the Hasmonean and Herodian periods (no Herodian pottery or lamps were found). Aerial photographs from 1945 show a siege camp with circumvallation west of the hill. Only Herod the Great's action against the "bandits" (*lêstai*) would account for such siege works, so this is the only archaeologically attested evidence of Herod's use of Roman siege techniques.

Another period of social protest followed Herod's death in 4 B.C.E., when several small spontaneous protest movements, some having leaders with messianic pretensions, broke out. Herod had left a will—indeed, a series of different wills[11]—but there was still much uncertainty. Popular uprisings destroyed some royal buildings, according to the literature: the Winter Palace at Jericho, the arsenal at Sepphoris, and a palace at Betharamphtha (*War* 2.55–65; *Ant.* 17.269–84). Only the Winter Palace at Jericho has been excavated and reported, and its excavations show evidence of fire in the *triclinium*, perhaps from the uprising.[12]

Jewish Revolts

The Jewish Revolt of 66–74 C.E., which left deep marks on both the Roman and Jewish numismatic records, is included here because of the clarity of its evidence for a successful popular movement. Masada, Herodium, Gamla, and Yodefat are well-known sites, with defenses and siege activities clearly visible. Josephus refers to the first two as strongholds of "brigands" (*War* 4.555); in both cases these brigands adapted a room in the existing buildings as a synagogue, emphasizing religious motivations. By contrast, Yodefat and Gamla were not connected with any specific sub-group.

The Bar Kochba Revolt of 132–135 C.E. also left physical remains. The primary evidence derives from inaccessible caves high up along the margins of the Dead Sea (the Cave of Horrors, the Cave of Letters, Wadi Muraba'at Caves), others under the main courtyard of Herodium, and some farther away from the center of things in the Shephelah. No conclusive evidence in the Galilee can be associated with the Bar Kochba Revolt.[13] The letters from the Nahal Hever Cave are the most important evidence from 132–135 C.E., for some pertain to the leader of the revolt, hinting at the tensions, issues, and relationships. Others pertain to Babatha, who left an archive of a woman's legal documents that has provided a rich tapestry of family life. Babatha carried documents that included the deed to her property, deeds authorized by military and political representatives of the very Roman government Bar Kochba sought to overthrow.[14] Taken together, textual and material remains (clothes, shoes, utensils) have provided a ground-level view of daily life within a revolutionary setting.

Both revolts were triggered by political, religious, cultural, and social aspirations. Their remains are important in providing among the best collections of materials reflecting widespread social unrest. All were deeply unsettling to Roman authorities. Analysis of social unrest in Judea and Galilee has been seminal in understanding similar movements in other locations (e.g., Britain, Germany, France, the Danube, North Africa). Having said that, there remains a question about the relevance of the evidence from the revolts for social protest. Both Jewish revolts had a higher degree of organization and deeper religious and political motivations than one might expect to find in a social protest movement, though economic factors certainly played a role as, for example, the oft-cited burning of debt records in the First Revolt indicates.

Watchtowers, Guard Posts, and Fortresses

The suggestion that there was a proliferation of minor fortifications to keep bandits in check in this period does not stand up well to scrutiny for three reasons. (1) Where watchtowers were common, especially in western Samaria (second century B.C.E. to second century C.E.),[15] there is no special evidence of banditry. (2) Both Hasmoneans and Herods had a substantial number of fortresses—the Herodian ones usually renovations of Hasmonean fortresses—but relatively few were in areas troubled by banditry and there is no record of their use against bandits. (3) The most troublesome areas—hilly borderlands in northern

Galilee, southern Lebanon, and southern Syria—had almost no fortresses. The notable exception, Keren Naftali, was occupied in the Hasmonean period but not in the Herodian. Had fortresses been utilized to suppress banditry, one would expect more forts with continuous occupation, especially in the Galilee. Despite the impression in later Roman sources (pp. 27–30 below), this particular strategy was not much used in Palestine.[16] Banditry may not have been endemic.

Peasant Life and Urbanization

The common opinion is that the early Roman Imperial period was a time of urbanization, with increases in land accumulation, monetization, and increased indebtedness.[17] In the Galilee, the cities of Tiberias, Bethsaida, and Caesarea Philippi were founded or refounded; Sepphoris, Caesarea Maritima, and Beth Shean were expanded; Phasaelis, Archelais, and Julias were created in Peraea. The Augustan peace ushered in a time of open borders and profitable trade, with central development of infrastructure projects such as harbors, warehouses, marketplaces, and roads. The Herods and other entrepreneurs took advantage of these opportunities. It is held that the actions of these urban elites threatened peasant life: fewer persons held increasing amounts of land, peasants lost their livelihood and were forced off the land, urbanization exploited peasants, and monetization threatened agrarian practices. In support of such views, social anthropology has been used to construct a necessary subordination of peasants whose surplus crops were taken away by the growing urban class.[18]

Material remains support this general picture in part, but hint at a subtler picture. The general shift to urbanization in the first century B.C.E. to the first century C.E. has likely been overstated. The more important movements towards urbanism in the east came earlier, in the late Hellenistic period (roughly second century B.C.E.), and later, in the middle Roman period (second century C.E.). The heyday of the great Hellenistic-Roman cities (e.g., Caesarea, Beth Shean, Gerasa) was in the second century C.E., in terms of expansion, range of institutional buildings, richness of detailing, imported materials, patronage, and benefaction. Bethsaida, for example (if et-Tell was in fact Bethsaida), which was refounded in the early first century C.E. as one of Philip's capitals, had little first-century building activity. It was busier in the

Iron Age than in the first century.[19] Both Sepphoris and Tiberias were modest cities in the first century, only a fraction of the second and third century cities.

Complementarily, small rural towns and villages increased both in number and size in this period.[20] Yodefat, for example, began as a small, late Hellenistic fortified farmstead and was taken over by the Hasmoneans as a hilltop village. In the late first century B.C.E. or early first century C.E. it expanded substantially southwards. Other small towns such as Cana seem similar. Rural village life expanded and improved at the same time that urbanization was proceeding gradually at Sepphoris and Tiberias (perhaps prompted by the increased opportunities of trade, commerce, and agriculture; Chapter 5). Decline of village life, abandonment of houses, and reduction of opportunities is not apparent. There was no reduction in village numbers or sizes; instead, there was an increase in numbers of houses, covering a range of types and sizes.[21] More critical assessment of these factors is still needed.

The degree of monetization in the period has also been overestimated. Galilean excavations usually have a majority of Hasmonean coins, with relatively few Herodian, procuratorial, and Roman coins, amplified somewhat with Tyrian shekels, sometimes in hoards. This counterintuitive situation might be accounted for on several grounds, but it is incorrect to claim intense monetization with the pressures that would bring to bear on a peasant population.

Sources for Understanding Social Protest, First Century B.C.E. to First Century C.E.

Roman sources are relatively rich for understanding banditry (*lêsteia*) over a two-century period in the Empire generally and in Syria-Palestine specifically. Only rarely, though, do the sources permit differentiation among organized political revolt, socially or religiously motivated revolt, spontaneous protest with social causes, robbers singly or in bands without social motivation. The commonest word in the Greek sources for most of these activities is *lêstês* and cognates, the focus of the following discussion. It is hardly coincidence that the *Mishnah* adopts *listîm* as a loanword (applied sometimes even to Roman authorities!).[22]

Sources: The Roman World

Paul's troubles, set out in 2 Corinthians 11:26, provide an overview of typical dangers; *lêstai* are included alongside natural problems (rivers, wilderness, sea) and social difficulties (Paul's kin, Gentiles, false brothers). Tombstones of persons "killed by bandits" support this impression (*interfectus a latronibus:* e.g., Rome, *ILS* 2011, 20307; Dalmatia, *ILS* 5112; Dacia, *CIL* 3.1559; Africa, *ILS* 5795; cf. *CIL* 3.8242). Pliny the Younger names three persons plus slaves that have "disappeared" or "vanished" (*Ep.* 6.25), two of them on the Via Flaminia. Another inscription refers to a fort erected by Commodus (189–192 C.E.) in Numidia "between two highways, for the safety of travelers" (*CIL* 8.2495). Death by bandits was common, according to Roman law (*Digest* 13.6.5.4).[23] The evidence spans a broad period, though no doubt the difficulties rose and fell within the period.

Local support of bandits was illegal. A prefect of Egypt says, "it is impossible to root out the bandits apart from those who protect them" (*P. Oxy* 1408; ca. 210 C.E.). Antoninus Pius, when proconsul of Asia, "declared by edict that irenarchs, when they captured brigands, should question them about their associates and about those who sheltered them" (*Digest* 48.3.6.1). Later formalizations in the *Digest* echo this view: "receivers [supporters] are punished as the bandits themselves. All those persons who could have apprehended the bandits but who let them escape, having received money or part of the loot, are to be treated as in this same category [of bandits]" (*Digest* 47.16.1). "It is the duty of a good and serious governor to see that the province he governs remains peaceful and quiet. . . . [He] must hunt down . . . bandits (*latrines*) . . .[and] must use force against their collaborators" (*Digest* 1.18.13).

Strabo (64 B.C.E.–24 C.E.) considered deteriorating social conditions a significant factor in banditry and piracy (which he thought of as a valid occupation in Augustus's day as earlier). He likened Pamphylians to Cilicians, among whom are some who "do not wholly abstain from the business of piracy (*tôn lêstrikôn ergôn*)" (*Geogr.* 12.570). Mount Corycus, a similarly rough area, was a pirate haunt; Lycians also inhabited rough lands but were not pirates (they were *hypo anthrôpôn sôphronôn*; 14.1.32). Rough areas of northern Italy sheltered brigands, a problem solved only by building better roads into the Alps under Augustus (4.204; 4.207, for Pannonia). Strabo was primarily concerned with

piracy (*hoi lêstêrioi*; 3.144), which extended west to "the Pillars." In
17.792 he speaks of seaborne activity (*stasis*) of Greeks (for the Black
Sea, 7.311), and in 5.232 he describes how even the residents of
Antium, near Rome, engaged in acts of "piracy" or banditry, though
they had no harbor. He knows of Egyptian "shepherds who were
pirates" (17.802: *hypo boukolôn lêstôn*), and Sicilian horse herders, cow
herders, and shepherds who "turned to brigandage in a sporadic way,
later they both assembled in great numbers and plundered the settlements." He watched one, Selurus, die in the Forum (6.273). Strabo's
descriptions of widespread but similar conditions (mountainous and
marginal) are important. Some cases, of course, may not have reflected
social protest of the kind discussed here, but some certainly did.

Declamation exercises of the elder Seneca (ca. 50 B.C.E.–ca. 40 C.E.)
in the *Controversiae* often presuppose a person's capture by pirates: a virgin (1.2), a man who later married the pirate chief's daughter (1.6), a
man who killed two of his brothers (1.7), a good son redeemed by a
debauched son (3.3), a youth cast adrift who became a pirate chief and
later captured his father (7.1), and a son who ransomed his father (7.4).
Little light is thrown on the historical situation, but these show that in
the late 30s C.E. there was still public concern with piracy and a perception of "humane" piracy. The younger Seneca (4 B.C.E.–65 C.E.)
advises readers to have "as little booty as possible on your person . . . if
you are empty-handed, the highwayman [*latro*] passes you by; even
along an infested road, the poor may travel in peace" (*Ep.* 14.9; cf.
Josephus on Essenes, who "carry nothing whatever with them on their
journeys, except arms as a protection against brigands"; *War* 2.125).
Seneca advises avoiding crowds (*Ep.* 7); he parodies the crowd's
reaction when a bandit was executed in the amphitheater for killing a
traveler.

Plutarch (ca. 50–120 C.E.) details Pompey's elimination of piracy
(*Pomp.* 24–28), giving a sense of widespread support for piracy despite the
threat it posed. His 500 ships, 120,000 infantry, and 5,000 cavalry meant
speedy success, followed by a very liberal settlement of captured pirates in
existing and new cities. Pompey thought "that by nature man neither is
nor becomes a wild or unsocial creature; . . . the habit of vice makes him
become something which by nature he is not, . . . he can be civilized again
by precept and example and by a change of place and of occupation"
(*Pomp.* 28). Plutarch, too, thought banditry had social causes and required
social solutions.

The *Roman History* of Appian (b. late first century C.E.) emphasizes that piracy was a major problem in the first century B.C.E. (*Bell. civ.* 1.111) and was resolved only when Pompey was commissioned to eradicate it in 67 B.C.E. (2.23). Rome was even threatened with famine as a result of pirates, who are likened to robbers (*Mithridatic Wars* 91–96). They afflicted the Mediterranean as far west as the Pillars of Hercules (93), but they were a severer problem in the east, especially in Cilicia Tracheia, where piracy began. Piracy extended to Syria, Pamphylia, Cyprus, and Pontus—indeed, to almost all eastern nations (92). Pompey's eradication of pirates was incomplete, for in 40–38 B.C.E. Octavian accused Pompey's son Sextus of encouraging a "mysterious robbery infesting the sea," so that famine threatened Rome (*Bell. civ.* 5.77, 80). In fact, Rome itself was "openly infested with bands of robbers" (cf. also *Bell. civ.* 5.132; Suetonius, *Aug.* 32–33).

Philo of Alexandria (ca. 15 B.C.E.–50 C.E.) presupposes banditry, despite Julius Caesar's clearing the Mediterranean of brigands and pirates (*Legat.* 146: *lêstai, peiratikai*). The ascetic Therapeutae near Alexandria clustered their solitary cells together for fear of robbers (*Contempl.* 24); parents ransomed captured children (*Prob.* 37; cf. 121); the wilds posed general dangers (*Spec.* 1.301). When discussing the commandment not to steal, Philo refers to oligarchs who perpetrated banditry (*Decal.* 136), and he likens Alexandrians to robbers when they attacked Jews (*Legat.* 122), while he praises Flaccus for paying his soldiers well enough so they would not turn into robbers (*Flacc.* 5).

When Dio Cassius (ca. 164–229 C.E.) looks back to Pompey, he claims that "large numbers had turned to banditry" (*Hist. Rom.* 36.20.2; also 5.28.1–3; 75.2.4), including some ex-soldiers and slaves (75.2.5–6; 77.10.5). Varus "distributed many of the soldiers to helpless communities . . . for the alleged purpose of guarding various points, arresting brigands, or escorting provision trains" (56.19.1; cf. Suetonius, *Tib.* 37). He mentions especially Bulla Felix—"never really seen when seen, never found when found, never caught when caught" (77.10.2)—who spoke up for slaves and peasants (77.10.5).

Not all brigands were popular. Galen says of a bandit who killed a traveler, "None of the local inhabitants would bury him, but in their hatred of him were glad enough to see his body consumed by the birds which, in a couple of days, ate his flesh, leaving the skeleton as if for medical demonstration" (*De anat. admin.* 1.2). In sum, from Marius and Sulla through to the second century C.E., brigandage and banditry were severe problems that demanded constant vigilance and strong measures. The problems, however, were not continuous or uniform. And while evidence of popular support for such bandits is not outstandingly strong, there is sufficient evidence, allowing for the upper-class status of the writers on whose comments we must rely, to suggest that much—though certainly not all—banditry had dimensions of social protest and social support. Perhaps occasionally it was even aimed at righting social grievances.

Sources: Syria and Palestine

The sources for Syria and Palestine are both fuller and more limited; there are fewer texts but those we have offer more circumstantial detail. Strabo is especially helpful as a bridge, since he alludes both to this region and to the broader Roman world. He describes the Lebanon and anti-Lebanon ranges, saying that the Itureans and Arabians were all robbers (*kakourgoi*), while the plains people were farmers (*Geogr.* 16.2.18). Pompey destroyed their fortresses, while others later removed threats to Arabian traders (16.2.18, re: Trachonitis) by breaking up Zenodorus's band (16.2.20; cf. also *OGIS* 1:424, reign of Agrippa I or II; *War* 1.304–14).[24] Strabo includes the Hasmoneans as robbers (*tôn lêstôn lêstêria*; 16.2.28), interpreting their tyrannies (*ek de tôn tyrannidôn ta lêstêria*) as a result of following Moses' laws, so that "some revolted and harassed the country," subduing much of Syria and Phoenicia (*Geogr.* 16.2.37). In his view there was little to choose between Zenodorus and the Hasmoneans!

Josephus: Hasmoneans and Herod

The Hasmonean Revolt (167–142 B.C.E.) began as a popular movement that had similarities—to judge from 1 Maccabees 2:42–48—with social banditry: trouble with authorities, flight to the countryside, and popular support. It is unsurprising that Strabo alluded to its leaders as bandits. Certainly the movement's main characteristics (religion, politics, and tradition or nationalism)[25] were similar to those of social protest, even if it was characterized only for a short time by small bands of dispossessed motivated by the struggle for sustenance, of which they had been deprived. For Strabo, banditry was more an abusive epithet than accurate description.

We hear nothing of banditry in Jewish sources during most of the Hasmonean period. But in the second quarter of the first century B.C.E., when Hasmonean internal conflict prompted Pompey's invasion and led to the triumph of Hyrcanus II and Antipater (64–63 B.C.E.), groups emerged that may have been socially motivated, though their activities do not fit the model well. Some were losers in a power struggle rather than social bandits. The upshot of these conditions (75–40 B.C.E.) was the rise to power of Antipater's second son, Herod, named King of Judea by the Romans in late 40 B.C.E.[26]

Josephus, on whose accounts of Herod we are so dependent, first uses *lêstês* and cognates (in both *War* and *Antiquities*) of groups fighting with the young Herod.[27] The hilly location between Galilee and Syria fits well the general conditions described by Strabo. They supported themselves and their families by plundering wealthy travelers, a form of violence prompted by revenge for their exploitation or social justice. Herod faced protests of two kinds, bandits who had fled from society but retained support from neighboring towns, and bandits supported by the politically powerful.[28] The difference between them was that in the second case the exploiters lined their pockets from the activities of the exploited. Initially Herod was a governor in Galilee under Hyrcanus II (*War* 1.204–15; *Ant.* 14.158–84).[29] When he executed Hezekiah (an *archilêstês*) for brigandage, Josephus alludes almost accidentally to popular support for brigands, for some of the Jerusalem elite persuaded Hyrcanus to try Herod for Hezekiah's murder. Support for Hezekiah may have been simply dislike of Herod; still it shows how Galileans could be linked with persons in Jerusalem.[30] Herod's aggressive opposition to social brigandage brought him to Rome's attention, and he was appointed governor of Coele-Syria and Samaria (47–46 B.C.E.; *Ant.* 14.160).[31]

Herod's long campaign to win control of Judea after being named King (40–37 B.C.E.) was interrupted to eliminate brigands in caves above the road near Arbel, who were raiding passing traffic (*War* 1.304–14; *Ant.* 14.415–30). He subdued them by lowering cages from the cliff tops.[32] Later, he returned to Galilee and pursued the brigands, partly to the (Huleh) swamps and partly to a fortress (Keren Naftali) (Plate 2) just west of the swamps (*War* 1.315–16; *Ant.* 14.431–33; see above).

Not all events using similar language refer to similar situations, so interpretive caution is necessary. The incidents of 38 B.C.E. may have been primarily a military campaign by Antigonus's supporters against Herod. Josephus's linking of Antigonus's strongholds with brigands in caves (*War* 1.303; *Ant.* 14.414–15) need not refer to social protest; military opposition to Herod is a plausible alternative, as suggested by the garrison Herod left behind, the pitched battle at Arbel, the use of an abandoned fortress, and the drowning of Herod's partisans in the Sea of Galilee (*Ant.* 14.450). The "noble death" motif in the account of the caves (a father kills seven children rather than allow them to go out to Herod) implies a religious rather than a social background; despite Josephus's vocabulary, he may not be describing the same phenomenon.

Because Herod effectively opposed banditry, Augustus ceded him Batanea, Auranitis, and Trachonitis (*Ant.* 15.343–49; *War* 1.398–99),[33] whose two major trade routes—the King's Highway from Aqaba and the Wadi Sirhan from Arabia—were vulnerable to bandits. Clearing the brigands from Trachonitis was a joint operation of Herod and M. Terrentius Varro (governor of Syria 24–23 B.C.E.). Josephus and Strabo agree on the complicity of Zenodorus (tetrarch of the Ituraeans; see *Ant.* 15.344–48; Strabo, *Geogr.* 16.2.20).[34] Bandits had been constructively resocialized by settling them on land from which they supported themselves, says Josephus; in 11 B.C.E., however, they returned to their old ways. This may have been simple banditry. More likely, it was revolt against Herod's rule (*Ant.* 16.271–75), since Syllaeus of Nabatea and Zenodorus protected the brigands in exchange for some of the profits. Later, Herod adopted the Roman policy of allotting land to those who would keep the peace, veterans in Trachonitis and Babylonian Jews in Batanea (*Ant.* 17.23–28; cf. 16.292).

At Herod's death uncoordinated revolts broke out in various locations.[35] Josephus notes the following: Herod's demobilized veterans in Idumea armed themselves and fought Archelaus's troops (*War* 2.55; *Ant.* 17.269–70); Judas, son of Hezekiah, broke into the Sepphoris armory, equipped his supporters, and attacked Antipas's supporters (*War* 2.56; *Ant.* 17.271–72); Simon gathered a group of robbers in Peraea, attacked Jericho, and burned Herod's palace (*War* 2.57–59; *Ant.* 17.273–76); other Peraeans attacked and burned Herod's palace at Betharamphtha across the Jordan from Jericho (*War* 2.59; *Ant.* 17.277); Athrongeus, a shepherd, raised a band in Judea and attacked Romans and Jews (*War* 2.60–65; *Ant.* 17.278–84).

Josephus uses *lêstrikos* of the group of incidents, and *lêstai* specifically only of Simon in Peraea. The difficulties were put down by
Varus (*War* 2.65–79; *Ant.* 17.285–98). He burned two cities, Sepphoris
and Emmaus, because they supported the revolutionaries, but in other
cities there was insufficient popular support to warrant such actions
(he sent any leaders related to Herod [!] to Rome for Augustus's judgment). At least Simon and the Peraeans, and perhaps Judas, were
social bandits; the other incidents involving military confrontations in
Judea are less clearly banditry.

Josephus: Prefects up to Pilate

Josephus knows almost nothing from Archelaus's exile in 6 C.E. until
Pilate, so little can be said about social protest during this period. The
major point of discussion has been whether Judas was the founder of
the "Zealot" movement (a question that is of no concern here), with a
continuous pattern of revolt through the first six decades of the first
century C.E., as Josephus thought. The prevailing view rejects this
claim[36] as part of Josephus's apologetic concerns. Unlike his earlier picture of individuals and families who resorted to banditry, he emphasizes
widespread disturbances, though he details important incidents under
Pilate, especially the "standards" and "aqueduct" incidents.

Josephus: Procurators after Pilate

His focus on "Zealots" is unmistakably apologetic, yet he can keep
groups separate, as he does with Eleazar, "who for twenty years had
ravaged the country with many of his associates" (*War* 2.253), until he
was captured and executed by Felix (procurator 52–60 C.E.). When
Samaritans murdered a Galilean going up to Jerusalem and Cumanus
(procurator 48–52 C.E.) did nothing, Jews allied themselves with
Eleazar and sacked and burned several Samaritan villages (*War*
2.228–31; *Ant.* 20.113–17), which illustrates neatly the officials' presumption of popular support for social protest movements in Palestine,
as elsewhere in the Roman world.

Illustrating the other side of conditions first observed under Herod,
Florus (procurator 64–66 C.E.) protected brigands, according to

Josephus, so that they "were at liberty to practice brigandage, on the condition that he received a share of the spoils" (*War* 2.278–79; *Ant.* 20.255–56). As conditions deteriorated following Eleazar's actions, "the whole of Judea was infested with bands of brigands" (*Ant.* 20.124; also 20.121, 185–86; *War* 2.271), so that eventually there was a coalition of brigands, whom Josephus calls "Zealots" (*War* 4.134, 160–62, 193, 196, 197, etc.). He believes conditions in the earlier period with individual bandits (sometimes with popular support) were continuous with conditions in the later period when various bands coalesced into a revolutionary movement. And that movement, according to Josephus, was continuous with the extreme Zealot movement, which broke out in 66 C.E. on the eve of the Revolt. The following scholarly views are only two among many: for Horsley and Hanson the Zealots coalesced only as a result of rural bandits moving to Jerusalem;[37] for Donaldson, city mobs were the equivalent of rural bandits and were already present in Jerusalem.[38] These conditions—volatile, politicized, and religiously informed—were similar to those of the Hasmonean Revolt.

HISTORICAL RECONSTRUCTION:
GALILEE, THE GOLAN, SAMARIA, JUDEA, AND SOCIAL PROTEST

Hellenism, Greeks, and Romans

Social conditions in the Holy Land changed frequently between the Persian and middle Roman periods, destabilizing society's institutions and structures and creating the backdrop for social protest. Israel's loss of identity was partially alleviated in the return from exile under the Persians, but those gains were eroded by Alexander the Great's conquest and the deliberate introduction of Greek cities (*poleis*), institutions, and ideals. After more lenient rule by the Diadochoi, the Seleucids wrenched away control of the land (200 B.C.E.). Antiochus IV Epiphanes attacked Judaism as a religion. The restrictions imposed were an essential background to the Hasmonean Revolt; as Strabo suggests, though he views it negatively, this was a form of social banditry that assumed revolutionary features (1 Macc 1).

As the Hasmoneans acquired the trappings of other late Hellenistic dynasties, destructive internal tensions (75–38 B.C.E.) created fresh conditions for banditry. Two consequences followed: the Hasmonean struggles (like similar struggles in Syria) led to Pompey's direct involvement (64/63 B.C.E.); the Roman conquest, though limited, altered social and religious institutions, so that banditry was indirectly encouraged. Herod's early reputation for ridding the Galilee of brigandage resulted in Rome's choosing him to rule. His dynasty then repeated a common pattern: accumulation of wealth, land, and power, with deprivation of small landowners and small businessmen. The localized uprisings on his death reflect the resulting underlying tensions.[39] Following the division of the kingdom, Archelaus was unable to rule effectively, though neither Antipas nor Philip experienced similar difficulties; either both were abler, or their regions had been more pacified. The shift in Judea in 6 C.E. to direct Roman rule under prefects (6–41 C.E.) and proconsuls (44–66 C.E.) created new conditions. After the short interlude under Agrippa I (41–44 C.E.), those difficulties got worse. Roman ineptness—together with an ineffectual Jewish elite respected by neither side, a heavy debt load and religious tensions, all of which are too frequently downplayed—led almost inevitably to full revolt in 66 C.E.

Jesus' Movement as an Instance of Social Protest: The Gospels

The difficulties in discerning what are and are not core Jesus traditions are notorious, but cannot be considered here. Q, like the gospels themselves, contains important information about the early movement (Chapter 5). When drawing on material that fits the periods outlined above, it must be recognized that theological and literary interests may well govern the presence and presentation of some material. But theological agendas need not a priori negate the possibility of material reflecting early traditions. While the speeches and specific encounters may be later, the framework or environment, if it fits what we know of the period, may legitimately be used to reconstruct the situation. Looking at selected features of the traditions about Jesus will enable an assessment of the Jesus movement against the forms of social protest discussed above.

Early Christian literature reflects conditions similar to those Josephus and the Roman literature describe. The difficulties with brigandage of the first century B.C.E. continued in places, especially in the

east, into the first century C.E. While the gospels refer frequently to the
lêstês group of words, they quickly disappear from other Christian literature. Paul uses *lêstês* once in 2 Corinthians 11:26, but generally speaking brigandage is missing from this literature, as it is also from some
secular literature of the same period (e.g., Pliny the Younger).

Jesus was executed between two *lêstai*, despite the implicit embar-
rassment to the narrative in this admission (Mark 15:27, 32//Matt
27:38, 44; cf. Luke 23:33, 39–43). There is palpable irony in Pilate's
including on the *titulus* the phrase "King of the Jews" (whether historically accurate or not matters little); literarily it ameliorates the offense
of the historical fact. Was Jesus, however, seen as a bandit? On the one
hand, three gospels make it seem that the decision to execute Jesus had
little basis in the facts of the case: Mark and Matthew hint at spurious
charges against Jesus, while John has Pilate prefer Jesus to be tried
according to Jewish law (John 18:31). Only Luke, more satisfactorily,
permits the notion that Jesus was a popular leader who was "pervert-
ing our nation, and forbidding us to give tribute to Caesar, and saying
that he is himself Christ a King" (Luke 23:2). This is close to the language of social protest; in general, Luke makes the most historical
sense of the trial accounts,[40] even though in the end Pilate concludes,
"I find no crime in this man" (Luke 23:4).

At Jesus' arrest the Synoptics have Jesus say, "Have you come out as
against a robber with swords and clubs?" (Mark 14:48 pars.). Did the
authorities really believe Jesus was a brigand, because they arrested
him as a *lêstês*? The evidence for urban brigands (above) may imply that
the authorities had ways to deal with them; certainly his arrest, the
charges (according to Luke), and his execution between *lêstai*, cohere to
give the narrative plausibility. The Jewish authorities—and in the first
instance the authorities are Jewish—dealt with Jesus as a brigand.
Perhaps Jesus really was seen as leader of a social protest movement
who needed to be eliminated.

The Synoptics report Jesus quoting Jeremiah 7:11 about a "robbers'
cave" in the "temple tantrum" incident (Chapter 14), contrasting that
text with Isaiah 56:7 about the temple as a "house of prayer for all
nations" (Mark 11:17 pars.). The irony occurs at two levels. On the one
hand, all the authors know their stories end with Jesus crucified
between two brigands, so a "robber-look-alike" who proclaims the
sacred place of Judaism a place for "robbers" has a wry ring to it. On
the other hand, the coin exchanges and the sale of sacrificial animals

were services provided for pious pilgrims who came up to Jerusalem from distant places,[41] not opportunities for profit; as John puts it, the temple should not be a "house of trade" (John 2:16; Chapter 14, below). In John, it is Jesus' "zeal" that "consumes" him, right in the place where he is viewed by the authorities as a "brigand."

Jesus' story in these scenes from the last week of his life intersects with social-political-religious circumstances in Palestine. Jesus was arrested like a robber, tried on charges similar to those that might be used against such a person, executed between two brigands, while another brigand—Barabbas—was set free (John 18:40), at a time when there were public concerns over brigandry. Despite the report that Jesus accused temple authorities of being "robbers," he himself was dealt with as a robber.

According to the Gospels, of course, Jesus was not really a robber. John presents Jesus as the good shepherd (John 10:1-18) who watches at the door of the sheepfold for the robber who climbs over the wall to steal sheep. The parable is heavily christologized—"all who came before me are thieves and robbers"—but its core imagery contrasts Jesus' program to the program of social bandits. The same impression is conveyed by the parable of the Good Samaritan (Luke 10:29-37; Lukan redaction), whose setting is rooted in the social conditions surveyed in the first half of this chapter: brigands terrorize the road between Jericho and Jerusalem along the Wadi Qelt; a traveler is set upon by bandits, robbed, and left for dead. Contrary to Seneca's advice, he carried money, identifying him as a "have" rather than a "have not." Yet Jesus' sympathies were with the critically wounded person, not the social bandits.

In both parables—and parables aim for verisimilitude—the vocabulary of social banditry is used, but there is no implied approval. As in the passion narratives, Jesus does not follow a program of "social protest" in the classic model. This is not to say, of course, that Jesus does not have strong peasant sympathies; he does. His attitudes to debt and moneylenders, tenant farmers and laborers, dispossessed and weak, show this sympathetic attitude very clearly.

The sayings and parables of Jesus refer to debt, indebtedness, moneylending, financial jeopardy, and debt forgiveness: the unforgiving servant in Matthew 18:23-35 (M); the unjust steward in Luke 16:1-9 (L); the two debtors of Luke 7:40-42 (Lukan redaction); the Lord's prayer in Q 11:4; love of one's enemies in Q 6:34; the parable of the talents in Q 19:11–27; the saying to lend without return in *Gos. Thom.* 95; and the Lord's Prayer (Matt 6:12). These accounts presuppose rural agrarian folk in small villages who are in danger of losing everything because of aggressive loan, interest, and repayment policies. The persons most directly criticized are middlemen, the "steward" or "servant" who is carrying out his master's real or perceived intentions. In turn, these sayings presume estates, accumulation of land, tenant farming, and leases,[42] as in the parables of the tenant farmers (Mark 12:1-9 pars.; *Gos. Thom.* 65), laborers in the vineyard (Matt 20:1-16 [M]), and make friends with your accuser (Q 12:57–59).

Jesus fit well into a world containing both exploited peasants who were threatened with losses, debts, and imprisonment, and absentee owners and middle management who placed additional burdens onto the agrarian poor. The above evidence shows that it was exactly these conditions that led to social banditry among some who had to flee their land to eke out a living preying on those who had exploited them. This is a case worth making, even if one holds back from full endorsement. One must note that only seldom did Jesus protest these conditions directly.

The evidence pulls in different directions, and raises three relevant questions. Did those outside his movement view Jesus as a part of such radical forms of social protest? To what extent was Jesus sympathetic to the more radical social protest that swirled through Palestine during his period? Did his immediate followers hold varying views of Jesus' attitudes to social protesters? On the last question, it seems likely that various persons among his followers held different views on society and social protest: Simon the Cananean (or Zealot?); James and John, the sons of "thunder"; Judas Iscariot (= *sicarius* or "dagger man"?). On the first question, it seems almost indisputable that some outside his movement thought of Jesus as just another leader of a minor group of *lêstai*, so that he could be arrested, tried, and executed on these grounds. On the question of Jesus' own views, although he was sympathetic to the plight of the exploited peasants, there is little indication that he was sympathetic to the means of those who adopted the life of *lêsteia*.

CHAPTER THREE

3-D VISUALIZATIONS OF A FIRST-CENTURY GALILEAN TOWN

INTRODUCTION[1]

Virtual Reality for Educational Television

> More alarming even than the engines was their whirring drone, more frightful than the missiles the crash. Then there was the thud of the dead falling one after another from the wall. Fearful shrieks from the women within the town mingled with the moans of the dying victims without. The whole surrounding area in front of the fighting lines ran with blood, and the piles of corpses formed a path to the top of the hill. (Josephus, *War* 3.247–49)

In July of 1996, a crew of five from WXXI-TV (a PBS affiliate in Rochester, N.Y.) arrived at the archaeological dig at Yodefat (Jotapata), Israel, to shoot a one-hour PBS network documentary, "Echoes from the Ancients." Flavius Josephus's eyewitness account of the siege of Yodefat was no small factor in the station's decision to undertake the project. It is a vivid tale of courage, treachery, and tragedy. Until the excavations had begun, Josephus's narrative had given the world the only known details of Yodefat's role in first-century history.

It is rare to have a defeated general's account of a Roman siege. Josephus was sent to the Galilee in 66 C.E. to command the northern forces in the First Jewish Revolt against Roman counterattack. In 67 C.E., the Roman general Vespasian and his son Titus—sent by Nero—closed upon Yodefat, the first walled city that resisted. Others fleeing Rome's forces had swelled the hilltop community much beyond its capacity. Though Josephus's account is exaggerated and politically colored, most of his description was borne out by the excavations.

Yodefat lies on a steep hill about half way between the Mediterranean Sea and the Sea of Galilee (Plates 3, 5). From the second century B.C.E. to the first century C.E. it flourished as a small Jewish town. Its archaeological and historical importance lay in several factors: (1) the site had not been built over since 67 C.E.; (2) Josephus's account provided a literary context alongside which the excavations could be placed; (3) the town offered the likelihood of a pristine Galilean Jewish town of the first century—the time of Jesus—thus anchoring all first-century studies; (4) it shed light on the transition from a small Hellenistic farmstead to a Jewish town following the Hasmonean resettlement of the Galilee. The last two factors give Yodefat international significance and affirmed WXXI's commitment to the project.

The Israel Antiquities Authority (IAA) and the University of Rochester (U of R) jointly carried out the excavations at Yodefat between 1992 and 1997. The IAA's Mordechai Aviam, then district archaeologist for Western Galilee, was director and archaeological supervisor, the U of R's William Scott Green, specialist in Second Temple Judaism and early Rabbinism, codirected and supervised the educational and administrative aspects of the dig. The team—drawn from Israel, the U.S.A., and Canada—consisted of experts in pottery, numismatics, mapping, surveying, AutoCAD, architecture, and history of religion. Students from the U of R and other institutions, with some nonstudents, did the volunteer fieldwork, reinforced with trips, explanations of what they were finding at the site, and evening classes.

Challenges

WXXI's goal for the documentary was to give viewers a new perspective of the evolution of two world religions through information revealed at Yodefat. Simply capturing images of the various activities would not result in an interesting television program. A general audience would not understand the significance of the history being discovered, and being made. Archaeology is an imaginative science; experts called on years of experience and stores of multidisciplinary knowledge to reimagine the first-century city. WXXI's responsibility was to bring the past alive for a national audience.

The storytelling obstacles were daunting: (1) the siege of Yodefat happened over 1,900 years earlier, so there were no contemporary artistic depictions of the battle; (2) in 1996 the excavation was still in the discovery stage, not in the final analysis stage; (3) daily life in Second

Temple Judaism—with its emphasis on ritual purity—was not familiar to the general public; (4) the more significant finds—aside from Roman *ballista* stones, catapult bolts, and arrowheads—were not self-explanatory. A central focus for the program gradually emerged from the compelling link between military events in the life of Mordechai Aviam and similar events involving Josephus and the first-century people of Yodefat. On this backbone, a mechanism had to be built that would allow viewers to "see" what ancient life in the Galilee was actually like.

Tools

WXXI decided on a series of virtual-reality recreations of Yodefat based on three factors that ensured the end product's historic and archaeological integrity. First, the Yodefat excavation was one of the first in Israel to employ AutoCAD technology, useful to archaeologists to store information in an easily retrievable form. At Yodefat, the dig's digital expert, Wolf Schleicher, employed AutoCAD to store six seasons of excavation results, which could then be merged with the mountain's topography and known physical features, such as cisterns. Once stored, each artifact could be shown as it related to other discoveries in each excavated square, or expanded to show it in relation to the entire site. Second, WXXI found a digital partner in the United States capable of using the stored AutoCAD information as a basis for three-dimensional recreations. CartesianFX, the digital animation arm of Bergmann Associates, a large national architectural firm, is expert in the art of transforming AutoCAD information into virtual reality reconstructions. Third, I served as the site architect for the 1996 excavation, as a New Testament scholar and former architect, who concentrated his efforts on understanding Yodefat's first-century community in three-dimensional form.

SITE EXCAVATIONS AND SMALL-TOWN ARCHITECTURE

Josephus

The town of Jotapata [ancient Yodefat] is almost entirely built on precipitous cliffs, being surrounded on three sides by ravines so deep that

the sight fails in the attempt to fathom the abyss. On the north side
alone, where the town has straggled sideways up a descending spur of
the mountains, is it accessible. But this quarter, too, Josephus, when he
fortified the city, had enclosed within his wall, in order to prevent the
enemy from occupying the ridge that commanded it (Josephus, *War*
3.158–59)

Josephus is more concerned to titillate his readers with the drama of
the site and the events there than to give informed architectural
descriptions. The architectural information in the account in Josephus
War 3.110–408 is slender, and can be summarized briefly. After
describing the town's situation and the wadis around it with great
enthusiasm (3.158), Josephus remarks that he built the wall around it
(3.159; in 3.111 he says that Yodefat was the strongest of all the fortified towns in Galilee). He claims to have increased the height of the
walls to twenty cubits (3.171–75; about 10 m or 33 feet); no surviving
walls substantiate this claim and it is probably an exaggeration (Plate
5). The defenders, Josephus explains, had sufficient food but not
enough water, because the town had no water source (3.181) and the
siege took place in mid-summer, when there was no rain. The Romans
knew the Jewish plight, because sentries could see the townspeople running to a central spot to distribute the limited water supplies
(3.184–85). The topography allowed Roman observers to see directly
into the lower plateau from the higher hills to the east and west and to
pinpoint *ballista* fire. Josephus describes the progress of the Roman
siege ramp, the effect of the battering ram on the defenders (3.213–21),
and efforts to ameliorate its destructive effects (3.222–28). He does not
describe, however, one important defensive stratagem that was seen
in the dig, the filling in of rooms adjacent to the walls to increase the
walls' resistance to the battering rams.

When the Romans entered the city at dawn on July 20, 67 C.E., they
took "the citadel" (*akra*), implying that the hilltop had an inner fortress
(3.326). This put them "in the midst of the city," permitting them to
"drive the people down the hill from the citadel, slaying them as they
drove them down" (3.329), an accurate description of the relationship
of the hilltop to the remainder of the city to the south. The defenders
were hampered by narrow streets (*clivi*) and the steepness of the hillside
(3.330). Josephus describes the great number of cisterns distributed
through the town (3.334); in the Roman underground search-and-
destroy missions during the following days, he says they found 1,200
persons hidden below ground in addition to the 40,000 who had

already died in the siege (both exaggerated figures, no doubt). The city was razed and burnt, as the excavations have vividly attested (3.336–39).

Josephus was the main actor in the final scene. He went to ground in a large cistern, which 40 "leading persons" had stocked with provisions (3.340–42). After several days, the 41 persons entered into a mutual death pact by drawing lots (3.390–91), at the end of which Josephus and a friend were fortuitously the last two alive. When Josephus surrendered and was brought to Vespasian, he predicted Vespasian's future rise to the Imperial purple, thus beginning a long friendship with the Flavian family (3.399–408).

Excavation Strategy and Results

A three-pronged excavation approach was developed: (a) the whole site of just over four hectares (40 dunams; 10 acres) was mapped and surveyed; (b) extensive areas relating to defensive walls and the Roman siege were investigated in detail; (c) selected areas of housing reflecting the character of the first-century Jewish town were explored. This permitted some general assessment of the urban layout of Yodefat.

Mapping

The keyhole-shaped town sat on a round, bald hilltop, with narrower, straight-sided extensions to the south occupying a plateau, some 30 m below the top of the hill. Most of the main hill was incorporated into the walled town, with some slopes on the southeast and the southern plateau, but the hillsides down into the surrounding wadis were not included. There were some steeply raked housing areas on the main hill, but on the lower plateau the housing sloped more gently. Nothing north of the main hilltop was built up. The north face of the main hill sloped down to form a saddle that was the main line of approach to Yodefat, both normally and for Vespasian's siege. The siege ramp ascended the less steep northern slope. Contrary to usual practice, Vespasian built no formal siege camp; presumably he believed the siege would finish quickly. His main camp was on the hill overlooking Yodefat from the north, with subordinate observation points on the hills around; Vespasian could see inside Yodefat from several posts.

The survey traced the walls around the perimeter of the town and demonstrated that almost the whole area inside the walls was built up, though more intensely occupied on the hilly areas than on the southern plateau. Rock-cut cisterns were concentrated in the area of the hilltop, with a large open rectangular pool where the hill joined the plateau. There were extensive rock-cut architectural features, especially on the bare hilltop, the interpretation of which has not been concluded, though it is clear that the cuttings originated in different periods of occupation, some going back to the earliest Hellenistic occupation of the site. There may also be evidence of a fortress.

Since the town had no natural water supply, cisterns were crucial to the town's existence. Yodefat survived entirely on what could be collected and stored during the winter rainfall in private and public cisterns and in the large rectangular open pool. The cisterns were of several types, some very large for communal water supplies (or for a fortress, perhaps), but most were domestic. Some had rock-cut stairs (with circular or rectangular shafts), others were accessed by lowering a jug through an opening (both rounded horizontal openings and rectangular vertical openings).

Walls

The Roman siege ramp was built at the northwest. These walls are of special interest, for walls from five periods have been identified: Hellenistic, Hasmonean I, Hasmonean II, Early Roman I and Early Roman II. Extensive excavations were conducted here during each season; in addition, the walls were explored at other points on the east, southeast, and southwest. The latest walls were built under the threat of Vespasian's attack, presumably Josephus's walls.[2] In some places, use of existing houses resulted in a kind of casemate wall. Deposits of stone chips formed a makeshift glacis outside the walls on the northwest. In one square there were glacis in two different strata, suggesting that the defenses had been reinforced earlier, probably in the Hasmonean period. Excavations on the east, southeast, and southwest sides disclosed simpler walls, 2 m or less wide, in relatively straight segments; on the east there was a redoubt and on the southeast there were towers, about 50 m apart, projecting 2 or 3 m from the line of the wall. Construction was of rough fieldstones, with hewn stones limited mainly to the projecting towers. Though the towers suggest carefully planned fortifications, in the very same area the wall cut across pottery kilns, suggesting very hastily built walls. At places on the west, the walls intersected or paralleled domestic walls. In general, the walls of the southern plateau were built just before or during the Revolt.

Near the top of the Roman ramp on the northwest, a complex stratigraphic record emerged, with parallel, superimposed, and bisecting walls, indicating that (1) the northwest corner was always the weakest point, (2) occupation had never expanded in this direction, and (3) additional defensive installations were hurriedly constructed because of Vespasian's threat. The earliest walls were Hellenistic, with subsequent impressive wall-building activity at two different Hasmonean periods, and less impressive building during the early Roman period. Part of the northwest casemate wall had been filled with rubble and debris to strengthen them against the force of the Roman attack. The town's main gate must have been in the northern wall, east of the Roman ramp; no subsidiary gates were located certainly, though there was likely one in the middle of the west wall and another on the east side near an olive press cave.

Housing

Several promising locations to investigate the various kinds of first-century housing and evidence of daily life were identified: the areas just inside the complex walls on the northwest corner; an area of steeply terraced housing just inside the wall on the east side of the main hill; lower down the hill to the south, where the plateau meets the hill; still farther south, another area just inside the wall on the plateau; and an area in the middle of the southern plateau (Chapter 5; see Plates 6–10).

Urban Layout

The lower plateau, representing just under a third of the total area of the town, may have been laid out on a Hippodamian plan between the two long parallel north-south walls. Though not fully investigated, there is sufficient evidence of streets that this seems probable in the southern portion of the city. No street plan could be traced on the hill, where a Hippodamian plan would have been impossible; the streets on the hill (*vici* and *clivi*) would have followed the hill's contours irregularly.

In the south, a narrow street 2 m wide and surfaced with stone chips was left immediately inside the wall. Where the steeply terraced housing on the east abutted the wall and just inside the wall at the Roman ramp, there was no intervening street.

Most of the site was devoted to housing. There was little evidence of communal activities: no cemetery, no market area, and no public buildings. In the southeast area, however, a large open rectangular pool or cistern had access steps (partly rock-cut, partly built) and waterproof plaster, with surface remains of a rock-cut balustrade at one corner near the steps. This was probably a communal water supply, used for such purposes as watering sheep or goats, laundry, and emergency water supplies, as Vespasian observed. The pool would have been filled by runoff water from streets, lanes, roofs, and courtyards. On the hilltop, the earliest section of the site to be settled and the location of the Hellenistic farmstead, there may have been a fortress. Rock-cuttings that crisscross the top may eventually yield a sensible reconstruction of the hilltop structures. It has been tentatively concluded that there was a roughly circular wall around the hilltop —whether only at an early stage or until the end of occupation is not clear—consistent with an acropolis. Any public buildings were likely on or near this now bare top.

Architectural and Small Finds

Remains of the seven-week siege in 67 C.E. were everywhere: arrowheads, catapult bolts, *ballistae*, rolling stones, and sandal nails. The pottery was typically Galilean (the majority local), shards of earlier Galilean common ware (GCW), and evidence of wine amphorae from the Greek islands. Yodefat also had its own pottery industry. An almost complete olive press was found in a cave just outside the east wall, with intact crushing stone, weights, pressing pits, and slots for beams in the walls of the cave. The numerous loom weights and fine decorated spindle whorls demonstrate existence of the raising of sheep and goats for wool.

Among the architectural fragments, a piece of architrave (about a meter long, with three simple bands and moldings) lay on the surface at the bottom of the hill outside the west wall, without context. Two column drums were found in the southeastern area, one inside a *mikveh*, which had rolled down the hill at the time of the Roman destruction

of the town. Another column drum was found in a balk at the northwest corner, again a result of Roman destruction. A large doorjamb
(over 2 m tall, about a meter deep, half a meter wide) was found in situ
but in secondary usage. The jamb-stone had been removed from its
original location and reused as a corner-post in a (first-century?) house.
A small, poor, Byzantine synagogue built in the saddle between Yodefat
and the hill to the north of the site had reused several column drums
of varying diameters, along with several capitals. All were in secondary
usage, no longer used as columns and capitals. This later synagogue
was constructed partly, perhaps mainly, from fragments of ancient
Yodefat.

Resulting History of the Site

The earliest construction on the hilltop was a fortified Hellenistic fort-
let or farmstead, perhaps owned by a citizen of Tyre. The hilltop was
taken over in the extension of the successful Hasmonean revolt into
the Galilee. A small Jewish town, perhaps initially contained within
the Hellenistic fortifications, took its place. Its attraction to new Jewish
settlers would have been that there were sufficient facilities (walls, cisterns, buildings) to offer the basis of a town. The town was later
expanded into a Jewish regional walled town, with extensions of the
settlement down the southern slope and later still onto the lower
plateau. These later developments may have begun under Herod the
Great (40–4 B.C.E.) and continued under Herod Antipas or Agrippa I
(4 B.C.E.–38 C.E.; 38–44 C.E.). If this surmise is correct, usual formulations of Galilean social history that emphasize the rapacity of the
Herodian period and the tendency for land and wealth to become
accumulated in relatively few hands with the consequent diminishing
of the lower middle class may need correction. The expansion of
Yodefat represents a period of significant development, with associated trade, commerce, and even wealth.

3-D Reconstruction

Though the layout of Yodefat is not fully understood (the excavated
area is small), the general outline was communicated to the consulting

architects preparing the virtual-reality visualizations. Much of the work preliminary to the 3-D reconstructions had focused on the neighborhood with two houses with *mikvaoth*, an unexcavated cave, the partially excavated open pool, two squares north of the open pool that exposed more housing, and surface rock-cut features in adjacent areas. The neighborhood included streets, lanes, the town wall, and the olive press.

A sustained analysis of this neighborhood by the site architect was passed on to the architects, using rough freehand sketches of these houses and likely elements in the urban layout (Plates 6, 8). Key indicators included construction features such as width of walls, drainage, doors, types of floors, along with functional elements such as the *tabun* (oven), olive crushing basin, cisterns, cave, and *mikvaoth*. Decisions had to be made about the limits of each house, indoor versus outdoor space, existence of second floors, and so on.

First-century housing in rural Galilean villages and towns is still under study, so the reconstruction was developed from first principles. First-century houses similar to Yodefat's terrace housing have been excavated at Gamla (Plates 21, 22), though Galilean building traditions differ in materials and methods of construction from those in the Golan Heights, where columnar basalt permits strong, lengthy beams, with arches and "window walls" common. Villages such as Capernaum (Plates 23, 24), Magdala, Meiron, and Beth Yerah have comparable early Roman housing. Converting archaeological results into an educational film demanded attention to the reconstruction of first-century housing in the Galilee.

DIGITAL ANIMATION AND TV PRODUCTION

Digital Animation and Virtual Reality

In the world of architecture, digital animation and virtual reality have become key design and presentation tools to convey and express the architect's vision. When Bergmann Associates was contacted to create animation for the Yodefat site, it seemed a natural progression beyond their more usual architectural responsibilities. Both architectural and archaeological disciplines utilize detailed record keeping to track a project and both use the same elements needed to create digital animation. The main difference is that architecture builds up while archaeology breaks down. The two disciplines are the reverse of each other and have a close intellectual connection.

Digital animation provides four functions or tools for the architect. (1) It can be used as an interactive design review and *scientific analysis* tool: design options can be assessed faster and at less expense, reducing field changes that cost time and money later. (2) *Interference detection* is easier and better, allowing identification of design flaws or potential interferences. (3) Digital animation can assist in *construction sequencing*, coordinating the various disciplines necessary to construct a building and keeping the general and sub-contractors better informed. (4) Digital animation can be a powerful tool in *public review and approval*, informing public opinion and educating the public.

This last function was the most relevant to the challenge of interpreting Yodefat for a broad public. Instead of having the television viewer try to comprehend complicated CAD data or still renderings, digital animation could convey a sense of the town as it might actually have looked. Animation could help the viewer understand the beauty of design and construction in an ancient community, transporting the viewer more directly back in time.

Team Process

Bergmann Associates' first task was to understand clearly the history of Yodefat and the vision of the town's recreation by the archaeologists and site architects through in-depth interviews and research in the period and location. It was critical to know as much as possible about how the people of Yodefat lived and how they built their homes. The digital artists had to rely heavily on those directly involved. They had to "see" the site accurately and follow the vision of the archaeologists.

The most creative events were meetings between the digital artists, architects, the TV crew, and the excavators at the beginning of the 3-D reconstruction process. They discussed videotapes of the site (aerials and various shots of the mountain and countryside), rocks brought from the site (providing color and texture for the visualizations), free-hand sketches, site drawings, and CAD data in AutoCAD (version 12) format. The excavators described the significance of the various finds. The digital artists prodded the excavators to clarify the basis of the reconstructions, and the film team clarified the dynamic visual needs of a national television production.

This talking-through of the issues created trust between the excavators and the architects, which survived the whole process. The digital artists developed confidence in proceeding on the basis of what they understood and the excavators were confident that the artists were capable of developing responsible animations. Draft virtual reality reconstructions were circulated to the excavators in three countries on two continents; frank critiques of those drafts were communicated to the architects. E-mail, Internet web-based services, file transfer protocols such as ftp, and telecommunications were necessary. There were actually only three face-to-face meetings with the entire project team over the course of six months. The process saved significant amounts of money.

Several general features needed to be conveyed to the large public audience that was anticipated. (1) The overall character of the town and its walled perimeter had to be faithfully portrayed, set in an accurate rendering of the topography, together with an understanding of the process of recording, storing, and utilizing the information about contours, squares, rock-cut features, and finds. (2) The neighborhood about which the most was known would provide insight into the domestic scale of the town, especially the character of one house with its cave. (3) Educating a large audience required attention to details that could be readily grasped and would be informative about Jewish life in antiquity: the house's outdoor living arrangements, *mikveh*, and cistern.

The digital artists needed a feel for people, customs, the architecture of the region and the period. The fundamental features of the site were in the excavation reports and AutoCAD data. The reconstructions emerged from the characteristic aspects of houses at Yodefat and other first-century communities. The key elements were its simple one- and two-story buildings, the relative poverty of most of the dwellings, the simplicity of the materials used, the modest size of the rooms, and their sparse furnishings.

The digital artists worked closely with the producers at WXXI to determine what should be modeled and animated for the production. Since digital modeling and animation take weeks to accomplish, changes in the scope of the project could not be permitted once the modeling process had begun. To ensure that all parties understood what was being created, storyboards were prepared. Decisions such as scene settings, viewpoints, materials, colors, textures, and animation paths were included in the storyboards, which had to match up with the already written script. Several meetings were needed to discuss the storyboards and their revisions. Digital modeling began after final approvals.

Technical Process

The CAD data from the site was the key factor in replicating the city and its buildings. The site had been surveyed and the survey points recorded in AutoCAD, permitting a digital terrain model (DTM), a series of triangles that creates a three-dimensional representation of the terrain. The DTM, the basis for all the digital modeling, allowed the digital artists to place the buildings and walls of the city properly and to grasp the scale of the terrain's elevation (Plate 5). Photographs and sketches did not clearly represent the severity of the terrain; the DTM did. The CAD data for each individual excavation square would have been insufficient without the DTM. With the DTM in place, the CAD data for each square could then be used intelligently. Since the data was in two dimensions, it was used as a template to extrude the forms into three dimensions. To add substance to the buildings, intense conversations were held between the digital artists, the site architect, and the archaeologists. Aesthetic elements such as window placements, flooring, and wall textures were discussed. For example, since only partial CAD data existed for the *mikveh*, the insights and reconstructions of the historians and archaeologists were invaluable in completing the digital model (Plates 7, 10).

Once these issues were resolved, the creation of the digital model began. Four high-end Silicon Graphics workstations running Alias Power Animator 6.0 (with its superior digital modeling tools and fast render times) were used to recreate the city of Yodefat. CartesianFX (CFX) chose the Silicon Graphics product line based on its capacity for handling complex graphics. Adding elements such as water and local vegetation increased the complexity of the digital model, so that it eventually exceeded 12 million polygons in size (most digital models are in the range of 1–2 million polygons). The Yodefat model required the most advanced computing power then available (CartesianFX utilized a Silicon Graphics R4400 onyx with 512MB of RAM).

The next step was to complete the "texturing" of the digital models, assigning the model coloring, lighting, shading, and textures. To match accurately the textures of the houses, especially the walls and floors and ceilings of Yodefat, individual samples of stones and pottery were examined. Where possible, artifacts were scanned for accurate coloring and textures. These scanned images (24-bit color) were brought into the software program Adobe PhotoShop 5.0. PhotoShop allows the digital artist to "clean up" scanned images, correcting anomalies such as poor image quality or lighting for the final animation. Again, interviewing was needed to settle authentically some issues, such as the intensity of first-century lighting, since correct lighting values would bring the model to life. The digital artists also viewed WXXI's videotape footage and photographs of other first- century cities in the area to understand how walls were assembled and mudplastered or how ceilings and roofs were constructed.

The animation required CartesianFX to work closely with WXXI to match existing video footage with the digital model, so the digital animation would blend with the actual footage of the site. The overall aim was to permit the viewer to understand not only what the site might have looked like in the first century but also what it is like today. Footage was selected for the aerial fly around of the city and the *mikveh* scenes. Once the video footage had been selected, the animation path could be laid out on the digital model. At this point, CartesianFX's Silicon Graphics Onyx supercomputer power was needed. To create one second of animation takes 30 frames or renderings. Each frame takes the supercomputer approximately ten minutes to calculate. Thus, one second of animation could require up to 300 minutes of raw computing time. On a normal PC, rendering times were over 45 minutes per frame, much too long to produce effectively. In all, approximately 60 seconds of animation were completed. To create a seamless blend, all viewing elements had to match perfectly, so the CFX team had the difficult task of matching the camera angle and speed when laying out the animation path. With the animation path defined, the computer produced the frames needed for the animation: a total of 1,800 frames were required, taking about 18,000 minutes (more than twelve days) to render. From the individual frames, several still renderings and graphics were used throughout the production. With the animation complete, all the electronic files were turned over to WXXI for post-production work.

The work requires a highly trained digital artist with expert knowledge in computer systems and software and a background in art and photography. Instead of ink, pencil, and paint, the medium is the computer. But even with the high technology hardware and software, the most important requirement was communication.

REACTIONS AND BENEFITS

The success of a television program is often gauged by ratings, the size of the audience, where they live, their ages, and their incomes. "Echoes from the Ancients" was a feature presentation of the Public Broadcasting System in December of 1998 and again in August of 1999. It was carried by affiliates in two-thirds of the United States, and seen by over 20 million people in the U.SA. and Canada; 18,000–20,000 people have accessed the program's companion Web site each week. Perhaps the best gauge of impact is the feedback from a wide range of viewers. The consensus was that the program enabled them to see history not as texts but as people. "Once I could see how they lived," remarked one viewer, "they were no longer esoteric. I saw where and how they lived, how they practiced their religion. Suddenly, first-century Israel had meaning."

The centerpiece animation of a *mikveh* at Yodefat achieved its goal. The evolution of Second Temple Judaism into Rabbinic Judaism, the influence of the Hasmoneans, and the religious roots of Jesus of Nazareth are complex and controversial concepts to present to a general television audience. The animation, however, enabled people to see a central feature of first-century Judaism in the Galilee. A viewer told WXXI, "I understand Judaism and Christianity in a way I never thought possible. The influence of Judaism on early Christianity is not something I learned in the classroom. It was intriguing!"

The 3-D animations contained in the WXXI documentary testified to the effective combination of scholarly research, digital science, and integrity of content. The goal was not to dazzle, but to place them in a programmatic setting that enhanced the content, and enlightened and informed the widest audience possible. Digital animation helped everyone, whether archaeologists or architects or viewers, to hear the faint "Echoes from the Ancients."

CHAPTER FOUR

KHIRBET QANA (AND OTHER VILLAGES)
AS A CONTEXT FOR JESUS

INTRODUCTION[1]

The Cana of Josephus (*Life* 86) is no doubt the same site as New Testament Cana (John 2:1-11; 4:46; 21:2 with 1:43-45), but there has been disagreement over which is the correct site. Recent excavations have tipped the scales decisively in favor of Khirbet Qana as the location of Cana.[2] Khirbet Qana sits on a 100-meter-high hill on the north side of the Beth Netofa Valley, across from Sepphoris (8 km south-south-west) and within sight of Nazareth Illit (13 km due south), at the mouth of the Wadi Yodefat. It was occupied from the Neolithic to the Ottoman periods, with peaks of settlement in the early Roman and Byzantine periods. Sometime in the Byzantine period, a cave halfway up the hill was adapted to meet the needs of pilgrims.

The extensive literature describing pilgrimages to the Holy Land contains numerous references to Cana, some of which (both in the Byzantine period and in the Crusader period) presuppose that Khirbet Qana was the pilgrim site (Chapter 6). Sometime during the Middle Ages attention shifted to Kefr Kenna, today's tourist stop northeast of Nazareth. By the early modern period both sites were known; in the early seventeenth century, Francisco Quaresmius decided between the two sites on the grounds that Kefr Kenna had a church and Khirbet Qana did not.[3] It is likely that an important factor in this shift was that the main road from Sepphoris to Tiberias passed by Kefr Kenna, while Khirbet Qana was not on any major road. Whatever roads may have served it earlier must have gone out of use by the early modern period. It has been argued that a major "Jewish road" went from Tiberias through Arbel, and thence along the north side of the Beth Netofa valley to Cana, at which point the road split, one branch going northwest up the Wadi Yodefat and the other south to Sepphoris. The claim could be correct. Beginning with nineteenth-century investigations of the Holy Land,[4] scholarly opinion has shifted to Khirbet Qana as New Testament Cana, a deduction now being borne out by excavations begun in 1998.

Jesus' context within first-century Palestine is illuminated by appreciation of small towns and villages, whether those associated with him, such as Cana, or others useful for comparative purposes, such as Yodefat and Gamla. This chapter presumes that a more sophisticated understanding of the architectural and urban features of towns provides a sounder basis for literary scholars who interpret the texts,[5] especially the social, economic, domestic, religious, architectural, and urban features of small-town life. Primary sites are Cana, Yodefat, and Gamla, along with other relevant towns (Capernaum and Chorazin), small villages (Nazareth), and capital cities (Bethsaida, Panias, Tiberias, and Sepphoris). Cana is an intriguing case study because the Gospel of John almost presents it as Jesus' early center, much as the Synoptic Gospels portray Capernaum (Chapter 6).

Towns and villages in all regions associated with Jesus could be drawn into this discussion,[6] especially where archaeological work has taken a broad approach, as in the case of the Meiron project in the upper Galilee, including Gush Halav and Khirbet Shema‘.[7] In the lower Galilee, comparisons of small towns with capital cities (*poleis*), especially Sepphoris, are of fundamental importance, and comparisons among the four capital cities (Sepphoris and Tiberias in Galilee, Bethsaida and Panias in Gaulanitis) would help in interpreting Jesus' back-and-forth movements between the realms of Antipas and Philip. Comparisons with Samaritan and Judean towns should isolate distinctive characteristics, if any, of the Galilee. This chapter, however, has a limited goal, to describe the character of small towns in the light of the new excavations at Khirbet Qana.

OVERALL CHARACTER

Khirbet Qana persisted through several occupational periods with few major changes; it was a hilltop village, approached from a saddle to the north; its informal plan was set by access and topography (Plate 4). Natural contours and slopes established its general layout, though some aspects of its plan are now partly obscured by a later trapezoidal wall that hides some hilltop features of the late Hellenistic and Roman periods. It spread partway down both eastern and western slopes, and farther down on the shallower north side. The steep south slope—overlooking Sepphoris and the Beth Netofa Valley—had no buildings until the plateau halfway down, where a separate small village was built later, laid out on approximately rectangular coordinates with informal *insulae*.

Nearby Yodefat provides an instructive comparison.[8] Its occupation period was much shorter (late Hellenistic to early Roman), but it had a similar layout: it was a hilltop town walled from the Hellenistic period through to the Revolt, approached from a saddle to the north, with a late first-century B.C.E. or early first-century C.E. extension onto a lower plateau, which had an approximately rectangular layout (Chapter 3). Gamla, in the Gaulanitis, was also a hilltop town, though it was on a steeply inclined plane and had an informally rectilinear plan. Thus, all three towns shared a kind of modified Hippodamian plan in some parts, not unlike the layouts of Capernaum and Chorazin, with their roughly rectangular coordinates that gave them an informal, late Hellenistic feel. Whether it is correct to refer to this as Hippodamian—or even quasi-Hippodamian—planning needs careful consideration.

The interpretation of Khirbet Qana's hilltop, after three seasons of excavations, is clearer but more complex. The Roman-Byzantine structures below the later trapezoidal wall were (where investigated) arranged almost exactly due north-south, though on the slopes below the hilltop a natural contour-hugging layout and street arrangement was used. It is too soon to say whether the hilltop buildings formed a coherent plan in the first century C.E., organized in blocks, or whether its generally orthogonal layout was simply a function of the hilltop's shape. In the two areas within the trapezoidal walls investigated in detail (the northeast and southwest corners) the layout seems more than accidental, though the site's contours could have prompted such an arrangement.

In the cases in which small towns had informal or quasi-Hippodamian elements, none had the formal Hippodamian plans of Hippos, Dor, or Caesarea Maritima at the same period, or Sepphoris and Tiberias at later periods. This may indicate one element in late Hellenistic cultural influences in the Galilee and Golan. While it would go too far to argue that there was a uniform late Hellenistic urban design throughout the Galilee and Golan in rural towns and villages as well as in major cities, there may be some general planning influence in a number of towns at a relatively early period, well before the second century C.E. The highly formal rectilinear plans at major Roman sites clearly draw on late Hellenistic and Roman urbanism, while the towns have a vaguely similar but much less clear influence.

ROAD PATTERNS AND CONNECTIONS TO MAIN SYSTEMS

A main approach road, identifiable by a retaining wall on the lower edge of the roadbed, entered Khirbet Qana on the east from a small wadi; it doubled back and approached the town from the northeast. A second road may have come into Khirbet Qana from the west (Wadi Yodefat), though the evidence is less good. Both approaches crossed the northern saddle, where there was a large public reservoir. At the northeast edge of town there was an outer informal "gate" (between bedrock and a large standing stone) and a more formal inner gate (with ramp and right-angled turn); the area is unexcavated, so the date is unclear.

Road connections with other towns are uncertain. There would have been a minor road west and north to Yodefat along the wadi, but the main roads of the Galilee (perhaps even before 70 C.E.) lay 6 km away across the Beth Netofa Valley. Major roads connected Sepphoris with Tiberias and Ptolemais, and beyond those with Lebanon, Samaria, Gaulanitis, and the Decapolis. In the early first century such roads were still unpaved and relatively informal.[9] Like Cana, neither Yodefat nor Gamla was on a major road, a feature common (and perhaps important) to all three towns. They were rural communities, though in all three cases within easy distance of a capital city. They were neither remote nor in the thick of things.

WALLS

Cana was unwalled for most of its life, including the early Roman period. It is absent from Josephus's list of walled towns (*War* 2.573–76; *Life* 185–88),[10] and Vespasian ignored it in the Revolt of 66–74 C.E., though he probably marched right by it going to Yodefat. No *ballista* stones, arrowheads, or catapult bolts have been found, though there are sling stones for ordinary hunting. Josephus's silence on military engagements at Cana during the Revolt seems accurate.

There were, however, meter-wide walls forming a trapezoidal structure on the hilltop. Initially these were interpreted as the walls of a monastery referred to in the pilgrim literature. Where the walls' foundations have been exposed on the northeast corner, however, they were poorly built, founded on dirt or rock tumble; cross walls, some of which were earlier than the trapezoidal walls, were not bonded to it, but merely filled open spaces between them. The large trapezoidal structure was in fact a shoddy late defensive wall enclosing the hilltop—and presumably the extent of the town during the unsettled seventh century C.E. In contrast to the north and east, the walls at the southwest corner were earlier and better built (perhaps early or middle Roman period) and it is likely that there was a public building on the southwest hilltop. The later portions of the trapezoidal walls were an extension of—and took their orientation from—the walls of the earlier southeast building.

One obvious fact should be underlined: the density of buildings in an unwalled town resulted from traditional social organization and principles of layout, not from containment by walls. The tight clustering of buildings in towns and villages in early Roman Galilee was simply the way towns developed, and reconstructions that show dispersed buildings in built-up villages and towns are likely to be wrong.

The town walls at both Gamla and Yodefat, despite the impressions in Josephus and the *Mishnah*, were built mainly at the time of the Revolt, under pressure of Roman attack, primarily by joining existing walls with short pieces of new walls to present a continuous front to the enemy.[11] Gamla's walls did not predate the Revolt. Yodefat's walls had a more complicated history: the hilltop, but only the hilltop, was fortified both in the Hellenistic and the Hasmonean periods, so that Yodefat was always a partly walled town, no doubt a main reason why it was chosen as one of the villages to be further fortified and defended at all costs during the Revolt of 66–74 C.E. (Chapter 3).

Most first-century towns and villages had no walls (cf. Capernaum and Chorazin). Yodefat and Gamla were exceptions that highlight the norm. Major cities or *poleis*, however, were walled as a matter of course. Thus, Sepphoris, Tiberias, Bethsaida, and Panias/Caesarea Philippi were walled, if not from their foundation as capitals, then soon after. (The case of Tiberias was unusual: though there was a major southern gate between Tiberias and Hammat, no walls were connected to the gate until later; in the first century C.E. it was unwalled.) Three typical conditions can be established: capital cities and *poleis* were walled; towns and villages were typically not walled; atypically, a very few towns or villages were walled, some from earlier periods (Yodefat) and some from the time of the Revolt (Gamla).

AGORAS AND COMMERCIAL STRUCTURES

Sepphoris and Tiberias had one or more market places by the second century. By contrast, there seems to have been no marketplace (*forum* or *agora*) at Cana, Gamla, Yodefat, Capernaum, Chorazin, and most other small towns and villages. In the first centuries B.C.E. and C.E., market forces had not, by and large, led to the creation of a *forum* in the center of rural towns where goods were bought and sold, along the lines of a Hellenistic or Roman town,[12] though the economy could have been changing in that direction. Commercial activity was conducted, no doubt, from houses or from near the town's entrance—the "gate" as it was described in earlier periods, especially in the Iron Age.[13] The popular view that there should be a formal prescribed commercial space does not apply to small towns and villages; that view is conditioned by Hellenistic and Roman patterns, as the terms *agora* and *forum* suggest.

Several possible locations for commerce in Khirbet Qana exist on the town's north side, informal spaces at the edge of town where roads entered the built-up area, particularly on the northeast where an irregular area by the "gate" may have served the village's needs. Huge rough boulders, not foundations of walls but intended merely to define spaces, surrounded the area. This was probably a commercial area both for itinerant travelers and townspeople. Presumably shops were in dwellings where pottery, glass, or other goods were manufactured, though no such shop-dwelling has been identified at Khirbet Qana yet.

STREET PATTERNS

The town core at Khirbet Qana in the late Hellenistic and early Roman period was, in the parts excavated, a densely packed hilltop, organized relatively regularly. Streets and lanes provide a sense of how the town's circulation patterns worked. Around the hilltop, the housing on slopes on three sides followed the contours, with streets along the contours (*vici*) wider than the streets climbing the slopes (*clivi*). Stairs are still visible in a few of the *clivi* on the north.

It is impossible to trace a street plan on the hilltop at Yodefat because of erosion, though the plan was probably adapted to the hill's contours. On the hillsides to the east and the south, the street pattern was like that at Khirbet Qana. When the town expanded onto a relatively level plateau to the south (late first century B.C.E./early first century C.E.), the "suburb" was laid out roughly on a gridiron, either because that naturally suited the shape of the site (the east and west edges of the plateau were nearly parallel) or because of cultural preferences. Certainty is impossible.

At Gamla, the *vici* followed the contours in a more or less parallel layout and were the main streets of the town, though there were irregularities in the layout due to the topography. The *clivi* were narrower and stepped, like Khirbet Qana, due to the steep hillside. Capernaum and Chorazin had flatter sites, and as a result the street layout was almost rectangular, with somewhat irregular *insulae*. The same was true at Sepphoris, even in the older (western) parts of the *polis*. It is safe to make two contrasting statements: (1) topography was a determining factor, shaping the layout of the town in traditional ways; (2) irregular orthogonal layouts ("quasi-Hippodamian" plans) appear more frequently than expected, so that imported cultural factors in village plans should not be ignored.

CISTERNS AND RESERVOIRS

Villages and towns were differentiated from *poleis* by water supply. *Poleis* such as Hippos, Beth Shean, Ptolemais, Dor, Caesarea Maritima, Tiberias, and Sepphoris had aqueducts with permanent water sources and extensive communal water storage facilities to ensure regular supply. In towns and villages, however, households subsisted on water stored in domestic cisterns filled during the winter rains. Towns may have provided public cisterns and reservoirs for the population at large, whether for regular needs or emergencies. Khirbet Qana had a public reservoir (undated) in the saddle north of the town, at a level where it was of relatively little use except for watering animals. Some of the cisterns on the hilltop are much larger than domestic scale, probably providing a publicly available water supply on the top. Most of the cisterns at Khirbet Qana were older, bell-shaped designs; some of the exceptions were obviously later, such as a large rectangular cistern near the lower village. The dominant bell shape may derive from earlier phases of the town. (Samples of plaster have been taken for carbon dating, so many of the features mentioned in this chapter as undated may soon be given dates.)

Yodefat had two public reservoirs, one on the southern plateau (first century) and another, like Khirbet Qana, on the northern saddle (undated). Yodefat's assemblage of cisterns included a mix of household cisterns and large public cisterns. Like Khirbet Qana, the public cisterns were in the older parts of town at the top of the hill. Yodefat's cistern typology was richer than Khirbet Qana's, with several styles and shapes. The reason for the differences in cistern typology between the two towns is not immediately apparent, but may have to do in part with Yodefat's Tyrian background and Khirbet Qana's longer occupation.

INDUSTRIAL AREAS

Khirbet Qana had several industrial areas. On the eastern slope a bell-shaped plastered dovecote (*columbarium*) was hewn from bedrock. A second tower-style *columbarium* may have been located on the lower slope in the north. Both *columbaria* were in domestic areas and typical first-century B.C.E./C.E. forms.[14] East of the trapezoidal wall several natural caves have collapsed; some were probably industrial installations (perhaps an olive press). Glass wasters have been found on the hilltop, suggesting a small glass-blowing activity. On the southeastern shoulder between two large cisterns was a two-room industrial operation of uncertain date but plausibly early Roman, probably for dyeing wool or leather, with four or five vats or pools in each room.

The most important industry at Yodefat was pottery manufacturing. Several kilns on the southern plateau produced a pottery similar to Kefar Hananiah ware. One kiln was destroyed when Josephus's wall was built hastily right through it. Just outside the wall, also on the southeast, a natural cave held a large olive-oil factory with two intact presses. The main industry at Gamla was also olive oil; a large two-press factory was located at the western end of town in a well-built, roofed structure near a wealthy residential area. There were also a substantial number of flour mills in the same general area.

ECONOMIC DIFFERENTIATION

Even this brief summary raises general economic issues. Khirbet Qana visually controlled one of the most fertile areas in the Galilee, second only to the Jezreel Valley. The site was occupied through a very long period, with peaks of settlement in early Roman and Byzantine periods and smaller peaks in the Iron Age and the Arab period; the long occupation implies that the town's location was prompted by natural agricultural advantages, probably crop farming similar to Bedouin practices today. Soil cores taken in the 2000 season should provide information both about grain crops in the Beth Netofa Valley and environmental fluctuations. To date, however, while there is a large repertoire of basalt grinders of various sizes and shapes, there is no evidence of large flour mills, threshing floors, or traditional storage bins, as one might expect.

Comparisons of economic activities in adjacent towns or villages would reveal whether neighboring towns differentiated their roles by developing complementary activities. Khirbet Qana and Yodefat, 2.5 km apart, offer an excellent opportunity to add to our limited knowledge of such differentiations, so a trial comparison of the two sites might be helpful.

The preliminary table below (Table 4.1) suggests there was relatively little overlap in industrial and agricultural activity in the two villages. One reason, no doubt, is that despite their proximity they lie in geographically different regions, with different exploitable opportunities. A geographic explanation, however, may be only a partial explanation; the overall picture suggests adjacent towns may have been complementary. Did the region function as a coherent economic unit? This could only be known from comparisons with other nearby towns and villages, but such an analysis would assist scholars of the social setting to understand better economic exploitation (frequently claimed for this period in the Galilee), city-rural relationships (also a matter of much discussion), peasant social protests (Chapter 2), and the like.

Table 4.1: Economic Activities at Yodefat and Khirbet Qana

	Yodefat, 6 seasons	Khirbet Qana, 3 seasons
Olives	Double press	Household size only (to date)
Grapes	—	—
Pottery	Three kilns	None
Grain crops	Some terraces	Beth Netofa Valley
Sheep & Wool	Numerous loom weights and spindle whorls	Relatively few loom weights
Dyeing	—	Major installation
Glass	—	Some wasters
Lime	?	?
Quarrying	Some	Some
Goats	?	?
Doves (dovecotes)	—	One certain, another probable
Other domestic animals	?	?

DIFFERENTIATED NEIGHBORHOODS

In both Khirbet Qana and Yodefat, and less clearly at Gamla, major industries were located near the edges of the town, with a preference for the eastern side of built-up areas because of prevailing westerly winds. Pottery kilns, olive presses, *columbaria*, and dyeing were situated on the eastern sides in one or both of Khirbet Qana and Yodefat; the same would be expected of lime kilns, glass blowing, forges, and other industries that produced smoke or waste products. Industrial activity shaped neighborhood patterns.

Neighborhoods were differentiated; at Khirbet Qana a housing typology is gradually emerging (Chapter 5; Plates 11–14). The structures on the hilltop under the Byzantine reconstruction of the town were mainly early Roman, with occasional small finds suggesting longer occupancy (Persian and Iron Age, mostly in first-century fills). Neighborhood and housing differentiation has not yet received enough attention. Concentrated work at recent excavations will eventually illuminate the social character of the towns and identify social strata. The strong scholarly opinions sometimes expressed on the basis of a study of texts have rarely had adequate roots in archaeological evidence.[15] Houses on the less steep northern slope at Khirbet Qana were larger and better equipped (one had a *mikveh* and storage cave), and in some cases had a side courtyard. While we have no evidence of columns for peristyles, we anticipate finding larger houses organized around a central courtyard on the lower north slopes. So we are gradually developing a three-item typology: terrace housing without courtyards, side courtyard houses, and central courtyard houses.[16] All the houses excavated to date were built of simple materials and basic, typically Galilean, construction.

Houses at Yodefat were equally simple, one or two stories, possibly three in the terrace housing. About the same range of houses can be distinguished as at Khirbet Qana: terrace housing, houses with informal courtyards, central courtyard houses. A remarkable frescoed house was discovered on the eastern slope, with a Pompeian style decoration and a painted plaster floor (Chapter 5), suggesting that the top end of the social scale was higher than anticipated at a rural site. The lower end of the social scale was a pottery-making neighborhood on the southern plateau. At Gamla, the steep slope makes almost all houses terrace housing (Plates 21–22). But there were still differences among neighborhoods, identifiable by size, finishes, artifacts, location, and courtyards.

By comparison, the first-century C.E. housing at Capernaum (Plates 23–24) was relatively modest, analogous to but different from the houses at Yodefat and Khirbet Qana. Several of the houses had small, irregular central courtyards. In the central parts of Chorazin near the synagogue, there were two (later) *insulae*, where housing units were grouped around a large, irregular, common courtyard. (No information is available on first to second centuries C.E. northerly areas or the southern areas.) The clearest results to date are from Yodefat, where a spectrum of wealth and status has emerged. Further examination of these housing types needs to be undertaken before definitive results can shed light on Jesus' context in rural towns and villages in the Galilee and the Golan. Comparisons should include material artifacts and house styles in different areas within the same site, and comparisons more broadly from one site to another. Careful consideration also needs to be given to change over time in the towns and villages of rural Galilee. Were they contracting or expanding? Were houses being abandoned in the first century or still being occupied?

Synagogues/Public Buildings

The trapezoidal wall, enclosing an area of approximately 45x75 m on the crown of the hill with an orientation about 18 or 20 degrees east of true north (in fact, oriented directly to Sepphoris and approximately towards Jerusalem), dated from the seventh century, either the Persian invasion of 614 C.E. or the Muslim conquest of 636 C.E. It was not the perimeter wall of a monumental public building complex.

The southwest parts of the trapezoidal wall, however, were carefully built with genuinely monumental features. Its regular courses were founded on bedrock, and the wall intersections that can be examined were well bonded. This portion of the wall was relatively early, and probably formed part of the walls of a public building complex. The main room (10x15 m) had regular 5x5 m bays in the nave, with 2.5x5.0 m bays in the aisles, and each of its columns sat on three dressed foundation stones (Plates 15–18). The floors in the aisles were plastered, but dressed bedrock in the nave. The room had a discontinuous single bench of varying widths on parts of three sides. A smaller room (3x4 m), east of and higher than the large room, had a single low bench on the three sides that have been exposed, and probably on all four, with a floor of bedrock. The juxtaposition of two adjacent benched rooms suggests a synagogue and *Beth ha-Midrash*. A soft, chalky limestone mock-Ionic capital—decorated with what looks like grape clusters in low relief—found in secondary usage as part of a later rebuilt wall, supports this identification, for the capital has formal analogies with capitals at Beth She'arim and Gamla (Plate 15). The date of the complex has not yet been determined; it was in use for some time, judging from the successive plaster floors, and it may be first century C.E. If this Roman-period structure is a public complex, the later trapezoidal walls adopted its orientation, suggesting that there was still occupation in this sector in the seventh century C.E.

In the northeast quadrant where the trapezoidal walls were flimsy, a pilaster made from well-dressed plastered stones with a finely carved rectangular capital in hard limestone, decorated a larger house (Plates 19, 20). The pilaster's top surface was only about 1.5 m off the floor. While this could suggest another public building (originally we hypothesized a monastery room) it is more likely a well-appointed house. No *voussoirs* and matching capital have been found, so an arch that springs from the pilaster and supports a second floor cannot be confirmed yet. In the adjacent square a finely bossed lintel, perhaps a door lintel, was discovered. There was a well-laid flagstone floor and an entry room off the street, with a large, bell-shaped cistern and another rectangular pit, the latter filled with first-century debris.

In the lower village halfway down the hill, a cave complex with two in situ stone water pots (and room for four more) was venerated in the Byzantine period. One of the signs of veneration was Greek graffiti on the ceiling on several of the multiple layers of plaster. There may have been a church, perhaps with associated monastic structures, contiguous to the cave. The character of these buildings awaits further excavations, and is in any case not relevant to questions about Jesus, except that this Byzantine evidence confirms that in the sixth century Khirbet Qana was identified as the Cana of the Gospels and Josephus. The veneration site was an altar-like construction, into which stone pots were plastered. Most of the front face of the altar was constructed from a sarcophagus lid on edge, with the flat inside surface facing out; it was rubbed smooth and had "Maltese" crosses inscribed into it. Part of the bottom of the sarcophagus was found 40 or 50 m away. The complex had four caves that communicated with each other; stairs and a tunnel suggest a deliberate processional way through three of the four caves.

No in situ evidence of a synagogue at Yodefat has survived, but there is scattered evidence of a public building, whether Jewish or pagan is hard to say: a monumental door jamb in secondary usage, several column drums found in destruction layers, column drums and capitals reused in a Byzantine synagogue at the bottom of the hill to the north, a piece of architrave lying loose on the site (and now lost). These could be the remains of a Tyrian late Hellenistic structure, though it would be surprising for its fragments to be found in early Roman destruction layers. It is more likely that these are remains of a public building (a synagogue?) at the top of the hill from the pre-destruction period.

The question of pre-destruction synagogues continues to be debated. On the one hand, inscriptional evidence confirms the presence of synagogues or Jewish public buildings (Part 3).[17] On the other hand, the limited archaeological data suggests a relatively limited presence of synagogues in first-century C.E. towns. One thing seems clear: in assessing structures as possible first-century Jewish public buildings, a procrustean bed that demands some combination of essential elements before the name synagogue can be used, must be avoided. There was a range of types and styles of buildings that defies simple categorization or typologies.

GRAVES

Khirbet Qana had a large necropolis of thirteen or fourteen tombs, with at least nineteen chambers, in four areas in a rough oval pattern around the site. Their general form was the same: one or more chambers per tomb, with between one and eleven loculi per chamber, with no *arcosolia* and no inscriptions. All were located about 500 m or more from the hilltop. With one exception, they were typologically similar, with a vertical shaft entrance, with no steps to give access to the courtyards. None was decorated, though surface features hint at some external architecture connected with the tombs.

The shaft entrances—1 to 2 m deep—functioned as courtyards; in some cases a *dromos*-style entrance would have been easier. The unusual shaft design must have been deliberate. There was no evidence of tomb closures, such as "buttressing stones," rolling stones, or stones fitting the chamber entrance, as noted in the *Mishnah*. The chambers and loculi conformed to the general *mishnaic* dimensions mentioned, and were similar to, though plainer than, those found in Jerusalem. No ossuaries were found, but there seems to have been provision for secondary burials in an extra-wide *loculus*, two joined *loculi*, and a small room.

Though there was no decoration inside or outside, there is evidence of water-related rock-cut installations. None had channels or drains to remove water from the shafts, so how the runoff water problems were solved is unclear. The tombs fit late Hellenistic through Second Temple tomb design; they relate to Jerusalem tombs as rural, peasant tombs to urban tombs. Evidently village burial practices correlated closely with Jerusalem practices, and with customs of the first to second centuries

C.E., as discussed in the *Mishnah*. These Jewish tombs of the Second Temple period, or just after, imply that there were not great differences in burial practices between south and north, between city and countryside, between rich and poor.

CONCLUSION

I raise several questions in the place of conclusions, with provisional comments on those questions, though the answers must still be determined.

To what extent were the towns of rural lower Galilee and the Golan planned towns of a kind characteristic of centralized economies and centralized control? There is evidence of modified or quasi-Hippodamian plans, especially in the early Roman period, suggesting Hellenistic cultural influences. In areas of lower Galilee and Gaulanitis, one might expect more traditional, informally laid out towns.

Have differences been exaggerated between major urban centers such as Sepphoris, Tiberias, Panias, and Bethsaida, on the one hand, and rural villages such as Cana, Yodefat, and Capernaum? The differences, which seem real and pervasive, are most persuasively seen in the small finds from Tiberias or Sepphoris or Panias (Bethsaida is less clear), which reflect a sophistication and urbanity that is not found regularly in small towns. The frescoed wall in a Yodefat house is a genuine surprise, for it fits more easily into the artistic and decorative vocabulary of a *polis* than a rural village. The small piece of fresco at Khirbet Qana came, perhaps, from a Jewish public building.

Was there a substantial difference in the degree of Hellenization evident in the urban centers and the rural villages? In a word, yes. Hellenistic influence was not absent in rural villages; indeed Yodefat's origins lay in a late Hellenistic settlement. But once "Judaized" in the Hasmonean period, small towns and villages were more conservative religiously and more constrained in expressions of wealth and culture. Even though a city such as Sepphoris had *mikvaoth*, as Khirbet Qana and Yodefat and Gamla also did, Sepphoris had more objects that suggest diversity of religious affiliations and more wealth for acquiring objects that reflected those mixed elements in the population.

Were rural towns and villages planned? There were elements of planning in such aspects of town life as the expansion of Yodefat onto the lower plateau, where the layout was more regular than might be expected of an unplanned, gradual expansion. Khirbet Qana seems to have had no similar elements.

What is the evidence for exploitation and economic development? Two factors point to economic development: a substantial number of new towns in the post-Hasmonean period, and new areas of development within existing towns. Both factors may have been due to an influx of Judean settlers. On the other hand, there is little evidence of evacuation of houses because of economic exploitation. Those interested in questions of social protest and peasant exploitation need to accumulate the material data to address the question of the balance between development and deprivation.

What does the material evidence in villages and small towns suggest about the economy, especially about dependence upon agriculture versus a manufacturing or industrial economy? Most small towns were self-sufficient agriculturally, or had interlocking, agriculturally based economies. Most Galilean towns and villages depended on either olives or grapes, sometimes both. Most would have grown root crops, and those that could, likely grew grain crops. Adjacent towns may have developed differentiated economies, perhaps in both agricultural and industrial-manufacturing fields. Since much manufacturing was household-based and labor was episodic, most towns had some balance between the two forms of employment and occupation. The balance at Khirbet Qana was probably typical of the balance at most other small towns: grain crop farming, herding of sheep and goats, wool and leather, raising of doves, glass manufacture; these are different from but not unlike what was found at Yodefat or at Gamla. More study needs to be given to the complementary and interlocking features of adjacent small towns.

Is there material evidence of social differentiation and social stratification in the organization and layout of these towns? Khirbet Qana has hints of social differentiation, especially in the variety of the village's housing types, similar to Yodefat or Gamla. Gamla's evidence is somewhat clearer, but Yodefat's fresco is important evidence for an upper class. One might have suspected this in the abstract and have questioned a too uniform "peasant" model. An informed answer to this question would influence substantially how Jesus' context is understood and how his words are interpreted.

Is there evidence of socio-religious differences in first-century towns, or should we think of an undifferentiated "common Judaism"? If the data from the three main sites we have discussed is homogenized, the answer is yes to both questions. There was a dominant "common Judaism," along the lines Sanders has suggested,[18] though his picture needs modification: this common religious understanding included use in some places of a communal meeting hall or public building and access to a communal *mikveh*; wealthier citizens who wished to highlight their concern for ritual purity built private *mikvaoth*. Some used stoneware if they could afford it. On the other hand, not all had a private *mikveh*, not all used stoneware, some had objects drawn from the pagan Roman world that offended against torah, and so on. In burial practices, Khirbet Qana followed Jewish customs more consistently than can be verified for other similarly sized towns.

In sum, Khirbet Qana provides another touchstone for study of the historical Jesus, one that, like Capernaum, is identified in the literary traditions as a place frequented by Jesus. While its stratigraphic evidence is not as neatly delimited as Yodefat or Gamla, like those towns it gives strong evidence of first-century life in a village whose occupation extended from the Iron Age to the Crusades and beyond. Its evidence will take on special importance when interpreted alongside other nearby evidence: towns and villages such as Yodefat, Shikhim, Ruma, Nazareth, and cities such as Sepphoris and Tiberias. Through comparative analyses, we may eventually be able to make more precise statements about some of the cities, towns, and villages linked with Jesus and his movement.

CHAPTER FIVE

FIRST-CENTURY HOUSES AND Q'S SETTING

INTRODUCTION[1]

Q's Setting in Judaism

This chapter presupposes that behind the gospels of Matthew and Luke lies a source, Q, which reflects the social conditions of an early group of believers in Jesus. "In terms of the fundamental beliefs of Judaism the Q Christians were a conservative grouping," marked by a concern for "inclusion and association and inseparability" from features of Judaism such as the temple.[2] Though Pharisaism concerns the group, the woes do not separate Q's community from either temple or law. "The tradition seems throughout to be comfortable within Judaism, uneasy about Pharisaism, and, in view of the rarity of any comment on the authority of the law (Q 16:17), not at all preoccupied with the problem which threatened to tear apart other early Christian communities." "We have a picture of a community whose outlook was essentially Jerusalem-centered, whose theology was Torah-centered, whose worship was temple-centered, and which saw (with some justice) no incompatibility between all of that and commitment to Jesus."[3] Similarly, C. M. Tuckett states, "Q's polemic is directed against only a part of the Jewish community among which the Q community existed."[4] This conservatism should neither be equated with nor set against Pharisaism, nor any specific group within Judaism; it may merely express a "common [and conservative] Judaism,"[5] characteristic of many Jews.

The *realia* of early Christianity and Second Temple Judaism, as exposed in recent archaeological research in the Galilee and the Golan, suggest that Catchpole's views are correct.[6] This chapter explores how my interests and his—both substantially altered from our interests as students 40 years ago—now intersect. I discuss archaeological data from towns and villages, which can help define a realistic context within town life in the lower Galilee and the Golan that offers a plausible concrete setting, and will argue that thinking coherently about some of this evidence might lead to a more refined view of some of Q's emphases.[7]

Q's Archaeological and Architectural Setting

Archaeological work over more than a century has deeply influenced approaches to the setting of early Christianity, through analyzing inscriptions, Christianity's urban setting,[8] architecture of early synagogues,[9] religious and social structures, adaptations of houses for religious activities,[10] voluntary associations,[11] and specificity of settings.[12]

New Testament scholarship has concentrated on Paul and focused on major cities, especially in Asia Minor and Greece: Paul's (and Ignatius's) letters, for example, reflected their social settings in the household, set against the rich tapestry of Greek culture and urbanism. The model of urban, upper-class Hellenistic and Roman houses that followed from this analysis of setting has illuminated how house churches developed in cities such as Ephesus, Corinth, and Rome. Sometimes, however, this urban Roman model, predicated on one set of local conditions, has been applied to other settings, without sufficient consideration of social and architectural and cultural factors in these other locations.[13] Neglecting the local particularities of each region in which Christianity became rooted or projecting an Asian model onto other early Christian developments will not do.

It is difficult to utilize *realia* in Galilee, Judea, and South Syria in descriptions of the rise of the Jesus movement, in part because no *realia* can certainly be associated with it in these early stages. The same is true, of course, of Paul and his communities, but this has not prevented Paul scholars from making substantial gains in understanding Paul's social location in Greece and Asia Minor. We need, however, to move beyond generalities to a refined social description of the setting of Jesus and communities that shaped the earliest gospel materials, utilizing relevant material evidence. The Jesus movement in Palestine was lodged for some time within Palestinian Judaism. How does first-century Palestinian Judaism reflect, and in turn shape, the movement's

social setting and literary products? How did the early Christian movement develop in northern Palestine—Galilee and Gaulanitis? Within
what architectural setting did its development occur? How did the Q
movement fit into its religious and sociocultural setting? I focus on
housing, because the movement among the first two generations of
Jesus' followers was essentially a house-based movement.

Local Housing and Religious Life in the Galilee and Golan

Housing

Palestinian housing is now receiving some attention. Archaeological
excavations explore housing with increasing frequency, though archaeological reports do not always emphasize domestic questions as
innately important. Since houses were often occupied for centuries,
their evidence is usually complex. The evidence is now being sifted in
fresh ways, though data for the study of first-century houses is still
somewhat sparse and not broadly available.[14] I describe three sites—
Yodefat, Gamla, and Khirbet Qana—among those that inform us of
first-century houses in Galilee and the Golan, followed by observations
on how this material might contribute to a reading of Q.

The northern parts of the land, especially Galilee and Gaulanitis
(with related regions in Auranitis, Trachonitis, Batanea, and Hulitis)
were less than half of Herod the Great's kingdom. They comprised,
however, the majority of Antipas's and Philip's tetrarchies, and later
most of Agrippa I's and II's regions, during and after the time of Jesus.
These northern regions—especially the towns—were likely Q's context. Yodefat in Galilee and Gamla in the Gaulanitis, both well excavated though not yet well published, are the most important sites,
sharing two important features: both were destroyed by Vespasian in 67
C.E. and both subsequently remained deserted. Both, therefore, offer
pristine first-century sites where excavation of the housing has been an
important goal, so they get scholars as close to the setting of Jesus as is
currently possible. I add Khirbet Qana, though it continued to be
occupied much later, for its intrinsic interest.

Yodefat

Yodefat lay on a steep hill halfway between the Mediterranean Sea and
the Sea of Galilee, concentrated on a bald hilltop, with a narrower
southern extension on a plateau about 30 m lower (Chapter 3).
According to Josephus, the town's population was 40,000, though it
could have held no more than a few thousand during a siege and its
normal population was probably below 1,000. The small town, built
around a Hellenistic fortified farmstead (a stage I ignore here), had
flourished since the Hasmonean resettlement of the Galilee in the second century B.C.E. The earliest Jewish village was contained within the
late Hellenistic fortifications; without a natural water supply, its walls,
cisterns, and buildings formed the basis of the later Jewish town. It
attracted new settlers, who occupied buildings on the southern slope
and the lower plateau that dated from the late first century B.C.E. to
first century C.E., probably under Herod the Great (40–4 B.C.E.),
Antipas (4 B.C.E.–38 C.E.) or Agrippa I (38–44 C.E.). Josephus strengthened Yodefat's defenses with additional walls to resist Rome's forces
during the early stages of the Revolt of 66–74 C.E., taking advantage
of steep hillsides above the surrounding wadis. The excavations (especially in 1999) have shown this hurried strengthening of the defenses.
The town fell after a 47-day siege in 67 C.E.

Rock-cut cisterns, some immense, were distributed around the site,
with the largest concentration around the hilltop; they were crucial to
Yodefat's existence. Most cisterns were domestic installations with rock-
cut stairs or an opening to lower a storage jar. The town also had two
large open rectangular pools, one on the plateau, and another in the
northern saddle.

Houses from the first centuries B.C.E. and C.E. have been excavated
around the site (see Plates 3, 5–10). They were relatively simple, one or
two stories of rough masonry construction, with almost no hewn stones
even around the openings; there was no mortar bonding the masonry
and few plaster or stucco wall finishes. The walls were bonded with and
finished in mud plaster, all of which has disappeared. Second floors
and roofs would have been constructed from small locally cut wooden
beams, with sticks and branches and mud forming the finished floor
and roof surfaces. No stone beams or arches were found (in contrast to
the volcanic areas of Gaulanitis, where different building materials and
methods were used) and no roof tiles. Ground floors were equally

simple, of beaten earth or roughly leveled exposed bedrock, and occasionally plaster or rough flagstone.

The lower plateau (roughly a third of the total area) had an orthogonal street pattern between two north-south wadis. A narrow street 2 m wide and surfaced with stone chips ran immediately inside the eastern wall. At other points (e.g., the steeply terraced housing on the northeast, inside the wall at the Roman ramp, and on the west side of the plateau) houses abutted the wall directly or, in several cases, were cut through by the wall, suggesting that there the wall was hurriedly constructed under threat of attack.

There is little evidence of public facilities, neither *agora* nor public buildings. The largest cisterns and the two large open rectangular pools were probably communal: the pool inside the walls had rock-cut steps and a balustrade at one corner. There may have been a public building at some stage, either Hellenistic, perhaps destroyed during the Hasmonean period, or Jewish, or both (Chapters 3, 4). It would have been situated on the now bare hilltop, where Hellenistic and later rock-cuttings may eventually yield clues for such a building.

Jewish ritual concerns are well attested. With stoneware having been found in disparate locations and in varied social locations, it is no longer possible to argue that only one group—Pharisees, for example—were concerned with ritual purity. Numerous stone-cut cups, bowls and jugs, in a wide variety of shapes and sizes, implied a common concern for ritual purity at Yodefat and a determination to avoid impurity in everyday utensils. Two *mikvaoth* (ritual bathing pools) in adjacent houses in the southeastern area also pointed to purity concerns. Both stoneware and *mikvaoth* imply strong domestic attention to purity; both suggest continuity between Galilean and Jerusalem purity concerns. Indeed, some of the stoneware may have originated in Jerusalem. Much the largest group of coins was Hasmonean, suggesting close links with Jerusalem. Jonathan Reed notes that similar numismatic evidence appears at Khirbet Qana, Gamla, and other sites. He observes, "although the number of sites with abundant first-century evidence is limited, the existing finds consistently mirror the finds of Judea."[15]

Housing was of several types. Terrace housing on the steep east slope just inside the wall was similar in form to the housing at Gamla and Khirbet Qana. The foundations and lower floors were rock-cut; houses were generally two stories; adjacent houses at a higher level were built on the walls of the houses below, so some walls were three stories high. Buildings abutted the town walls and rooftops of lower houses were used as additional living areas of higher houses.

In the 1997 season one unexpectedly different room was discovered on the east side of the town. Almost 5 m of painted-plaster wall (fresco) was found in a geometric style reminiscent of Pompeii (a kind of simplified first style) with similar colors. The floor of the frescoed room was also plastered and painted. This was a major exception to the other housing: (1) it pointed to more wealth than the other housing; (2) its nearest Jewish analogies were wealthy houses in Jerusalem and Judean palaces built by Herod the Great (Jericho, Herodium, Masada, Machaerus, Caesarea Maritima); (3) the house's frescoed wall was the most vividly painted and intact found from first-century Israel; (4) no frescoed floor has been found dated to the first century in Galilee. Further excavations will be required to understand this 1997 evidence properly. Was the rest of the house consistent in style and decoration? Was this a peristyle house in a town that had no evidence of such a style? Did other houses in town share these features? Did Yodefat have a continuously differentiated social structure? Or was this one house the sole example? No explanation for such a wealthy house in Yodefat is forthcoming. Nothing in the historical record suggests a social setting for a sophisticated urban style house in a small agrarian peasant town.

Where the slope was less steep the houses followed the contours closely, with floors adjusted to suit the levels. The foundations and floors were sometimes rock-cut; one floor was roughly plastered on bedrock. The rooms were a little larger than in the terrace housing, and more artifacts illustrative of daily life were found in this area. Short lanes off streets provided access. Two houses with private *mikvaoth* formed a complex that could be reconstructed in more detail (Plates 6–10 and Chapter 3). Floors were rock-cut, beaten earth, or roughly paved. Rock-cut cisterns were filled by water from the roofs; at ground level, a collecting pool and channel survived in one house. An adjacent cave for storage or a shelter for animals was integrated into the same house; there was an oven (*tabun*) in the courtyard and a small olive crushing installation in another. One *mikveh* had a room of its own, the other was in a rock-cut cavity adjacent to a cistern; both appear to have had water channels from their own water sources, providing running or "living" water. The large open pool, on which the neighborhood focused, was beside this complex. A narrow street separated the houses from the town wall, and a short lane gave access to other houses whose plans could be read from rock-cut foundations. A nearby cave had an industrial-scale double press olive-oil installation, so the *mikvaoth* inside the wall may mean the olive press operated under conditions of ritual purity.

Simple first-century housing with one or two rooms was laid out orthogonally on the lower plateau. A large (unexcavated house) had rock-cut remains that still stood half to 1 m high, which included the main door and all four walls. It was planned around a central court-yard, though the floor had collapsed into cisterns below. Near the Roman siege-ramp on the northwest a housing complex showed the vigor of the Roman siege. First-century houses (below which were late Hellenistic houses) were built against the town wall. They formed case-mate rooms that were filled during the siege to strengthen the defenses. The kitchen was the most revealing room, full of pottery broken dur-ing the siege, with a *tabun* (oven) and a piece of stone table top or kitchen "counter," all on a beaten earth floor with an adjacent bedrock floor at a higher level.

Gamla

Gamla was built on a much earlier Bronze Age site, a ridge between two very steep ravines with rivers (Plate 1). There may have been a rudimentary water supply by aqueduct but cisterns supplied most of Gamla's water needs. Like Yodefat, the town had flourished from its Hasmonean re-Judaization onwards. The earliest housing was in the northeast, but it expanded into new neighborhoods to the south and west. Most housing was terraced, with the rear wall of a lower house acting as the front wall of a house higher up the slope (Plates 21, 22). Gamla was protected on three sides by deep ravines, but the natural approach from higher land to the east required extra efforts; during the revolt that ridge was cut away. As at Yodefat, Josephus used a com-bination of existing and new walls to create a casemate wall prior to the Roman attack, with a round tower high on the northeast corner where the casemate wall met the ridge. These precautions worked well, for Gamla survived a seven-month siege in the spring of 67 C.E. before Vespasian took it in the fall of that year.

Early in the Gamla excavations a public building was uncovered that served various religious purposes associated with a synagogue: a simple multipurpose communal building with columns, varied capitals, complex entrance, niche in one corner (possibly for the Torah scroll), separate large *mikveh* with water channel and connecting *otzer*, and small *Beth ha-Midrash* for study and education, acting as part of the casemate wall (Plate 25). Another community building has since been discovered, whose presence was long anticipated from a lintel decorated with a central rosette and flanking palm trees lying on the surface. Its purpose is uncertain, for the structure has no obvious Jewish analogies. It seems unlikely that it was a second synagogue, since it had three equal-sized rooms side by side, connected by doorways; these inner rooms opened onto a broad space through wide openings framed by decorated pilasters. Had the building been found in a Roman context, it might have been thought dedicated to Rome's Capitoline Triad! That is obviously impossible, and all that can be said so far is that Gamla had more complex and organized social-religious facilities than are usually found in a rural town site.

Gamla's neighborhoods, like Yodefat's, included some that were wealthier than others. The excavators identified a higher quality neighborhood on the west, a Hasmonean neighborhood (perhaps no longer in use at the time of the Revolt) on the upper hillside, a neighborhood around the synagogue, and still other (unexcavated) neighborhoods lower down the hill. The wealthier buildings were larger, better constructed, better finished, had frescoed plaster surfaces, with more artifacts, and paved courtyards of dressed stones. A street running up the hill (*clivus*) had wide stairs, and adjacent houses included industrial activities such as olive oil or flour production. A complete first-century c.e. olive-oil installation occupied its own building, with two large industrial-scale presses, an adjoining "office," and an attached *mikveh* to ensure ritual purity. Perhaps its olive oil was used in the Jerusalem temple. (A hoard of Tyrian shekels from the time of the Revolt, possibly connected with the press, was found outside the door of this factory.) The oil factory was roofed with slabs of columnar basalt about 2 m long, supported by an intermediate longitudinal arch to create a single large room, in a typical Gaulanitis style. Most houses, and the recently discovered public building, were also roofed with columnar basalt supported on consoles projecting from the walls.

The northeast houses were smaller and earlier (time of Herod or before), with plastered floors, within which were washing and purification installations, including a low pool and a bathtub; one was a *mikveh* with a floor of undressed stones in front.[16] Near the synagogue, houses survive to about 4 or 5 m: rooms typically had small cupboards incorporated into one or more walls, and in some cases stairs to a second floor. The simplicity of the domestic organization in such modest housing can still be appreciated; no rooms were specifically set aside for dining or "public" entertaining. Hirschfeld suggests *triclinia* and entertaining areas were regular features, but there is little evidence of either in these early simple houses.[17] More significant was the concern for ritual purity, both publicly alongside the synagogue, and privately within the Hasmonean housing and in the western neighborhood.

Khirbet Qana

The historical situation is different with Khirbet Qana. Whereas Yodefat and Gamla were destroyed in 67 C.E., most structures at Khirbet Qana were occupied through a number of periods. The town occupied about 20 or 25 dunams on the upper slopes of the hill, most of which derived from the early Roman period or before. There was a "suburb" (later, but still undated), halfway down the south slope, of about 12 dunams. In total, Khirbet Qana was about 35 dunams (3 1/2 hectares; 8 to 9 acres). Gamla was about 60 dunams (6 hectares; 15 acres); comparatively Yodefat was about 40 dunams (4 hectares; 10 acres). There are clear resonances between Khirbet Qana and Yodefat and Gamla. Stoneware, in two cases lathe-turned rather than chiseled, was used. The concern for ritual purity was accentuated, as at both Yodefat and Gamla, by *mikvaoth*: one *mikveh*—in use in the Byzantine period though its date of origin was first century C.E.— has been excavated and several other possible *mikvaoth* have been identified. One *mikveh* had been abandoned because the mason carelessly broke through into a large bell cistern, making both cistern and *mikveh* useless.

On the steeper eastern and western slopes late Hellenistic or early Roman houses were reused through the Byzantine period. They were terraced in the same way as at Yodefat and Gamla; on the east slope a party wall between two houses had joist supports for the floor of the house lower down the slope. It is too soon to sketch in any detail the urban layout at various periods or to describe differentiated neighborhoods.

Social Setting of Q

The Origins of Q

Some opening presumptions might be stated at the outset.[18] (1) Q is not the product of "wandering charismatics" but of a sedentary scribal setting, as William Arnal argues (emphasizing economic issues such as a Roman policy of urbanization, more effective collection of taxes, monetization, cash cropping, and consolidation of holdings). He suggests Capernaum as a place where a village scribe might have produced the earliest stratum of Q.[19] (2) While stages in Q's composition can plausibly be posited,[20] (3) Q profits, nevertheless, from analysis as a carefully structured and complete document in its final—if not original—stage, (4) so that Q is not so much *Kleinliteratur* as carefully composed (*pace* Harnack, et al.).[21] (5) Cynicism, which some consider relevant to Q's origins, was a near neighbor to Jewish areas. While I am not persuaded by the "wandering Cynic" hypothesis, it must be granted that there were Cynics in the Decapolis, and probably in Gaulanitis and lower Galilee.[22] The essentially Greco-Roman but multiethnic character of the Galilee[23] as a setting of Q is often assumed.[24]

The first part of this chapter rehearsed the material evidence of first-century towns and villages in the region.[25] What follows is a modest contribution to concretizing Q's social setting.[26] It starts from Alan Kirk's reconstruction of Q's macro-composition: "Each macro-composition articulates, aggressively and *protreptically*, a set of social interests. Q is a particularistic 'boundary' text whose paraenesis functions both to *recruit* and *resocialize*."[27] Kirk makes attractive and illuminating sense of Q, so I build on his "ring composition," despite general reservations about such approaches.

Macro-composition

Kirk argues for four main compositional macro units that collectively form a single larger composition. My summary strips away a few elements irrelevant to my purpose, though his overall scheme is still represented, sometimes by summaries of compositional units; the highlighting of words and phrases is mine.

I Q 3:7–7:35
John introduces Jesus, including his <u>baptism</u>, John and Jesus together
(3:7–9, 16–17, 21–22)
    Temptation narrative (4:1–13)
        Inaugural sermon; love enemies, judge not (6:20b–49)
Central saying   *Disciple not above teacher* (6:40)
        <u>Trees</u>, <u>fruit</u>, builders
    Healing of Centurion's child (7:1–10)
Jesus' ministry, speaks of John, John and Jesus viewed together (7:18–35)

II Q 9:57–10:22
<u>Homelessness</u>, give up <u>family</u> and patrimony (9:57–58)
    Lord of <u>harvest</u> sends <u>laborers</u>, "I send you" (10:2–3)
        Peace, <u>Houses/cities</u> accept; <u>houses/cities</u> reject; towns,
        cities (10:4–11)
Central saying   *More tolerable for Sodom than that city* (10:12)
        Woes, <u>cities</u> reject [<u>Chorazin</u>, <u>Bethsaida</u>, <u>Capernaum</u>];
        cities accept [*Tyre, Sidon*]; <u>towns</u>, <u>cities</u> (10:13–15)
    Receives you, receives me, receives him who sent me (10:16)
Exalted Son of the <u>Father</u>, new <u>family</u> (10:21–22)

III Q 10:23–13:35
Sightedness, presence, prophets and kings (10:23–24)
    Prayer: <u>household</u>, <u>daily bread</u>, <u>debts</u>, <u>poverty</u>, <u>purity</u> (11:2–13)
        Beelzebul controversy (11:14–23)
        Unclean spirit (11:24–26)
Central saying   *Last state worse than first* (11:26b)
        Demand for sign controversy (11:29–35)
    Official <u>purity apparatus and cult</u>: <u>temple</u>, <u>tithes</u>, <u>wealth</u>, <u>pollution</u>
    (11:39–52)
Blindness, withdrawal, Jerusalem prophets (13:34–35)

IV Q 12:2–28:30
Followers judged by <u>hostile authorities</u> (12:2–12) and anxious about <u>food
and drink</u> (12:22–34)
    <u>Servants</u>, <u>master</u>, <u>rewards and punishments</u> (12:35–46)
        Judgment and <u>families</u> sundered (12:49–59)
        Mustard seed and leaven (13:18–21)
            The <u>narrow door</u> and <u>Banquet</u> parable
            (13:24–29)
Central saying   *Last first, humble exalted* (13:30; 14:11)
            <u>Banquet</u> parable and discipleship
            (14:16–24, 26–27, 34–35)

Lost <u>sheep</u>, lost <u>coin</u>, <u>law</u> and divorce, mustard
seed (15:4–10; 16:16–18; 17:5–6)
Judgment; <u>divisions</u> and separations (17:23–37)
<u>Servants</u>, <u>master</u>, <u>rewards</u> and <u>punishment</u> (19:12–25)
Followers judge <u>Israel</u>; followers <u>eat and drink</u> in kingdom (22:28–30)

In Kirk's display of Q, the macro-structure flows from John's relationship with Jesus in the wilderness by the River Jordan in unit I, to a
familial setting among towns and cities, contrasting three towns that
oppose Jesus with two (actual? potential?) that approve him in unit II.
The emphasis on households continues in unit III, where the poverty
and purity concerns of households favorably disposed to Jesus contrasts
with the Pharisees' purity and torah concerns and also with Jerusalem's
treatment of prophets. In unit IV, Q continues to emphasize household
activities associated with daily life in a rural and agricultural setting:
eating and drinking, masters and servants, divisions within families.
Thus Q progresses in an orderly way from a remote setting in Judea (I),
to a town/city setting somewhere near the north end of the Sea of
Galilee and Phoenicia (II), through an emphasis on household concerns (III–IV), some of which focus on purity (III), while others focus
on status relationships, rewards and punishments, within an agricultural context (IV). Curiously, none of the four central sayings in Kirk's
macro-composition is fundamental to the social description; I take the
reason to be that these sayings characterize central elements in Jesus'
message as recalled by Q, and are not elaborative or adaptive features
of the Q scribe, introduced to apply Jesus' central sayings to his community. To put it differently, the scribe of Q is freer in the surrounding
materials to introduce features that directly reflect his own setting,
though it would be incorrect to suggest that the surrounding material
is therefore entirely secondary.

Q's Emphases as an Indication of its Setting

Only a careful redactional and compositional analysis can disentangle
those elements in Q that most directly reflect its setting. In place of
such a fine tool I use a blunt tool and gather a few elements together
to assess the coherence of the picture of Q. My interest is not in the
redaction but in the reflected setting and its correspondence to archae-

ological, architectural, and religious features found in the representative towns briefly surveyed above.

Households

Q's core imagery is house and householder as models for community behavior. A householder returns from a wedding feast to find lights burning and rewards his faithful servants (Q 12:35–38); a householder punishes unreliable servants (Q 12:42–46); a careless householder's house is broken into (Q 12:39–40); a householder answers the door cautiously after dark (Q 13:25–27); a householder rewards and punishes servants for their handling of monetary affairs on his behalf (Q 19:12–26). (The realism of the picture of the servant who hides his talent resonates with archaeological evidence of buried coin hoards. See Gamla, above.) A [one-room] house lit by a lamp functions as an analogy for the eye (Q 11:33–36); a house on a rock is an analogy for doing Jesus' words (Q 6:46–49); an orderly and swept house is an analogy for exorcism (Q 11:24–26). There is a similar analogy, drawing on the roughness of rural floors, in Q 15:8–10 (Lukan special material).

Poverty, debts, and supply of daily bread are endemic issues within some households (Q 11:2–13), while other households have servants and laborers, who are subject to domestic punishments and rewards (12:35–36; 19:12–25). Some followers leave the domestic responsibilities of ploughs and graves (Q 9:57–62) to take up temporary accommodation in others' houses, where they are provided for (Q 10:4–11), perhaps sundering familial relationships to acquire new ones (Q 12:49–59; 10:21–22). The Q community throughout presupposes householders in towns and villages or as small landowners, with servants as factors in the domestic economy of the household, suggesting that Q's immediate context lies less among dispossessed or itinerant than among those who have houses or land.

The descriptions of small northern towns correspond to and amplify Q's core emphasis on the household within rural town life. The social organizations were tight and close, with houses packed together into a relatively dense matrix, where—if it was hilly, as many towns were—houses shared common walls for different levels of floors and roofs, where living and working activities were in the courtyards overlooked by roofs, where the roof of one house was an important addition to the living space of another (Q 12:3; Lukan Redaction in 17:31). Conglomerations of housing dominated small Palestinian townscapes with some variety in building types—though not comparable to equivalent Roman towns—that might have stretched to include a multipurpose communal building and a few other public facilities.

Agricultural Imagery

Q presumes plentiful harvests that require laborers (Q 10:2) and oxen (Q 14:18–19), with sowing and reaping, gathering into barns and granaries (Q 12:24–8), winnowing and threshing (with burning of chaff; Q 3:17; cf. Q 17:35). These presuppose a crop-farming background in lower Galilee (for example, Beth Netofa or Jezreel Valleys) or Gaulanitis, both of which had rich agrarian lands that correspond to Q's ethos. If more general considerations did not pull the setting towards Galilee or the Golan, other areas in Judea, Batanea, Auranitis or Peraea would also be possible. Q's neglect of the natural imagery of lakes, fishing, and boats (slightly present in Q 17:2, 6; 11:11) suggests that the Sea of Galilee is outside Q's field of vision, just as its neglect of grapes and olives (allusion in Q 6:44) suggests that upper Galilee is beyond its view.

Towns and Villages

Q is interested in towns and cities, naming polemically Chorazin, Bethsaida, and Capernaum (within a few kilometers of each other) and pointing in a surprisingly positive way to Tyre and Sidon (Q 7:1–9; 10:13–15). Jerusalem is mentioned polemically (Q 13:34–35; cf. 11:51), though probably proverbially, as Tyre and Sidon may also be. The polemic against Capernaum, Bethsaida, and Chorazin is remarkable, for otherwise Q's setting might naturally gravitate to that region. Because the polemic is rhetorically gratuitous, these towns cannot be the actual setting of Q, despite Arnal's arguments for Q's location at the north end of the lake.

The strong man in his house (*aulê* may suggest peristyle; Q 11:21–22) hints at a city house, though the new evidence that an agrarian town such as Yodefat could have sophisticated upper-class houses, possibly even peristyle houses, calls for careful consideration of the degree of uniformity of houses in a particular town. Further, the commonplace observation that the Synoptics never mention Tiberias or Sepphoris (Antipas's capitals)—often used to claim that Jesus was not interested in the city—must be qualified with the observation that Q mentions Bethsaida (one of Philip's capitals), and even Tyre and Sidon; Mark also mentions Caesarea Philippi, Philip's other capital. Generalizing that Jesus was hostile to cities from the omission of Tiberias and Sepphoris is unwarranted and misleading, for silence on Galilee's capitals is balanced by mention of Gaulanitis's capitals. Galilee and Gaulanitis are equally good candidates for Q's setting. Indeed, Q's description of the kingdom divided against itself (Q 11:17–18) resonates with the division of Herod's kingdom between his two sons, specifically with the consequences of that division during their later years or the middle years of Agrippa II.

The *agora* is the backdrop for children's games (Q 7:32) and Pharisees' activities (Q 11:43). None of the three towns surveyed above had an *agora*, though all must have provided for communal sale of goods. Community proclamation occurs in cities (*poleis*; Q 10:8–12; cf. 10:1), which either accept or reject the messenger (Q 10:13–15; cf. Matt 10:23). *Polis* (city) properly alludes to capitals of the brothers Herod, Decapolis cities (Beth Shean, Hippos, Gadara), or coastal cities (Dor, Ptolemais), though Matthew (11:20) thinks Chorazin and Capernaum are also *poleis*. Followers must enter by the narrow gate, as in a walled town (Q 13:24 should perhaps be read in its Matthean form in 7:13–14) or even an unwalled town; Yodefat, Gamla, and Khirbet Qana provide examples. Towns near capitals offer a suitable setting for Q.

Ritual Allusions: Baptism

The ascetic John warns of Isaiah's vision of coming judgment and the separation of the wheat from the chaff (Q 3:2b–4, 7–9, 16–17, 21–22). His baptism by water will be by fire and Spirit at the end (Q 3:16). So Jesus comes to John for baptism (Q 3:21–22), a rite intended for the children of Abraham, and by extension for those not genetically Abraham's progeny (Q 3:7–9). When John reappears in the account, he thinks of Jesus in terms of Isaiah's description of the coming one (Q 7:18–28): the sociable townsperson contrasts starkly with the wilderness ascetic (Q 7:33–34). Still, Q's Jesus, true to his Baptizer roots, threatens metaphorical fire and baptism (Q 12:49–53), resulting in division among members of the household and fire upon the earth.

The emphasis on baptism seems not to accord well with the socio-geographic setting I am proposing for Q until we recall the widespread provision for ritual immersion in *mikvaoth*. Purity concerns, including rituals dealing with uncleanness, were common within the towns that are within the horizon of the Q community. One possibility is that baptism in this earliest period would be appropriate in a *mikveh*, or in other water sources such as public reservoirs. *Didache* 7.1 requires baptism in "living water" (cf. Lev 15:13) and contrasts this with ordinary cold water, hinting at the use by this community of *mikvaoth* for baptisms. John's baptism was in the wilderness, but "this generation's" baptisms took place in towns and public places (Q 7:31–35).

Ritual Allusions: Eating and Drinking

Differences in eating and drinking are fundamental elements in Q's John/Jesus contrast. John ignored the table. Since Jesus did not (Q 7:33–34; cf. Q 10:7) he was thought a glutton and a drunk like tax collectors and sinners. Similar allusions appear in the Great Supper parable (Q 14:16–24), the account of Diaspora Jews ("east and west") sitting at table (Q 13:28–29), and negatively in the eschatological sayings about the Son of Man (Q 17:27). Luke emphasizes this theme redactionally in the Marriage Feast parable (Q 12:36, Lukan special material) and the closed door (Q 13:24–27).

Eating and drinking in Q's social situation occasionally implies substantial dining rooms for communal activities, "reclining" as in *triclinia*. While it is not impossible that wealthy followers of Jesus had such rooms, and while occasionally a Palestinian town might have houses with *triclinia* or second-floor rooms for entertaining guests, this was probably uncommon. In Morocco, 500-year old Berber village houses, similar to Palestinian houses, commonly include a second- or third-floor "guest room," the only decorated room in the house, used exclusively to entertain visitors. Yizhar Hirschfeld observes the same pattern.[28] If *triclinia* were not available, where did community social/religious activities occur? Though we have no direct evidence that followers of Jesus used community buildings—like Gamla's—there is no reason for this not to have happened. The issue, of course, is the period when an early Christian group was so marginalized or "self-identified" that it might no longer do so. Since Q and the community that spawned it came before the "parting of the ways," there is no reason to exclude Q's community from use of such multipurpose communal facilities (see Part 3).

Ritual Allusions: Woes, Purity, and Prayer

The woes (Q 11:39b–52) reflect Q's setting: ritual purity of utensils (cleaning the outside and/or inside, Q 11:39b–41), tithing (Q 11:42), synagogue attendance (Q 11:43; cf. 12:11–12), corpse impurity (Q 11:44; cf. also 11:47), Torah interpretation (Q 11:46, 52), and relationship to prophets (Q 11:47–51). The community's relaxed handling of ritual and quasi-ritual issues is striking. Q's arguments, more subdued than Matthew's polemical expansion of the woes (Matt 23), were directed against Pharisees and legal interpreters (*hoi nomikoi*), but the community tithed, interpreted Torah, and recognized prophets. It probably also was concerned for ritual purity, attended synagogue, and avoided corpse impurity. A more positive understanding of these relationships, including use of local synagogues for communal meals, is likelier than deep-seated antagonisms. Q contains strong injunctions to regular prayer (Q 11:2–4; cf. 11:5–8, 9–13), the clauses of which emphasize purity, poverty, and debts, on the view that Q 11:5–8 are original and not Lukan redaction.

Summary

Q's reflections of its social and geographical setting imply that Q was part of an agriculturally oriented community involved in grain farming and related pursuits in lower Galilee or Gaulanitis. It was set in a town, one in competition with those towns condemned by Jesus, possibly walled, and in a location where Tyre and Sidon were within the situational horizon. Houses and householders were a dominant factor in the town. There was a synagogue, which may have been used for the group's ritual activities: eating and drinking, prayer, baptism, and ritual purity.

CONCLUSION

Some features could reflect a stage prior to Q, perhaps Jesus' setting rather than Q's. This is a valid caveat, but two further observations may be made: (1) even if this were the case, Q's overlay is largely consistent with the earlier setting, for most of the indications cohere; (2) by contrast, the setting of the "historical Jesus" would probably emphasize factors such as fishing, the Sea of Galilee, Jesus' trips to the "other side," the place of Capernaum, and so on. I have deliberately left uncertain whether Galilee or Gaulanitis is the likelier geographical location, partly because I cannot decide and partly because at this juncture more studies of these questions are needed. Some indications ("other side," Tyre and Sidon) pull towards lower Galilee; other indications (Bethsaida) pull towards Gaulanitis. The lower Galilee is the most logical, if not the only, choice.

The social and geographical setting of Q can be identified relatively precisely. Q was set naturally in towns (and cities?), not within the activities of wandering charismatics. Householders were the primary social referent, some of whom were masters with servants. They worked in a region where grain crops were common sources of income. The community practiced ritual purity, including the cleansing of utensils; baptism, perhaps including the use of *mikvaoth*, was observed; eating and drinking were important rituals. It was thus a group that had found a solution to carrying on such activities.

CHAPTER SIX

WHAT HAS CANA TO DO WITH CAPERNAUM?

INTRODUCTION[1]

The third quest of the historical Jesus has created an explosion of research into Jesus' geographical setting, much of it focused on the Galilee.[2] By comparison, relatively little work has concentrated on Gaulanitis, often considered merely a subdivision of the Galilee. Yet it, too, is important for the historical Jesus.[3] Though I do not deal with Gaulanitis, distinctions between the two northern regions in character, culture, history, and social and religious makeup should be recognized.

This chapter links evidence from texts and material culture, from "the dirt and the word."[4] It is prompted by three interrelated concerns: (1) the geography and chronology of the historical Jesus; (2) archaeological, architectural, and sociohistorical investigation of Galilean villages, especially Cana (to be located at Khirbet Qana in my view) and Yodefat (Jotapata);[5] and (3) uneasiness over claims about Capernaum. I link these *realia*-related concerns to the Gospel of John (and its putative source, the Signs Gospel), though my interest in John is less acute than in Galilean and Jesus issues. In dealing with the importance of place I wish to draw Cana as a known "place" more fully into discussions of Jesus traditions.

Josephus, like the New Testament, mentions Cana, Capernaum, and Bethsaida in connection with events of 66–67 C.E. After an injury near Bethsaida/Julias (*Life* 399–403), Josephus was taken to Capernaum, stayed one day, and left for Tarichaea. Cana, however, was his center for part of the time he was in Galilee preparing for the Roman counterattack: "Now at this time my abode was in a village of Galilee, which is named Cana" (*Life* 86); he also said he lived in the Beth Netofa Valley (*Life* 207, "Plain of Asochis"; other references in Josephus to Cana are textual errors or refer to other sites). Cana was strategically sensible, since neither Tiberias nor Sepphoris was fully under

Josephus's control, and Cana—unlike nearby Yodefat, whose defenses
he was strengthening—easily overlooked Sepphoris and visually controlled the Beth Netofa Valley. Thus, Josephus uses Cana administra-
tively but Capernaum only for emergency.

Recent studies of geographical "place" have broadened the discussion to include regional, ethnic, urban, economic, social, symbolic,
political, and religious factors, as well as textual "place." Earlier studies
are still important for stressing the texts' handling of geographic mark-
ers as aspects of the authors' theological purposes and constructions of
reality, whether in the Synoptics or the Gospel of John.[6] Despite this, the
Synoptic emphasis on Capernaum has been little challenged; it has
been an archaeological bedrock of gospel study.[7] Since its relevance has
long been emphasized, I will say little about it, instead underscoring
Cana's significance, partly by viewing Cana and Capernaum as literary
rivals for Jesus' home base. The Cana tradition was as early and almost
as strong as the Capernaum claim, though whether Cana was actually
a center of Jesus' activity is a separate question.

GEOGRAPHY OF THE GOSPELS

The geographical assumptions of the Gospels and their sources, especially the Galilean allusions, show considerable variety. The only specific
indication of place in the *Gospel of Thomas* is an incidental reference to "a
Samaritan carrying a lamb on his way to Judea" (*Gos. Thom.* 60), which
merely implies a journey through or near Samaria. The Synoptics sometimes attribute locales, lacking in *Thomas*, in pericopes both share. This
suggests, depending on the direction of influence, a process of either
localization or delocalization. The *Gospel of Thomas* as a whole is firmly
set in rural villages ("in his own village," *Gos. Thom.* 31), presumably but
not explicitly in the Galilee. Other documents without locales are
Dialogue of the Savior and *Apocryphon of James*. The *Infancy Gospel of Thomas*
describes situations that may take place in Galilee; some manuscripts
locate Jesus' home in Bethlehem (near Nazareth; *Inf. Gos. Thom.* 1; cf. also
4, 12 for "village").

Q contains relatively few references to specific locations, though
more than the *Gospel of Thomas* (Chapter 5). It opens with John at the
Jordan; by the time Jesus enters Capernaum (Q 7:1) many of Jesus' sayings have already been reported, but always without a setting. Jesus'

approval after the Capernaum healing ("not even in Israel have I found such faith") is soon undercut by his woes on Capernaum, Chorazin, and Bethsaida (Q 10:12–15), which are compared unfavorably to the Phoenician cities Tyre and Sidon. The setting of the woes on the Pharisees is unstated, but Jerusalem may be presupposed (Q 11:51; 13:34). Like the *Gospel of Thomas*, Q identifies no center for Jesus' activity other than generalized rural towns and villages.

Mark knows that Jesus is from Nazareth (Mark 1:9; cf. 1:24; 10:47; 14:67; 16:6), from which he goes to the Jordan to see John. Jesus returns to Galilee but relocates to the area around the lake, making Capernaum his main location, where he teaches and heals (Mark 1:21, 23).[8] Capernaum is his and his followers' home (2:1; 1:29), from which place he travels around the region by land and water, including visits to Bethsaida (6:45; 8:22). At Mark's narrative climax, Jesus travels to the regions of Tyre and Sidon, the Decapolis, Panias, and Mount Hermon (7:24–9:32), before returning to Capernaum (9:33-50) and then heading to Judea and Jerusalem (10:1).[9] Since Mark knows nothing of the woes on Bethsaida, Capernaum, and Chorazin, his allusions to Capernaum take on additional significance.

In Matthew's more complicated scheme, Bethlehem is both Jesus' birthplace and home (2:1-8, 16), while Nazareth is merely Jesus' adopted home (2:23; cf. 26:71; 21:11). Following Mark, Matthew's Jesus sees John at the Jordan; he settles in Capernaum when he returns, in order to fulfill prophecy (4:13-17; cf. 17:24). Matthew's inclusion of Q's woes on Capernaum, Chorazin, and Bethsaida balances his positive notices of Capernaum. He shortens Mark's itinerary outside Galilee (15:21, 29), though Jesus still visits Panias (16:13). Matthew's construction of Jesus' place (born in Bethlehem, moved to Nazareth, selected Capernaum as his center) is the most influential geographical tradition.

Luke's variant on Matthew's view is complicated by the question of sources. Since the Proto-Luke hypothesis still seems persuasive, its geographical thread is relevant. After regional allusions to Judea, Galilee, Ituraea, Trachonitis, and Abilene, Proto-Luke's Jesus makes the requisite visit to John at the Jordan (Luke 3:1-3; 2:1), returns to Galilee (3:14), to Nazareth where he was brought up (3:16). He is challenged (4:16-30) to do in his "own country" works like those he had done in Capernaum (4:23-24, though none has been mentioned yet). He goes to Lake Gennesaret (5:1), Capernaum, and Nain (7:1, 11). Jesus perambulates "through cities and villages" (8:1; 11:1; 13:10, 22; 17:11) before setting his face to go to Jerusalem (9:51) via Samaria (9:52). R. H. Lightfoot observes that "no district receives any notable preference" in Luke (Galilee 275 verses, Samaria 350 verses, Judea 320 verses).[10] The woes on Chorazin, Bethsaida, and Capernaum occur, illogically, in this section (10:13-15). When Luke adds Mark and other material to his first edition he makes Bethlehem Jesus' birthplace (2:4, 15), but retains Nazareth as Jesus' original hometown (1:26; 2:4, 39, 51; 4:16; cf. "Nazarene" at 18:37 and seven times in Acts). Luke ignores Mark's itinerary to Tyre, Sidon, Panias, and the Decapolis despite its obvious relevance to his theology (see Table 6.1).

A regional Galilean ambience for Jesus is deeply, no doubt correctly, rooted in various traditions, though this regional setting is not always noted specifically. There is wide recognition of time spent in Jerusalem and Judea, even in the *Gospel of Thomas* though not explicitly in Q. Some gospels are explicitly set in Jerusalem: *Papyrus Oxyrhynchus* 840, *Papyrus Egerton* 2, *Gospel of Peter* (with Galilean post-resurrection incidents), *Acts of Pilate*, and *Protevangelium of James*. There is, thus, no unanimity on Jesus' central place:

- Q and *Thomas* know no center; Q's woes work against Capernaum, Chorazin, or Bethsaida.

- Proto-Luke also has no real center, but balances time in Galilee (Nazareth, the Sea, Capernaum, Nain) with time traveling on the road towards Jerusalem.

- Mark views Capernaum as Jesus' center, with connections to Bethsaida, Tyre and Sidon, Panias, and the Decapolis.

- Matthew imagines Bethlehem as Jesus' hometown, Nazareth as his family's adopted home, and Capernaum as his chosen new location, following Mark.

- Luke, however, sees Bethlehem merely as Jesus' birth town, while Nazareth is his family home, with which he stays in contact after relocating to Capernaum.

Two general points: (1) most traditions presuppose a two-part ministry, first in Galilee and later in Judea and Jerusalem; the Fourth Gospel, however, has a back-and-forth pattern between Galilee and Jerusalem, which some scholars prefer: "the sort of itinerary that John presents makes much more sense than the one-year, one-way itinerary in Mark."[11] (2) While there is no uniform tradition about Jesus' specific "place," there is a tendency to focus on Capernaum, following Mark;

Table 6.1: General Geographical Patterns of the Gospels

G Thom	Q	Mark	Matt	Luke	Proto-Luke	SG-Fortna	John
	Jordan	Jordan	Jordan	Jordan	Jordan	Jordan	Jordan
[Galilee]	[Galilee?]	Galilee -Capernaum -towns -Capernaum -lakeside -hill country -lakeside -Sea+Golan -Capernaum? -Nazareth	Galilee -Seaside -Capernaum -Sea+Golan -Capernaum? -towns -lakeside -Nazareth -Sea+Golan	Galilee -Nazareth - Capernaum -remote place Judea (?) -lake - Capernaum -Nain	Galilee -Nazareth -lake - Capernaum -Nain	Gaulanitis Galilee	Gaulanitis Galilee -Bethsaida? -Cana -Capernaum
		Villages Bethsaida? Gennesaret	Gennesaret	Cities and Villages	Cities and Villages		
		Pagan areas -Tyre -Sidon -Decapolis -Bethsaida -Panias	Pagan areas -Tyre+Sidon -seaside -Magadan -Gaulanitis -Panias	Gaulanitis			
	Capernaum	Galilee -Capernaum	Galilee -Capernaum	Bethsaida to Jerusalem	to Jerusalem		Judea
Samaria				Samaria	Samaria	Samaria	Samaria
				Villages and towns	Villages and towns		Galilee -Cana
							Judea
							Sea/Golan
							Galilee
							Judea
							Peraea
[Judea]	[Jerusalem?]	Judea/Peraea	Judea/Peraea	Judea	Judea	Judea	Judea

yet support for Capernaum as a center is not as strong as usually assumed, since other early gospels such as Q, *Thomas*, and Proto-Luke have a different scheme from Mark's. Both propositions have been widely, perhaps too readily, accepted; both questions are viewed differently in John.

JOHN

Fourth Gospel

British scholars such as C. H. Dodd and John A. T. Robinson have examined synoptic-like historical traditions underlying the Fourth Gospel.[12] The Cana material is especially important. Robinson argues, "history belongs to the bedrock of the Johannine tradition."[13] He thinks the Fourth Gospel a primary gospel alongside—sometimes as reliable as—the Synoptic Gospels, though not necessarily the earliest.[14] Robinson followed Dodd, who found traditional material in the Cana meal and the healing of the nobleman's son, though he doubted the Nathanael tradition; it belonged to "a Jewish environment, and . . . [was] barely intelligible to a Hellenistic public," deriving from "the Christian mission in controversy with Jewish opposition."[15]

Alternation between Judea and Galilee dominates the Fourth Gospel's geographical schematization; many note that Jesus' homeland (*patris*) in John is Judea, not Galilee. Jesus' Galilean role begins in Cana and only later includes Capernaum and the area around the lake. Nathanael of Cana plays a special role, bracketing the Fourth Gospel in an introduction (1:43-51) and flashback (21:2); the implied rivalry with Nazareth in Nathanael's comment simply reflects that the two villages are within sight of each other. The primary Cana incident, the wedding (2:1-11), has a village setting, a household, large stone jars for purification, and storage cisterns, to which I will return. This first "sign," together with a second one also set in Cana but operative in Capernaum (4:46-54), "led his disciples to believe in him" (2:11; cf. 4:54). The final redaction has slightly altered the role of Cana by having Jesus deliberately return there after a visit to Judea and Samaria (its source, the Signs Gospel, implies a continuous stay in Cana). When the royal officer comes to Cana asking Jesus to go with him to Capernaum, Jesus merely tells him his son is well. Though these are the first two explicit signs, the final redaction has squeezed in others set in Judea, creating gaps at 2:23 and 3:2.

Underlying Traditions

If it is correct that a Signs Gospel lies behind the Fourth Gospel,[16] the earlier gospel—even more than the finished Fourth Gospel—is dominated geographically in its opening scenes by the conviction that Jesus' own place is Cana. The later *Epistle of the Apostles* 5 extends the Cana activities beyond "water to wine" to include "and awakened the dead and made the lame to walk; for him whose hand was withered, he stretched it out again, and the woman who suffered twelve years from a hemorrhage touched the edge of his garment. . . ."

Nathanael of Cana is the first Galilean follower of Jesus, since John sets the earlier three followers (Andrew, Peter, and Philip) in Bethsaida-in-Gaulanitis (incorrectly located in Galilee at 12:21). John 21:2 lists an inner group of seven followers that includes Nathanael from Cana-in-Galilee who get a miraculous catch of fish on the Lake of Tiberias and see the risen Jesus. The identification of Nathanael, from Cana, was probably found in the Signs Gospel: "the absence of a major role for Nathaniel [sic] in the [Fourth Gospel] argues for this [1:47b-48] having been primitive material."[17] Raymond E. Brown is less certain: "it is difficult to be sure whether this [21:2] represents traditional knowledge or is a deduction from Nathanael's knowledge of the local Galilean situation in 1:46, combined with 2:1-12."

The first sign, water into wine (2:1-11), follows Nathanael's first mention and is immediately followed by the official's son restored to life (2:12a; 4:46-54). Robert Fortna notes that the awkwardness of the two seams at 2:12 and 4:46 is solved either by the healing that takes place in Capernaum (Bultmann) or on the Cana–Capernaum road (Wilkens). But 4:49 ("come down before my child dies") presupposes that Jesus is still in Cana, not already on the road; so a more likely transition to the second sign is: "While Jesus was still in Cana. . . ."[18] Next comes the catch of fish ("third" in 21:14 naturally extends "second" in 4:54; the Fourth Gospel relocated it to a resurrection setting). The first Galilean disciple, the first two acts of Jesus, and the catch of fish (through Nathanael's identification; 21:2) are all related to Cana. The Signs Gospel then puts Jesus on the other side, in Gaulanitis, before he

Table 6.2: Detailed Comparisons, Jesus' Itinerary

John	Signs Gospel-Becker	Signs Gospel-von Wahlde	Signs Gospel-Fortna	Proto-Luke
Jordan 1.28	Jordan 1.28	Jordan 1.28	Aenon 3.23 + 1.36	Jordan
[Gaulanitis?– Bethsaida?] 1.43-44 to Galilee	[Gaulanitis?– Bethsaida? 1.44]	[Gaulanitis?– Bethsaida? 1.44]	[Gaulanitis?– Bethsaida? 1.43-44]	
Galilee–Cana 1.45-2.11	Galilee–Cana 1.45-2.11	Galilee–Cana 1.45-2.11	Cana 1.45? 2.1-11	Galilee–Nazareth 4.14-16
Capernaum 2.12	Capernaum 2.12	Jerusalem 2.23	Capernaum 2.12	[Capernaum?] 4.23
Jerusalem 2.13	[Judea 3.22?]	Judea 3.22	Sea 21.2	Sea 5.1
Judea 3.22	Samaria 4.5	Samaria 4.4	Sea + Gaulanitis 6.1	Capernaum 7.1
Samaria 4.4	Galilee–Cana 4.46	Galilee–Cana 4.43, 46	Samaria 4.4	Nain 7.11
Galilee–Cana 4.43, 46	Sea + Golan 6.1	Jerusalem 5.1	Judea–Bethany 11.17	[Judea?] 7.17
[Capernaum 4.47?]	Capernaum 6.16-17	Sea + Gaulanitis 6.1	Jerusalem 9.1; 5.2; 2.14	To Jerusalem 9.51
Jerusalem 5.1	Galilee 7.1	Capernaum 6.16-17	Bethany 12.1	Samaria 9.52
Sea + Golan 6.1	Jerusalem 5.1	Jerusalem 7.25	Jerusalem 12.12	[Bethany?] 10.38
Capernaum 6.16-17	Peraea 10.40	Peraea 10.40		Near Jerusalem 19.11
Galilee 7.1	Judea–Bethany 11.7, 17	Judea–Bethany 11.17		Jerusalem 19.37-41
Jerusalem 7.10	Ephraim 11.54	Ephraim 11.54		
Peraea 10.40		Bethany 12.1		
Judea–Bethany 11.7, 17		Jerusalem 12.20		
Ephraim 11.54				
Bethany 12.1				
Jerusalem 12.12				
+ Passion Narrative	No Passion Narrative	+ Passion Narrative	+ Passion Narrative	+Passion Narrative

crosses the lake to Capernaum; when he arrives, the village remains unnamed and nothing happens. Fortna's Signs Gospel shifts to Jerusalem where Jesus remains (he supposes a one-way trip to Judea, like the Synoptics).[19] This source narrative emphasizes Cana's role, downgrades Capernaum's, and locates Jesus' proper "place" in Galilee differently from Mark (see Table 6.2).

John's Geography

Studies of the geographical references in John emphasize redactional and theological factors.[20] Fortna, for example, stresses differences between the geographical patterns of the Signs Gospel and the Fourth Gospel, so that the bipolar alternation between Galilee and Judea is characteristic only of the final redaction: "John has made conscious use in his gospel of geography as a theological device. . . . It is likely that the places he adopts as pivotal for this purpose (Cana, Bethany, Jerusalem) were simply taken by him in the first instance from the source." Fortna also states, "[E]ach story is inseparably attached to a specific locale and so seems to fit closely into a scheme of the travels of Jesus common to all. By contrast many of the synoptic miracles have only the vaguest geographical reference or none at all. . . ."[21] Fortna's reconstruction, though attractive, is unpersuasive when made to conform to a synoptic pattern.

At a sociohistorical level, the allusions to specific towns and villages may mean there were small Johannine communities in Judea, Galilee, Samaria, and Peraea in the early period, rivaling, for example, Petrine communities, especially in Capernaum.[22] Was Cana a leading Galilean center of Johannine Christianity and Capernaum a more conservative center? Several features of the Signs Gospel and the Fourth Gospel are striking when set alongside the Synoptic Gospels.

- The Fourth Gospel knows, but ignores, that Nazareth is Jesus' hometown (1:45-46; cf. 18:5; 19:19).

- Cana is Jesus' main place in John's source, while Capernaum is merely a destination in the two instances it is named, not a center; in neither instance is it important that Jesus even reaches it.

- Later redaction adds more Capernaum references (John 6) and alters the Cana references, relocating the catch of fish as a resurrection appearance (John 21).

- The geographical references in Fortna's Signs Gospel and Proto-Luke are similar (Table 6.2), though Cana replaces Nazareth; neither emphasizes Capernaum.
- Gaulanitis's importance is recognized; Bethsaida is the hometown of Peter, Andrew, and Philip (1:46; cf. 12:21).

These redactional changes in the Fourth Gospel may occur through "interference" from the Synoptic narratives,[23] especially Mark, in which Capernaum's role is exaggerated; the Signs Source, followed by the Fourth Gospel, locates Jesus' place distinctively in Cana. Schmidt's warning needs to be taken seriously: "It is illegitimate to proceed automatically from recognition of the historical worthlessness (*historische Wertlosigkeit*) of the Markan outline to endorsement of the Johannine outline."[24] The Johannine picture significantly differs from the other Gospels in portraying Cana-in-Galilee as Jesus' first center of activity, prior to any references to Capernaum.[25] What then can we say about this small town or village highlighted in the Fourth Gospel?

Cana in Pilgrim Literature

There are four possible locations for Cana:[26] Kefr Kenna, Khirbet Qana, 'Ain Qana (near Kefr Kenna) and Qana El-Jaleel (Lebanon).[27] Pilgrim literature from the fourth century on refers to Cana; the following are the most important texts.[28]

- Jerome to Marcella in Rome (Letter 46, 392/3 C.E.): ". . . we shall go to see Nazareth . . . not far off Cana will be visible, where the water was turned into wine"; Jerome to Eustochium (Letter 108, 404 C.E.): "Then she went quickly on through Nazareth, the nurse of the Lord; through Cana and Capernaum which witnessed his miracles. . . ."
- Epiphanius (*Panarion Haereseis* 51.30.1–2; 375 C.E.) refers to a *martyrium* (probably the cathedral built over a Temple to Dionysus) and miraculous fountain in Gerasa [Jerash], where every year the spring ran with wine on the anniversary of the miracle at Cana, i.e., Epiphany.
- Theodosius (*de Situ Terrae Sanctae*, early sixth century C.E.): "From Joppa it is thirty miles to Caesarea Palestinae . . . from Caesarea it is thirty miles to Diocaesarea, from which came Simon Magus. . . . From Diocaesarea it is five miles to Cana of Galilee. From Diocaesarea it is five miles to Nazareth."
- The Pilgrim of Piacenza (560–570 C.E.): "At Ptolemais we left the coast and traveled into the Galilee region to a city called Diocaesarea. . . .

Three miles further on we came to Cana, where the Lord attended the wedding, and we actually reclined on the couch. On it (undeserving though I am) I wrote the names of my parents [. . . .] Of the water pots two are still there, and I filled one of them up with wine and lifted it up full onto my shoulders. I offered it at the altar, and we washed in the spring to gain a blessing."

- Willibald (724 C.E.; after Hugeburc, late eighth century: *The Life of Saint Willibald*, ch. 13): he and his companions "continued their journey [from Nazareth] and reached the village of Cana, where the Lord changed the water into wine. There is a large church there, and on the altar of the church is one of the six water pots which the Lord ordered to be filled with water, and it was turned into wine; they drank some wine from it."

- *Commemoratorium* (808 C.E.): "Summary of a memorandum on the churches and monasteries. . . . In Galilee: In the holy city of Nazareth 12 [monks]. One mile from Nazareth . . . a monastery and a church built in honour of St. Mary, 8 monks. In Cana of Galilee, where the Lord made water into wine [?] monks."

- Saewulf (1102–1103 C.E.), the first western pilgrim after the Crusades to leave a narrative, says that "six miles to the northeast of Nazareth, on a hill, is Cana of Galilee, where our Lord converted water into wine at the marriage feast. There is nothing left standing except the monastery called that of the Architriclinius."

- Burchard of Mount Sion (1283 C.E.): "The place is shown at this day where the six water pots stood, and the dining-room wherein the tables were. . . . To the north Cana of Galilee has a round mountain, on whose slope it stands. At its foot, on the south side, it has a very fair plain, which Josephus calls Carmelion; it reaches as far as Sepphoris, and is extremely fertile and pleasant. . . . Two leagues to the south of Cana of Galilee is Sepphoris."

Cana was not yet a customary pilgrim's veneration place at the time of Jerome; by the time of Epiphanius it was so venerated, since Gerasa, which reflected Cana,[29] was regularly visited. By the sixth century (Theodosius and the Pilgrim of Piacenza) Cana had become important. The Piacenza Pilgrim's account requires that Cana be Khirbet Qana for three reasons: (1) the distance of three miles from Sepphoris works better; (2) his route proceeded onwards to Nazareth after Cana, a route that works poorly with Kefr Kenna; (3) archaeology now shows that there was a veneration cave with water pots on an altar with benches around. I will allude to this account later; Willibald's circumstantial account is also important. Crusader notices, including two maps,[30] also identified Khirbet Qana with Cana, as does—very clearly—the account of Burchard of Mount Sion (1283 C.E.).

Burchard saw a round mountain to the north, the Beth Netofa Valley to the south, and a dining room and water pots in a veneration cave.[31] Not all accounts point to Khirbet Qana. A second location for Cana emerges at Kefr Kenna, perhaps at some point in the Middle Ages. Francisco Quaresmius (early seventeenth century), the papal emissary to Palestine, notes that there are two Canas:

> Cana of the Galilee (the first one) is located West of Nazareth, a little to the North, on the hill that dominates the beautiful and spacious plain of Zabulon [Beth Netofa Valley]; it is about 6 miles from Sepphoris and 10 miles from Nazareth; it is a small village of nothing, reduced to a few houses; there is no church, neither are there signs that there ever was a church. . . . Kefer Cana is located 4 miles from Nazareth; it is located on the mountain in the northern part facing toward the east; all around there is a wide and spacious plain and there are quite a few trees and many houses; and I learned that there, there is a church. . . . Perhaps at the time of Christ it was a small city reduced later to being a village.

A half-century later Henry Maundrell (20 April 1697) locates Cana at Khirbet Qana: "The next morning we took our leave of Nazareth. . . . We directed our course for Acra, in order to do which, going first northward, we crossed the hills that encompassed the vale of Nazareth on that side, after which we turned to the westward, and passed in view of Cana of Galilee, the place signalized with the beginning of Christ's miracles. In an hour and a half more we came to Sepharia." Later still, Edward Robinson says that "the Cana of the New Testament" is not at Kefr Kenna but rather at "a ruin called Kâna el-Jelil, on the northern side of the plain el-Buttauf . . . in the time of Quaresmius, the church and the convent at Nazareth were first built up, after the desolations of many centuries, and this circumstance conspired to give currency among travelers, to the view which monks adopted respecting Cana."[32]

Quaresmius's account underscores how a tourist preference for Kefr Kenna, the rival site, arose and has been maintained more or less continuously since. The modern turning point was Robinson's use of linguistic criteria to establish the geography of the Holy Land; though his views were strongly contested, they have stood firmly. Recent analyses have confirmed that Khirbet Qana is the site of the Cana of Josephus and the New Testament.

CANA IN ARCHAEOLOGY

Excavations at Khirbet Qana have demonstrated the vitality of settlement from the Hellenistic through early Arab periods, concentrating to date on a Byzantine veneration cave, a possible Jewish synagogue with *Beth ha-Midrash*, and housing. The site has been occupied from the Neolithic period and the Iron Age through to the nineteenth century.

Khirbet Qana's extensive necropolis contains 13 tombs, at least 18 chambers, and up to about 100 *loculi* or *kokhim*. The plan and interior forms show that these are Second Temple tombs, a simpler form of tombs found in Jerusalem and elsewhere. The shaft design of the tombs was unusual, possibly influenced by cultural and/or ethnic influences from Phoenicia. In all but one case the entrance was not a *dromos*, as was common (Jerusalem and Beth She'arim, for example).[33]

There are three types of housing at Khirbet Qana in three different areas of the site:

(1) Terrace houses occupy the steep east and west slopes, similar to terraced housing at Gamla and Yodefat (Plates 12, 13). While the early date of such houses is clear, unlike Gamla and Yodefat the village was not destroyed, so that its housing was in almost continuous use from the late Hellenistic period through to the Byzantine period. The walls remained standing while the floors show stratified occupational levels through a sequence of periods. These terrace houses were simple, two-floor houses, without courtyards, densely packed, with adjacent houses using common party walls (Chapters 4, 5).

(2) Side courtyard houses occupied less steep ground, mainly on the north at Khirbet Qana (Plates 11, 14); these too were simple houses, with less complex floor levels and the living space extended into a courtyard, often with a cistern. One carefully excavated house (though in fact from the Byzantine period) had a courtyard with an enormous cistern, and a *mikveh* from the early Roman period beside the cistern (plaster samples have not yet been published), an important indication of Judaism's vitality at Khirbet Qana. The house had a nicely built bench and storage cave with intact Byzantine pottery. As more houses are excavated higher up the hillside, we expect to find similar houses from earlier periods.

(3) Central courtyard houses occupied the hilltop and the northern
    saddle. Excavation of an elite house on the hilltop has been cru-
    cial to understanding the occupation sequence (Plates 19, 20). The
    house was used over a long period, and while it is not yet clear
    when it was first built, much of the structure was early Roman.
    Several stages are visible in walls and floors, especially in the main
    courtyard, which had a large rock-cut cistern and rectangular pit.
    The courtyard was entered from a street or lane; opening off the
    courtyard was a monumental room with plastered walls and
    floors, which at a later stage had a beautifully carved capital on a
    pilaster. The pilaster must have supported an arch spanning the
    width of the room and supporting a second floor.

Trapezoidal walls (about 45x75 m) initially were interpreted as a
monastic complex covering the whole hilltop, including the elite house.
In fact, the hilltop walls were defensive walls from the Persian invasion
or Muslim conquest (614 or 634 C.E.). Another part of the wall in the
southwest, however, was early Roman, finer and more monumental
than the rest; it is from a public building of some sort, perhaps a synagogue (see Plates 15–18). Attached to it is a smaller room that may
be a *Beth ha-Midrash*. The main room is 10x15 m, with intermittent benches, column bases laid out precisely on a 5x5 m nave, with
2.5x5 m side aisles. The adjacent room is about 3x5 m, with continuous benches on three (perhaps four) sides. A monumental capital fits
this interpretation, though there is still no clear proof of the building's
identification as a Jewish public building. The building is unusual architecturally, though some features have parallels with public buildings at
Chorazin, Gamla, and Khirbet Shema', all of which have a room that
functions as a study house. In the squares associated with these two
rooms, roof tiles—some embedded in constructions from obviously
later periods—and one small piece of fresco reinforce the picture of a
monumental building. The fresco has pink, red, gray, and yellow-ochre
paint in a geometric pattern, not unlike the colors of the large first-
century house at Yodefat. Hasmonean coins (a majority of the coins
found on the site) and pieces of stoneware (a majority of which were
found in the vicinity of the monumental building) strengthen the evidence for a first-century Jewish community at Khirbet Qana.

    Reports since the 1950s have referred to a pilgrim cave half way up
the hill.[34] There are four interconnected caves with two entrances to

permit a flow of traffic. The main cave has four layers of plaster, three of which have graffiti and inscriptions, some of which are Christian; the other three caves have no graffiti. The floor has several layers of plaster, interspersed with layers of cobbles, surrounded by benches on the south and west sides. The east side had a kind of mini-apse. Interest focuses on an altar or bench on the north side of the cave, formed in part by a turned up sarcophagus lid that has at least one, and more likely three, incised "Maltese" crosses on what was originally the underside of the lid. The bases of two stone jugs were still in situ on the altar, held in place by plaster that was continuous from ceiling to altar; a third jug was on the floor of the cave. There was room for six jugs.

This cave corresponds closely to details of the veneration cave in the pilgrim accounts, supporting the identification of Khirbet Qana as pilgrim Cana (and thus the more probable site of Cana of the New Testament and Josephus). Some pilgrim accounts imply there should be a monastery on the site.[35] There is no monastery on the hilltop, it is now clear, but one corner of its walls may have been located beside the veneration cave below later Arab housing, in the village halfway up the hill. A north-south wall of over 2 m width bonds with an east-west wall of over 1 m width, implying a very large building at the cave mouth. Khirbet Qana was a town or village whose main periods of occupation are late Hellenistic, early Roman, and early Byzantine, with an important Christian pilgrimage installation, probably a monastery and possibly a synagogue/*Beth ha-Midrash* complex.

CANA AND CAPERNAUM

Capernaum's excavations feature a fifth- (sixth?) century limestone synagogue, now rivaled in impact by a flying-saucer church hovering above an octagonal fifth-century church. Corbo has claimed first-century C.E. precursors for both: a basalt synagogue below the limestone building and a fourth-century rhomboidal church below the octagonal structure, with a first-century venerated room from the house where Jesus healed Peter's mother below that.

Capernaum was fishing based and Cana was agriculturally based, but in other respects they were similar, with similar developments from the early Roman through early Byzantine periods. Both were small peasant villages, each within sight of a capital of Galilee; both were

associated with Jesus and with events of the First Revolt. Both may
have had early Jewish-Christian communities, though evidence for this
is slender and later. The character of the housing is similar, though
Khirbet Qana's seems more varied. The presence of a synagogue is
similar, though Khirbet Qana's is still uncertain. The evidence of social
and religious life is somewhat similar, though there is more evidence of
observant Judaism at Khirbet Qana than at Capernaum (*mikvaoth*,
stoneware, Hasmonean coinage, *columbaria*). The development of
Christian veneration is also similar, though we have no proof of a
church structure yet at Khirbet Qana.

The claim that Capernaum's Christian veneration site goes back
continuously to the first century is, however, doubtful. The detailed
excavation reports do not allow certainty, for the stratigraphy is unclear
and the drawings include details not founded on the reports. The venerated room at the center of the *insula sacra* was originally a courtyard,
in all probability: (1) the space was too big to be roofed; (2) the drawings show a "ghost wall," of which there is no physical evidence, to
solve the roofing problem; (3) an analogous area in a nearby house is
certainly a courtyard.[36]

Three comments form a conclusion:

(1) Khirbet Qana, like Yodefat and Gamla (which lack connections
    with Jesus) and Capernaum, gives an accurate sense of place for
    the historical Jesus. All were small, densely occupied rural vil-
    lages, thriving and self-confident in the first century, with obser-
    vant Jewish inhabitants across a range of status levels. The
    relationship between the villages and adjacent cities is still not
    clear, nor is it clear why both Josephus and Jesus should seem to
    have made Cana a base of operations.
(2) Christianity developed in Cana, though archaeological evidence
    is not earlier than the fourth century. Textual evidence makes
    Cana and Capernaum rival claimants as the main village of
    Jesus, the one possibly associated with John and the other with
    Peter.
(3) Cana, like Capernaum, challenges assumptions of an early and
    sharp cleavage between Judaism and Christianity. The material
    evidence of the fourth to sixth centuries suggests that both had
    Jewish and Christian communities living in proximity to each
    other. Khirbet Qana had a venerated site, possibly with a church

beside it, and, if present indications hold, a synagogue/*Beth ha-Midrash* complex serving a Jewish community into the Byzantine period. Capernaum, too, with physical evidence that is now more rather than less controversial, had Jewish and Christian communities. The number of sites with adjacent communities but no material evidence of conflict between them is limited: Capernaum, Beth Yerah, Nazareth, and now Khirbet Qana. All are around the Sea of Galilee and in the lower Galilee, and three of the four are intimately associated with Jesus' ministry. Khirbet Qana may assume substantial importance as Capernaum's rival as a place for the historical Jesus, as the location where early Byzantines located the water-to-wine incident, and as a site that reflects ongoing parallel Jewish and Christian communities.

PART THREE

SYNAGOGUES AND CHURCHES

CHAPTER SEVEN

PRE-70 SYNAGOGUES AS *COLLEGIA* IN ROME, THE DIASPORA, AND JUDEA

INTRODUCTION[1]

Simeon Guterman argued half a century ago that "on the basis of Josephus's specific evidence and the general similarity in the organization of synagogues and the *collegia* we may feel justified in regarding the Jewish communities as *collegia licita*."[2] Mary Smallwood affirmed that view a quarter century ago.[3] This chapter carries their views of the matter somewhat further. It is surprising that the view that synagogues were *collegia* has not caught on; many writers on synagogues ignore the claim. Debates on the origins of synagogue buildings are more likely to discuss such divergent and improbable origins as basilicas, council chambers, dining rooms, temples, and the like. In the equally vigorous debate over the functions and roles of synagogues there are few mentions of voluntary associations. The general sense of these debates is that the development of synagogues was *sui generis*, when in fact it was part of a larger movement. Synagogues functioned—and were perceived—as *collegia* in the Diaspora; the earliest evidence for synagogues is from the Mediterranean Diaspora, and this suggests that synagogues actually began life as *collegia* in a Diaspora setting. When they came into Palestine they continued to show signs of being *collegia* though that terminology was no longer appropriate; only gradually did they take on (especially in the Holy Land) a new set of features deriving from the loss of the temple.

I begin with a brief analysis and critique of an important major work on synagogues. The first volume of two volumes on synagogues contains an important selection of individual studies, many translated from the Hebrew for the first time, with a heavy emphasis on Israeli participation.[4] (1) There are important methodological issues at stake, with Israeli scholars tending to one side of the debate and American scholars on the other side.[5] (2) There is no agreement on what role the later literary evidence of Talmud and *Mishnah* is to play. (3) There is still a strong attachment to a typology of synagogue development that according to many scholars is outdated and no longer viable. The fundamental question is whether the evidence from the earliest period—the focus of this paper—is to be heard and followed.

J. Gwyn Griffiths complains, correctly, that only a minority of scholars has recognized that the synagogue had its origins in Egypt: "The possibility of an Egyptian influence is not even considered" by most (8). He is tolerant of the idea of the influence of "Hellenistic associations," but in the end he retreats from granting them substantial influence. Aryeh Kasher also rehearses Egyptian evidence, arguing that while synagogues were for Torah reading and prayer, "they should resemble the Jerusalem temple in their functions . . . not involved with the sacrificial worship" (200, cf. 209); he links this with an insistence that Leontopolis (and Elephantine) were insignificant in Egyptian Judaism (Chapter 10). Lester L. Grabbe claims that Judean synagogues were not Pharisaic, and that there is only the slenderest of evidence before the first century C.E., while Paul V. M. Flesher comments, in an important footnote (29, n. 8) that "none of the rabbinic texts published prior to about 250 refer to synagogues prior to 70 . . . [including] the Mishnah." He assesses pre-70 synagogues helpfully, though he gives too much weight to such matters as orientation, and not enough to the presence of *mikvaoth* at Gamla and Herodium (37). He distinguishes between Galilee and Judea, and is not much interested in the party affiliations of those building the structures.

Dennis Groh provides an important fresh analysis of datable archaeological evidence for synagogues, a model of care, precision, and accurate analysis.[6] His view is clear: "stratigraphic excavation has flat-footedly destroyed the sequential development" of (1) a basilican type; (2) the fourth-century broadhouse type; (3) a Byzantine synagogue with apse toward Jerusalem. He concludes, "The first-century Galilean synagogue . . . is essentially a room to gather the community" (60). The first basilican synagogues were mid-third century and orientation towards Jerusalem appeared first in the second century (69). Yoram Tsafrir fights a rearguard action against the newer views, both with respect to typology and also supporting the view that "prior to the third century synagogues did not exist as special structures, with external identifying signs" (79); "the Galilean synagogue is a third-century Jewish invention"(80). Alf T. Kraabel's views on Diaspora synagogues are represented by reprinting his well-known *ANRW* article (1979): we must abandon the basilica model, there is no one pattern, Rabbinic statements are irrelevant, and Diaspora synagogues were often deliberately inconspicuous community buildings for various functions. Dan Urman argues that the house of assembly was "first and foremost . . . a community center"; only later did it become a house of prayer in the land of Israel. Further, the *Beth ha-Midrash* of the Second Temple was a real building: "a good part of the structures uncovered thus far and identified as houses of assembly were, in fact, houses of study" (255). Ronny Reich presents cogent evidence for a link between synagogues and *mikvaoth* in the Second Temple period (295), though not in the later period when there is a "drastic decrease in the construction and use of *miqwaot* in general" (296). The book is a mixed bag. It shows that helpful insights emerge from continued archaeological work and analysis, but efforts to construct a typological development of synagogues have run their course;[7] there is still no consensus on synagogue origins, though there is a growing inclination to look to the Mediterranean Diaspora.

Viewing synagogues as voluntary associations, or *collegia*, deriving their status from decisions of Caesar and Augustus in the first century B.C.E., illuminates the character of their buildings. Conversely, examining synagogues both in Judea and the Diaspora sheds light on *collegia*. I use several kinds of data from the late Roman Republic and the early Empire: evidence about *collegia* in general and their treatment in various areas of the Empire, inscriptional evidence about the roles and activities of synagogues and their distribution, and archaeological evidence bearing on their physical character. These all overlap to some extent, showing the character of synagogues as they were found in the Diaspora or in Judea. The evidence is diffuse geographically and chronologically, but I draw my ammunition from one period, the last half of the first century B.C.E. and the early first century C.E.

JEWISH SYNAGOGUES AS *COLLEGIA* IN THE FIRST CENTURY B.C.E.

Synagogues were viewed as *collegia* by Roman authorities in the first century B.C.E., yet their status was special. Two figures dominate the interpretation of the evidence, Julius Caesar and Caesar Augustus. Others have summarized the main outlines of the legal position.[8] In 64 B.C.E. the Senate prohibited all *collegia* on principle because of their danger to the state as private institutions.[9] It was characteristic of the political and social turbulence of the period that in 58 B.C.E., during the First Triumvirate, *collegia* were permitted again, and that in 56 B.C.E. the Senate again dissolved political clubs, a specific class of *collegia*. A few years later (sometime between 49 and 44 B.C.E.), Julius Caesar prohibited all *collegia* Empire-wide except the most ancient. One exception, perhaps because it conformed to the notion *ancient*, was Judaism,[10] and this exception was also Empire-wide. By this action Caesar made Judaism a *religio licita*, and Jewish gratitude for this status was demonstrated by Jewish attendance at Caesar's funeral (Suetonius, *Jul.* 84.5). The character of the period emerges clearly from Cicero's defence of Flaccus:

> There follows that ill will stemming from Jewish gold. . . . Although it is the practice annually to send gold in the name of Jews to Jerusalem from Italy and all the provinces, Flaccus ordered by an edict that it was forbidden to export it from the province of Asia. . . . "But," you will say, "Gnaeus Pompey, when he captured Jerusalem, although a victor, touched not a thing in that shrine." In this especially, as in many other matters, he acted wisely, for, in the case of such a suspicious and abusive state, he left no occasion for gossip on the part of his opponents. For I do not think that it was the religion of the Jews and of his enemies that acted as an obstacle to this very distinguished general, but rather his sense of honor. (*Flac.* 66–69)

Jews first reached Rome probably about 161 B.C.E., when a delegation from Judah the Hasmonean went to the Roman Senate to establish a connection between Rome and Judea (1 Macc 8:1–32). This was repeated on two later occasions (1 Macc 12:16; 14:24; about 150 and 139 B.C.E. respectively). During this period the Jews' position in Rome was tenuous. Numbers increased throughout the early first century B.C.E., accelerated by Pompey's conquests in the East, when Jews from Syria and Judea were sent to Rome as slaves following Pompey's settlement of the eastern questions. Others came because of the opportunities in Rome following Rome's continued expansion in the East, as it assumed the position of the main Mediterranean power. Though initially resident aliens and slaves, some Jews acquired freedom and Roman citizenship. Most of the Jewish community lived in the suburbs, initially Transtiberinum, later the Campus Martius and the Subura. By the first century B.C.E. there was a Jewish community in Ostia, Rome's port city.

During the chaotic period of the civil wars the law against *collegia* fell into abeyance. At some unknown date Augustus reenacted it, and synagogues were again exempted under his law against *collegia*. Philo, though not a contemporary, provides good evidence for Augustus's generosity:

> . . . he did not expel them from Rome or deprive them of their Roman citizenship because they remembered their Jewish nationality also. He introduced no changes into their synagogues, he did not prevent them from meeting for the exposition of the Law, and he raised no objection to the offering of first fruits. . . . Moreover . . . if the distribution [in Rome of money or food] happened to be made on the Sabbath . . . he instructed the distributors to reserve the Jew's share . . . until the next day.[11]

The pattern sketched above is this: in times of factionalism and strife *collegia* tended to be permitted, but in times when reconstruction and consolidation were important, *collegia* were restricted—in 64 B.C.E., in the 40s under Julius Caesar, and in the 20s (?) under Augustus. In the latter two cases, synagogues were exempted. In the Augustan legislation Judaism acquired status as a licit religion everywhere in the Empire.

INSCRIPTIONAL AND LITERARY EVIDENCE OF SYNAGOGUES IN THE DIASPORA

Inscriptional and Literary Evidence

The earliest datable evidence for synagogues is a group of inscriptions from Egypt. They refer to buildings for cultic and community purposes, in almost all cases calling them prayerhouses (*proseuchai*). Most of the inscriptional evidence from Egypt is described or reproduced in Schürer.[12] All eight presuppose a building, not just a worshiping community.

- Schedia, *CIJ* 1440, 246–221 B.C.E.: "On behalf of King Ptolemy and Queen Berenice, his sister and wife, and their children, the Jews [dedicated] this prayerhouse."

- Lower Egypt, *CIJ* 1449, 246–221 B.C.E.: an older inscription was included in a later one; it read "King Ptolemy Euergetes [bestowed the right of asylum] on the prayerhouse."

- Athribis, *CIJ* 1443, 180–145 (?) B.C.E.: "On behalf of King Ptolemy and Queen Cleopatra, Ptolemy son of Epicydus, the commander of the guard, and the Jews in Athribis [dedicated] the prayerhouse to the Highest God."

- Athribis, *CIJ* 1444, 180–145 (?) B.C.E.: "On behalf of King Ptolemy and Queen Cleopatra and their children, Hermias and his wife Philotera and their children [dedicated] this *exedra* for the prayerhouse."

- Nitriai, *CIJ* 1442 (not 1422 as Schürer says), 144–116 B.C.E.: "On behalf of King Ptolemy and Queen Cleopatra his sister and Queen Cleopatra his wife, benefactors [*euergetai*], the Jews in Nitriai [dedicated] the prayerhouse and appurtenances."

- Xenephyris, *CIJ* 1441, 144–116 B.C.E.: similar to previous, but ". . . the Jews of Xenephyris [dedicated] the gateway of the prayerhouse when Theodoros and Achillion were benefactors [*prostatai*]."

- Alexandria, *CIJ* 1433, second century B.C.E.: "To the Highest God [who hears prayer] the holy [precinct (*peribolos*) and] the prayer[house and the app]urtenances [were dedicated]."

- Alexandria, *CIJ* 1432, 36 (?) B.C.E.: "On behalf of the Qu[een] and K[ing], Alypus made the prayerho[use] for the Highest God who hears prayer, in the fifteenth year in the month Mecheir."

Two important papyri from the same region and period match a ninth inscription, from Arsenoe-Crocodilopolis in the Fayum; a building is again presupposed.

- Arsinoe-Crocodilopolis in the Fayum, *CPJ* III.1532A, 246–221 B.C.E.: "On behalf of King Ptolemy son of Ptolemy and Queen Berenice his wife and sister and their children, the Jews in the city of the Crocodiles [dedicated] the prayerhouse."

- Fayum, a papyrus *CPJ* I.129, 11 May 218 B.C.E., refers to a thief who stole a cloak and desposited it "in the prayerhouse of the Jews."

- Arsinoe in the Fayum, a papyrus *CPJ* I.134, late second century B.C.E. has a list of properties with two references to "a prayerhouse of Jews" that owned a "holy garden" (*hiera paradeisos*).

One papyrus from Egypt uses the term *synagôgê*, linked with the more common word *proseuchê*,[13] in which *proseuchê* refers to the building and *synagôgê* refers simply to the "gathering."[14] This evidence presupposes buildings from third to first centuries B.C.E. serving the needs of the Jewish communities, mostly in Lower Egypt.[15] The favored term in Egypt was *proseuchai*, but I have no doubt that—despite the absence of archaeological evidence about their size, shape, or form—they were synagogues.

Philo provides the most important literary evidence from Egypt (early first century C.E.). Generally he uses *proseuchê* for Jewish community buildings. This is frequent in both *Legatio ad Gaium* and *In Flaccum*, where the references are usually to buildings in Alexandria vandalized, burned or desecrated by the mobs in the violence surrounding the year 38 C.E.[16] Twice he refers to Rome and the *proseuchai* there that met on the Sabbaths and collected money for the temple in Jerusalem, which Augustus knew but did nothing about (*Legat.* 156, 157). He also refers to Jews occupying themselves every seventh day with the philosophy of their fathers: "for what are our places of prayer (*proseukêtria*) throughout the cities but schools of prudence and courage and temperance and justice, and also of piety and holiness and every virtue" (*Mos.* 2.216; cf. *Spec.* 2.62). Speaking of Sabbath worship, Philo says that Essenes "proceed to the sacred places (*topous*), which they call synagogues (*synagôgai*), where the young sit ranked in rows below the elders. . . ." (*Prob.* 81; cf. *Contempl.* 30).

Decrees in Antiquities *16.160–73 and 14.190–264*

Josephus cites decrees that we might have found as inscriptions, had we been so lucky. There are six in *Antiquities* 16, two from Augustus (to Asia, probably from 2–3 C.E.; and to Norbanus Flaccus, probably between 31 and 27 B.C.E.), two from Marcus Agrippa (to Ephesus, perhaps 14 B.C.E.; and to Cyrene, before 12 B.C.E.); one from Norbanus Flaccus (to Sardis, between 31 and 27 B.C.E.), and one from Julius Antonuis (to Ephesus, 4 B.C.E.). In the earliest (Norbanus Flaccus), Augustus made the essential point that Jews could send "sacred moneys up to Jerusalem without interference" (*Ant.* 16.166), a reference to the temple tax. Flaccus confirmed this right in his decree to Sardis, adding, "however great [the sums] may be" (*Ant.* 16.171), indicating perhaps that Jews could send special gifts in addition to the temple tax. In the longest of the decrees, inscribed on a column in a Temple of Caesar (in Ankara?), Augustus added as his rationale the favorable disposition of Judaism and especially Hyrcanus II towards Rome and towards Julius Caesar. Augustus extended the rights beyond the half-shekel tax to include exemption from appearing in court on the Sabbath, and protection of Jewish sacred books and sacred monies. Two decrees of Marcus Agrippa reinforced these general provisions, and added (to Ephesus) that anyone stealing sacred Jewish money forfeited the right of asylum, just as temple-robbers did. Julius Antonuis, Mark Antony's son, confirmed the decrees of Augustus and Agrippa.

Josephus's record of these decrees and letters has sometimes been considered inauthentic, but current views are more generous.[17] If the decrees are authentic (though perhaps not always accurate translations), as I think, the evidence for Augustus's lenient treatment of Jews in various parts of the Diaspora is solid, especially with respect to the collection and transmission of the temple tax (probably including additional free-will gifts) and exemption from attendance at court. Both protections went beyond what was usual in *collegia*: transmission of money to Jerusalem implied a degree of foreign allegiance unparalleled in *collegia*, and exemption from court attendance also seems unparalleled. Judaism's status went beyond that of other *collegia*.

The details in the longer collection of decrees in *Antiquities* 14 are less clear: nevertheless, the following summarizing comments can be made.

(1) Those attributed to Julius Caesar (the first six: 14.190–212) must date from 49 to 44 B.C.E.; the issues had to do as much with Judea as the Diaspora. They referred in every instance to Hyrcanus II,[18] High Priest and Ethnarch, and they focused on the right of his sons to hold the same offices; they shed little light on the question of synagogues as *collegia*.[19]

(2) Two others confirmed decrees of Julius Caesar, one by Julius Gaius to Parium (or Paros) and the other by Mark Antony and Publius Dolabella (April 11, 44 B.C.E.: 14.213–22).

(3) Yet another referred to the decrees of the Senate (Gaius Fannius to Cos: 14.233).

(4) The main theme of the rest was exemption from military service, an important issue during the civil war; this appeared first in a decree of Lucius Lentulus to Asia and Ephesus (September 19, 49 B.C.E.: 14.228–29), was repeated by him in two other decrees, and was cited in three more decrees. Dolabella also dealt with the exemption from military service in another decree to Asia and Ephesus, probably in 44 (14.223–27).

(5) Two decrees, one by Lucius Antonius, son of Mark Antony (14.235), and one a decree of Sardis (14.259–61), allowed Jews to build their own place (of prayer in the case of Sardis); the former confirmed Jews' right of association and right to decide civil cases, the latter confirmed the right to adjudicate suits among themselves, and added the right to a place to build and inhabit

(a quarter set aside for them?); it also added the right to approved food.

(6) Other rights in this collection included making offerings (presumably in Jerusalem), deferring court appearances on the Sabbath, managing produce as they saw fit, celebrating festivals, and keeping the Sabbath.

(7) A decree from Pergamon (14.247–54) referred to Hyrcanus I (135–104 B.C.E.), and was therefore earlier; its concerns were markedly different: harbors, taxation, and the movement of goods. A second may also have referred to Hyrcanus I (14.241–43), though this is less certain.

With those exceptions, the decrees showed the conditions of Judaism in the Diaspora and in a couple of cases in Judea during the last half of the first century B.C.E.

Judaism was strongly affirmed in the decrees. Jewish communities were regularly sustained in their claims to be sanctioned as a *religio licita* (frequently against the opposition of local authorities), able to run their affairs in the same way others did. In these decrees Judaism in the Diaspora was well protected. Much of that protection was contingent upon actions of Julius Caesar and the Senate of Rome.

The degree of protection went beyond what was usual for other *collegia*. Despite the fact that a *collegium* was not a legal person, in some matters the protection applied to the group as a whole. Jewish communities could collect the half-shekel temple tax and could send it to Jerusalem; apparently, judging by the frequent references to the temple tax, this arrangement was resented and delegations were attacked. Many would have seen this degree of independence as a dangerous allegiance to another power, to an exclusive God outside the Roman pantheon, a local god who was intolerant of rivals. A related prerogative—the collection and transmission of produce being sent as fulfilment of the requirement for tithing first fruits—was interfered with and also caused grief.[20]

The decrees underscore the rich group life of Diaspora Jewish communities, with common meals, observance of festivals, carrying out of religious rituals, special gatherings, educational opportunities, and special food. They carried out their traditional rites and customs. They also enjoyed rights they could exercise individually: exemption from military service, observing the Sabbath, and adjudicating their own civil suits. Local communities of the Diaspora were able to preserve

their way of life against the weight of opinion in many of the cities in
which they settled, for which they had official support from Roman
officials. They were like and unlike other *collegia*.

SYNAGOGUES IN ROME

Twelve or thirteen named synagogues are known in Rome;[21] it is likely
the earliest was a "Synagogue of the Hebrews," for two reasons. First,
a similarly named synagogue at Corinth provides an analogy: a reused
lintel carried an inscription that originally read *SYNAGÔGÊ
HEBRAIÔN*. Second, the generic name was inherently likely to be earliest. Differentiating themselves in Rome (linguistically?) from the
"Synagogue of the Hebrews" was the "Synagogue of the
Vernaculars," whose adherents may have spoken Latin.[22] Some Roman
synagogues were named after neighborhoods (Campus Martius,
Subura, and Calcaria) or foreign cities (Elea, Tripolis, Skina [?], Arca
in Lebanon). Three or four were named after persons.

This evidence is relatively late and imperfect, with no descriptions
of the synagogues or—with the important exception of nearby
Ostia—archaeological remains. Nevertheless, the list of synagogues in
Rome is impressive, even if the allusions were rather casual. When did
they originate? In the cases of those referring to neighborhoods or foreign places, no convincing arguments can be mounted about dates. In
the cases of those named after persons, a date of origin close to the
time of that person's influence is plausible.

The three or four Roman synagogues named after persons are of
direct interest to this study: one refers to Augustus, one to Agrippa, and
one to Volumnius, with a fourth debatable one. In the light of the introductory section of this chapter, it is not surprising to find Rome having
a Synagogue of the Augustans (or Augustesians).[23] I do not think
Augustus was the patron or that his freedmen (*libertini*) formed the synagogue. The synagogue was probably so named to honor the emperor
under whom Judaism flourished in the Diaspora. The community must
have agreed to name the synagogue while Augustus was still alive, otherwise the point would have been lost. Since most of the inscriptions come
from the Monteverde catacomb, the oldest in Rome, it is likely that the
synagogue was located nearby in Transtiberinum, the oldest Jewish area.
Augustus's (implied) approval of the naming of the synagogue underscored his tolerance of Judaism and its institutions, right in Rome.

There was a synagogue of the Agrippans or Agrippesians, presumably named after Augustus's chief lieutenant and heir, Marcus Vipsanius Agrippa, who died in 12 B.C.E.,[24] though it is possible that it was named after either Agrippa I or Agrippa II, both of whom had lengthy contacts with Rome. In either case, the origin of the synagogue was likely to have been in the late first century B.C.E. or early first century C.E. If it were named after Marcus Agrippa, as I think likely, it would have been because he upheld Jewish privileges in the East, in Asia Minor particularly. Like the synagogue of the Augustans, the synagogue of the Agrippans likely stood in the Transtiberinum.

A synagogue of the Volumnians or Volumnesians was named after Volumnius.[25] It is debatable whether this Volumnius was the official active in Syria from 9 to 7 B.C.E. If this Volumnius were the Syrian official, then there was a third synagogue named after a person involved in Jewish history in the eastern part of the Empire.[26] At the least we have evidence of two synagogues in Rome named after the highest officials in the land; Augustus and Agrippa were instrumental in alleviating the conditions of Jews in the Diaspora. In all three cases the origins of the synagogues were likely to be contemporary with the persons themselves, late first century B.C.E. or early first century C.E.

In sum, the earliest synagogue in Rome was simply the "Synagogue of the Hebrews." Two other synagogues were named after the highest officials, Augustus and Agrippa. Further, a synagogue may have been named after Volumnius, tribune of Syria. All four originated in the period just before or just after the turn of the eras; all four were probably located in the suburb across the Tiber.

I have tacitly assumed in the above discussion that these early synagogues were buildings, not informal communities of Jews. Since the earliest known buildings go back to the late-third century B.C.E. in Egypt and others are attested in second and first century B.C.E. contexts elsewhere in the Diaspora, it is not unreasonable to imagine synagogues in Rome, perhaps as many as four or five, at this relatively early period. The synagogue in Ostia (Chapter 12) had a first-century C.E. level, so synagogue buildings in Rome seem likely.

A Synagogue of the Herodians?

A fragmentary inscription from the Roman catacombs may have referred to a "Synagogue of the Herodians" (*CIJ* 173); the arguments about it are vigorous and convoluted.[27] If it alludes to a synagogue named after Herod the Great, what is the significance? It was found on a large (57x45 cm) broken marble slab from the Via Appia. Its lettering is unusually large—unequalled in the inscriptions from this location—varying from 6 to 9 cm. Only part of the text remains in four lines, three with writing:

 ....]x   x   x
 ....]ΓΩΓΗΣ
 ....]ΡΟΔΙΩΝ
 ....]ΕΥΛΟΓΙΑΠΑΣΙ

The debate over the inscription has taken three forms, though only the first two are actively held. (1) H. J. Leon, followed by David Noy in the latest publication of the inscription,[28] argues for a personal name, some variant on "Rhodion." (2) J.-B. Frey, followed by a museum catalogue,[29] argues for "Herod." (3) Emil Schürer proposed a reference to the island of Rhodes.[30] The arguments are evenly balanced, and conclusions are insecure. I argue for a reference to a "synagogue of Herodians." Discussions have ignored the first line with the three "X"s, on which I make three observations: (1) no inscriptions in *CIJ* (nor in Noy's volumes) have a similar device (note *CIJ* 491); (2) some inscriptions have a highlighted name in the first line; (3) other inscriptions have iconographic devices bracketing the first line.[31] I suggest a key to the correct reading is reading the Xs as a design motif decorating both ends of the first line, with a name in the nominative or dative.[32] The first line, I suppose, was thus:

 X X X NAME X X X

This supposition helps to establish limits for the original size of the marble slab, probably just over a meter wide, consistent with the monumental size of lettering.[33]

 Several inscriptions that highlight the name in one line go on in the next to name a position: head or scribe, also in the nominative (*CIJ* 221, 277, 284, 353), analogies that work well here. Line two likely read "head of the synagogue," "scribe of the synagogue," or "father of the synagogue" (*archôn/grammateus/patêr tês synagôgês*).[34] Using the first as an example, notice how the relative position of the Xs and the surviving letters *gôgês* is just about right; lines one and two then read:

 [X X X NAME] XXX
 [archôntêssyna]GÔGÊ S

Immediately before the *rho* in]RODIÔN is the vertical stroke of either an *iota* or an *êta*.[35] Leon reads an *iota* and interprets it as the final letter in a dative of the deceased's name, while he takes "Rhodion" as the name of the donor setting up the inscription.[36] Frey reads *êta* and reconstructs the middle line of text as HÊRODIÔN. Against Frey's reconstruction are two difficulties. First, while one might have expected HÊRODEIÔN, Latin influence and the way the name was pronounced might have given rise to the inscription's reading, analogous to the Latinisms in "Augustesians" and "Agrippesians," though the form is not "Herodesians" (as in the other named synagogues). Second, the first "O" in the surviving letters is an *omicron*, not an *omega*, as "Herodians" properly requires. Two facts soften this latter difficulty: first, since the Greek of the inscriptions is often barbarous, misspellings should be expected; Augustus was misspelt in one (*CIJ* 368) and Volumnius in another (*CIJ* 417). A misspelling of Herod, in Rome a less commonly heard name, is not much of a problem. Second, the name Herod was in fact occasionally spelled in this fashion; one inscription makes the same mistake and a coin type of Herod of Chalcis has the name misspelt in the same way with an *omicron*.[37] An error here is not implausible. Line three is best completed with a reference to "the Herodians," in the genitive plural. Since this reading does not fill the whole line, it is obvious that the carver was not under any pressure to compress his letters at the end of line three. This in turn suggests a space on the left, which I propose was filled with a symbol (a menorah or some such symbol, found not infrequently on the lower left), following Frey's suggestion and numerous examples in the corpus.[38]

Line four preserves the final encomium; here the carver misjudged his line length and had to squeeze the letters as he neared the end, in contrast to the generous spacing of lines two and three. My reconstruction proposes reference to the deceased's age before the final blessing, a standard feature that would account for the decreasing space of the letters at the end of the line (cf. *CIJ* 176). The final blessing was frequently "in peace your sleep"; the simple form of blessing found here, though not unique, is rare. In over 500 inscriptions only one is somewhat similar (*CIJ* 204; cf. 652, 694, and 515, a piece of gold glass); it too has a menorah.[39] Putting these observations together gives a reconstruction of the missing portion of the text (the space on the lower left would be occupied by a drawing of a Jewish symbol, such as a menorah).

[x x x n a m e] x x x	[x x x n a m e] x x x
[archôntêssyna]GÔGÊS	[ruler of the syna]gogue
[tôn hê]RODIÔN	[of the He]rodians
[etê - -]EULOGIAPASI	[age?] A blessing to all

This reconstruction gives a grammatically correct and sensible result, without straining the evidence as Frey, Leon, and Noy do. Frey's reconstruction—place of the synagogue of the Herodians—is attractive but unparalleled, creating problems of reconstruction and layout. Leon's views require too large a slab. The reconstruction presented above, however, conforms in its details to other evidence from the catacombs. If this reasoning is correct, Herod the Great, who was influential in Diaspora affairs and familiar to the Roman Jewish community, was a fourth person indirectly honored in an early synagogue inscription in Rome.

This would be the only known dedication of a synagogue relating to Herod, and would add an otherwise unknown element to his portrait. The reason for a Roman community honoring him in this way cannot be known. The simplest view is that he was known as being active on behalf of Diaspora Jews and was seen as King of all Jews everywhere. In parentheses, I note that even if this reconstruction of the inscription were correct, the Herod referred to here could be Herod Agrippa I or II, not Herod the Great. In such a case, this synagogue could be the same as the synagogue of the Agrippans. Either conclusion would affect the details but not the main point of this chapter.

If this line of argument is convincing, there may have been four first-century B.C.E. synagogues in Rome named after persons instrumental in bettering the conditions of Jews in the Diaspora in the circumstances discussed earlier. These four knew each other well, were well disposed to the maintenance of the Jewish communities, and in three cases were good friends. This is not incidental, for these allusions to four highly placed individuals came close to the time when Jewish privileges and exemptions from laws against *collegia* were debated, even disputed. With the other evidence linking Augustus, Agrippa, and Herod to the welfare of the Diaspora, the evidence is mutually confirming.

HEROD AND IMPERIAL POLICY

The shorter collection of decrees (*Ant.* 16.160–73) follows an incident in which Ionian Jews appealed to Marcus Agrippa for support in connection with attacks on their keeping of their laws (*Ant.* 16.27–61). Herod the Great directed Nicolas of Damascus to defend the Jewish appellants. They won the suit. Marcus Agrippa's decision was based on Herod's good will and friendship, and perhaps also Herod's benefactions to cities in which large numbers of Jews lived. His concern for the Diaspora was the motivating factor in his substantial gifts throughout Syria, Asia Minor, the Aegean Islands, and mainland Greece. Instead of donations benefiting a Diaspora Jewish community, his benefactions were for the larger community. They portrayed Jews as good citizens, not concerned for their own limited welfare but actively part of the larger social group. Such a policy would have minimized resentment towards, or because of, their special status under the *collegia* laws.

Three names stand out as persons active in upholding Jewish rights: Julius Caesar, Augustus, and Marcus Agrippa. Herod's name should be added to these. The four names dovetail with the inscriptions in Rome, where three of the four had synagogues named after them directly or indirectly. The actions of the Roman Jewish community in naming synagogues after Augustus, Marcus Agrippa, Herod and Volumnius (if he was the Syrian official) was a response to their important roles in the Diaspora, supporting the rights and privileges of the Jewish communities.

ARCHAEOLOGICAL EVIDENCE IN THE DIASPORA AND JUDEA

The earliest archaeological evidence for synagogues comes from Egypt[40] (where they are referred to as "Houses of Prayer"[41]), the Aegean islands, especially Delos[42] (and perhaps Aegina, where the remains are slim and debated),[43] and Ostia (Chapters 8–12). Despite the number of Diaspora communities in which synagogues were to be found, most of the building evidence is later than the first century.[44] The two most helpful sites from the Diaspora are Delos and Ostia.[45] This situation prompts consideration of Judea for early building remains on which reconstructions can be based.[46] I will consider four pieces of evidence: Gamla, Masada, Herodium, and the Theodotos inscription.

Gamla

The community building at Gamla was a synagogue, perhaps the earliest from Judea, from the first century B.C.E. It was located at the high side of town, adjacent to a casemate wall (in this respect not unlike Masada), with a room within the wall functioning perhaps as a *Beth ha-Midrash*, and with a ritual pool (*mikveh*) a few steps away outside the front entrance (Plate 25). The building was constructed of black basalt ashlar masonry, with columns supporting the roof, the corner columns being heart-shaped; the capitals were carved in varied but relatively unornamented style. The interior was plain: around the walls were benches; the main portion of the floor was packed dirt. There were two entrances: the main door with an unusual, indirect entrance on the axis of the large room faced approximately southwest, and a side entrance faced approximately southeast, dropping down via stairs to the street that ran along the south wall. Jerusalem lay to the southwest.

The building was a simple community hall suitable for a variety of functions. There was little to differentiate functions in the building. The evidence is unclear whether it provided for liturgical functions. A niche in the northwest corner might have been a Torah niche and a row of stone pavers across the middle of the dirt floor has been thought suitable as the location of a reading desk. I will comment on these features later.

Masada

Assessments of Masada have been hampered by publishing delays.[47] Yadin's main publication of his work at Masada included the conclusion that an earlier phase underlay the synagogue from the time of the First Revolt; he thought it likely to have been a synagogue, within the same walls but with a different configuration of the space (Plate 26). If the original building were also a synagogue, it was early, perhaps earlier than Gamla.[48] This structure, usually called Masada I, was also very plain: it lacked the benches almost uniformly found in Judean synagogues, had an entrance and a pattern of columns similar to the Gamla synagogue. Like Gamla, Masada I was against a casemate wall, but

Masada I had no separate room within the width of the wall. In Masada's case the outside wall of the synagogue was the defensive wall. There was no evidence of provision for liturgical functions in Masada I: no niche or reading desk. The door faced roughly southeast; Jerusalem lay slightly west of north. The casemate wall and the adjacent structures were part of Herod's building program in the last third of the first century B.C.E. If the building were a synagogue, it would be the only synagogue from Herod's own building activities.

The defenders of Masada renovated the space during the First Revolt. In the changes that were made in Masada II, a *genizah* was created with an under-floor compartment to store biblical scrolls no longer in use. The renovators compensated for this loss of space by removing the entrance area and incorporating that space within the main hall. Some of the columns were apparently reused from Herod's Northern Palace. Benches were added around the now awkwardly shaped room. Though no *mikveh* was provided adjacent to the synagogue, there was a fine *mikveh* on the diametrically opposite side of the site, and another in the northeast corner of the administrative building, nearer the synagogue. Masada II was certainly a first-century C.E. synagogue, with no provision for liturgical functions and no effort to alter its orientation or the door's location. Yigael Yadin muddies the issue by saying "it was wholly oriented towards Jerusalem as required."[49]

Herodium

The synagogue inserted by Herodium's defenders during the First Revolt into the upper palace was contemporaneous with Masada II. The room was originally Herod's *triclinium* (Plate 27); in renovating it to accommodate the religious needs of the defenders, benches were placed around the walls, and a *mikveh* built outside the door, but relatively few other alterations were made. The door faced due east; Jerusalem was almost due north. There is little evidence to indicate how the defenders altered the decoration or other fittings of the *triclinium*. There was no niche for Torah scrolls, and no provision for a reading desk. The room was a simple community hall with little decoration or artistic elaboration.

Theodotos Inscription

An important inscription found in the City of David excavations in Jerusalem may date from the period before the destruction of the temple, though if it is pre-70 how long before cannot be said (Chapter 12).[50] The text is well known:

> Theodotos, son of Vettenus, priest and head of the synagogue [*archisy-nagôgos*], son of an *archisynagôgos*, grandson of an *archisynagôgos*, built the synagogue for the reading of Torah and the study of the commandments, and the guest-house and the rooms and the water installations, for the needy travellers from abroad. The foundations of the synagogue were laid by his fathers and the elders and Simonides. (*CIJ* 1404)

The inscription sets out some functions of a synagogue:[51] reading of Torah and study of commandments for the residents of Jerusalem who attended this synagogue regularly; beds and washing facilities and other rooms for Diaspora visitors. Regrettably we have no plan to show how these functions were given architectural form. If this were pre-70 C.E., the inscription broadens our understanding of building remains, for it provides the first description of areas that might be included in a more urban synagogue. The other pre-70 evidence is limited to synagogues that are basically one communal room, perhaps with a porch or small ancillary room. The extra facilities that are mentioned were needed for visitors, of course, who were in Jerusalem for a festival. How large and complex the structure was, how such a synagogue would have fitted into Jerusalem's streetscape, how it might have been recognized by the visitors that it served, how it would have been oriented in the holy city, how it might have been decorated—all these are unanswerable questions. I draw two conclusions from the inscription: (1) the variety and complexity of pre-70 C.E. synagogues was greater than the variety in the few synagogues just described suggests; (2) synagogue functions focused on intra-group (and visitors' needs); there is no hint, other than Theodotos's role as a priest, of a connection with the temple in Jerusalem.

Orientation

There was no consistency in the orientation of pre-70 synagogues. The synagogue at Gamla was oriented with its door almost towards

Jerusalem (see Figure 7.1). This comes as close to the assumed correct orientation as any of these early synagogues. It is likely, however, that this orientation was purely accidental; its location in the town would hardly admit of any other arrangement since the contours shaped its orientation, it was bounded by a street on the south, the casemate wall on the east, an embankment and a street on the north. In Masada, the wall opposite the door came closest to being in the direction of Jerusalem, but it was by no means on that alignment. If it be objected that the circumstances there were awkward for getting the right direction it can be replied that Masada II, the revolutionaries' synagogue, could have been located elsewhere within the overall complex, had orientation been an important factor. If the first stage were a purpose-built synagogue, the original builders could have chosen a location that would have been oriented differently.

Herodium offered its renovators little opportunity for choice in the location of the synagogue or its orientation. Once it was decided to squeeze it into the existing spaces available in the fortress complex, the *triclinium* offered the best possibility. The orientation of all rooms is north-south or east-west; the orientation of the *triclinium* was east-west, with one long sidewall more or less to Jerusalem. The most one can say is that the orientation was not so important that it prohibited the inclusion of the synagogue in the *triclinium*.

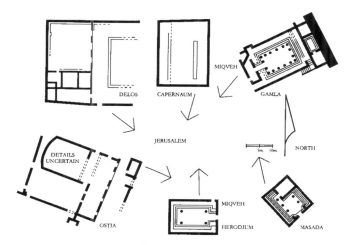

Figure 7.1. *Synagogues, comparative plans to a common scale. None of these six pre-70 CE synagogues had a Torah shrine, and only Gamla had a cupboard that might have stored Torah scrolls in the northwest corner). The large arrows show their orientation relative to Jerusalem. In a late phase Ostia's Torah shrine was oriented to Jerusalem.*

The much later synagogue of Capernaum—"the limestone synagogue"—was oriented with its door on the south towards Jerusalem,
the then-correct orientation. Excavations below that building uncovered parts of what may have been a first-century synagogue; the orientation was almost identical, but at that stage there were two
doors—apparently, one on the west and one on the east wall, an
unusual arrangement—with the doors at right angles to the direction
of Jerusalem. The Magdala building had a door on the northwest,
more or less away from Jerusalem but without any particular reference
to Jerusalem.[52] The earliest evidence leads to a simple conclusion: orientation towards Jerusalem was irrelevant. It mattered little to the
builders how the buildings faced.[53]

Liturgy

None of Masada I, Masada II, or Herodium provided for liturgical
functions.[54] Gamla may have, but the niche was not obviously for Torah
scrolls, though it may have been. The line of stone pavers across the
middle may, but need not, have been intended as a location for a reading desk and thus evidence for a movable desk. None of the pre-70 synagogues had symbols recalling the temple in Jerusalem. Such
symbols—found profusely in later synagogues in mosaic floors, capitals, lintels, and other architectural features—were completely absent
in pre-70 buildings. The use of menorah, *lulav*, and *ethrog*, in synagogue
art all date after 70.[55]

In addition, any indications of a separation between men and
women were also absent from early synagogues. None of the ones
described, or other potentially pre-70 buildings, had a gallery that
might be held to be a women's gallery. If there were to be a division
between men and women, it would have had to be by means of a barrier in the middle of the benches. Yet the space itself, with all participants looking at each other from the benches around the walls, was
designed to highlight the communal, almost democratic, character of
the space (Chapter 10). It is unlikely that the builders would have
created a space that expressed the community's oneness and then
have subdivided it in such a way as to call that sense of oneness into
question.

Social Meaning

Buildings have social meaning, expressing the goals, aspirations, and values of a community or society. The case of all these pre-70 synagogues is strikingly consistent, despite their differing religious backgrounds. They all express a high sense of community, especially in the arrangements of the benches around three or four walls so that members—presumably both male and female—could all be equally involved in the activities of the community. There was nothing to focus the participant's attention elsewhere, no reflection of Jerusalem, no liturgical foci, and no distracting visual decoration. The nearest analogies are found in the puritan and left-wing streams of Reformation Christianity, with their rejection of explicit liturgy, visual symbolism, and reminders of other traditions. While I would not press these comparisons, the primary emphasis on a communal experience of a democratic type is striking.[56]

The importance of these observations is largely negative: they define, however, the stage of development of the synagogue in the first century and suggest that provision for worship was not highly refined. These early synagogues, which differ markedly from later ones, were flexible; the use of the space was not constrained by fixtures or holy functions that required architectural definition. Further, there were no elements in pre-70 synagogues that showed attachment to the temple in Jerusalem. The synagogue had not yet become (as it would later come to be) a replacement for the center of worship in Jerusalem, and none of its features was intended to call the temple to mind. Quite the contrary, it conveyed an architectural character radically different from—almost diametrically opposite to—the temple. All the evidence is consistent with spaces intended for multiple communal functions, not spaces in some way modeled on temple architecture with its highly articulated separations of holiness and functional responsibilities (Chapter 16).

General Character

The four synagogues just considered were plain, uncomplicated structures, more like Mennonite or Quaker meeting houses, Plymouth

Brethren assemblies, even Orange Order or Women's Auxiliary halls, than liturgically sophisticated religious buildings. The synagogue remains are consistent with the impression gained from the inscriptional evidence discussed above. Synagogues were community-oriented *collegia*, groups gathered together for multiple purposes as portrayed in Josephus and the Theodotos inscription. In those vignettes of synagogues (mainly in the Diaspora) we observed small communities that ate meals together, observed festivals, organized the collection of dues, arranged for the transmission of firstfruits, heard civil law cases within the community, and so on.

Several questions remain to be asked. (1) Are the above observations on the architectural character of Judean and Galilean synagogues likely to hold true for places within the Diaspora at large? (2) Is it possible that there were other, more advanced or liturgically developed synagogues coexisting with these relatively primitive buildings, of which we have no evidence yet? (3) Are the remains best explained as the natural result of the definition of the roles of synagogues as *collegia*? I take the answer to (1) to be yes (the reconstruction drawings of synagogues at Delos and Ostia suggest this; Chapters 11, 12), and the answer to (2) to be maybe, but we need more to go on (a Torah niche at Gamla would raise this issue). Since (3) is the main interest of this chapter, I offer a few more sentences.

I have argued that synagogues as *collegia* had a special place in the early Roman Empire; their status and privileges were spelled out and went beyond what other *collegia* claimed. Further, I have suggested that the process of definition occurred in the last half of the first century B.C.E., when synagogues in Rome were dedicated to some of the leading protagonists for Judaism. This was also a period when the earliest synagogues of which we have helpful archaeological remains were built in Judea. In addition, I have sketched the range of functions that our earliest sources ascribe to these synagogues. Finally, my interpretation of the physical remains concludes that there is direct evidence of exactly the kind of buildings one would anticipate in this early period to meet such a broad range of needs. It is a minor theme of this assessment that pre-70 synagogues were not modelled on the Jerusalem temple and that no effort was made to replicate the motifs, character, or divisions of the temple.[57]

Synagogues in Judea provide examples of the kinds of buildings provided elsewhere in the Diaspora to serve as "places of their own" for the Jewish community (Chapter 11). It may go too far to claim that the architectural models for synagogues were other *collegia*, not the temple (though see Chapter 12). A more cautious way of putting it will stand scrutiny: the development of synagogues before 70 C.E. was of a piece with the legal definition of *collegia* in the same period and the decision to consider synagogues as *collegia*. What we see in these Judean synagogues were *collegia*.

CHAPTER EIGHT

ARCHITECTURAL TRANSITIONS FROM SYNAGOGUES AND HOUSE CHURCHES TO PURPOSE-BUILT CHURCHES[1]

> Christianity stresses the formation of "kinship" community either where it had not existed before (1 Peter 2:10) or where it had been disrupted by the Jesus revolution (Mark 10:23-31). Early Christians undoubtedly met in private homes (Colossians 4:15), though it should not be forgotten that Christians, like the Jews (Acts 16:13), also met in open places (Pliny, *Letters*, 117), markets, and hired halls (Acts 20:8). There is no literary evidence nor archaeological indication that any such home was converted into an extant church building. Nor is there any extant church that certainly was built prior to Constantine. Consequently, *we have no evidence regarding the intentional structure of a Christian meeting place prior to the "peace."* But there are homes that were restructured to accommodate the Christian assembly.[2]

The emphasized words in Graydon Snyder's description are almost a commonplace: there is no evidence of purpose-built churches before 313 C.E. (the Edict of Milan). It is likewise a commonplace that Constantine inaugurated Christian basilicas in the period after 324 C.E. when he was sole emperor, to assume tacitly that later basilican churches derived from Constantine's initiative, and to imagine that this is a sufficient explanation.[3] This chapter emphasizes that there was a transitional period in the third century during which the example of Jewish synagogues was a critical factor.

SNYDER AND WHITE ON HOUSE CHURCHES AND HOUSE SYNAGOGUES

Snyder has gathered archaeological evidence for the character of early Christianity, emphasizing the breadth of the evidence and the importance of the social-historical framework. The study remains a skillfully devised compendium, useful for its drawings, bibliographies, analyses, and evaluations. One concern was to identify the earliest stages of the architecture of Christian meeting places, and he rightly put first the church at Dura Europos, alongside the more complicated evidence of Capernaum, Aquileia, and the *Titulus* churches in Rome.[4] He argues that "Christians of the third century were not building new churches, but taking over existing architectural structures," as Dura Europos (a house converted to Christian use sometime between 232 and 256 C.E.) shows unmistakably. He was more reticent about Capernaum, holding that it had little to tell us about house churches. Some evidence, he said, was "borderline." He thought the north church at Aquileia "may be the first Christian edifice created *de novo*," for he doubted that there was an earlier *domus ecclesiae* below it, emphasizing that these are "simply halls with mosaic floors." He considered Titulus Crisogoni a rival for this honor: "If this hall was built in 310 . . . then this, or possibly the north church at Aquileia, must be the earliest-known structure built specifically for the Christian assembly. We can note that this building . . . was a meeting hall."[5]

Snyder also considered evidence for *insulae* or tenement churches, suggesting that in addition to remodeling middle- or upper-class houses, a similar practice obtained lower down the scale, when a church member turned over a modest apartment (in which much of the population lived) to the church. The best example is SS. Giovanni e Paolo in Rome, where renovations carried out in the mid-third century C.E. created a two-story meeting hall.[6] Snyder thought it likely that the third-century alterations were for Christian purposes, since early fourth-century changes were certainly Christian.

This general picture fits well the complex social-historical developments of the third century. While Snyder allowed the possibility that there were purpose-built pre-Constantinian churches, he was skeptical because the evidence was slender. He cited several relevant inscriptions: e.g., *P. Oxy* I.43 (ca. 295 C.E.) refers to two streets named after churches and *P. Oxy* XXXIII.2673 (5 Feb 304 C.E.) refers to church possessions, both of which might presume publicly visible meeting places. Basically, however, "Christian culture began to appear at approximately the end of the second century," when several features coalesced, "when they became involved with legal title to land and property; when they used organized labor . . . when their church had public functions such as buying and selling; when the Church had visible, known leadership; and, above all, when Christians were willing to make their presence known to the larger public."[7]

Snyder's work has been partly replaced by L. Michael White's study, which is fuller in its documentation of the relevant archaeological and literary evidence but narrower because it is limited to architecture.[8] White emphasizes the social context of early Christian architecture. Volume 1 analyzes early archaeological evidence for church buildings alongside evidence for Mithraea, synagogues, and other religious structures. Volume 2 provides a collection of primary data bearing on those analyses.[9] White accepts a widely recognized view, that churches had their earliest origins in the house-church, and then examines "pre-basilican" churches in volume 1 archaeologically, emphasizing the successive adaptations to fit houses for use as churches. When patrons turned over their houses to groups, they provided for renovations to make them more useful. The most informative archaeological materials come from Dura Europos, where almost contemporaneous structures for Jews, Christians, Mithraists, and others, can be compared. These structures were generally located against the city walls, in contrast to traditional religious structures in the urban center. The same situation obtains in Priene, where a synagogue, a Mithraeum, and a cult dedicated to Alexander, were beside each other in a residential district near the western city wall. In both cities, substantial temples in the center contrasted with new house-based cults on the periphery.

Early Christianity was rooted in a specific set of social conditions involving patrons wealthy enough to have houses that could be renovated and given away. The status of Christians, the roles of patrons, and the honor system that lay behind such munificent gifts allow a better understanding of the Church as it moved from being a movement within Judaism to the religion of the Empire.

White includes discussion of synagogues but limits the evidence to the Diaspora. Though understandable, the decision is regrettable: it eliminates instances of early purpose-built synagogues and overlooks important adapted synagogues; it exaggerates the closeness of some comparisons and overlooks other useful comparisons. The data, however, in volume 2, imply that not all pre-Constantinian churches were adaptive structures. Sometime in the third century Christians tentatively began to build more self-confident, more publicly visible meeting places that were purpose-built. The evidence suggests a transitional

phase between the early informal adaptations of houses and the "true"
basilicas of Constantine, though this period can be neither precisely
dated nor fully described. Such a transition period is potentially important and needs concentrated study, along the lines of the questions suggested at the end of this chapter.

CHRONOLOGICAL AND GEOGRAPHICAL CONSIDERATIONS

House-synagogues are relevant chronologically.[10] At Dura a house was
converted to a synagogue (second half of the second century C.E.), earlier than the church adaptation. The same pattern was present in Stobi
(second or third century C.E.), Priene (probably second century C.E.; see
Plate 31), Ostia (second century C.E.; see Plate 34, Figure 12.1), and
Delos, the earliest such adaptation (second or first century B.C.E.).[11]
While the social processes were the same, adaptations for synagogues
were usually earlier than those for churches. Geographically, the Jewish
Diaspora provides excellent physical evidence for patron-inspired
adaptations of houses as synagogues, extending from the second century B.C.E. through the third century C.E. There is good inscriptional
evidence for patrons' roles.

On the Christian side, the evidence is both better and worse. Early
Christian literature coheres with archaeological evidence from a
slightly later period, as many have demonstrated,[12] that churches met in
houses of patrons, who either continued to share the house or donated
it outright. A *domus ecclesiae* probably did multiple duty as meeting
place, house, workshop, and social center, though as time passed the
religious uses probably became more important, the earliest unassail-
able evidence being Dura. Most of the literary and physical evidence
pertains to areas outside Palestine. We will not be far wrong to think
that by the mid-second century C.E. Christians used adapted houses as
churches.

The evidence for both house-synagogues and house-churches is
weaker in Judea. Excavations at Caesarea Maritima suggest a (perhaps)
second-century house-synagogue, though the information is not well
published; the house may have been late Hellenistic.[13] Adaptation of
the *triclinium* in Herod's Upper Palace at Herodium and an alteration
at Masada provided synagogues for use by revolutionaries (66–74 C.E.),
adopting naturally the pattern elsewhere (see Plates 26, 27).[14] Both

renovations emerged from the exigencies of war in the late first century
C.E., not from patronage. The pre-70 C.E. purpose-built synagogues at
Gamla (see Plate 25) and elsewhere do not compromise the importance
of adaptation as a synagogue strategy, especially among less socially
significant groups. Inclusion of Judean evidence leads to a more
nuanced view of these Jewish developments. Christian architectural
adaptation is less clear: in Galilee Capernaum is usually cited, though
there are serious difficulties (Chapter 6). Several examples nearby in
Syria are better, especially Qirqbize, Umm al-Jimal, and Dura.[15] Thus,
the evidence of Diaspora and Holy Land, while not identical, coheres,
and any history of general architectural developments should avoid too
sharp a contrast. What follows will focus on relevant data from the eastern provinces, especially Palestine, in order to focus on this innovative
transitional period.[16]

Purpose-Built Jewish Synagogues

The above description might imply that Christian communities
learned how to adapt houses for their needs from Jewish and other
communities, a likely but not yet demonstrable view. Certainly they
developed similar strategies and thought about their buildings in similar ways, though the evidence is not well balanced.[17] One aspect of this
emerges from an unlikely source. Though Eusebius did not know it,
Judaism had both eremitic and coenobitic monasticism, as did the
church of Eusebius's day; both communities had developed the same
types of monastic communities two centuries apart (Chapter 9).
Eusebius quoted Philo's description of the Therapeutae's buildings and
practices—those of a Jewish group—claiming that he was describing
early Christian practices in Alexandria. Did he know what he was
doing when he borrowed from Philo, or was he deliberately obfuscat-
ing? The two Jewish monasteries known to us, Qumran and the
Therapeutae, had long since been destroyed and probably no trace of
them remained in Eusebius's day. Since there was apparently no continuing tradition of monastic Judaism, Eusebius (whether knowingly
and tendentiously or ignorantly and innocently matters little) applied
Philo's description to Christian monasteries. Were the two developments totally independent or was there some residual borrowing by
Christians from earlier Jewish practices? We cannot say. The literary

evidence is insufficient to settle the historical and architectural questions, though most would assume the complete independence of the two architectural developments.

Basilican churches paralleled basilican synagogues, though later. Were they, however, independent developments?[18] Lee Levine holds that "many buildings, especially those in the Galilee and Golan, were patterned after some form of Roman civic building, others were patterned on the Christian basilica and featured a central nave, two aisles, an apse (or bema), a narthex (forehall), and an atrium."[19] This formulation obscures the situation somewhat, since Jewish basilican synagogues preceded churches.

The word "basilica" is regularly used of churches and synagogues. The Roman basilica was a civic building, used for a variety of purposes: market, bank, stock exchange, tribunal, law court, and meeting place.[20] Basilicas emerged in the Roman world by the second century B.C.E.[21] Although the word is Greek ("royal building"), there is no known example of a Greek precursor to Roman structures. The word indicates function, not architectural form. The form it came to have was rectangular, of varying proportions, with entrances in either the short or long sides, and with a higher central portion divided from two lower side aisles by rows of columns. Usually there were clerestory windows above the columns to light the central space; often there was a second floor over the side aisles. Sometimes there was an apse or a projection, used as a "tribunal," on one end or one side (later, sometimes at both ends).[22] Christians and Jews adapted this shape for their purpose-built religious structures.[23] Although the word is frequently used loosely of any room with columns, it is best to use it only when a number of basilican elements are present. Large halls without basilican elements are here called "meeting halls," following Snyder and White.

Roman basilicas appeared in the Roman East from the first century B.C.E. onwards. The most important and probably the earliest (late first century B.C.E.) was Herod's Royal Basilica, located on the south side of Jerusalem's temple precinct. The basilica in Sebaste may also have been a Herodian construction. In the second century C.E. a basilica with apse was built in Tiberias alongside the street leading to Hammat Tiberias. Another late second-century C.E. basilica appears in Beth She'arim. Beth Shean, Bostra, Canatha (Qanawat), Maximinianopolis (Shaqqa), and other important eastern cities, both Hellenized and Jewish, had basilicas.

Table 8.1: Synagogues in the Roman East[24]

Pre-Constantinian

	Eastern Diaspora	**Palestine**[25]
Meeting Halls	Aegina	Jericho, Hasmonean Palace, 70–50 B.C.E.[26] Gamla, 1 c. B.C.E. or C.E. Shuafat, pre-70 C.E.[27] Kiryat Sefer (pre-70 C.E.?) Nabratein synagogue 1 (2 c. C.E.) En Gedi, phase 1 (late 2/early 3 c. C.E.) Khirbet Shema (3 c. C.E.) Caesarea, stratum 4 (3 c.) Capernaum, phase 1? (1/early 2 c. C.E.) Qasrin, phase 1 (3 c. C.E.) Hammat Tiberias, phase 1 (3 c. C.E.)
Basilicas	Gerasa (3 c. C.E.)[28] Sardis, stage 3 (3 c. C.E.)[29]	Arbel, phase 1 (2 c. C.E.) Qazyon? (197 C.E.)[30] Nabratein synagogue 2a (3 c. C.E.) Chorazin, phase 1 (3 c. C.E.) Baram, large syn (3 c. C.E.) Gush Halav (3 c. C.E.) Ma'oz Hayyim (3 c. C.E.) Meiron (3 c. C.E.) Horvat Sumaqa, phase 1 (3 c. C.E.)? Hammat Gader, phases 1–2 (3 c. C.E.?) Horvat 'Ammudim (end 3 c./early 4 c. C.E.)

Post-Constantinian

	Eastern Diaspora	Palestine
Meeting Halls		Hammat Tiberias, phase 2 (4 c. C.E.)
Basilicas	Sardis, stage 4 (4 c. C.E.) Miletus ? (3 c. C.E.?) Apamea (ca 391 C.E.?)	Qasrin, bldg. A (4 c. C.E.) Chorazin, phase 2 (early 4 c. C.E.) Beth She'arim (late 3/4 c. C.E.) Rehov (4 c. C.E.) Meroth (4 c. C.E.) Capernaum, phase 2 (late 4 c. C.E.) *Samaritan Synagogues* (all 4 c. C.E.) Khirbet Samara, narthex, atrium Zur Natan (Khirbet Majdal), atrium el-Khirbe (Mt. Gerizim) Hazzan Ya'aqov Synagogue (Shechem)

Jewish communities began building a version of basilican synagogues relatively early. This basic architectural form was soon fashionable, though the significance of the basilican form itself is often ignored. Not all synagogues were basilican. Alongside this form were a number of meeting halls. In Table 8.1 I have excluded house-synagogues but included meeting halls and basilicas; the line between them is not clear, and a more adequate typology still needs to be attempted. Though the division pre- and post-Constantine was not significant for synagogue architecture, that convention helps clarify their relation to church architecture.

Table 8.1 suggests that (1) there is a more even chronological distribution from pre-70 C.E. synagogues through the fourth century than is usually thought; (2) the practices of Jewish communities in the Eastern Diaspora and Palestine were parallel; (3) architectural form within both Diaspora and Palestinian communities shifted from more or less evenly balanced numbers of meeting halls and basilican synagogues to a substantial preponderance of basilican style; (4) while numerous synagogues were built on models other than basilicas, from the third century onwards (when Roman basilicas had become common in the area) basilican synagogues gradually became dominant, especially in the Holy Land. These synagogues did not ape in size or detail true Roman basilicas, but there was sufficient similarity to basilicas that their formal origins are not much in doubt. Thus, the fundamental observation is that basilican synagogues predated basilican churches.

Purpose-built "houses of prayer" in Egyptian Judaism originated in the second century B.C.E.; inscriptional evidence refers to *exedrae* (*CIJ* 1444; for texts, Chapter 7), gateways (*CIJ* 1441), *periboloi* (*CIJ* 1433), appurtenances (*CIJ* 1422, 1433), and gardens (*CPJ* 1134). The allusions are not as clear as we might wish, but some prayerhouses had basilican features, though most of these earliest Jewish community structures were, no doubt, more like meeting halls than basilicas. We may have here important antecedents of later basilican synagogues, an architectural development traceable first in the Diaspora, and developed a little later in the homeland.

Post-destruction Judaism had a strong tradition of purpose-built synagogues. These developed in several types, but by the third century the strongest and most widespread form was modeled on Roman basilicas. Like basilicas, they had multiple communal purposes, had large crowds in view, with higher nave and lower side aisles, a double row of columns, clerestory windows, occasionally apses, doors typically (though not always) in the shorter end, and located in a central area. Most decoration was concentrated in the interior, frequently embellished with mosaic floors. Their functional, chronological, and design features suggest that synagogues drew much of the inspiration for their form and decoration from Roman basilicas. Just at the time synagogues followed the basilican model, however, they also began to mimic features of the temple in Jerusalem. Decorative motifs reminiscent of the temple began to appear only when Judaism had the self-confidence to construct once again purpose-built structures in the Holy Land. Thus, alongside a deep sense of loss of the central shrine went, ironically, an accommodation to Roman standards of taste.

These later synagogues differed from basilicas in several respects, especially interior features: seating was on benches around the walls,[31] they were oriented towards Jerusalem, they provided for Torah scrolls, they might be located away from the city center.[32] While earlier structures were relatively simple halls, purpose-built synagogues soon adopted the Roman basilica as the model of choice, both in homeland and Diaspora.

Purpose-built Christian Churches

From 324 C.E. onwards Imperial basilicas were built, the finest being those ordered by Constantine himself:[33] in Jerusalem, the Holy Sepulcher and the Eleona on the Mount of Olives; in Bethlehem, the Church of the Holy Nativity; at Mamre, within Herod's enclosure of the oak tree associated with Abraham.[34] Yet, significant as Constantine's architectural program was, purpose-built churches preceded him, during some reigns and in some places where Christianity was especially self-confident. House churches no doubt became gradually more visible and public, as White emphasizes in connection with the Ostia synagogue, but when a Christian community acquired a site and erected its own structure, churches became significantly more public. This seems to have happened by the late third century, before the Constantinian settlement, according to White and Snyder's evidence. The possibility of earlier examples in out-of-the-way places should not be excluded altogether. In the following I have used White, limiting the evidence to sites and sources from the East; I include only those that may presuppose purpose-built churches prior to the flowering of "true" basilican churches after 324 C.E.

Documentary Evidence

- *P. Oxy* I.43 (Egypt, ca. 295 C.E.): the papyrus alludes to North Church Street and South Church Street, more likely if they were purpose-built churches but not impossible of house churches (White, No. 45).

- Lebaba, Syria (318/319 C.E.): an inscription referring to a Marcionite "synagogue" built under the direction of the Presbyter Paul (White, No. 39).

- Laodicea Combusta, epitaph of M. Julius Eugenius (307–340 C.E.): outlining his life, the inscription mentions that he "rebuilt the entire church from its foundations and all embellishments around it, which contain *stoai* and *tetrastoa*, paintings, mosaics, a fountain and an outer gateway . . ." (White, No. 48).

Archaeological Evidence (See Also Table 8.2)

- Qirqbize in Northern Syria (early fourth century): a small basilican church was found adjacent to a villa. (White, No. 38)

Non-Christian Literary Sources

- *Edessene Chronicle* I (VIII), 1–2 (Nov. 201 C.E.): "... in the reign of Severus ... the spring of water that rose in the great palace of Abgar the Great flowed more strongly than ever ... so that the royal halls, the *stoai* and apartments began to stand in water. ... [T]hey destroyed the great and magnificent palace of our Lord the King and tearing away everything that lay in their path and all the beautiful and splendid buildings. ... They even destroyed the temple of the church of the Christians" (White, No. 26). The juxtaposition of church and king's palace implies a large visible structure.

- Porphyry, *Adversus Christianos* frag. 76 (268–70 C.E.): the Syrian Neoplatonist (234–305 C.E.) contrasted temples (*naoi*) and houses (*oikiai*): "But the Christians, imitating the construction of temples, erect great buildings in which they meet to pray, though there is nothing to prevent them from doing this in their own homes ..." (White, No. 29).

- Maximinus, Rescript (after Eusebius, *Historia ecclesiastica* 9.10.10) concerning Christians (313 C.E.): the language could refer to house churches or to basilicas: "And they are given concessions so that they might construct their dominical houses (*ta kyriaka ta oikeia*)" (White, No. 34).

- *Edessene Chronicle* XII.2 (313 C.E.): "bishop Kune laid the foundations for the church of 'Orhai [Edessa]; bishop Sa'ad built and completed it after him" (White, No. 26).

- Licinius and Constantine, *The Edict of Milan* 7(13 June 313 C.E.): "... if any appear to have bought them ... let them restore the same to the Christians without charge and with no price on demand. ... And since the said Christians are known to have possessed not only those places in which they were accustomed to meet, but others as well ... you will order them ... to return the same to the Christians, that is to their corporations and conventicles" (White, No. 33).

Christian Literary Sources

- Eusebius, *Historia ecclesiastica* 8.1.5 (ca. 303 C.E.), looking back before the turn of the century: "with what favor one may observe the rulers in every church being honored by all procurators and governors. Or how could anyone describe those assemblies with numberless crowds and the great throngs gathered together in every city as well as the remarkable concourses in the houses of prayer? On account of these things, no longer being satisfied with their old buildings, they erected from the foundations churches of spacious dimensions in every city ..." (White, No. 23).[35]

- Eusebius, *Historia ecclesiastica* 10.4.37–45 (324 C.E.), describing the new church, dedicated in 317 or 318 C.E., built by Bishop Paulinus in Tyre: ". . . the whole area that he enclosed was much larger. The outer enclosure he fortified with a wall surrounding the whole, so that it might be a secure courtyard for the whole. He spread out a gateway, great and raised on high to ward off the very rays of the rising sun. . . . Marking off a great expanse between the temple and the first gates he adorned all around it with four transverse *stoai*, which enclosed the area in a kind of quadrangular figure with columns raised on all sides. He enclosed their intermittent spaces with wooden lattice-work partitions which reached an appropriate height, and he left an atrium in the middle for beholding the sky . . . he erected opposite the front of the temple fountains . . . he made the entry passages to the temple wide openings by means of still more innermost gateways . . . he arranged the number of gateways for the *stoai* on either flank of the whole temple, and in addition to these he designed up above different openings to the building for still more light. . . . Now the Royal House [Gk. *basileion oikon*] he fortified with richer and even more lavish materials. . . . Nor did the pavement escape his care. Indeed this, too, he made brilliant with all kinds of ornate marble . . . he constructed ornate *exedrai* and large buildings on either side . . ." (White, No. 23).

- Eusebius, *Historia ecclesiastica* 10.2.1–3.1 (ca. 324), again looking back: "we beheld every place which, a short time before, had been torn down by the impious deeds of the tyrants. Reviving as from long and deadly mistreatment the temples were raised once again from the foundation to a lofty height and received in far greater measure the magnificence of those that had formerly been destroyed. . . . There came to pass many festivals of dedication in every city and consecration of the newly built houses of prayer . . ." (White, No. 23).

Alongside evidence for eastern churches in a transitional period should be placed sites up to the end of the fourth century (thus paralleling Table 8.1). Table 8.2 distinguishes in a preliminary way between halls, small churches or chapels, and major basilicas.

There was a good bit of architectural variation, but the dominant form for purpose-built churches came to be the basilica, after a bridge period during which large meeting halls were created.[36] Even within the one architectural form there were variations in size, proportions, embellishment, apsidal arrangements, and so on; but most examples in the east resembled the form well known from Roman architecture. (1) The pre-Constantinian period had purpose-built churches, some of which may have been basilican; (2) Constantine adapted the basilica for most of the noble structures he sponsored; (3) after Constantine, basilican churches that were not merely scaled-down

Table 8.2: Early Churches in the Roman East

Meeting Halls
Nazareth?, phase 1 (below Byzantine monastery), 3–4 c. C.E.[37]   Capernaum, phase 2 (domus ecclesiae?), 4 c. C.E.

Chapels (usually basilican)
Tabgha, Church of the Loaves and Fishes, phase 1, 4 c. C.E.   Tabgha, Church of the Sermon on the Mount, 4 c. C.E.   Tabgha, Church of the Primacy of Peter, 4 c. C.E.   Nablus, Jacob's Well, cruciform church, ca. 380 C.E.   'Agur, late 4 c. C.E.   Mamre, church within Herodian enclosure, ca. 330 C.E. (apse earlier?)   Shavei Tzion, late 4 c. C.E.   Magen, Building C (flanking Building B, below), 4 c. C.E.   Burj Haidar, mid-4 c. C.E.   Kharrab Shams, 4 c. C.E. (before 370 C.E.)   Serjillah, small church, perhaps before inscription of 372 C.E.   Fafertin, apse with semi-dome, bema, inscription 372 C.E.   Antioch, St. Peter's, 4 c. C.E.   Barad, Syria, Julianos' Church, 399–402

Basilicas
Jerusalem, Church of the Holy Sepulchre, 326–35 C.E.   Bethelehem, Church of Nativity, 320s–330s C.E.   Jerusalem, Eleona Church, 330s C.E.   Gerasa, Cathedral Church (reconstruction of Temple of Dionysus?), ca. 365 C.E.   Jerusalem, Gethsemane, Egeria's Church, 379–84 C.E.   Damascus, Church of St. John the Baptist, 379 C.E.   Bosra, 3 c. Roman basilica converted to church, 4 c. C.E.   Qanawat (Canatha), Roman basilica converted to church, 4 c. C.E.   Pella, Civic Complex Church, ca. 400   Elusa, East Church, 4 c. C.E.   Mamshit, East Church, 4 c. C.E.   Sobata, South Church, late 4 c. C.E.   Dor, late 4 c. C.E.   Magen,[38] Building B, 4 c. C.E.   Ephesus, Church of the Councils, conversion of Roman basilica, 4 c. C.E.

versions of Constantine's creations proliferated; but (4) basilican synagogues had already emerged as an architectural type a couple of centuries earlier, and (5) these structures were the nearest analogy for the
modestly scaled fourth-century churches.

Synagogue and church developed in parallel fashions, but were they
architecturally independent? Early on, both used houses donated by
patrons; both shifted to purpose-built structures; in a transitional phase
both used meeting halls and basilicas; both eventually adopted the
Roman basilica.[39] These circumstances nuance the view that early
Christianity and post-destruction Judaism were bent on differentiating
themselves from one another; in this regard Jewish and Christian communities behaved similarly. Now that White has elucidated the early
adaptive strategies of both communities, the transition to purpose-built
strategies—especially within Christianity—needs examination, as do
the formal similarities (especially between some early Galilean synagogues and some early Syrian churches). Further research might consider the following:

- Can comparison of formally similar churches and synagogues clarify the
  architectural relationships between Jewish and Christian basilicas?[40]

- How similar were Jewish basilican synagogues to the Roman basilica,
  and do eastern Roman examples influence specific Jewish structures?

- How similar were small Christian churches to Roman basilicas, on the
  one hand, and to Jewish basilican synagogues, on the other?

- Did Judaism influence Christian architectural developments in the transitional period (late third and early fourth centuries), or was Christian
  practice a parallel and unrelated acculturation?

- Would architectural influence imply that "sibling" relationships were relatively close for a long period?

- In a later period did Judaism borrow from Christianity?

- Can efforts at self-definition by both communities be architecturally dis-
  cerned?

- Were similar social changes (e.g., altered roles for patrons, increased
  resources) occurring in both Christian and Jewish communities, and can
  they be traced, in the shift from house churches to basilican churches? If
  so, would this require major revisions in understanding Jewish history?

- Could an architectural inventory of both groups of buildings from the
  same period establish reliably the relative wealth and resources of the
  two communities?

- Would different architectural solutions to such matters as entry rites, seating, roles of leaders and participants, attitudes to patrons, place of martyrs and relics, and the like, provide a guide to differences in the character of each community?

Ultimately, perhaps, there may be no assured answers, for the evidence is still thin for the transitional periods. But there is a need for deeper and better understandings of the relationships between Judaism and Christianity during the crucial *ante pacem* period.

CHAPTER NINE

PHILO AND EUSEBIUS ON MONASTERIES AND MONASTICISM: THE THERAPEUTAE AND KELLIA

This chapter attempts two experiments:[1] first, to assess whether one can use ancient literature to develop an architectural reconstruction of buildings used by a Jewish group in the early Christian period; secondly, and more speculatively, to enquire into the influence of that group and its structures in a later period of Christian history. Philo knew this Jewish group as the Therapeutae/Therapeutrides. It flowered in the first century B.C.E. and the first century C.E., and adopted several remarkable practices: complementary names for female and male participants, complementary activities, and equivalent leadership positions. It was an unusual group that provided a setting for religious Jewish women in Egypt within a celibate but mixed community (Chapter 10). My focus is on the group's buildings, which formed one of the few monastic complexes known to us from that period. The other well-known monastic community, also from the Jewish world, was the one at Qumran (Plate 28).[2] The latter was a communal enterprise, whereas the Therapeutae/Therapeutrides was a quasi-communal group—both male and female—in which the emphasis was on a life of solitary contemplation. To use later Christian terms, Qumran was coenobitic while the Therapeutae were quasi-eremitic.

My main point of comparison is a monastic group of buildings at Kellia in Lower Egypt that reflects the activities of a quasi-eremitic group. I emphasize the curious similarities between Kellia and Philo's description of the Therapeutae. The middle term between the two is Eusebius's description of early Egyptian monasticism.

EUSEBIUS ON THE THERAPEUTAE

Eusebius (born about 260 C.E.) enters the picture because he reported the Therapeutae having so many features similar to the Christianity of his day that he claimed they were Christians.[3] Eusebius's *History of the Church* (*CH*) Book 2, deals with the apostles from Tiberius to Nero. When he introduces Peter (2.13-14), he deftly connects him with Mark, Peter's follower and the author of the Gospel (2.15). He suggests Peter was the first Christian to preach and establish churches in Egypt, especially in Alexandria:

> So large was the body of believers, men and women alike, built up there at the first attempt, with an extremely severe rule of life, that Philo decided that he must record in writing their activities, gatherings, meals, and everything else about their way of living. . . . [U]nder Claudius, Philo came to Rome to have conversations with Peter, then preaching to the people there. This would not be improbable, as the short work to which I am referring, and which he [Philo] produced at a considerably later date, clearly contains the rules of the Church still observed in our own day. And again, when he describes the life of our ascetics with the greatest precision, it is plain enough that he not only knew but welcomed with whole-hearted approval the apostolic men of his day, who it seems were of Hebrew stock and therefore, in the Jewish manner, still retained most of their ancient customs. (*CH* 2.16–17)

The passage is a blend of fact and fiction, knowledge and speculation. Eusebius knew Philo had visited Rome during Claudius's reign (fact, see earlier in 2.4–5) but he asserted that he came to talk to Peter (fiction). He knew of *On the Contemplative Life* (fact) but he believed it spoke of ascetic Christians (fiction). He understood the earliest Christian apostles were Hebrew in manner of life and race (fact) and thought that Philo was almost one of them (fiction). He claimed that there was a large body of Christians in Alexandria (fact?) and thought they behaved like ascetic Jews (fiction?). He argued that Peter preached in Rome (fact?) but that it was as early as the reign of Claudius (fiction).

The features of the Therapeutae that attracted Eusebius included their renunciation of property, their life of contemplation ("the prophetic way of life"), their location near Lake Mareotis,[4] their seclusion in houses with individual sanctuaries, their spiritual discipline (*askêsis*), including their study of Scripture,[5] their self-control in matters of food, and the conduct of their meetings (see Figure 9.1). He quoted liberally from *On the Contemplative Life* and was careful to attribute it to Philo, pointing out that he selected these items for comment because they were "those in which the characteristics of Church life are displayed."

But beginning at this point in his description his comments on the Therapeutae take on a defensive ring, suggesting that his view that they were Christians was controversial:

- "If anyone does not agree that what has been described is peculiar to the gospel way of life but thinks it applicable to other people too, he will surely be convinced."

- "These statements . . . seem to me to refer plainly and unquestionably to members of our Church."

- "If . . . someone insists on denying it, he will surely . . . be convinced by still clearer evidence which cannot be found anywhere but in the religious practices of Christians."

- ". . . the regular spiritual discipline still practiced among us . . ."

- ". . . in precise accordance with the practice observed by us and us alone to this day."

- ". . . anyone can see that he [Philo] had in mind the first preachers of the gospel teaching and the customs handed down by the apostles from the beginning." (*CH* 2.17)

Two observations flow from this curious situation: (1) Eusebius did the best he could to make sound historical reconstructions with the information available, though he sometimes led readers wildly astray;[6] (2) in the fourth century he valued—and wished the Church to emulate—the ascetic life of a first-century group he thought was Christian. Two points bearing on monasticism are also significant. First, Eusebius showed that Christian monasticism had developed in his own day to a point at which its characteristics, even if in terms borrowed from Philo, could be described; Egyptian monasticism manifested some of the same features as Philo's description. Second, monastic history must have been sufficiently long that he could claim with some plausibility that its features went back 250 or more years to the time of Mark's supposed founding of Egyptian Christianity. Whether Eusebius himself believed this does not matter as much as the fact that he could make this claim.[7] He provides important evidence for Egyptian monasticism in the late third and early fourth century.[8] Can his inferences about early Christian monasticism be substantiated by archaeological evidence? The short answer is no. There is no verifiable archaeological evidence in Egypt—or indeed anywhere else—for Christian monasteries so early. There is, however, a suggestive site.

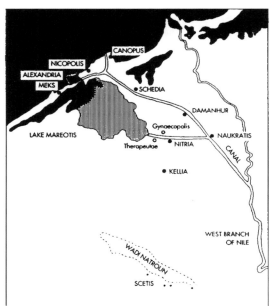

Figure 9.1 *Lake Mareotis area, map. The map attempts to indicate the first-century size of Lake Mareotis (the shaded area), the location of the canals, and the relative locations of the Therapeutae, Gynaecopolis, Nitria, Kellia, and the Wadi Natroun. The locations of the first two are hypothetical, based on Philo's description (Therapeutae) and Strabo's description (Gynaecopolis).*

THE KELLIA

About 55 km south of Alexandria is the site of the Kellia, a large collection of monastic establishments from antiquity,[9] lying just south of Nitria, another monastic center, and north of Wadi Natroun—or the Scetis—which still has four monastic establishments today. (Nitria is said to have had 5000 monks, Kellia 600, Oxyrhynchus 10,000 monks and 20,000 virgins; a nineteenth-century estimate was 70,000 monastics altogether.) All three areas lie within 60 km of each other on the edge of the great Western Desert. Together they formed one of the greatest examples of the urge to flee society and go into the wilderness to live a life of prayer, self-denial and worship of God.

Kellia derives from a Greek transliteration (*kella*) of the Latin *cella* ("room," "chamber," or simply "cell"). The name indicates the character of the buildings that have been recovered there (Figure 9.2). This site contains some of the earliest structures thrown up by the fledgling monastic movement. It has attracted intensive yet sporadic archaeolog-

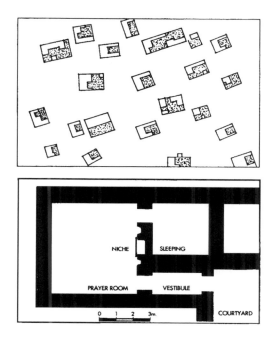

Figure 9.2. *Kellia, map and typical monk's apartment. The upper drawing reproduces in sketch from a small section of the excavations of the site of Kellia, with its numerous individual "houses" (apartments or cells). A typical early apartment for one monk had a prayer room, niche (always oriented towards the east), and small sleeping room, entered through a vestibule off a courtyard.*

ical rescue work since 1964, for agriculture has already taken over much of the site and threatens to take over the whole area. The excavated structures emphasize the individual cell and express, in built form, the ideal of a life of solitary devotion (Figure 9.2). Nearby Nitria was used as a kind of novitiate before monks adopted a more withdrawn life at Kellia.

Excavations at Kellia give strong fifth-, sixth- and seventh-century evidence of quasi-eremitic monasticism. Apparently they emphasized withdrawal but blended it with communal elements, so it was distinct from total seclusion with no communal elements and from communal, or coenobitic, monasticism.[10] Though most of the buildings at Kellia derive from the sixth and seventh centuries, some reflect fifth-century practices,[11] and the excavators have concluded that the earliest stages go back to fourth-century structures. Literary evidence confirms the development of the site in the late-300s. The excavators have done an exemplary job in the difficult context of emergency excavations.[12] The following summary is confined to the earliest substantial evidence—the fifth century—but much applies to the evidence that pertains to the fourth century.[13]

- There was a pattern of clusters of mud brick houses with vaulted rooms already in the fifth century (it probably applied to the fourth century as well), all oriented to the east.

- A low wall enclosed house and courtyard; there was a suite of rooms for a monk, the most important space being for prayer and meditation, entered through a small vestibule. Off this room was a small sleeping cell and storage rooms. In the earliest buildings the prayer room was typically in the northwest corner.[14]

- The prayer rooms usually had a niche on the east wall (a customary direction for prayer), with a fresco of Christ or something similar to aid devotion.[15]

- The houses became more complex as the site developed, first admitting two persons, a senior monk and a junior disciple, then accommodating a number of monks in one larger structure, often around a central courtyard.[16]

- There were few major communal buildings, although primitive ones may have existed in the fifth century; others certainly developed later.[17] For some purposes communal functions were carried out (perhaps only in the very earliest period) at Nitria, some distance away but still functioning as a kind of motherhouse.[18]

EGYPTIAN MONASTICISM

Eusebius wrote just at the time that Egyptian monasticism emerged out of the activities of three persons: Antony (251–356 C.E.) the first anchorite, whose activity was originally just south of Alexandria;[19] Pachomius (290–346 C.E.) the first cenobite;[20] and Athanasius (296–373 C.E.) the Bishop of Alexandria who encouraged these earliest monks. Athanasius's *Life of Antony* (*Vita Antonii*, ca. 357 C.E.) introduces the terms "monk" and "monastery" into Christian literature. Antony's long career included two periods as a hermit, the earlier in the last quarter of the third century. The *Life of Antony* purports to describe the period around 306 C.E.[21] Antony's first period of activity prior to 306 C.E. was located in the desert south of Alexandria and west of the Nile Delta, near the remains at Kellia, Nitria, and the Wadi Natroun.[22]

Literary evidence puts these monastic foundations in the early fourth century (between 330 and 340 C.E.); the archaeological evidence (which is strong for the fifth to the seventh centuries) confirms their origins in the fourth century,[23] so that the literary and archaeological evidence converge in a satisfying way.

Eusebius wrote his church history with its account of the Therapeutae in this setting; most of the first seven books were written before 303 C.E. and the final version ca. 324 C.E. In his description of the Therapeutae, whom he believed to be Christian, Eusebius carefully quoted Philo's reference to the "monastery" (*monastêrion*), the only time prior to Athanasius's use of the word in connection with Antony that the word has been found in Greek literature. So Athanasius (ca. 357 C.E.) uses *monastêrion* of Antony's activities, referring to a half-century earlier. Eusebius derived *monastêrion* from Philo's description of the Therapeutae (ca. 306 C.E., quoting Philo from the early first century). The earliest instance of individual withdrawal can be found in Antony in the preceding few years; he withdrew from society immediately south of Lake Mareotis. Fourth-century remains of quasi-eremitic establishments have been found in the same region. The Therapeutae, another quasi-eremitic group, was also located on the margins of Lake Mareotis. Is this a remarkable set of coincidences or is there something historically significant in these associations?

PHILO ON THE THERAPEUTAE AND THERAPEUTRIDES

Having claimed in *CH* 2.16 that this was a large group, "both men and women alike," Eusebius then refers to Philo's *On the Contemplative Life* and to the group's name (in *CH* 2.17): "Therapeutae and their womenfolk Therapeutrides." He thought the name (following Philo) came from either the root "to heal" or "to worship" and that this name was used "because the title Christian was not yet in general use." Eusebius was intrigued by the emphasis on women. He thought the clearest evidence of the Christian character of the group was the presence and the roles of women, "most of them elderly spinsters who have remained single": inclusion of celibate women was evidence they were Christian (Chapter 10).

Philo's account itself included more material than Eusebius borrowed; it is now agreed—after nineteenth-century doubts—that it is genuine and that it describes a Jewish group in Egypt. It may even be firsthand,[24] for the buildings were somewhere near Alexandria.[25] The members had fled from society to Lake Mareotis[26] where there was a community of farm buildings or "houses collected together" (*Contempl.* 22–24). Distinctive activities set the group apart: laws and oracles, dream activity, prayer, meditation and contemplation, reading and interpretation of Scripture, singing of hymns and psalms, seventh-day assemblies, hierarchical seating, and so on (*Contempl.* 25–31).

Buildings of the Therapeutae

We have no archaeological evidence of the structures but Philo provides an important description of the group's buildings. He describes imprecisely their "houses" (*oikia*, *Contempl.* 24; *oikêma*, 25), perhaps with the emphasis on cells or cubicles, clustered along Lake Mareotis but "neither near together as in towns . . . nor yet at a great distance" (*Contempl.* 24). They had a dispersed character, as compared with Qumran,[27] though not so dispersed as to destroy the sense of *koinônia* (*Contempl.* 24). Each house had its own *hieron* or "shrine," also called a *semneion* or "sanctuary" and *monastêrion* or "cubicle" in which persons were initiated into the mysteries of the sanctified life (*Contempl.* 25). Philo's use of these words is confusing; it is difficult to imagine how he visualized the "houses" or "cells." For example, towards the end he refers to each member going back to a *semneion* after the vigil (*Contempl.* 89), meaning the private contemplative space; in *Contempl.* 30 he uses *monastêrion* for the same function; in *Contempl.* 25 both words are used to explain *hieron*, which is merely part of an *oikêma* though it (like *oikia* in *Contempl.* 24) is used of the space that each person had, not of a group house.[28] The most obvious solution is that he visualized a "shrine" (not more accurately described), inside a special room for contemplation and devotion, within a somewhat larger house—all set within a garden or field that contributes to its solitary character (Figure 9.3).

They had two larger buildings. The first was a "common sanctuary" (*koinon semneion*, *Contempl.* 32) for seventh-day worship. Philo referred to the degree of isolation of the individual cells (*Contempl.* 30) when introducing the description of this building: the members did not pass beyond the courtyard (*auleios*)[29] of their individual houses, "not even looking out from their isolation." The individual chambers for contem-

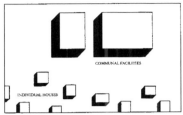

Figure 12.2 Therapeutae: Schematic Community

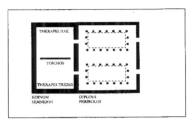

Figure 12.4 Therapeutae: Schematic Assembly Room

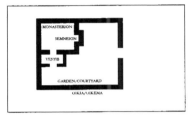

Figure 12.3 Therapeutae: Schematic "House"

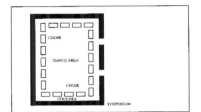

Figure 12.5 Therapeutae: Schematic Banquet Room

Figure 9.3. *Therapeutae, hypothetical reconstructions. The four drawings attempt to give form to Philo's description of the monastic community: on the upper left a general layout with large communal structures and small "houses," on the lower left a typical small "house" or cell, and on the right the assembly room and triclinium or banquet room. There is, regrettably, no archaeological evidence for these hypothetical reconstructions.*

plation were far enough away or else arranged in such a fashion that the members could not see the communal building. Within the common sanctuary was a double enclosure (*diplous peribolos*) providing space on one side for men, on the other for women: "for women too regularly make part of the audience with the same ardour (*zēlon*) and the same sense of their calling" (*Contempl.* 32). Then Philo describes a "dividing wall" in a Jewish building for ritual purposes, the first and perhaps only time in antiquity:

> The wall between the two chambers rises up from the ground to three or four cubits built in the form of a breastwork, while the space above up to the roof is left open. This arrangement serves two purposes: the modesty becoming to the female sex is preserved, while the women sitting within ear-shot can easily follow what is said since there is nothing to obstruct the voice of the speaker (*Contempl.* 33).

It is common to argue that synagogues in this period did not have a dividing wall between men and women,[30] a view I share. There is no literary or archaeological evidence for a division, whether horizontal or vertical, at an early stage of synagogue development. Here, however, is a description of just such a division in an assembly building, though in a structure different from a synagogue. The division (*toichos*) could recall the barrier (*soreg*) between the outer court and the so-called Court of Women in the Jerusalem temple (Chapter 16),[31] though I consider that to be a remote analogy. Philo describes a combination of an outdoor space (*peribolos*) and a roofed room attached to it, like the space before or around a temple. The hints suggest a double *stoa* enclosing a defined double space, off of which is an assembly room divided down the middle by a breast-high wall.

The other common building was a refectory (*symposion*), not divided in the same way as the first (see *Contempl.* 83; "they rise up all together and standing in the middle of the refectory"). Initially men reclined on one side and women on the other, but as the meal progressed towards the vigil they all came together into a single choir. The benches were not soft, says Philo, but "plank beds of the common kinds of wood, covered with quite cheap strewings of native papyrus, raised slightly at the arms to give something to lean on" (*Contempl.* 69). The guests were arranged in rows in order of precedence according to years in the community (*Contempl.* 75, 80). Portable tables were brought in filled with food after scripture exposition and hymns (*Contempl.* 81). When the meal was over, the members remained in the dining room and held the sacred vigil.[32]

The *symposion* itself was not unusual, but I know of no building similar to the assembly room in antiquity (Chapter 12); Philo describes a unique solution to the group's unusual equivalence between men and women (perhaps strengthening the view that Philo may have seen the buildings for himself). The combination of the two large structures with a number of smaller cells in a single complex was also unusual, though it had obvious resemblances to later Christian monasteries, just as the dividing wall had resemblances to later synagogues.

One final observation on the Therapeutae. It is not known how the group ended; scholars tacitly assume it did not survive beyond the first century C.E. This assumption is precarious. As compared with the temple community at Leontopolis (Chapter 10), which filled Egyptian military functions and may have been a place of last resort for Judean revolutionaries after the fall of Jerusalem, there is no suggestion of military importance attaching to the Therapeutae and no reason for Roman military action against it in 73 or 74 C.E., when the Romans destroyed Leontopolis, 150 km to the southeast (*War* 7.421, 433–35).

The community could have been involved in some way in the Jewish revolt in Egypt in 115/116 C.E., but this is never said. I see no way to infer from any literary or historical datum when the community disappeared; it may have lasted for some time.

THE THERAPEUTAE AND KELLIA

There were strong resemblances between the buildings excavated at Kellia and Philo's description of the Therapeutae. Those resemblances can be summarized as follows:

- the Therapeutae and Kellia had houses resembling farm houses clustered together, allowing complete privacy for each individual; both communities emphasized withdrawal, seclusion, the life of individual contemplation;

- a life of seclusion was balanced with communal activities;

- individual living quarters contained shrines on which devotion focused;

- the main assembly buildings in both cases were remote (though it later changed at Kellia);

- both communities met in weekly assemblies, in both cases with community meals and community worship in common facilities;

- both communities were located near Lake Mareotis, perhaps in both cases on the far side of the lake;

- the two communities were the only ones during the whole period to have the word *monastêrion* applied to them;

- literary descriptions suggest that women participated in both groups in a celibate life of withdrawal.

The resemblances apply to the built forms and the organization of life of the two monastic settlements. There were differences, the main one being the difference in the relationship between the cells at Kellia and the mother house at Nitria (15 km away); there is no hint in Philo's description of a similar distance among the Therapeutae. There also may have been differences in the exact nature of the individual shrines and in the size of the community. In general, however, if one wants an impression of the buildings of the Therapeutae, one cannot do better than to look at the structures at Kellia.

ONCE AGAIN, EUSEBIUS AND PHILO

The distinct echoes of Philo's description of the Therapeutae in the monastic practices of Eusebius's own day at sites such as Kellia prompted Eusebius, I suggest, to identify the Therapeutae as Christians. Christian groups similar to the Therapeutae developed quasi-eremitic monastic establishments; the fact that this occurred in Egypt does not mean that there was any influence of one on the other. It may be that the resemblances are indirect, fortuitous, or unexceptional—there are only so many ways to build and organize a monastery. Because monasteries existed before Eusebius's time, he could imagine when he came to write his history that Philo's description of the Therapeutae was simply a description of an early version of the Egyptian Christian monasteries he knew firsthand. It is not difficult to understand why Eusebius applied this earlier description to something he knew; it squared closely with his observations. There may, then, be no great mystery in Eusebius's application of Philo to Christians of Eusebius's period. It was an honest mistake.

Was Eusebius, however, not just making a mistake, as I first thought, when he applied Philo's description to Christian monks? Or did he know what he was doing when he took a Jewish group of the first century and called it Christian, as I now wonder? The evidence is slight, but tips in favor of the latter view. (1) The statements referred to earlier indicating controversy over his claim tumble over each other in the last portion of *Church History* 2.17, suggesting opposition to Eusebius's view that the Therapeutae were Christians. Perhaps Eusebius's opponents knew the group was Jewish, not Christian, and believed that one should not use Jewish customs to establish Christian practices. (2) Eusebius certainly knew that Philo was not a Christian, so why would Philo have written about a Christian group? Eusebius went out of his way to make up a reason—the size of the group (*CH* 2.16)—for Philo's interest in Christianity. (3) Eusebius's personal contacts might have informed him of the true character of the Therapeutae, for he had spent some time in Egypt. Whether Eusebius knew what he was doing or not, the gap between the apostolic period and his day made it relatively easy for him to absorb the group into his history of Christianity as one of the original forms of behavior and organization, even though others doubted this model for Christian activity. Eusebius saw the Therapeutae as an explanation, perhaps even a defense, of the fledgling monastic movement of his day. He was convinced that if it existed in his day it must have existed in the apostolic period also.

This much may be a reasonable inference regarding Eusebius's motivation. Even if true, however, it does not go very far towards accounting historically for the development in a Christian group of the same monastic practices and monastic structures as Judaism had earlier developed. To put the issue differently, did one influence the other? Was monasticism before Eusebius's day being influenced by direct or indirect knowledge of the practices of the Therapeutae? This is ultimately an unanswerable question. Since we do not know how long the Therapeutae survived as a group we cannot guess how much knowledge there was of the group's organization and buildings nor what impact they might have had. Is it plausible that Christians in an earlier period (second century? early third century?) knew of the group, and that they found themselves attracted to it? In such a scenario the attractions would be the quality of the life, its emphasis on celibacy and virginity, its attention to the contemplative spiritual life, and the devotion of the group to Scripture and worship. We cannot know the answer to this question; it is only barely plausible speculation. What stands out as remarkable is the close similarity of the life of two groups and the closely similar buildings they developed to meet their needs.

THE THERAPEUTAE, CONCLUDING COMMENTS

My main interest here is the first-century group, the Therapeutae; is it worth asking whether it had other lasting influences on either Christianity or Judaism? Within Judaism the only close contemporary parallel for this type of closed community with a distinctive set of buildings was Qumran.[33] In important respects Qumran was not closely similar. Yet Qumran helps to underscore significant aspects of the Therapeutae; both communities were dedicated to scriptural exposition, common life, withdrawal from society, and full-time religious activity (see Plate 28). For a period of time, Judaism had a monastic tradition, perhaps more influential than we can now recover with confidence. When it disappeared is not known. To emphasize a point made earlier, there was a correspondence between two accessible forms of Jewish monasticism—Qumran being coenobitic and the Therapeutae being quasi-eremitic—and two forms of Christian monasticism—

Lower Egypt being mainly quasi-eremitic and Upper Egypt being mainly coenobitic. It is a desideratum to investigate as carefully and thoroughly as possible this monastic stream in post-biblical Judaism. Perhaps as we understand Christian monasticism better we can begin to understand Jewish monasticism and its impact better.

Despite the fact that the Therapeutae left no footprints in Judaism, there was one slight but suggestive later connection with this almost forgotten Egyptian group: the division between males and females in the assembly room (*Contempl.* 32). Ironically, the group that experimented most successfully with equivalence between males and females may have bequeathed to Judaism a wall that has symbolized the division between the sexes ever since. I cannot prove that later synagogues that used such a wall derived it from the Therapeutae; yet there are no other documented first-century walls (except for the temple in Jerusalem which is hardly similar; Chapter 16).[34] There were later barriers, and the description of the wall in Philo sounds similar to such later walls. The Therapeutae's buildings offer a fascinating possibility of a step on the way towards later synagogues.

Did the Therapeutae influence the earliest stages of Christianity? There is only slight first-century Christian flirtation with monasticism so such a thought may seem unlikely.[35] It is worth recalling that there were similar attitudes to women, marriage, the celibate life and virginity in the church in Corinth.[36] Pierre Benoit, not known for radical views, hinted long ago at the possibility of the Therapeutae being a middle term between Judaism and the Gnosticism of Asia Minor, with Apollos being a vehicle for that influence.[37] Some persons in the church in Corinth, influenced by leaders other than Paul, held exaggerated views—as Paul saw things—of women's right to act independently alongside men; the same persons may have held stringent views of flesh, the body and self-denial. In several respects these views were similar to the independent virginal and celibate lifestyles of the Therapeutae, though without the secluded life of contemplation. If Benoit is right that members of the church in Corinth learned these views from Apollos, who learned them in turn from the Jewish monastic group in Egypt,[38] then the Therapeutae would have left two footprints on later Christian monasticism, one through the shaping of ascetic ideas in the influential church in Corinth, and the other through the shaping of the ideal of the withdrawn life and the outlines of its practice.

CHAPTER TEN

JEWISH VOLUNTARY ASSOCIATIONS IN EGYPT AND THE ROLES OF WOMEN[1]

One of the distinctive traits of social relations in Egypt, at least among the upper classes, was the more nearly equivalent roles of women and men, symbolized by the complementary roles of the Pharaoh and Queen,[2] roles recognized by Jewish synagogues in Egypt (Chapter 7). Two Jewish groups in Egypt showed the importance of women in their organizations. One was a celibate monastic group near Alexandria in which men and women participated equally (Chapter 9); the other was a military temple-oriented community at Leontopolis, where women were involved in the priesthood.

PART 1. THE TEMPLE COMMUNITY AT LEONTOPOLIS

INTRODUCTION

The *Tosefta* relates a tradition about the founding of the Temple of Onias at Leontopolis:

> When he [Simeon] was dying, he said to them, "My son Onias will serve in my place." Then his brother Shimei envied him, being older than he by two years and a half. He said to him, "Come, and I shall instruct you on the order of the temple service." [Shimei] put on him a light gown and girded him with a girdle and set him up by the altar and then said to his brothers, the other priests, "See what this man has promised and carried out for his girlfriend: 'On the day on which I shall take up the office of high priest, I am going to put on your gown and gird myself with your girdle.'" His brothers the priests wanted to kill him [for coming to the altar in a woman's garments]. He fled from them and they pursued him. So he went off to Alexandria in Egypt and there he built an altar and presented on it burnt offerings for idols. (*Tosefta Menahot* 13.II.1)

165

Could this tradition connecting the cultic practice of Onias with women's garments be a reference to the presence of women priests at Leontopolis? This rather whimsical account differs substantially from the more believable accounts found in Josephus, 2 Maccabees and the *Mishnah*. What is its origin? One plausible explanation is that it reflects the involvement of women in cultic activities at Leontopolis. Priests connected with the Temple of Onias wore women's garments. Why? Because some of them were women. An inscription on a tombstone at the site corroborates this possibility, highly speculative when based only on the Toseftan tradition. The inscription refers to Marin, called a priest:

> O Marin, priest [*hierisa*], excellent one, friend of all, who caused pain to none, a friend to your neighbors, farewell. About 50 years old. In the third year of Caesar, Payni 13.[3]

In the light of this inscription, it is possible to interpret the *Tosefta* passage as mocking the practice of Onias' temple for including women among the priestly personnel. This chapter reviews what is known about the community associated with the temple at Leontopolis and investigates the possibility of women priests at the site.

BACKGROUND OF THE COMMUNITY ACCORDING TO JOSEPHUS

Josephus alone among ancient authors gives a detailed description of the Jewish community at Leontopolis and its temple, though *War* and *Antiquities* give conflicting accounts of its origins. Onias (III or IV?), having been deprived of his right to the high priesthood, went to Alexandria, and, according to *War*, "being graciously received by Ptolemy, owing to that monarch's hatred of Antiochus, told him that he would make the Jewish nation his ally if he would accede to his proposal" to build a temple "somewhere in Egypt and to worship God after the manner of his fathers" (*War* 7.423–24). Ptolemy gave him a tract of land in the nome of Heliopolis, where Onias erected a fortress and a temple, thus colonizing the district (*War* 7.421), implying that the area had not been previously settled. In *Antiquities* we are told that, while living in Alexandria, Onias (here Onias IV) requested of Ptolemy and Cleopatra permission to build a temple in Egypt "similar to that at Jerusalem, and to appoint Levites and priests of his own race" (*Ant.*

13.63). Josephus quotes a letter, purporting to be written from Onias to Ptolemy and Cleopatra, whose authenticity is widely disputed:

> Many and great are the services which I have rendered you in the course of the war, with the help of God, when I was in Coele-Syria and Phoenicia, and when I came with the Jews to Leontopolis in the nome of Heliopolis and to other places where our nation is settled; and I found that most of them have temples, contrary to what is proper, and that for this reason they are ill-disposed toward one another, as is also the case with the Egyptians because of the multitude of their temples and their varying opinions about the forms of worship; and I have found a most suitable place in the fortress called after Bubastis-of-the-Fields, which abounds in various kinds of trees and is full of sacred animals, wherefore I beg you to permit me to cleanse this temple, which belongs to no one and is in ruins, and to build a temple to the Most High God in the likeness of that at Jerusalem and with the same dimensions, on behalf of you and your wife and children, in order that the Jewish inhabitants of Egypt may be able to come together there in mutual harmony and serve your interests. (*Ant.* 13.65–67)

This letter suggests that Onias was in the military service of Ptolemy and Cleopatra (possibly even before he went to Egypt) and probably in a high position.[4] Onias was engaged in this service when he first went to Leontopolis, a location he suggested to Ptolemy as the site for a temple, rather than Ptolemy choosing it for him, as *War* implies. In contrast to *War*, the letter suggests that prior to the building of the temple Leontopolis had already been settled by Jews; Onias merely increased the population of the settlement by coming with more Jews, though it is possible that Onias had already created a Jewish (military?) settlement prior to the writing of the letter and only added the Jewish temple later. The letter says that a fortress and an Egyptian temple were already on the site.[5] Further, the involvement of the Jews and Egyptians with numerous temples in the area is attested, as well as disputes amongst them over forms of worship. Onias expected that his temple would allow Jews to come together in mutual harmony and serve the interests of Ptolemy and Cleopatra.

The origin of the Jewish community at Leontopolis lay in a military settlement, a kind of border post near the point where Jewish, Idumean, and Egyptian interests met. Onias was the leader of the settlement, to which a Jewish temple was added. It was intended to end religious disputes and unite Jews by serving all the Jews in the area surrounding it, and possibly even further abroad.

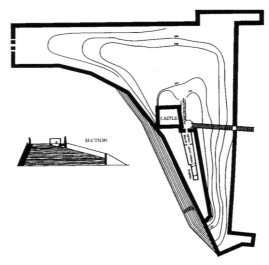

Figure 10.1. *Leontopolis (Tell el-Yehudiyeh), plan and section. The very rough section shows the hill on which the Jewish temple was situated, with its long stair up; the plan indicates very approximately what was discovered in ninteenth century excavations. A large fort or castle was northwest of the two (or three) courtyard temple, somewhat similar to Jerusalem (after Petrie,* Hyksos and Israelite Cities, *Plate XXIII).*

ARCHAEOLOGICAL REMAINS

The site of Tell el-Yehudiyeh, 35 km north of Cairo in the Delta, has been identified as the site of the temple of Leontopolis (Figure 10.1).[6] A brick retaining wall surrounded the mound atop which the temple once stood. The temple was approached from the bottom of the hill by a large staircase on the eastern slope, or from the north where the slope was gentler and an approach ran through an area of three or four acres, probably covered with houses. A road going from east to west led through the town and out to the cemetery and the desert.[7] At the time of W. M. Flinders Petrie's excavation only portions of the foundations of the temple walls remained, but Petrie was able to conjecture the plan of the temple. A very broad outer enclosure wall (about 65 feet wide) ran around the temple structures. Inside this wall there was evidence of both an outer and an inner court. The outer court was 32 feet wide at the front and 27 feet at the back, with a length of 44 feet (9.7x8.2x13.4 m). The inner court was 27 feet wide in front, 21 feet wide at the back and 63 feet in length (8.2x6.4x19.2 m). The temple (*naos*) was rectangular, 16.75x54.8 feet (5.1x16.7 m).[8] Little else can be known about its structure, except that a marble column was found which Petrie believed, based on its dimensions and material, to have been one of two columns supporting the porch.[9]

At the head of the stairway, northwest of the temple, Petrie uncovered foundations of a large rectangular building, about 52x73 feet (15.9x22.3 m). This seems to have been a defensive fortress, commanding a view of the entire surrounding region, including the ascent up the stairway from the town and the entrance to the temple and its courts. Other finds included Corinthian capitals of limestone and an ostracon inscribed with the names Harkheb son of Zeho and Abram, followed by the word "bricks." This led him to the conclusion that both Egyptians and Jews had worked on the construction of the temple.[10] He also found a number of limestone *ballista* stones, most likely from the Roman destruction of the temple in 73 C.E. (since if they had been from an earlier siege they would not have been left around the site). Supporting the idea of a siege was the fact that the bricks of the east and north walls, as well as the brick pier that would have supported the stairway, had been burnt. Petrie also discovered "cylinders of pottery containing burnt offerings" in the base of the mound, usually a bed of white wood ash one to three inches thick with bones of lambs.[11]

THE COMMUNITY'S MILITARY ROLE

Some information can be gleaned about the community and its temple between the building of the temple (ca. 160 B.C.E.) and its destruction in 73 C.E. It was best known for its military role. Victor Tcherikover points out that Onias led a force into Alexandria in support of Cleopatra after Philometor's death.[12] Chelkias and Ananias, Onias's descendants, also became generals for Cleopatra (*Ant.* 13.287). Particularly relevant for the Marin inscription, since the event occurred in her lifetime, was an encounter between Antipater's troops and "Jews who occupied the district which took its name from Onias" (*War* 1.190; *Ant.* 14.133), about 48 B.C.E. At first they barred Antipater's way but were then prevailed upon to refrain from opposition and give him supplies.[13] In Marin's time the district of Onias had military resources sufficient to bar the way of a force large enough to have taken Pelusium immediately beforehand (*War* 1.187–89). The fact that the temple was closed in 73 C.E. by order of the Roman emperor suggests that its military as well as its religious importance was maintained up to this time. Josephus says:

> The emperor, suspicious of the interminable tendency of the Jews to revolution, and fearing that they might again collect together in force and draw others away with them, ordered Lupus to demolish the Jewish temple in the so-called district of Onias. . . . Lupus, the governor of Alexandria, on receipt of Caesar's letter repaired to the temple and, having carried off some of the votive offerings, shut up the building. Lupus dying soon after, Paulinus, his successor in office, completely stripped the place of its treasures, threatening the priests with severe penalties if they failed to produce them all, prohibited would-be worshippers from approaching the precincts, and, closing the gates, debarred all access, so as to leave thenceforth no vestige of divine worship on the spot. (*War* 7.421; 433–35)

There would have been little reason for the emperor or the governor to think it necessary to close the temple at Leontopolis if it were insignificant in the life of the Jews of Egypt. The Roman officials must have been concerned that it could become a unifying institution for Egyptian Jews and a rallying point for those supporting the Jewish revolt. Moreover, the fact that it was necessary, even after Lupus had "shut up the building," for his successor to strip it completely, threaten the priests and force away those who wished to worship there, reveals that, even under persecution, priests kept it in operation and Jews worshiped there. The account implies the temple was important for some Egyptian Jews. In fact, if the account is accurate, there must have been enough worshipers for them to be a threat to Rome. Perhaps Josephus has exaggerated the details, stressing the threat it posed to emphasize Jewish bravery and strength. The discovery of *ballista* stones and burnt walls, however, supports the outline of his account. The temple was only overcome after a siege, so Jews defended it to the end.

THE COMMUNITY'S CULTIC ROLE

Leontopolis was a cultic community, rivaling Jerusalem. Information emerges from archaeological, literary, and epigraphic evidence. Josephus tells us the temple was staffed by Levites and priests of Onias's race (*Ant.* 13.63), perhaps a large number (*War* 7.430).

Archaeological remains showed evidence of animal sacrifices made there.[14] The *Mishnah*, too, in referring briefly to the House of Onias, reveals its cultic practices:

> [If he said,] "I pledge myself to offer a Whole-offering," he must offer it in the temple. And if he offered it in the House of Onias he has not fulfilled his obligation. [If he said,] "I will offer it in the House of Onias," he should offer it in the temple, but if he offered it in the House of Onias he has fulfilled his obligation. . . . If priests have ministered in the House of Onias they may not minister in the temple in Jerusalem; still more does this apply to [priests who have ministered in] that other matter; for it is written, "Nevertheless the priests of the high places came not up to the altar of the Lord in Jerusalem, but they did eat unleavened bread among their brethren"; thus they were like them that have a blemish; they may share and they may eat [of the Holy Things] but they may not offer sacrifice. (*m. Menah.* 13:10)

It was acceptable to sacrifice at Leontopolis as long as the worshiper did not pledge to make the offering in the Jerusalem temple. This ruling, while not necessarily indicating an opinion about the legitimacy of the House of Onias on the part of the Jerusalem authorities, indicates that people were indeed offering sacrifices at Leontopolis. The Jerusalem leaders had to decide how to treat these sacrifices. The ruling implies they did not express unrelieved opposition to Leontopolis. The passage continues by saying that priests who had ministered in the House of Onias could no longer minister in the Jerusalem temple, although they did not thereby lose their Levitical status. For this to be an issue priests must actually have come from the House of Onias and asked to minister in the Jerusalem temple. This was probably not an isolated incident, considering that the ruling was preserved until the compilation of the *Mishnah*. This point is important. First, it suggests that the Leontopolis temple was in regular operation for a lengthy period. Second, it shows that it continued to employ regular Levitical priests, who claimed legitimacy on Jerusalem's criteria. *Mishnah Menahoth* 13:10 reveals a surprising interplay between the two temples. The worship and priesthood at Leontopolis were not considered illegitimate by Jerusalem, simply inferior. Third, this situation underscores that the disqualifying element had to do with the rivalry between Jerusalem and Leontopolis, not with the conditions of service or worship.

The Community's Social and Religious Character

Leontopolis was a Jewish community with evidence of some assimilation to the surrounding culture. Remains of an underground Jewish cemetery, which was excavated by Édouard Naville in the late nineteenth century, were found northeast of the temple. According to Naville, the plan of the tombs was unlike Egyptian tombs, but closely resembled tombs found in Phoenicia and Judaea, where they are known as *fours à cercueils*.[15] Though both Greek and Hebrew names appear on the tomb inscriptions in almost equal numbers, together with a few Egyptian names, the arrangement of the tombs and remains of the bodies suggest that the tombs were for Jews. Several fathers with Egyptian names gave Hebrew names to their children (*CPJ* 2.145). In one of the inscriptions the deceased responds to the question of her country of birth, "the famous land of Onias reared me" (*CPJ* 2.1530). Most inscriptions address the deceased in the vocative, followed by *chaire*, "farewell," the epithet *chrêste*, "excellent one," and *aore*, "untimely dead." Their contents suggest no dominant religious or cultural outlook, not even predominantly Jewish content, but neither is there any other notable leaning.[16] Kasher argues from the funerary inscriptions that the community was large and economically well established. He suggests there were different qualities of rock in the cemetery, and thus "good" and "bad" sections, necessitating a burial society to allocate them.[17]

Other evidence for the formal organization of the city comes from two inscriptions, *CPJ* 3.1450, and *CPJ* 3.1530A. The reconstructed reading of *CPJ* 3.1450 discusses a decision (*psephismata*) by the whole community (*plêthos*) of the sacred district. This vocabulary agrees with that in the *Letter of Aristeas*, used to refer to a *politeuma* (roughly, "community of foreigners"), leading Kasher to conclude that Leontopolis was also a *politeuma*. Further evidence comes from inscription 1530A in which a man named Abramos is named the *politarchês*, a title used in Egypt for the city governor subordinate to the *stratêgos* of the nome.[18] This inscription sheds light on the community organization of Leontopolis, where the presence of a Jewish *politarchês* suggests that Jews administered it. Abramos is said to wear "the wreath of magistracy for the whole people" (*ethnikê*), vocabulary fitting the ethnic criterion for the formation of a *politeuma* and the same term applied to the Jewish community in Alexandria. Kasher concludes that Alexandria and Leontopolis were both organized as *politeumata*.[19] The organized nature of Leontopolis emerges from other vocabulary found in the inscriptions, such as the plea that both "citizens and strangers" weep for Rachelis (*CPJ* 3.1513) and Theon's claim to have been a "friend to all the citizens" and "renowned in council" (*CPJ* 3.1489). Josephus himself may have considered Leontopolis a *politeuma*. According to Borgen, a *politeuma* was "confirmation by the king that an ethnic community was permitted—within limits—to live in accordance with its ancestral laws."[20] This description is strikingly similar to Josephus's report of the correspondence between Onias and Ptolemy: he asked permission to build a temple to the Most High God "in order that the Jewish inhabitants of Egypt may be able to come together there in mutual harmony" (*Ant.* 13.67). Even though Josephus may have fabricated this correspondence, he may still reflect the perception (and perhaps reality) of the legal status of Leontopolis.

Would a community situated around the temple of Onias have been viewed as an association? That seems quite possible. It served the needs of a Jewish *ethnê* living in a military and cultic community. Associations in Egypt usually met in a public temple. Greek terms and Egyptian names in the building records of the temple and in its grave inscriptions show that Greeks and Egyptians probably lived in the vicinity, too, and influenced its culture. The Jewish temple was likely one religious option among others. Foreigners formed associations in Rome and other places (Chapters 7, 11, 12), where they maintained their national identity by adherence to their own deity. Jews in Leontopolis, initially foreigners, would have been viewed as setting up their own religious association. Since most associations assumed funerary obligations, the organization of the catacombs may have been a function of the temple association.

On the other hand, if Kasher's analysis of the community as a *politeuma* is correct, the above interpretation is less tenable. The function of a *politeuma* was to create a community of people that shared the same identity. If Leontopolis were a *politeuma*, according to this definition its sole religious affiliation would have been Judaism. If the temple was the focal point of their religious expression, the temple may not have been viewed as a voluntary association. Instead it would have been an integral part of the life of every member of the community. Ultimately, however, there is not enough information to determine the status of the temple. We know for certain neither the cultural composition of the community (perhaps the Greek and Egyptian names simply reflect linguistic and cross-cultural influences) nor its structure.

THE MARIN INSCRIPTION AND THE MEANING OF *HIERISA*

Activity at Leontopolis probably revolved around the temple and the military. Traditionally, then, women would not be expected to have had a large role in the administration of the city. The Marin inscription found in the catacombs at Leontopolis, however, indicates otherwise. Marin's designation *hierisa* has traditionally been translated "of priestly descent," because Jewish women could not be priests.[21] Bernadette Brooten's study suggests the term should be translated with its usual meaning "priest."[22] *Hierisa* was the Greek equivalent of *kohenet*, a rabbinic term used to denote a woman who has either been born into a priestly family and is unmarried or one who has married a priest. "Such an identification," Brooten states, "would in no way imply congregational leadership or a cultic function, other than the right to eat the priestly offerings." Thus it is possible that the term simply designated Marin as the daughter or wife of a priest and that she had no cultic function in Onias's temple. For a number of reasons, however, it is not sufficient to accept this reading of the term in Marin's case.

As Brooten points out, the more common translation of *hierisa* in the Greco-Roman world is "priest," and in any context other than a Jewish one "no scholar would have thought of arguing that 'priest' does not really mean 'priest.' The composers of [this inscription] must have been aware that they were employing a term which normally implied a cultic function."[23] *Hierisa* appears not to have been as common as *hiereia*, which also designated a priestess, but there are some examples: a Roman Jew, Gaudentia, designated *hierisa* (*CIJ* 315), and two instances in lists of Egyptian priesthoods, where *hierisson* are listed alongside *athlophorês*, *hieron*, and *canephorês* (*P. London* 880 and *BGU* 994). In Egypt, women designated *hierisa* and *hiereia* had definite cultic roles, both in indigenous Egyptian and in Hellenistic religious organizations.[24] Finally, there is an example in which a Jewish inscription uses the expression *Maria hê tou hiereos* to designate the wife or daughter of a priest. If the term *hierisa* were commonly used as the term for wife/daughter of a priest it would be highly unusual for someone to use this more cumbersome expression for the same idea. Moreover, as

Brooten points out, the expression shows "that there was a way in Greek to express such a relationship without this title [*hierisa*] which a Greek speaker would have understood as meaning 'female cultic functionary.'"[25]

Further evidence comes from the cultic roles of women in both Jewish and Hellenistic Egyptian religion. There are no examples in the Septuagint where *hierisa* is used; in the one place *hiereia* is used it denotes a religious assembly. A number of passages, however, refer to women filling a cultic role. In Exodus 38:8 and 1 Samuel 2:22 the same root, SMS, is used for the "service" of women as for Levitical service in the Tabernacle.[26] The Targum on Judges 5:24 refers to Jael, the wife of Heber, as similar to one of the women who minister in the houses of learning. Again the word "minister" is the same as that used of the ministry of the high priest and the common priests.[27] Miriam's descent is traced back to Levi (Num 26:59; 1 Chr 6:3) and she is viewed as a prophet. Miriam, like Samuel, may have been an example of the fusion of the offices of prophet and priest.[28] According to Peritz, these examples of Jewish women who served cultic functions were precedents for the participation of women in priestly functions in Judaism. The temple at Leontopolis seems part of this tradition. Jews there were a priestly community in a setting far from Jerusalem, and they would likely have interpreted biblical texts independently in defining their identity in their new cultic situation. They may have adopted the Miriam tradition as a model for the women of their community since they, like Miriam, lived in Egypt.

This possibility is strengthened by the priestly roles of women in classical and Hellenistic Egyptian religion. Women played a large part in cultic activities in Egypt, both in the indigenous and Ptolemaic cults. *Hiereia*, the more common term for priestess, occurs in 31 documents from Roman Egypt, referring to a priestess of indigenous Egyptian or Hellenistic religion (e.g., Anubis, Isis). It is used loosely to designate any temple functionary, rather than strictly to refer to one officiating at animal sacrifices. A prominent role played by *hiereiai* was that of musician-priestess. According to Blackman, "all temples in Ptolemaic times had musician-priestesses attached to them,"[29] as this example in service of Hathor shows: "These musician-priestesses, when dancing and rattling their sistra in her worship, consciously impersonated the goddess. . . . During their performances they held out their sistra and bead-necklaces for their onlookers to touch, so imparting to them the blessing of the goddess. . . . [Hathor] was regarded as actually immanent also in her emblems, the sistra and bead-necklaces."[30]

The musician-priestesses played an important cultic role, since they symbolized the presence of the goddess in the temple. Inscriptions at Edfu record the name of a female officiant immediately after the high priest of the nome. Aylward Blackman comments: "that the title of the female officiant should appear side by side with that of the high-priest indicates that she occupied the same position among the women who served in the temple, i.e. the musician-priestesses, as he did among the men, and quite justifies our speaking of her as a high-priestess."[31]

Women were linked to the temple cult in the New Kingdom in the role of musician (*shemayet*), a title employed by large numbers of elite women. Gay Robins notes, "except for 'mistress of the house,' it must be the commonest title found for women in the Theban tombs."[32] Troupes of musicians, consisting of both men and women, were in the charge of a woman called "great one of the troupe of musical performers," who was the wife of one of the high officials, or the chief priest. Robins suggests that the "great one of the musical troupe" may have been responsible for the training, practice, and rotas of the performers, ensuring all went well during the ritual. She stresses that in the New Kingdom a distinction was made between the roles of men and women in the temple cult, with women's roles limited to the musical aspects of worship. This does not mean, however, that their role was low status. On the contrary, the "great one of the musical troupe" was high status, while "male singers and musicians usually remained anonymous, and clearly ranked lower than female singers from elite families."[33]

Though the bulk of the evidence suggests that women's cultic role was primarily musical, it was not limited to music. Francoise Dunand sees two roles for women in association with temples, one musical and one analogous to priests' roles.[34] In one example a high priestess was depicted as pouring out a libation, in another Princess Nebttowi at Thebes consecrated the offering. In the Ptolemaic period women made funeral libations.[35] Both Dunand and Blackman interpret the evidence as indicative that women in many cases performed the same daily temple liturgical duties as male priests.[36] These roles of women in the priesthood in Egypt seem to have been influenced by the roles of women monarchs. In Egyptian custom the pairing of the king and queen was central. Because monarchs were important cultic figures, queens had priestly positions alongside their husbands. Blackman gives an example from predynastic Egypt: "[The] king of Heliopolis was high priest of the sun god and was also regarded as his embodiment—Horus. The Heliopolitan queen, as wife of the sun-god's high-priest, would have acted as the sun-god's high-priestess, and would also surely have been identified with the goddess Hathor, the sun-god's wife, both in her capacity of high-priestess and also in that of wife of the embodiment of the sun-god."[37]

Some royal women in the Eighteenth Dynasty—for example the wife of king Ahmose, Hatshepsut, and her daughter Neferura—bore the title "god's wife of Amun." The god's wife had an active role in temple ritual, as scenes from the Red Chapel of Hatshepsut show, and she, like male priests, entered the sanctuary of the god.[38] In Ptolemaic Egypt, too, it was customary for a king and queen, often brother and sister, to hold the throne. In many cases the monarchs were deified and this led to other priestly positions for women. Ptolemy Philopator, for example, inaugurated a special cult in honor of his mother Berenice II; a new eponymous priesthood, reserved for women, was created, the holder entitled *athlophore*. There were other offices for women connected with female monarchs, such as the priestess of Arsinoe Philopator and the *canephore* of Arsinoe Philadelphus.[39] Egyptian priestesses apparently came from all social classes and age was no limitation. Inscriptions record priestesses from the age of 15 to 79. Two priestesses were called *agrammatos* ("illiterate")[40] and two were the wives of weavers.[41] This last example, as well as indicating the social standing of the priestesses, shows that they did not need to be connected with male priests as wives or daughters in order to be priestesses. Dunand concludes that although there is evidence that priests were more numerous than priestesses in Egypt, there were many priestesses and they assumed analogous functions to those of their male colleagues, both in classical and Ptolemaic Egypt. He states that Egyptian women, "benefited from right and privileges comparable to men's. . . . In contrast to most ancient societies, their situation was almost one of equality."[42] Cleopatra showed the power a woman could hold in Roman Egypt, holding sole, undisputed power for most of her reign.

ASSIMILATION OF THE JEWISH COMMUNITY AT LEONTOPOLIS

Jews in Egypt assimilated to the ways of Egyptian religion; documents and charms mention the names of both the Jewish God and various Egyptian and Greek gods in the same item. One example has a prayer to Zeus, Sarapis, and the Jewish God; another to Apollo, God, Michael, and Gabriel.[43] The catacombs at Leontopolis also show Jewish assimilation. One mentions that the departed is in Hades (*CPJ* 3.1511), and another refers to the "shadowy region of Lethe" (*CPJ* 3.1530). Even if this vocabulary was simply that of a hired Greek poet, as the note accompanying *CPJ* 1530 suggests, it indicates the presence of non-Jews in the Leontopolis community. Egyptian names in other inscriptions underscore this presence. The evidence for Egyptian priestesses and for assimilation of Jews in Egypt to Egyptian religious practices provides a plausible background for the claim that the temple at Leontopolis had priestesses. The *Toseftan* account of the escape of Onias from Jerusalem provides further support. The prime reason for opposition to Onias was his connection with wearing feminine garments during cultic practice. Perhaps the passage expresses rabbinic censure of Onias's temple because it included women in its priestly personnel.

Marin's title *hierisa* probably indicates that she was a temple functionary at Leontopolis. Unfortunately the inscription gives no indication of her role; on the analogy of priestesses in Egypt, her role may have involved music or other daily temple duties, such as pouring libations or preparing sacrifices. While it may initially seem implausible that Onias's temple, founded by one who had held the position of high priest of the Jerusalem temple, could stray so far from Jewish orthodoxy as to have female priests, one can envision a gradual progression away from Jerusalem practice. In Egyptian practice, it was common for the priesthood to involve various members of one family. Perhaps the priests at Leontopolis, after some time there, shared this practice.

Marin was born in 77 B.C.E. By the time she was old enough to be a priestess roughly a century had passed since the founding of the temple. This provided plenty of time for assimilation of Egyptian practices. It may be that other Jewish temples in the vicinity at the time when Onias built his temple (*Ant.* 13.66) already had women priests. The transition to the participation of women priests in Leontopolis may have been easy and natural. The combination of cultural influences and the recollection of women serving in ancient Judaism (Exod 38:8; 1 Sam 2:22) may have prompted Jews at Leontopolis to include women as priests as religious practice developed in their community.

PART 2. THERAPEUTAE AND THERAPEUTRIDES AT LAKE MAREOTIS

PHILO'S ACCOUNT

The Therapeutae-Therapeutrides formed a group known only from a lengthy and enthusiastic account in Philo.[44] He describes a number of important features of the Therapeutae, some of which were common to other associations (Chapters 9, 11). The relevant features can be briefly listed.

(1) In his introductory description of "these philosphers," and in several later references, Philo refers to the group as a *proairesis*, a word with a wide range of meanings.[45] In several instances *proairesis* implies something like a "sect." Philo also refers to them as a *systêma* (*Contempl.* 72)—a "college" or "association," with a lifelong commitment—for new members sought "never to leave their place in this company" (*Contempl.* 12) and they gave up their property to their children or relatives, "thinking their mortal life already ended" (*Contempl.* 13, cf. 18).

(2) Philo says that those who desired "justice" and "equality" (*dikaiosynê* and *isotêtos, Contempl.* 17) fled from society to Lake Mareotis where there was a community of farm buildings (22–23) or "houses collected together" (24).

(3) Each house had a *hieron/semneion*, a "shrine" in which persons were "initiated" into the "mysteries" of the sanctified life (*en hoi monoumenoi ta tou semnou biou mystêrion telountai,* 25), language that points to an association with initiatory rites and ritual provision for daily life.

(4) Distinct activities—use of laws and oracles, dreams, prayer, meditation and contemplation, reading and interpretation of scripture, singing of hymns and psalms, seventh day assemblies, hierarchical seating—set the group apart (25–31).

(5) The community had a common sanctuary (*koinon semneion*, 32) with distinctive architectural features for meetings of the whole group, both male and female members.

(6) Common meals (64–82), sharply contrasted with Roman and Greek meals (48–63), were an important feature of the group's activities, occurring weekly and in a special form every seventh week (65).

(7) A sacred vigil (83–89) complemented the festal meal every seventh week.

Most Greeks or Romans observing these elements, some definitional and some functional, would have thought of it as an association—a *collegium* or *thiasos*. There are, however, no references to other features—provision for burials, a patron—that might ordinarily have been found in voluntary associations.[46] The indications are sufficient, however, to suggest that the community was perceived as an association and perceived itself in the same way. This unusual community is important when sketching the religious variations of the Greco-Roman and Jewish worlds.

ACTIVITIES

The Therapeutae prayed in isolation twice a day, at dawn and at evening (27–28). Between these times they contemplated Scripture as allegory, studied the writings of their founders, and composed hymns and psalms "in all sorts of metres and melodies" suitable for processions or in libations at the altars. These daily activities occupied them for six days during which they ate and drank only at night, some eating only every third day while others abstained for seven days.

There was a general assembly on the seventh day (30–31), when the *presbytatos* ("eldest") gave a discourse, they ate common bread flavored with salt and hyssop, and drank water. On the fiftieth day they were called by the *ephêmereutai* ("member of the rotation," 65–66)[47] to line up in an orderly manner and pray. The elders (*presbyteroi*) reclined in rows according to rank (75). The *proedros* ("president") discussed a question arising from Scripture or one propounded by a member, treating the Scripture allegorically (77–78). Then young male servers brought in food on tables, followed by a sacred all night vigil (77, 81, 83). After this they all departed to their houses or cubicles to repeat the 50-day cycle again.

Therapeutrides

As compared with Qumran[48] the most outstanding feature of this group was the careful attention paid to women, the Therapeutrides.[49] Women had parallel, equal, and almost identical roles to men. Philo himself expresses a touch of condescension or surprise in his reactions, but his description offers a rare glimpse into a group in which women were involved as equals. The Lake Mareotis community stood apart from similar religious communities dominated either by males (Qumran, Mithraea, most *collegia*) or by females (Demeter and Kore).[50] This group was a radical experiment in a withdrawn communal life of contemplation, characterized by equal rights and more or less equal leadership. The main features pertaining to women were these:

(1) Though Philo begins in paragraph 1 referring to the "virtue of these men" he immediately thereafter refers to "Therapeutae and Therapeutrides," using masculine and feminine names for the group. He does not comment on this pairing and he only once again uses the paired names, being more interested in their etymological derivation from "heal" or "worship."[51] He does not intend two separate groups, for everything that follows, including the architectural and liturgical arrangements, implies an integrated organization in which male and female were joined in an equal "fellowship." Philo uses the two forms of the name merely to distinguish between male and female members. This separate nomenclature is, nevertheless, evidence of women's unusual position.

(2) Philo speaks of the members as "philosophers." This implies that women too were philosophers (89) as Philo used the term. At the time Philo wrote only Musonius Rufus argued similarly.[52]

(3) The seventh day meetings (32–33; no doubt Sabbath) included women as equals.[53] An impression of inequality may remain in Philo's description of a dividing wall between the sexes for reasons of modesty and ease of listening. He seems to assume that the speakers were all male. In what follows, however, no differences between men and women are noted (34–39).

(4) After a long digresssion on meals in pagan society (40–63), Philo turns to the community's 50th day assembly and banquet (64–65), stressing that the members of the community were

"disciples" of "the prophet Moses" (64). "The feast is shared by women also, most of them aged virgins who have kept their chastity not under compulsion, like some of the Greek priestesses, but of their own free will . . ." (68).[54] Men sat on the right and women on the left, but the fundamental fact was that women joined with the men. Exposition and singing followed, punctuated by chanting of closing choruses (80), when men and women participated equally.[55]

(5) In the following vigil (83–89) members formed two antiphonal choirs—one male, one female—in the middle of the dining room (*symposion*), each with its own leader and precentor, with clapping and stomping and complex rising and falling harmonies, perhaps accompanied by wheeling dances.[56] Then all joined together as a single mixed choir, "a copy of the choir set up of old beside the Red Sea in honor of the wonders there wrought" (85),[57] "so filled with ecstasy both men and women that forming a single choir they sang hymns of thanksgiving to God their Savior, the men led by the prophet Moses and the women by the prophetess Miriam" (87). Philo again uses the names Therapeutae and Therapeutrides of this mixed choir, "the treble of the women blending with the bases of the men, [to] create an harmonious consent,[58] music in the truest sense." When dawn came after their all night hymn sing and prayer, each went off to a private sanctuary to pursue philosophy.

This was a voluntary association. Unlike most associations, however, they formed a residential community with common meeting hall and dining room, and monastic living with contemplative cells. They lived ascetic lives of contemplation as "philosophers," with weekly meetings of the whole group and a pentecostal feast, characterized by exposition, singing, dancing, prayer, and a night long vigil. Women and men were equal.[59] There were almost no gender-determined roles, though most leaders may have been males, like the servants at the banquet. There were no stereotyped female roles. They did the same things as men, with similar cells for contemplation, defined but equal space in the meeting room, and common though defined dining facilities. In choral activities men and women had equal and parallel roles. It is less clear if equality extended also to the spoken word. The Therapeutae's leader was "the prophet Moses"; the Therapeutrides' leader was "the prophetess Miriam."[60] There was exact parallelism in leadership, then, founded on a brother and sister who played key roles in Israel's ancient history in Egypt, though we cannot say what this leadership involved. The choice of names for the leaders was deliberate.

THE ORIGINS OF THE THERAPEUTRIDES/THERAPEUTAE

This equivalence had two likely sources of inspiration: the Isis-Osiris cult, active and influential in this period, where a brother and sister played the crucial roles; the Hebrew Bible, with its stories about Moses and Miriam, another brother-sister pair with strong associations with Egypt.[61] The biblical narrative may have prompted scriptural exegetes interested in Miriam and Moses to adapt elements of the story to community needs. A blend of both Egyptian sources provides a sensible background for the impetus to create this community with radical equality between women and men.[62]

Isis-Osiris

(1) In the Herculaneum painting of the Isis cult meeting at dawn for sacrifice, two choirs are ranged up either side of the stairs singing. A precentor or leader directs the choirs in the middle distance. The two mixed choirs of men and women reflects the antiphonal choirs of the Therapeutae, who were arranged partly in two separate choirs and partly as a mixed choir.[63] (2) The Therapeutae's worship, like the worship of Isis, culminated in a dawn choral celebration. Other analogous features included (3) Egyptian provenance, (4) language of initiation, (5) provision in some instances for living within the precincts,[64] (6) dreams, (7) celibacy, (8) and periodic abstention from wine. Women in both participated in priestly and lay roles[65] and sometimes there was a rough equivalence of numbers.

Hebrew Bible

The Therapeutae formed a genuinely Jewish group, whose inspiration lay in Israel's ancient history. The Biblical narratives may have

prompted scriptural exegetes concerned for Egyptian traditions to create a community based on radical equality of women and men. (1)
Miriam was a prophetess (Exod 15:20-21) who danced and sang to the
Lord in the incident at the Red Sea. (2) She was firmly rooted in Egypt
from birth through childhood (Exod 2:4-8)[66] and adulthood. She died
at Kadesh according to one tradition (Num 20:1) before she could
enter the Promised Land, like her brother Moses.[67] (3) She had no children (Num 26:59) and is not usually described as being married,[68] so
she may have qualified as an aged virgin, though no surviving source
says this of her. (4) Miriam and Aaron claimed the Lord had spoken to
them as well (Num 12:1-15); when Miriam was afflicted with leprosy
because of the Lord's anger, Moses interceded and she was healed after
seven days in the wilderness. (5) Only Moses and Miriam appear as
prophet and prophetess in Philo's description of the Therapeutae; he
deliberately leaves Aaron to one side; priests, of whom Aaron was
the progenitor, are barely in view in Philo's description of the
Therapeutae.

The Egyptian ascetic community also reflected the biblical accounts
of Moses and Miriam. There was no reference to Aaron, and only the
slightest reference to priests, for this was a prophetic, not priestly, community. Yet Philo's description ignores their attitude to torah. The community was unusual in the way Miriam was paired with Moses. In fact,
more features of the community's life were taken from the story of
Miriam than of Moses. In the end, however, Miriam's leadership role
among the Therapeutrides, though hinted at in the Hebrew Bible, was
not derived so much from Judaism as from local Egyptian influences,
both Egyptian religion—specifically the Isis cult's liturgical, practical,
and behavioral details—and the Egyptian setting, where Pharaohs and
sister-consorts provided models for the strong role of Miriam.

SUMMARY

In two Egyptian Jewish communities, the Therapeutae and
Leontopolis, women held central religious positions. Among the
Therapeutae, women were the equals of men. While this was highly
unusual in Judaism at the time in which these communities flourished
it was not so unusual in Egypt, where women commonly held priestly
and even high-priestly positions. The status of women in Egypt was

heightened by a reduction in the polarity between the sexes, caused in turn by the monarchy, where "on the highest level, queens are to be found in the traditionally male spheres of government and warfare."[69] Egyptian women also shared power with men in religious spheres. The sharing of power between king and queen—often brother and sister— dovetails with Jewish stories about Moses and Miriam, traditions also connected with Egypt. The practices of both the Therapeutae-Therapeutrides and the Leontopolis community reduced the polarity between the sexes. Men and women at both sites shared cultic activities. This equality was the result, on the one hand, of assimilation to Egypt and, on the other, of exegesis of a Jewish tradition about Moses and Miriam leading the Jews out of Egypt. Both groups, then, viewed themselves as distinctly and purely Jewish.

Further, we have argued, strongly in the case of the Lake Mareotis community and less strongly in the case of the Leontopolis community, that both were viewed by their neighbors and by themselves as voluntary associations. The buildings, organizational structure, activities, and communal features would have suggested that both communities had distinctive and strong associational characteristics.

CHAPTER ELEVEN

BUILDING "A *SYNODOS* . . . AND A PLACE OF THEIR OWN"

INTRODUCTION[1]

In the opinion of most scholars, early Christian buildings derived from house churches on the one hand and Roman basilicas on the other, two useful and relevant models (Chapter 8). I propose, however, a broader architectural background—one that includes both those models—that derives from associations (Chapter 7). Architectural forms adopted by associations were varied; it should be no surprise that among the varied typologies of associations, the forms adopted by churches and synagogues were prominent, since both synagogues and churches were viewed as associations. Obviously, associations were only one model among several, but often the main model in the eyes of outsiders, who needed an analogy to understand this new movement.

I suggest the following general picture. (1) In the earliest period (to 150 C.E.), Romans viewed Christian communities on the analogy of synagogues, which were viewed as associations ("*synodos*" in the title refers to Josephus's description of the Sardis synagogue). (2) In a developmental middle period (ca. 150 to 325 C.E.), when Christianity and Judaism veered apart, churches continued to be thought of as associations. (3) In the post-Constantinian period (325 C.E. onwards), when the association analogy was less relevant, Christian use of the basilica—an architectural form that consciously expressed power, with civic and Imperial implications—contributed to the Church being viewed as part of the power elite (other Christian groups outside the mainstream continued to be more like voluntary associations). The book *Voluntary Associations* establishes the following points:

- associations included religiously discrete groups such as Mithraea, synagogues, and churches, in addition to other associations such as trade, merchant, and philosophical groups;[2]

- most voluntary associations valued patrons and benefactions highly;

- most associations carried on a similar range of functions (communal meals, cultic actions, burials, etc.), despite substantial variations in emphasis;

- the Roman state dealt with these varied groups on much the same basis, even if it sometimes needed to differentiate among them;

- their architecture was varied but shared common features.

ARCHITECTURE

I am convinced an analysis of associational architecture is relevant. The art and architecture of Mithraea, for example, proclaimed the aims and values and ideals of the group for insiders. Even though Mithraea were "self-revealing," Mithraic art was not meant for public display.[3] How then to interpret their cave-like spaces, with a pair of parallel inward-facing benches, on which a small group of participants reclined or knelt in communal meetings? Other evidence of the Mithra cult might imply a strongly hierarchical organization, but the bench arrangement may imply a more "democratic" group. Perhaps the social experience should be read from the archaeology rather than, or in addition to, written descriptions?

The social character of associations was expressed in the built-forms of the *synodos*, *collegium*, *thiasos*, *philosophia*, or *ekklêsia*, for two complementary reasons: (1) groups consciously constructed buildings that expressed their character, as with Mithraea; (2) groups adapted to the character imposed upon them by the built-form of their meeting space, as happened with synagogues' and churches' use of houses. Deliberate architectural expression, the first factor, must lie behind the choice of building type for structures of associations, as we shall summarize later. The second factor, architectural "determinism," is more controversial: nevertheless, both historical and modern examples suggest that the built-form of one's surroundings influences socioreligious developments, whether within church, synagogue, or mystery cult, whether in the modern period or antiquity. Groups take on the character of their spaces.

Social character was expressed in details, too. Statues, busts, and portraits in voluntary associations, along with inscriptions on walls, colonnades, columns, mosaic floors, and frescoes honored patrons and provided an implicit *cursus honorum* among the members. Members and visitors alike were reminded of the rewards of generosity, especially the *timê* ("honor") that accrued to patrons. Dedications attested to the privileges of wealth and social status, of patron-client obligations, and hierarchical relationships. Inscriptions attested to Jews' and Christians' use of this practice, as well; there was no difference between associations, synagogues, and churches, to judge from synagogue (second century B.C.E. to fifth century C.E.) and church epigraphs (fourth to fifth century C.E.). Both sought benefactions and engaged enthusiastically in patronage and honor systems similar to those of other private associations of antiquity.

Buildings for associations have attracted relatively little attention, partly because most were unassuming and partly because the category is flexible. *Collegia* or *thiasoi* turn up, but only infrequently have they been identified as having intrinsic archaeological or architectural interest. Associations have often been overlooked because of excavation strategies, not because they were socially or intellectually unimportant. Sometimes associations were readapted later for other uses, occasionally Christian churches (Mactaris), so that some associations disappeared beneath later uses. Only a few large excavations, such as Ostia, have revealed sufficient buildings to permit generalizations. Because associative buildings were sometimes adapted from houses of patrons and benefactors,[4] an association might be publicly invisible even in antiquity; it became visible only when extensively renovated. Groups were small; a house renovation might have accommodated 15 to 100 members.[5] A group of three houses in Priene adapted for voluntary associations illustrates such residential locations away from the city center.

RECENT STUDIES

Investigations of Egyptian Judaism lead to the conclusion that Egyptian synagogues (and synagogues elsewhere) were seen by members and by society as associations. The inscriptional evidence for Egyptian synagogues is especially strong (see Chapters 8 and 10). The buildings were dedicated to the Ptolemaic king and queen; donors were named alongside the honorees; the buildings were called *proseuchai* ("prayerhouses"); architectural features such as gateways, *periboloi*, *exedrae*, holy gardens, and appurtenances were mentioned. These features suggest that Egyptian *proseuchai* were complex structures, like associations, but since the inscriptions derived from different buildings, their details cannot be combined to provide a coherent building description. The early Jewish community building (*proseuchê* or "prayerhouse" for communal use) represented an important stage on the way to the community's self-definition, the *synagôgê* in its root sense as a group of people. Gradually the terminology altered so that *synagôgê*, originally expressing the communal character of the group, later came to be used for the building as well.

Equally important is the fact that monastic Jewish groups preceded monastic early Christian groups. An ascetic monastic establishment near Alexandria, the Therapeutae, was an early quasi-eremitic experiment emphasizing withdrawal, worship, and contemplation (Chapters 9 and 10). By contrast, the Qumran community was a coenobitic establishment from the same period. Both communities—Qumran and the Therapeutae—had ceased functioning by the early second century. While the sources of early Christian monasticism are unclear, it is remarkable that when significant documentary evidence begins (late third century), both eremitic and coenobitic monastic structures were being developed in both Egypt and Palestine. The only relevant model for the two tracks appears to be Jewish monasticism in Egypt and Palestine about two centuries earlier. This typological analogy is perplexing, yet the parallelism emphasizes the natural Christian takeover of Jewish models.

This quick summary permits emphasizing two points: there were close relationships between churches and synagogues, and both were part of the larger category of associations. The association model was particularly important during the formative period of Christian development. The architecture of churches developed along several main tracks—house-churches, meetinghouses, and basilicas—but the overall development should be interpreted within the context of associations. The differences among these various types should not be exaggerated, since associations utilized all three types. Christian use of these three architectural forms can be traced within the third century, paralleling synagogue developments closely. House-churches were earliest, but there were meetinghouses and purpose-built basilicas already before Constantine (Chapter 8). Speedy and sweeping changes followed Constantine's conversion. House-churches and meetinghouses tended to die out, while monumental basilican civic structures (together with octagonal or round memorial buildings) took over. But even when the basilica became the norm, the form was altered by the influence of features derived from the functional solutions for association buildings.

SOME STRUCTURES

Priene

Three small adaptive religious structures were located at the west end of Agora Street (or West Gate Street) beside the city wall. They provided facilities for Jews, adherents of Cybele, and an Alexander cult. The earliest of the three (soon after Alexander's death) housed a *heroon* for Alexander the Great. Another housed the orgiastic cult of Cybele, Mater Magna of Phrygia, with its strong sense of initiation and the mysteries, whose priests castrated themselves. The latest was a *proseuchê* or *synagôgê*, where Jews and affiliated non-Jews studied, worshiped, and established a communal identity. The juxtaposition of the three cults in neighboring houses implies that all three originated in similar communal conditions; each had matured sufficiently that a benefactor emerged to provide a permanent home, encouraging communal formation and accelerating further development. The three buildings reflected the conditions of many associations, located on the town's edge, relatively invisible, relying on patrons. When the association was given a building, each adapted the house to serve ritual and communal needs for meeting, dining, worship, administration, and storage.

The Alexander and Cybele buildings are so ruined that little can be said. A sacrificial pit and a statue of Cybele identified one building as Cybele's. Alexander reputedly lived beside it when he was at Priene in 334 B.C.E.; an inscription from elsewhere in the city mentioned an Alexandrium and another on this house's doorpost warned that only the pure clothed in white garments could enter the sanctuary. Figurines, including a bust and partial torso of an Alexander-like figure, were found in excavations. The *oecus* (living area) and a room on the north of the courtyard were modified for cultic purposes.

More can be said about the synagogue (second–third century C.E.), at the end of a short lane off Agora Street (see Plate 31). A stele with a menorah, a diagnostic indicator of the Jewish community, was discovered in the excavations (a smaller relief with menorah was found elsewhere). Remains of a Doric order, part of a colonnade that carried the roof over the new assembly hall, were found. Benches provided seating.[6] The Jewish community later negotiated with a neighbor to the east for an additional one square meter for a Torah niche, suggesting developing ritual needs. Other rooms surrounded the main assembly hall and a new entrance was arranged on the west.

A well-known inscription from Stobi amplifies the Priene synagogue's functional character: a patron donated a house as a synagogue but reserved a portion for his family's use (second–third century C.E.). After two phases of synagogue structures, the building was rebuilt as a Christian church.[7] Polycharmus, the original donor, was named in floor inscriptions in stratum I of the synagogue; the following inscription on a column was still in use during the church phase:

> [Claudius] Tiberius Polycharmus, also called Achyrius, father of the synagogue in Stobi, who has conducted himself with all the prescriptions of Judaism, in accordance with a vow, [gave] a house as the holy place, and the *triclinium* with the colonnades [*tetrastoa*], from his own funds, without touching in any way the funds of the sanctuary. But the right to and ownership of the upper story, I, Claudius Tiberius Polycharmus, reserve for myself and my heirs for life. If anyone wishes to make alterations contrary to my decisions, he shall pay the patriarch [of the synagogue] 250,000 denarii. This agreement was made by me. Repairs of the tiles of the upper level are to be made by my heirs and me. (*CIJ* 694, adapted)

A similar but earlier inscription from Acmonia in Phrygia (ca. 60 C.E.) mentioning several patrons is also relevant to Priene:

> This building constructed by Julia Severa was restored by Publius Tyrronius Clades, head of the synagogue for life (*dia biou archisynagôgos*), and Lucius, son of Lucius, head of the synagogue, and Popilius Zotikos, *archôn*, from their own funds and from money contributed: the walls and the ceiling; and they made safe the gates; and all the remaining decorations. The community (*synagôgê*) honored these men with a golden shield on account of their virtuous life and their good will and zeal for the community (*synagôgê*). (*CIJ* 766, adapted)

These inscriptions attest to the selective alteration of various building parts, embellishments to the structure, communal and individual gifts, acknowledgment of patrons, and even the reservation of some parts of the building for a patron's use. They flesh out the social-historical background of gifts of houses to associations, such as the three found in Priene, and make it clear that the use of houses should be seen as part of the larger pattern of association buildings.

Miletus

Though no buildings of associations have been found in nearby Miletus, some surviving inscriptions on the seats of the large Roman theater (second century C.E.) indicate that various associations held reserved seats. These inscriptions have not been published in full, so the range of groups reserving seats is uncertain. Two groups, however, illustrate associative life in a city of the Greek east. Side by side in the theater, seats were reserved for the "Jews and Godfearers" of Miletus, implying a synagogue group, and for the "emperor-loving [*philaugustoi*] goldsmiths."[8] That Jews and Imperial cult members sat side by side underscores the range, importance, and visibility of associations that had seats in the theater in a city such as Miletus.

Ephesus

Given the extensive excavations at Ephesus, it is surprising that no buildings for associations have been identified. About 100 of the 4,000 to 5,000 inscriptions from Ephesus refer to private voluntary associations,[9] comprising 60 groups: 41 trade associations (52 inscriptions) and 19 cultic associations focused on gods and emperors (20 inscriptions). Of the latter, seven refer to the Jewish god, one to Isis/Sarapis, one to Nero along with his mother and his wife, one to Trajan, three to Hadrian, and five generally to the *sebastoi*. Only eight inscriptions mention buildings or building renovations, but since inscriptions require structures on which they can be mounted, there must have been substantially more than eight buildings. The epigraphic information ranges from low-status trade associations (fishermen and fishmongers, cowherds, wool workers, linen workers, bread mixers) through various other groups (bankers, physicians, master builders, mystics, silversmiths, coppersmiths). Religious-cultic associations included Demeter, Dionysus, Hermes, Poseidon, Zeus, Asklepios, as well as the Jewish God and Isis/Sarapis. Among Imperial figures, Nero was the earliest named by a private association; no Flavians were named on inscriptions, though one inscription was dated to Domitian's reign (88/89 C.E.).

One inscription described an association of fishery tollhouse workers, who dedicated a building to Nero, Agrippina, and Octavia (ca. 54–59 C.E.), together with the citizens (*dêmos*) of the Romans and of the

Ephesians. Eighty-eight members, both males and females, contributed; the gifts ranged from four columns at the top end to five
denarii at the bottom.[10] The building, located near the southeast corner
of the harbor, has not been found. It was publicly prominent, to judge
from the stele's inscription, which lists the following architectural elements: 18 columns (including one painted column), Phokaian stone
paving in an "open area" and in the "colonnade beside the *stoa*," tile
roof (300 tiles), and a brick structure (4,000 bricks); rush mats for the
stoa's floor. The construction superintendent, L. Fabricius Vitalis,
donated two of the 18 columns plus the adjacent altars. The structure
was probably a utilitarian, freestanding, brick building with a tile roof.
Its most impressive feature was likely the courtyard with *stoa* (four
columns wide by six columns long would give 18 columns), both of
which were paved attractively in Phokaian marble. In Ephesus, this is
the closest we can get to precision concerning the architectural character of an association building.

Delos

Twenty-four voluntary associations are attested on Delos, including
groups based on ethnic, geographical, or professional factors.[11]
McLean analyzes provisions for the cultic activities of the groups,
examining the Italian Hermaïstai, the Heraclêsiastai of Tyre, the
Poseidoniasts of Berytus, two Serapeia, and a synagogue (in his view,
Samaritan). Most noteworthy is the typological similarity of several of
the buildings, especially the Hellenistic houses adapted for use of various associations, with cultic adaptations that, though different from
each other, had common elements.

The synagogue (early second century B.C.E.) was an adaptation of a
Hellenistic house, built around a large peristyle courtyard (though see
Chapter 12).[12] On one side were two large adjacent rooms, one with
benches and a marble *thronos*, with a suite of smaller rooms. The main
entrance was the peristyle courtyard. The Poseidoniasts (merchants,
shippers, and warehousemen) of Berytus constructed a building before
153 B.C.E., also with a peristyle courtyard, off which were two other
courts, one the cult center with three altars. Off the cult center were
four small parallel rooms, three of which were small shrines (*naoi*), and
along another side of the main courtyard a suite of rooms, partly for

commercial purposes, partly for living areas.[13] Sarapeion A (ca. 220 B.C.E.) was an early adaptation of a house for cultic purposes (known, according to a lengthy epigraph, as "Therapeutae"). A small temple was raised slightly above a sunken courtyard, off which were other rooms at different levels.[14] Sarapeion B had a courtyard with *stoa* on one side, a small temple fronting the court on another side, and a large meeting room with altars and small rooms as shrines (*naoi*).

Sardis

The Imperial court-bath-gymnasium-synagogue complex at Sardis is well known. A monumental Roman bath and a Greek *palaestra* (whose gymnasium rooms have survived in the mostly unexcavated north wing) framed the Imperial cult facilities (Plate 30). The synagogue (third century C.E.?) occupied the matching south wing of the gymnasium (second–third centuries C.E.). The gymnasium, with its educational and philosophical functions, may have seemed appropriate for adaptation by the "*synodos*" (association) of Jews in Sardis, though this portion of the gymnasium had already been remodeled earlier. The use of the space in the interval between gym and synagogue is unclear. Even though the synagogue structure was not likely the direct successor of the earlier building that Josephus describes, the decree he records is relevant (Chapter 7):

> Lucius Antonius, son of Marcus, proquaestor and propraetor, to the magistrates, council and people of Sardis, greetings. Jewish citizens of yours [*v.l.*, ours] have come to me and pointed out that from the earliest times they have had an association [*synodos*] of their own in accordance with their native laws and a place of their own [*topon idion*], in which they decide their affairs and controversies with one another. . . . (Josephus, *Ant.* 14.235, ca. 50–49 B.C.E.)

The Jewish community in Sardis (1) had been considered an association (*synodos*) since the mid-first century B.C.E., (2) with "a place of its own" (3) where it decided its own affairs. (4) Later it moved into grander quarters in the gymnasium's south wing, a major public structure, (5) where it was juxtaposed with the Imperial cult (see Miletus above). Its building was larger than typical for associations (though see below on Pergamon, Ostia, Pompeii, and Sufetula); its rich decoration, extensive inscriptions, large forecourt, and adjacent shops, can be paralleled among other associations.

Pergamon

Three important association structures in Pergamon are particularly relevant: a philosophical hall, a "hall of benches," and a Sarapeion.[15] They illustrate well the broad range of association buildings. These three very different associations on the main street were all purpose-built and shared strong cultic concerns; their formal differences prohibit facile generalizations about buildings for associations.

The philosophers' association (early first century B.C.E.) comprised an entry hall facing on the processional way, bath, meeting hall, and cult area (all opening off the entry) (Plate 33). The meeting hall was a raked theatral seating area (thirteen curved rows averaging six meters, holding about 150 persons), with a wide opening to the entrance. This unusually formal arrangement—like an *odeion* or *ekklêsiastêrion*—distinguished audience from teacher. East of this was a handsomely finished room with a niche opposite the door, probably used as a *heroon*, and busts, one of which was of Diodorus Pasparos, to whom the association was dedicated. His benefactions probably included the decorative marble work that identified this as a high-status association. West of the theatral room was a multiroom bath.

The nearby hall of benches was part of a complex of shops and houses on a lane off the processional way, overlying earlier houses but not constructed from them (first–second century C.E.) (Plate 32). Its main space was like two large *triclinia* (dining rooms), whose open ends faced each other; members reclined on high, wide dining benches around the room's perimeter. The fronts of the benches, which had niches in them, were so high that stairs were needed to get on the benches. The diners' attention focused on two cult altars associated with Dionysus. There may have been ancillary service rooms on the south, but these cannot be clearly identified. The hall of benches represents a form continuous with the *triclinium*-centered adaptations of houses familiar from other associations.

The Sarapeion ("Red Hall"; early second century C.E.) in the lower town was entered through a large *peribolos* (100x200 m) with landscaped gardens. The courtyard probably held an earlier temple to Isis, in addition to the large basilica (26x60 m), with reversed apse and stairs to the roof. Below the basilica floor, a tunnel gave access to a huge seated statue of Sarapis on a large platform, so that priests could speak from Sarapis's mouth. The high brick walls of the basilica (surviving to

19 m) originally faced with marble and alabaster still give the impression of wealth, power, and influence.

Pompeii

The extensive excavations of Pompeii have not disclosed as many associations as might be expected, perhaps because associations were suppressed after the riots of 59 C.E. (Tacitus, *Annals* 14.7.4). The Villa Imperiale, with its long promenade, three or four meeting rooms, barrel-vaulted banquet hall, ladies' dining room, and other facilities, likely could be "hired for an evening by a *collegium* or *sodalicum* that had no clubhouse of its own."[16] The Temple of Isis, rebuilt from the foundations by a patron, N. Popidius Celsinus, just north of the large theater, was a small temple within a four-sided peristyle, from which five wide doorways gave onto a large rectangular hall for ritual meals, with Egyptianizing frescoes.[17] The building's form repeats closely a fresco of the worship of Isis with priests, altar, and two facing choirs or groups of worshipers from Herculaneum (Chapter 10). Outside the walls of Pompeii, the Villa of the Mysteries was a large country villa with atrium, peristyle, *tablinum*, several *triclinia*, a large wine press and even larger kitchen. Though it is not certain if it was ever used as an association building, the frescoes in one large room illustrate clearly the ritual of a Dionysiac cult in the period, and are therefore useful evidence for the character of cult-associations. The Insula Iuliae Felicis was a military association with bath, swimming pool, dining areas, shops with mezzanines, upper story apartments, colonnades, and gardens.[18]

Ostia

Ostia's guilds were not suppressed, and numerous important, sometimes imposing, *collegia* can be identified, by one count fifty-nine.[19] Two buildings across the street from one another near the western end of town reflected Ostia's wealthy ambience. On the south side of the *Decumanus* was a handsomely articulated School of Trajan, on the north side an equally substantial Association of Shipbuilders. The same association built both, perhaps, as a coordinated effort to impress Ostia with the shipbuilders' influence. The School of Trajan had a columned entrance; a formal courtyard within was dominated on one side of the axial approach by a statue of Trajan; beyond, a long raised pool down the center dominated another courtyard, at the end of which was a fine *triclinium*. Across the street, the Shipbuilders Association's building had an entry, courtyard, axial temple, *stoai*, with another courtyard beyond—one of five similarly designed complexes in Ostia.

The guild of Ostia's firemen, the Vigiles, was altogether different. The barracks centered on a large courtyard surrounded by portico and rooms on several floors and shops along one side. The courtyard focused on an Imperial cult chapel, inside which a low platform held altars to Antoninus Pius, Lucius Verus, L. Septimius Severus, and two to Marcus Aurelius; outside the portico held statues to other Imperial figures. The association of builders (Julio-Claudian) met in a building with open courtyard, portico, five *triclinia*, chapel, kitchen, and other rooms. An inscription records details of another association building (143 C.E.), listing various contributions, among which were a statue and two busts of Marcus Aurelius, five busts of Antoninus, busts of Lucius Verus, Commodus, Concordia. Also recorded were six benches, four tables and two stools, hot baths with heating apparatus, candelabra, six mattresses, and four cushions, along with distributions of gifts to all the members.[20] These associations were closely tied to members of the Imperial family.

An imposing triangular courtyard just inside the Porta Laurentina held temples for Cybele, Attis, and Bellona,[21] including separate guild buildings for the *cannophori* (reed bearers), *dendrophori* (tree bearers) and the *hastiferi* (spear carriers), where the *taurobolium* was practiced. Near the Via della Foce was a building for Sarapis (127 C.E.) with living quarters; there was also a cult to Isis, though the building has not yet been found; and there were at least 15 Mithraea throughout the city, none suggesting wealth.[22]

Outside the Porta Marina was the well-known first-century and later synagogue, with successive adaptations of an earlier house (Chapter 12).[23] A large hall with *aedicula* (Torah shrine) dominated the final scheme; there was a second main room (with benches) for community meetings and meals, an adjacent kitchen, and ancillary spaces. The Ostia synagogue is a good example of a house adaptation that must initially have been invisible, but with successive renovations came to be a visible element in the neighborhood.[24]

North Africa

Among a number of relevant association structures I note two only. At Mactaris (modern Makhtar), an imposing association for the Iuventutes—an imperially sponsored quasi-military youth association that helped keep the peace—was designed around an attractive peristyle courtyard. A church, a later conversion of the Iuventutes' association, overlies part of the original association building; it entailed a substantial new structure built from earlier materials. And at Sufetula (modern Sbeitla) a very large and finely designed association provided for the needs of a guild of craftsmen, with hall, apsidal *triclinium*, and numerous workshops, all laid out around a handsome peristyle courtyard. These are two of the larger associations, and in the one case the appropriateness of the transition from voluntary association with Imperial overtones to church demonstrates an important aspect of the close relationship of associations and churches.

Syria-Palestine

The evidence from the east for associations is not very strong, but it is important for understanding the relevance of association structures for early Christian communities. The destruction of Dura Europos (about 257 C.E.), a military town on the Empire's fringe, preserved important second–third century C.E. evidence of several significant adaptive buildings: Mithra, Gaddes, Zeus, the Palmyrene gods, a synagogue, and a church, where the underlying houses can be traced with varying degrees of success.[25] Their urban locations in mainly residential areas beside the city wall parallel the Priene associations; they were richly decorated in a common Syrian/Parthian style. This group of associations provides a striking snapshot of developments as one moves from the second through the third to the fourth centuries, when houses were still being adapted but beginning to show differentiated—in some cases monumental—features, specific to the developing needs of the group.

I leave to one side the growing body of pre-70 C.E. synagogues in the region and other relevant structures (e.g., the late first century C.E. Mithraeum at Caesarea Maritima) to allude parenthetically to early church architecture in Jordan and Syria. The Dura church (230s C.E.) is the earliest significant Christian structure. Recently S. Thomas

Parker (North Carolina State) and Mary Louise Mussell (Ottawa) have
claimed that Aqaba in Jordan, only half a century later, boasted a purpose-built church (290s C.E.). If correct, this is the oldest known structure built as a church, built in a somewhat crude basilican style. Such
pre-Constantinian evidence of Christian structures, on the one hand
wholly similar to other cult-association buildings and on the other hand
rather novel in an informal adaptation of a basilican style for a purpose-built structure, is important for understanding early Christian
developments.

The situation in Jordan and southern Syria in the Byzantine period
was startling. Madaba had 14 known churches, nearby Umm er-Rasas
had 15, Gerasa (Jerash) and Umm al-Jimal each had 15, and nearby
Khirbet es-Samra had 8, all archaeologically established (by contrast,
Pella had six churches, Bostra three, and Canatha two). These are minimum numbers, since debris or still-inhabited areas of some cities may
hide other churches. No similarly small region had such a remarkable
concentration of churches, which suggests that Jordan may have been
the greatest early center of Christianity, more important and influential than standard histories suggest. With the lone exception of
Jerusalem, which had comparable but smaller numbers (11 in
Jerusalem proper, 8 on the Mount of Olives, by my count, though an
ancient pilgrim reports 24 on the Mount of Olives alone!), nowhere
else in Judea had similar concentrations of early church structures.
Even if one were to interpret the evidence from Madaba, Umm er-
Rasas, Gerasa, Umm al-Jimal, and Khirbet es-Samra as churches for
neighborhoods, there are many more churches than one would expect.
Larger urban centers such as Ephesus, Hierapolis, Laodicea, Corinth,
Philippi, Thessalonica—to name some with Pauline connections—had
nothing like these numbers. The combination of the large numbers (67
churches in five provincial towns) and the early dating of some church
buildings (ca. 230 C.E. at Dura; ca. 290 C.E. at Aqaba) in the region
underscores the importance of Jordan and southern Syria for the
developing history of early Christian communities. Thinking of
churches as associations may help understand this unusual situation.

ANALYTICAL COMMENTS

The architectural typology of these associations suggests something
about their contributions to community formation.

Domestic: Priene (Alexander, Cybele, synagogue); Dura (church, synagogue, Gaddes, Mithra); Delos (synagogue, Serapeia); Ostia (synagogue); Pompeii (mysteries)

Domestic-style associations were often cultic in function; religious convictions prompted the gift of a house for the cult's needs. In their initial phases they borrowed the general domestic character of the patron's house, but they gradually diverged from that model as they were renovated and adapted to meet developing needs of the community. They were organized architectonically around the house's peristyle courtyard, but the room most often used as the association's center was the *triclinium*, which often dominated the facilities. Especially in domestic association buildings, patrons continued to play significant roles in the life of the association (e.g., Stobi, Acmonia), and might continue to use parts of the house. Christian associations with domestic origins were like other religious or secular associations. Cultic activities were integrated with community-building activities, and the use of domestic facilities, especially the important *triclinium*, is noted in the literature (e.g., Luke–Acts, Paul, 1 Peter, 2–3 John, Didache, Ignatius, etc.).

Odeion-like: Pergamon (philosophia)

The theatral-style seating found at Pergamon was uncommon. The building distinguished between philosopher and audience, and emphasized the role and authority of the speaker in a kind of one-directional conversation. The group might still have functioned as a genuine community—as the bath and the cultic area with niche, altar, and statues alongside the lecture hall suggest—but its structures underplayed that communal character. A theatral model for church structures was not pursued, though churches developed a similar directional, focused, authority-based model of communal organization.

Study: Aphrodisias (philosophical building); Priene, Sardis, Delos, Dura (synagogues); Sardis and elsewhere (gymnasia for philosophical study)

Collective study was emphasized in several associations. The use of benches around several sides of a hall in synagogues conveyed architecturally the formal importance of study; some early synagogues had a separate *Beth ha-Midrash* (especially in the Holy Land as at Gamla and Chorazin, perhaps Cana). A special seat sometimes identified a "president" in the "seat of Moses," both a functional and a status differentiation (in selecting the "president" or *archisynagôgos*, wealth or benefactions probably played a role). Surprisingly, this was not a model adopted by the church, with the exception of two churches at Herodium, suggesting that communal study was rarely articulated as a communal priority.

Prayer: Mithraea, Synagogues, and Cultic Spaces

It was common to conduct prayers in association buildings, of course, but only the Jewish community created *proseuchai* ("prayer houses"). Though early Christians shared this religious activity with Mithraists and most other cult groups, churches were not specifically prayer-houses. Important as prayer was, architectural expression of prayer was relatively uncommon in the ordinary communal setting of early Christianity, except for monastic complexes. It might be noted that eremitic monasteries, both Jewish and Christian, had cells (*kella*) for individual monks that were specifically designed at a very early stage for prayer and meditation, focused often on a niche to which devotion was directed (Chapter 9).

Dining: Pergamon (Hall of Benches); Ostia (trade associations, School of Trajan); Pompeii (Isis, Villa of the Mysteries); Sufetula (trade association)

Dining in a *triclinium* was a core aspect of the life of *collegia, thiasoi, synodoi, philosophiai*, and *ekklêsiai*. The triclinium emphasized the importance of communal meals as a formative model, whether in synagogue, church, or Mithraeum. Among churches, this activity was crucial for two or three centuries, when house-churches were the norm. After Constantine, this activity disappeared, except in monastic—especially coenobitic—structures, where the refectory replaced the *triclinium*. In churches, the community-forming common meals were replaced by liturgical and cultic celebrations within the main basilican meeting space.

Insulae were used to accommodate voluntary associations in Ostia (military association; trade association) and other large cities. Churches also could be accommodated in rooms of an *insula*,[26] as archaeological evidence attests in Rome. The development is best thought of as a sub-category of the dining function of associations, since some of the associations that can be assessed accommodated their needs within street-front taverns, usually ground floor *tabernae* or *cauponae* in *insulae*.

Legal-cultic: Pergamon (Sarapeion); Aqaba (church)

Small local "basilican" churches, particularly in the early period (Aqaba), unlike later Imperial-style basilicas, were modeled either on adaptations of basilicas for associations or on basilican synagogues. When associations adopted a basilican model, with apse as the place of cultic veneration housing a god's, emperor's, or patron's statue, they might utilize a variety of configurations: with ancillary rooms, with the basilican structure on one side of a courtyard, with narthex, and so on. Some such structures were later adapted for use as churches (e.g., Mactaris in Tunisia; Sarapeion in Pergamon), emphasizing that this form of association was appropriate for a Christian community. The basilica became the model of choice for churches after Constantine adopted Christianity, primarily but not exclusively in cases of Imperial patronage (Bethlehem's Church of the Nativity, Jerusalem's Church of the Holy Sepulcher and Eleona Church, Rome's St. Peter's, etc.). Some features of these monumental basilicas may not have derived from earlier Roman basilicas but from association complexes, such as entry, courtyard, narthex, ancillary rooms. The basilican form, when absorbed into Christianity, was a hybrid.

Initiation-Sacrificial: Ostia (Cybele, Attis, Bellona, Shipbuilders, and others); Pompeii (Isis); Delos (Sarapeion A, Sarapeion B)

Associations whose main purpose was cultic tended to have structures whose forms reflected the sacrificial needs of the cult. Typically this meant the provision of a *naos*-like structure for the cult-statue, with additional facilities surrounding this, including provision for the group to meet, usually in a courtyard, and provision for communal dining. The courtyard-temple was usually raised above the courtyard on a podium, an arrangement not ordinarily found in churches, though occasionally other elements of the layout can be found in Christian buildings.

In some associations, exclusion and controlled access were important (Dionysiac or Eleusinian or Isiaian structures). Christianity as a mystery may have drawn from these models, especially the emphasis on entry into the community and its ritual. There was soon extensive refinement and elaboration of provision for baptisms in churches and monasteries, usually in a symbolically significant location, and even with symbolically significant tanks shaped, for example, as a vulva, symbolizing the new birth (Sufetula). The inspiration for these developments may have come more from mystery associations than from inherently necessary theological or communal concerns within Christianity.

Conclusion

This chapter has attempted a broad preliminary analysis of buildings for associations, as a basis for understanding early Christian practices. Though such a study should be carried out more fully and for its own sake (with narrower chronological and geographical limits), for the present purpose a few conclusions may be valid.

- Associations were a widespread fact of life, but buildings for associations fitted no one pattern. As a functional grouping of related activities, they formed a complex matrix of architectural types.

- Synagogues looked and behaved like voluntary associations. As they developed first in Diaspora, they shared in this architectural complexity (with communal emphasis, benches, meals, worship, courtyards, ancillary spaces, etc). Within the life of the *polis*, they adopted patterns of behavior similar to associations, such as reserving seats in the theater (Miletus) or finding a donor to give them a house (Priene, Dura, etc.).

- Churches, too, behaved like associations; sometimes they took over voluntary associations and reused them (Mactaris, Pergamon). Only occasionally did a church take over and reuse the *cella* of pagan temple (e.g., Olba in Turkey); more often the temple was torn down and the site reused (Gerasa, Jerusalem, Damascus). With the Constantinian triumph, the dominant architectural solution was the use of the basilica as the prototype for churches, yet associations were influential in providing some architectural elements in typical church buildings.

- Patronage and benefaction, with the typical memorials to them in inscriptions and images (and the veneration of images of influential figures), were found in numerous churches in all areas, similar to the practices of associations. Architectural features were also borrowed, such as atria, enclosed courtyards, narthexes, complex ancillary spaces, and so on. Monastic complexes, especially coenobitic monasteries, likewise had associational features.

- Recognizing the links between associational and early Christian building practices fundamentally influences an understanding of social-historical factors operative on the church. Church practices (initiation, membership, devotion to the gods, dining), and building typologies (adaptation of domestic spaces, utilization of sacrificial and basilican models) were comparable to other associations.

- The shift to formal, official, and powerful models of church building—the basilica—and away from communally oriented buildings of the kind found in associations was a decisive change in churches' self-definition.

AN ARCHITECTURAL CASE FOR SYNAGOGUES
AS ASSOCIATIONS

INTRODUCTION[1]

The general case for seeing various kinds of ancient religious buildings as associations applies especially to interpreting synagogues as associations, since the origins of synagogues are so controversial. Some synagogues discussed in previous chapters (Ostia, Delos, Priene; see Chapters 7, 8, 11) will be examined in more detail here. Ancient synagogues were complex social organizations; they took architectural form, especially in the Diaspora, in similarly complex ways. My concern in this chapter is architectural and comparative, though this concern is relevant to broader issues, because ancient buildings, like modern ones, both shaped behavior and were shaped by the actions and functions carried on within. Synagogues might be modeled architecturally on association buildings without needing to be viewed politically as associations or to operate internally exactly like associations, though I consider the similarities very close.[2] I argue that the strongest and most general hypothesis on synagogue origins derives from associations; to make the case, I concentrate on early buildings in the Diaspora, with only a brief glance at the Jewish homeland.

Synagogues' origins did not lie in a historical crisis or specific challenge but were the result of lengthy experimentation with building forms learned first in the Diaspora.[3] Evidence for the architectural origins of synagogues—as distinct from theoretical or causative explanations—is found in a combination of literary, archaeological, and epigraphic information, though none of the sources answers directly questions of origins or analogies. There is room for uncertainty and speculation. Nevertheless, the case is strong for claiming that associations were models for synagogues; cumulative lines of evidence converge on association buildings in a Diaspora setting.

Table 12.1: Comparison of Judean and Diaspora Synagogues
to the End of the First Century C.E.

DIASPORA			PALESTINE		
SITE	EVID	DATE	SITE	EVID	DATE
NORTH AFRICA			**JUDEA**		
Schedia	ins	246–221 B.C.E.	Jerusalem: Theodotos	ins	1 c. C.E.
Arsinöe/Crocodilopolis	ins	246–221 B.C.E.	Jerusalem: Freedmen	NT	1 c. C.E.
Fayum	ins	11 May 218 B.C.E.	Qumran	arch/lit	1 c. C.E.
Athribis	ins	180–145 B.C.E.	Jericho	arch	70–50 B.C.E
Nitriai	ins	144–116 B.C.E.	Herodium	arch	60s C.E.
Xenephyris	ins	144–116 B.C..E.	Masada	arch	60s C.E.
Alexandria	ins	2 c. B.C.E.	Modi'in	arch	60s C.E.
Alexandria	Philo	1 c. C.E.	Qiryat Sefer	arch	1 c. C.E.
Uncertain Location	ins	c. 130 or 40 B.C.E.	Horvat 'Ethri	arch	1–2 C.E.
Leontopolis	ins/lit	mid-2 c. B.C.E.			1 c. C.E.
Therapeutae	Philo	1 c. B.C.E.	**GALILEE**		
Naucratis	ins	30 B.C.E.–14 C.E.	Tiberias	Jos	1 c. C.E.
Uncertain Location	ins	1 c. C.E.	Capernaum	NT/arch?	1 c. C.E.
Berenice	ins	late 1 c. B.C.E.	Nazareth	NT	1 c. C.E.
BLACK SEA					
Panticapaea	ins	81 C.E.	**GAULANITIS**		
Chersonesus	ins	1 c. C.E.	Gamla I	arch	1 c. C.E.
Phanagoria	ins	16 C.E.	Gamla II?	arch	1 c. C.E.
Gorgippia	ins	1st c. C.E.	**COAST CITIES**		
SYRIA			Dor (Diaspora?)	Jos	1 c. C.E.
Damascus	NT/ Jos	2- 1 c. B.C.E.	Caesarea Maritima	Jos/NT/ arch?	1 c. C.E.
Antioch on Orontes	Jos	2 B.C.E.	**UNCERTAIN**		
			Migdal	arch	
			Chorazin	arch	
			Khirbet Qana	arch	

DIASPORA		
SITE	EVID	DATE
GREECE & ASIA		
Acmonia	ins	1 c. C.E.
Ephesus	Jos/NT	1 c. B.C.E.
Halicarnassus	Jos	1 c. B.C.E.
Sardis	Jos/arch?	1 c. B.C.E.
Delos-Judean	arch/ins	2 c. B.C.E.
Delos-Samaritan	ins	2 c. B.C.E.
Salamis	NT	1 c. C.E.
Pisidian Antioch	NT	1 c. C.E.
Iconium	NT	1 c. C.E.
Thessalonica	NT	1 c. C.E.
Beroea	NT	1 c. C.E.
Athens	NT	1 c. C.E.
Corinth	NT	1 c. C.E.
Philippi	NT	1 c. C.E.
Laodicea	unc	
Tralles	unc	
Miletus	unc	
ITALY		
Ostia	ins/arch	1 c. C.E.
Rome-Augustesians	ins	1 c. B.C.E.
Agrippesians	ins	1 c. B.C.E.
Volumnians	ins	1 c. B.C.E.
Hebrews	ins	1 c. B.C.E.
Herodians	ins	1 c. B.C.E.
Marano-Campania	ins	1 c. B.C.E.

ins = inscriptional evidence
lit = literary allusion
Jos = Josephus
NT = New Testament
arch = archaeological evidence
unc = uncertain

This list summarizes the evidence for synagogue buildings constructed before about 100 C.E.,[4] categorized as either Palestinian or Diaspora (though it is debatable how to list Dor and Caesarea). Each building stands separately to emphasize the relationship of Diaspora and Palestinian evidence (see Table 8.1).[5]

DISTRIBUTION AND DATING OF EVIDENCE

Diaspora / Palestine Comparison

Not all the locations in Table 12.1 are certain. Some implied by literary allusions (Acts, Josephus's decrees) should be accepted only with
caution;[6] yet the literary evidence for widespread distribution of synagogues is as important as the archaeological remains. (1) The Diaspora
evidence (40+ synagogues) strongly outweighs the Palestinian evidence
(about 15 synagogues, even when Caesarea Maritima, Dor, and
Tiberias, with their strong Hellenistic and Roman influences, are
included). (2) About 20 Diaspora buildings (mostly based on relatively
precise inscriptional evidence) precede the first century C.E., compared
with one or two Judean structures (Qumran and Jericho, both debated).
(3) There is only one reliable early inscription from Palestine against
more than 20 early inscriptions from the Diaspora, though in almost all
inscriptional cases no relevant building has been found. The Jewish
Diaspora followed the Roman "epigraphic habit" in marking their
buildings but this habit was less consistently followed in Palestine. (4)
Nevertheless, there are eight excavated buildings in the homeland,
against two in the Diaspora.[7] (This imbalance may be attributed to two
factors: the synagogue stands out as the sole public building in
Palestinian villages and towns, and Israeli archaeologists have focused
attention on such structures, whereas in larger Diaspora centers they
were relatively more modest and often unnoticed.) (5) The evidence is
complex and varied in both settings, with overlapping inscriptional, literary, and archaeological data; the juxtaposition of material and literary evidence provides a relatively coherent picture of early synagogues.

Architectural Comparison

Though in many cases we can only guess at size and form, these nearly
60 synagogues covered a range of building types. Some may have been
basilican (Tiberias, Alexandria); many were simple meeting places
(Gamla, Masada); some were house adaptations (Jericho, Priene, Dura);
some were complex structures (Delos, Ostia, Jerusalem, Qumran). The
later classic architectural form of the synagogue was the basilica, a
Roman form despite its Greek name (*basilikos*), implying it was for large

gatherings, often beside a public open space, with interior columns usually supporting a clerestory roof, with one or more apses, and a platform. Synagogues apparently used this form long before Constantine popularized its use for churches, so the common claim that Jewish synagogues copied Christian basilicas needs qualification.

Two other forms for synagogues developed alongside the basilican form. The simple "meeting place" was important, not only for synagogues but also for other religious communities and associations (Chapter 9). And the "house synagogue," as Michael White has shown, was an important strategy.[8] In various communities and associations (Christianity, Mithraism), houses of wealthy patrons were converted into community meeting places in a strategy that nicely suited an age of benefactions and patronal activity. The modifications were usually modest and lacked external visibility, unless they included raised roofs, inscribed lintels, or extensions.

Terminology

The terminology used of Jewish public buildings varied by region, period, and type of evidence. Outsiders preferred some terms; Jews may have preferred others (as the North African and Bosporan inscriptional evidence suggests). The range is wide: *proseuchê, synagôgê, synagôgion, synodos, collegium, thiasos, sabbateion, politeuma, therapeutai, amphitheatron, hieron*, and so on.[9] The preferred Jewish terms were *proseuchê* and *synagôgê*, terms utilized by other associations also. Occasionally Jews used terms preferred by non-Jews: *synodos, thiasos*, and *therapeutai*. In the early period *proseuchê* was the commonest term, but by the first century C.E. *synagôgê* was being used, initially as a term for the community but soon as a building term.[10]

Josephus illustrates the overlap in terminology between associations and Jewish communities (*Ant.* 14.215; set in Parium and Delos). He claims to have seen an inscription of Julius Caesar's forbidding "religious societies to assemble [*thiasous synagesthai*] in the city, but [Jews] alone he did not forbid to do so or to collect contributions of money or to hold common meals. Similarly do I forbid other religious assemblies [*allous thiasous*] to assemble and feast in accordance with their native customs and ordinances [*ta patria ethê kai nomima synagesthai te kai estiasthai*]." Since "other *thiasoi*" had been forbidden to meet, Caesar's treatment of Judaism was in one sense *sui generis*, but their general classification was among *thiasoi*. Josephus, following Caesar, used a term for Jews that he deemed appropriate. The *synagôgê* was not a unique category in first-century C.E. Roman society but viewed as part of a larger classification, *thiasoi*.

Architectural Details

Inscriptional and literary descriptions allude to architectural details that suggest that some early synagogue buildings were carefully articulated complexes. From Egyptian inscriptions we find: *exedra*, gateway (*pylôn*), *peribolos*, appurtenances, and gardens. Josephus's decrees refer to a dining room (*triclinium* for common meals), facilities for observing rites, sacrifice, courtroom, and library. The Theodotos inscription mentions facilities for assembly, reading, teaching, rooms, hostel, and water installations.[11] This inscriptional evidence from Egypt, Asia Minor and Judea confirms that prior to 100 C.E. synagogues commonly had complex architectural forms; it coheres with archaeological evidence from Delos and Ostia. Some synagogues had sophisticated design features.

If we include Qumran and Jericho as synagogues (Plates 28, 29), a roughly analogous picture emerges for Judea. In ordinary towns and villages, however, such as Gamla (Plate 25) and Qiryat Sefer, public buildings were simpler multipurpose structures that provided for a range of functions, without architecturally differentiated spaces. The literary and epigraphic records imply that Diaspora buildings were relatively more complex architecturally at an earlier period than Judean buildings. These design details of buildings align synagogues with association buildings.

DIASPORA SYNAGOGUES IN CONTEXT

Associations in the Greek and Roman worlds typically had a meeting room, *triclinium*, and a variety of other ancillary spaces. Their architectural forms and those of synagogues overlapped. The most instructive sites to demonstrate these analogies are Ostia, Delos, and Priene, all with relevant comparanda. We have already seen that the synagogues at these sites were found among other associations. In each case, the Jewish building had close analogies to nearby associations.

Regrettably, the absence of an inventory of association buildings makes comparisons difficult. We know association buildings best in cases of gradual decline in the cities' fortunes and where a large percentage of the city has been excavated (Ostia, Delos, and Priene), or where large numbers of inscriptions have been recovered (Ephesus; see generally Chapter 11). But we need an analysis of the strategies used in locating, constructing, adapting, embellishing, and identifying association buildings, including those religious groups of the ancient world that were perceived as associations. Was there implied rivalry or even overt competition among associations, which vied for the attention of the citizens? Comparative analysis of association buildings would shed light on the conditions under which Judaism and early Christianity operated.

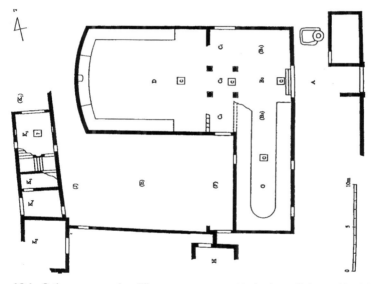

Figure 12.1. *Ostia synagogue, plan. The synagogue was outside the city walls in a residential area. The plan shows the first century C.E. phase, with entrance at A, meeting hall in D, and triclinium in G. The area in E-F was later enclosed to become a new triclinium, and G was converted to a kitchen. Plan courtesy of Anders Runesson.*

Ostia

About 60 associations or *collegia* are known archaeologically at Ostia, some rather impressive and complex. The distribution of cultic, trade, and civic associations follows no simple pattern, though they tend to be in secondary locations on main streets.[12] Some wealthy associations built their own structures, some met in temples; their activities included assemblies, worship, banquets, and provision of water.

The synagogue at Ostia, according to the Lund analysis,[13] was a purpose-built building from the latter part of the first century C.E. (Figure 12.1, Plate 34)[14] The synagogue's design—with provision for assembly, banqueting, worship, and a water supply—aligns it closely with other Ostian associations. The earliest plan included a *triclinium* (in the area subsequently utilized as a kitchen), assembly room, and cistern. The assembly had a gently curved west wall with benches on three sides and a bema at the center of the curved wall. The *triclinium* had benches on three sides of a narrow room, in the standard form but with relatively little space between the bench fronts. At this early stage, the synagogue lacked the later monumental Torah niche and the additional room on the southwest later used as the *triclinium*. Some issues are still being debated.[15] Was the area originally residential? Was the synagogue adapted from a private house? How prominent was it initially? When did it begin to function as a synagogue? It is certain, however, that when it began to be used as a Jewish communal building, Ostians would have viewed it as sharing the architectural idiom of other associations. Its most noticeable difference from others—though as the temple to Bona Dea shows, not unique—was that it stood outside the city.

The house builders' guild (*Caseggiato dei Triclini*) offers relevant comparisons. The shape of the synagogue's meeting room was repeated in the shape of the curved bench in the house builders' *tablinum*, and its *triclinium* was similar to three of the house builders' four *triclinia*. Their building was originally constructed early in the reign of Hadrian; an inscription on a statue base dedicated to Septimius Severus identifies the association as for the *fabri tignuari*.[16] It was designed around a central courtyard that gave it "an aristocratic air,"[17] though the upper floor and roof were carried on utilitarian brick piers. Ten shops faced the streets, four on the north and six on the south. Four stairwells served rooms on the upper floor(s). Four *triclinia* on the east opened into the courtyard, matched by four other rooms on the west.[18] The *tablinum*, with its gently curved "bench" that partly mimics the arrangement in the synagogue, was centered on the south side of the courtyard opposite the main door (the synagogue was not designed around a courtyard). A public latrine (*forica*) was introduced into two shops at the southeast corner in the fourth century C.E.[19] The house builders association may have had another "guild temple" on the eastern *decumanus*—the *Tempio collegiale*—to express loyalty to Pertinax; if so, the *Caseggiato dei Triclini* was used for guild affairs.[20]

Associations in Ostia did not hew to one line only. Different organizations constructed a variety of facilities in response to their needs. The Ostia synagogue's analogies with one of the wealthiest of all the associations—the house builders' guild—fit comfortably within the typology of Ostian association buildings.

Delos

For a century and a half Delos was an independent *polis*; Rome made it a free port (166 B.C.E.), challenging the dominance of Rhodes.[21] Numerous communities of Italians and easterners—Phoenicians, Egyptians, Jews, and Samaritans—established themselves on the island during the late second/early first century B.C.E. But Delos declined after two sackings (Mithradates VI, 88 B.C.E.; pirates, 69 B.C.E.), and its commercial opportunities were assumed by Corinth (refounded 44 B.C.E.).[22] More than 24 associations are known on Delos, primarily from inscriptions. Most foreign cults were on the higher ground below Mount Kynthos, though some foreign associations such as the Poseidoniasts of Berytos, were in the city by the sacred harbor.

Four Jewish inscriptions were found inside a building on the northeast coast, identified as a synagogue (area GD 80).[23] A fifth inscription was found in an *insula* (area GD 79),[24] between it and the stadium and gymnasium (area GD 76, 77, 78).[25] Two clearly Samaritan inscriptions were discovered in 1979–1980 about 90 m north of the synagogue.[26] Were there one or two synagogues? The epigraphic evidence is ambiguous.[27] McLean argues for only one, believing the building remains were those of a Samaritan synagogue, based on the recent inscriptions;[28] White argues for two buildings.[29] It seems likelier that White is correct, that there were two buildings, that the building remains were Jewish, and that the Samaritan synagogue has yet to be found.

To elaborate on the previous description (Chapter 11), the remains of the synagogue comprise a suite of rooms on the west with a peristyle courtyard on the east, though its eastern portico, if it had one, has fallen into the sea.[30] The suite of rooms may have been part of a larger (unexcavated) structure. A large benched meeting hall was subdivided into two rooms in one of the renovation phases, at which time the central of three doors was blocked.[31] In the subdivided form, a *thronos* occupied a central position on the bench on the west wall of the northern room, opposite its main door. There were also benches in the northwest corner of the courtyard's *stoa*. South of the meeting room(s) was a suite of six rooms, one with a large cistern partly under the southern half of the meeting room.

Michael White thinks the building was converted from a second-century B.C.E. house in two stages during the early first century B.C.E.[32] Donald Binder and Anders Runesson, argue for a purpose-built building (possibly a non-Jewish association originally, which was taken over by Jews after 88 B.C.E.),[33] on the basis of its similarity in plan and scale to the building of the Poseidoniasts of Berytos.[34] The size of the peristyle columns, and meeting hall were consistent with a purpose-built building (the column drums were 45–55 cm in diameter, and thus about 3.60 to 4.60 m. high, plus about 1 m entablature; White). The disagreements need not concern us, since the main point is that the synagogue was closely analogous to the Poseidoniasts' building, in just the same way as the synagogue in Ostia was analogous to the house builders' guild. This point stands independent of the debate over house-synagogue adaptation versus purpose-built synagogue.

Priene

To solidify the point about synagogues and associations, I refer again to Priene. Priene was refounded on a new site (ca. 350 B.C.E.) after an earlier site was abandoned because of the silting up of the Meander River.[35] The new harbor also became unusable by the time of Augustus as silting continued. Its subsequent history, though basically unknown, included Priene's gradual deterioration and abandonment. This meant that Priene remained relatively intact, like Ostia, with little Roman overbuilding, so the urban design is still an exceptional example of a Hippodamian plan molded over a sloping topography. Hellenistic civic buildings and houses survive. Three houses on the south side of Agora Street (West Gate Street) along the city wall were adapted to meet the needs of three cultic associations: one dedicated to Cybele (ignored here), another for the hero cult of Alexander, and a third for the Jewish community.[36] All were originally houses, adapted for associational needs at various periods.

The House of Alexander was the earliest to be converted to association use. Wiegand and Schrader referred to it as a *hieros oikos*, adapted from a typical Hellenistic private house with courtyard and smaller rooms surrounding it.[37] In its renovated state it included a sanctuary 9.2x19.0 m, with three columns down the middle and a podium in the northeast corner. Parts of two tables were discovered, one in front of the podium and another in the room northeast of the courtyard. The door to the courtyard, whose left doorpost had an inscription saying that none shall enter the "holy sanctuary" except those wearing white clothing, was from a lane on the west.[38] Between the courtyard and the sanctuary was a porch with three statue bases in a row. Portions of two statues of Alexander were found, and elsewhere another inscription was found referring to restorations to the sacred place devoted to Alexander in 140 B.C.E. The renovations were carried out in a somewhat slipshod manner, for much of the east wall utilized the wall of the house on that side.[39]

The synagogue was the latest of the three adaptations (Plate 31). There has been little discussion of the building's dating or of the history of the Jewish community in Priene and how that history connected with overall urban developments.[40] White's suggested three stages of adaptation may well be correct, but there is a need for precision on the timing of those stages and the house's architectural history, as White points out. The renovations turned the Hellenistic courtyard into a monumentalized meeting hall, with a new door from the west lane into a new porch area (built over some earlier small rooms that had opened off the lane), all axially related to a new niche on the east built in space borrowed from the neighboring house. The original *oecus* (living room) and *prostas* (vestibule) became ancillary spaces, with a new entrance directly into the *oecus*, though the excavation reports are unclear if there was a direct connection from this suite of rooms into the meeting hall. New stylobates were constructed in the meeting hall, the north one slightly splayed, with one column drum still roughly in place. A bench ran along a new north wall of the meeting hall. Beside the niche were a small basin, a tall rectangular stele (2.20 m high) decorated with a menorah (fallen, but still in place), a broken slab (0.52x0.60 m) with a relief of two peacocks and a *lulav* (neither of which has been properly studied).[41] The synagogue project was not as large as the renovation of Alexander's house, but was similar in several major respects: its use of an earlier house, disappearance of the domestic functions, creation of a new entrance, insertion of a major meeting hall with new columns and roof, providion of a new liturgical area (in Alexander's house, with a small podium, table, sacrificial area, and nearby statues of Alexander; in the synagogue, with a small niche, basin, and two menorah reliefs).

Three of the oldest synagogues in the Diaspora show that synagogues were constructed on the same lines as other association buildings. The three differed from each other, underscoring that there was no single model for synagogues, just as there was no single association model. Without a common model, each Jewish community used the example of near-at-hand associations as an appropriate solution for its needs.

LEVINE ON ASSOCIATIONS

Lee Levine considers three possible explanations of synagogue origins: the city-gate (which he prefers), the Jerusalem temple, and association buildings.[42] With respect to associations he argues (1) that Roman authorities used words such as *thiasoi* or *collegia* or *synodoi* without precision; (2) that Jewish communities were not simply associations because they had a "far greater range of activities" and "rights" than associations; (3) that Jewish communities were not "voluntary." These points are essentially correct and show how Jewish communities might be differentiated from other associations. But they do not subvert the claim that synagogues were associations, for the variety among associations was wide enough that—architecturally, organizationally, and behaviorally—synagogues fell naturally within those limits. He deals more extensively in his book with the bearing of voluntary associations on the analysis of synagogues. He says, amongst other things:

- Synagogues shifted gradually from communal centers with religious components to houses of worship with communal activities (2–4).

- Sometimes *proseuchai* incorporated associations, so that in Egypt we find a *synodos*, burial society, Sambathic association, and other professional associations (80–81, 87, 129, 368).[43] The same is true in Aphrodisias and possibly in Miletus, where the theater had seats for "Godfearers of the Jews" beside an association of *philaugustoi*.

- Josephus's decrees describe activities that complement and sometimes dovetail with the epigraphic linguistic evidence.[44] Levine grants that Jews "freely borrowed different frameworks from their surroundings, with models ranging from the *politeuma* (e.g., Berenice, 89–96) and *collegium*, through the *synodos*, *koinon* and *thiasos*" (121, cf. 106–7). He considers this a "high degree of Hellenization," though it might be merely a case of synagogues' "borrowing."

- Synagogue functions—both in Judea and Diaspora (124–25)—were analogous to those of associations: professional and social groups, benevolent societies, manumissions, dining and kitchens, courts, charity, study, library, residence, incubation (368–85). Synagogues were "not *sui generis*."

- Synagogues "borrowed much from Greco-Roman associations (*thiasos*, *koinon*, *collegia*, etc.)" yet "no analogy does justice to the unique role of this institution" (159). "Diaspora synagogues functioned, and indeed were often referred to, as associations; they followed one of several Greco-Roman models" (589).

Levine grants most of what this chapter claims, that the clearest analogy for synagogues—whether one thinks of architecture, functions, organization, popular perceptions, or legal status—was the association. Since associations developed in the Greek and Roman worlds, Judaism, I suggest, first borrowed from this model in the Diaspora. Levine draws back from this obvious conclusion, because synagogues had more functions, were more complex, and could not be contained entirely by an associational model. Though he rejects *sui generis* arguments, in the end he seems to make a *sui generis* argument for synagogues. If the difference were merely one of degree, it seems proper to include synagogues within the general classification associations. The institution of the synagogue emerged out of those social and religious groups called associations; the architectural similarities of their buildings reinforce that origin.

JUDEA

A brief addendum on Judea. The majority of early Palestinian synagogues were simple communal meeting halls: Gamla, Masada, Herodium, Qiryat Sefer, Modi'in, and Horvat 'Ethri (Chapter 7). Three cases, however, were analogous to complex Diaspora buildings: Jerusalem, Qumran, and Jericho. All three pose difficulties, however. The Theodotos inscription from Jerusalem is suggestively descriptive, but without archaeological remains all that can be said is it had an assembly hall for reading and teaching, chambers and water installation as an inn. Our knowledge of Qumran comes from the archaeological investigation of the buildings, but only parts of the notebooks and some of the photographs have been published.[45] The debates over meeting rooms and anything that might be called a "synagogue" are intense (see Plate 28). If the Qumran group was an association, like the Therapeutae in Egypt (Chapters 9, 10), it was appropriate that it should have had communal spaces: dining and pantry (rooms 77, 86, 89), kitchen (rooms 41, 38), benched meeting room (room 4), work areas, living areas, and water installations for ritual purity. The meeting spaces seem to have included a dining room (77), meeting room (30), and council room (4). The recently excavated building at Jericho has been published in limited detail to date (see Plate 29). It was a complex structure, adapted from a house, with *triclinium*, kitchen, meeting hall, *mikveh*, entrance, and other rooms. If Ehud Netzer is correct that this was a synagogue, it is another example of an early Judean synagogue that broke away from the simple meeting hall structure of the majority.

The above examples are suggestive: the Theodotos synagogue in Jerusalem met the needs of foreign visitors (*tois chrêzousin apo xenês*); the Qumran complex was for a group voluntarily assembled in the desert awaiting God's future decisive acts; the Jericho synagogue was set in the context of late Hellenistic elite palaces. All were early, and all three drew their architectural inspiration from traditions other than those that later led to the more common simple meeting halls.

I note two other considerations. (1) Caesarea Maritima,[46] Dor, and Tiberias all had synagogues from the late Hellenistic/early Roman periods. All three were in contact with the wider Roman world and may have had natural affinities with synagogues elsewhere. Lack of information about them prohibits their effective inclusion in this discussion. (2) Recent study of Samaritan synagogues suggests a distribution both geographically and chronologically similar to Judean synagogues, possibly with a similar range of types.[47] Future histories of synagogues in the eastern Mediterranean need to take this parallel information into account, which seems in general to reinforce the above conclusion. We might eventually construct a stemma of developments that bridged disjunctions between Diaspora and Palestine, between Judean and Samaritan synagogues.

CONCLUSION

I have located Jewish synagogues architecturally in the context of the eastern Mediterranean in a setting of Roman tolerance of Jewish communities. Jewish communal buildings fitted comfortably within the range of *synodoi*, *thiasoi*, and *collegia* in that Diaspora world. While Jewish communities might form a discrete subgroup among other associations, they adopted architectural forms that were part of a common vocabulary of buildings from the same period and met a variety of communal needs, like other associations.

The range of archaeological, epigraphic, and literary evidence for studying synagogues forces us methodologically to use logic, inference, intuition, and even speculation. But we must still begin with evidence, not hypothetical or theoretical constructs. Can one reasonably work towards a conclusion on origins? I think so. The literary and epigraphic evidence demonstrates early and widespread distribution of Jewish public buildings in the Diaspora. This creates a presumption, a hypothesis, a relatively simple explanation—but not proof—that synagogues originated in the Diaspora. Other hypotheses are possible, but they must posit either long silences or complex processes of which we have few hints. A more complex process of development is also possible that might include two discrete processes, one leading to simple meeting room synagogues, another leading to more highly articulated synagogues.[48] Still, chronological priority and weight of evidence falls clearly on the side of the Diaspora and within the context of associations.

PART FOUR

JUDEA AND JERUSALEM

CHAPTER THIRTEEN

LAW AND PIETY IN HEROD'S ARCHITECTURE[1]

> Herod's rule destroyed the internal organization of the Jewish commu-
> nity. In contrast to the Hasmonean kings who had ruled jointly with the
> popular institutions, Herod abolished all traditional autonomous institu-
> tions, and in practice did away with the authority of the Torah, although
> this never took official form. One of the aims of his policy was to
> strengthen the foreign element in Eretz Israel and to bring the kingdom
> into the Roman Hellenistic cultural orbit.[2]

Shimon Appelbaum summarized an earlier consensus on Herod the
Great in the *Encyclopedia Judaica*. He balanced this judgment to some
extent with more positive statements about Herod's actions, though he
took away much of their force when he said, "Herod had to try to make
himself accepted to some extent by the Jews." He listed these features as
follows: an unsuccessful attempt to win over the Pharisees; care not to
flout the external expressions of the religion of Israel; refraining from
putting images of idols or his own portrait on coins; refusal to allow his
sister Salome to marry an uncircumcised Nabatean prince; and the
rebuilding of the temple. Despite these actions, according to
Appelbaum, Herod could not win the hearts of the Jewish people. They
viewed him as "the destroyer of their traditional institutions, the mur-
derer of their kings and leaders, and the agent of a foreign government."
The result was that "Herod was more acceptable to the Jews of the exile
than to those of Eretz Israel."[3]

The evidence, especially the physical architectural evidence,
requires a subtler view of Herod. His attitude to torah, while no doubt
equivocal, was not destructive; his sense of piety, while not entirely
Jewish, was much larger; and his intentions should be more generously
stated. My hypothesis, briefly, is that Herod's buildings showed a complex form of piety—but a piety whose objects went beyond what was
acceptable in Judaism—and a concern for torah that worked within its
limitations, as he understood them. These concerns were expressed
both in Eretz Israel and in the Diaspora, but reaction to them differed

in accordance with the accommodation reached with Hellenism in different areas.

HEROD'S ARCHITECTURE

First, I survey Herod's buildings to assess the degree to which his buildings recognized torah's prohibition against figurative representations. The question is one that has not yet been thoroughly canvassed; indeed, it cannot be because of the incomplete state of the relevant excavations and the uncertainty of their results.[4] I suggest that one of the major influences operating on Herod in some of his buildings was the Jewish religious requirement not to represent living things figuratively, a stronger view of one of the points Appelbaum noted. Before turning to that, I briefly describe three major influences on Herod.

(1) Hellenistic architecture was obviously the most vigorous cultural determinant on Herod's buildings. This exuberant post-Hellenic movement, exemplified best in Asia Minor, expressed a kind of magnificence and richness that classical Greek architecture never achieved. Many scholars of the mid-twentieth century saw Hellenistic architecture—like Baroque—as a degeneration,[5] but for sheer pomp and excitement nothing exceeded some of the great urban developments of the late Hellenistic period, such as Pergamon, Palmyra, Baalbek, Gerasa, and Lepcis Magna. Herod drew on Hellenistic architecture and carried some of its tendencies even further than its earlier high points. Josephus says of Herod's Sebaste (*Ant.* 15.298), "He also made it splendid in order to leave to posterity a monument of the humanity that arose from his love of beauty."

(2) Herod was a Romanophile. Some aspects of his buildings can only be compared to and understood against the developments of Roman architecture,[6] itself influenced, of course, by both Greek and Hellenistic architecture.[7] Many Roman influences are best seen in technical and technological aspects of his buildings, such as the use of arch and dome, or *opus recticulatum* (a concrete wall faced with stones in a diamond pattern). In formal design-oriented questions the influence is not so great; in fact it is possible that occasionally an apparent influence may be evidence of

Herod's influence on later Roman structures. Some comparisons between Augustus and Herod might need to be turned on their ear.[8]

(3) Herod was influenced by the Orient. He was an oriental despot whose need for power, pomp, and pleasure could be understood better against the background of the east than as an aspect of western Imperial power. Augustus and Herod, though friends, were not alike. Augustus's building program, though like Herod's in many respects, was motivated by piety towards the Roman state and Roman gods. While Herod was also motivated by piety in part, his buildings often expressed power, pomp, and pleasure, revealing instead influences from the model of the oriental despot.

These three influences—Hellenistic, Roman, and Oriental—infused Herod's buildings with an eclectic excitement that was rare in the ancient world. His architectural conceptions were exhilarating, conveying a seventeenth-century Baroque sense of panache. The relative importance of these influences on Herod varied from building to building and place to place. It is crucial, however, to notice one remarkable phenomenon: in Herod's villas at Jericho (where we have the remains of three villas), at Masada (where we have the remains of two large and several small villas), and at Herodium (where we have the remains of Herod's upper villa and a large lower complex), there is no archaeological evidence of decoration that would have offended scruples based on the second commandment. This is remarkable in two ways. First, Herod's villas were the cutting edge of his architectural program, more advanced, more imaginative, and more Roman than many of his other buildings; it is surprising, if Herod were a radical Hellenist who only reluctantly acceded to Jewish scruples, that these buildings did not share the Roman and Greek love of the human figure. Second, his villas were his most private buildings; if Herod had no personal scruples about figurative representations, it is surprising that he felt it inappropriate in these villas to include images in the decor. The archaeology even suggests that the revolutionaries had no need to strip away or paint over Herodian decoration, 75 or 100 years later. It was not needed. The Western Palace at Masada, one of two large palace complexes, makes the point: the mosaics show Herod's sensitivity to Jewish religious views; they used geometric designs of a

Hellenistic kind mixed with designs prominent in Jewish art, such as olive branches, pomegranates, fig and vine leaves.

Herod had, of course, numerous other living quarters—the Antonia fortress, his Jerusalem palace, various residences (Caesarea, Sebaste, and Panias), and fortresses in numerous other parts of Judea. While we might naturally expect his residences in Jerusalem to have followed the practice outlined, the most revealing evidence would come from villas where Roman influences were stronger. While there is inadequate evidence for all these sites, only the palace in Caesarea Maritima, a largely non-Jewish city, seems to have had a statue.

The rebuilding of the temple in Jerusalem contained, with one important exception, no figures. Herod would be expected to be as careful as possible there, even by his detractors. It is surprising, however, that the building form itself did not cause any controversy, because that form was very strongly Hellenistic and Roman, especially in the features that Herod introduced (Chapter 16). The one exception was an eagle over a gate or door. At the announcement of Herod's death Judas and Mathias led a revolt "to pull down those structures which had been erected in defiance of the law," and specifically this notorious eagle (*War* 1.648–55; *Ant.* 17.146–63). At this stage we need only notice that it was the sole offending item in the temple complex and that Josephus did not list any other specific objectives for Judas' and Mathias' anger.

Herod also built a theater, a gymnasium, and an amphitheater in Jerusalem, according to Josephus. Any of these might have had decoration and appurtenances that would be offensive, just as they might have been the scenes of activities that contravened torah. The so-called "trophies incident" (*Ant.* 15.267–91) was one such: "Herod went still farther in departing from the native customs and corrupted the ancient way of life." Josephus refers this incident to the theater (or more likely the amphitheater), which Herod had decorated with "trophies," understood by some Jews to be "images of men." The gymnasium may also have had offensive aspects to it, though Herod's cannot have been the first such gymnasium (1 Macc 1:11–15). During the Hellenistic period the form of gymnasia underwent impressive developments that turned them into cultural centers with libraries and lecture rooms.[9] This made it a favored object of benefactions. It was also in Jewish eyes a place where nakedness was the rule, where pederasty might be encouraged, and where religious rites essential to the gymnasium were required. Yet Josephus says nothing of the second-century B.C.E. structure.

The situation away from Jerusalem may not have been the same as at Jerusalem, and the evidence is less good. Caesarea, Sebaste, and Panias were all new foundations or refoundations; each contained a temple dedicated to Augustus and Roma, with at least one major statue of the Emperor (*War* 1.417).[10] These temples reflected Augustus's practice to allow a greater degree of emperor worship in the provinces, especially in the east, than was tolerable in Rome. Herod was probably the earliest client-king to show his loyalty to Augustus in this way. He built his temples to Augustus and Roma where they would cause minimum offense: in the far north at Panias, already dedicated to the god Pan; at Samaria, renamed Sebaste in honor of the Emperor, where Jewish sentiment was hardly a factor; and at Caesarea Maritima on the coast, originally the Hellenistic city of Strato's Tower.

In the latter case light is shed on the religious situation by Josephus's comment on the origins of the revolt in 66–74 C.E. He refers to an armed revolt at Caesarea Maritima that the Greeks won, and in commenting on this he argues that Herod would not have erected statues and buildings there if he had intended the city for Jews (*War* 2.266–70, 284–92; contrast *Ant.* 20.173, 182, 184; Tacitus, *Annals* 14.65). If the implication is correct, Herod differentiated between the parts of his kingdom. He selected Caesarea Maritima as the site of a Temple to Augustus and Roma precisely because it was largely non-Jewish. Despite the pagan population, a synagogue may have functioned in Caesarea during the Herodian period, though we have no evidence for conflict between Jews and non-Jews prior to the time of Agrippa I.[11] Herod was able to satisfy the Jewish population that his actions were not contrary to Jewish religious interests, and it may be that one element in this agenda was a synagogue. Since Herod, so far as we know, built no synagogues, it may be arguable that his temple-oriented piety (Chapter 16) was a mark of religious conservatism.

Herod had something to do with the building of the Temple of Ba'al Shamim at Si'a (the temple itself? the forecourt?). A statue base (which was found in the nineteenth century but is now lost) once held a statue of Herod, the only known statue of him. I view this structure in the same terms as the Temples to Augustus and Roma, as evidence of Herod's desire to make a religious statement to non-Jews. Much could be said of his buildings in the Greco-Roman world. Here, too, he made bold statements by building gymnasia, theaters, halls, porticoes, marketplaces, colonnaded streets, aqueducts, and so on. They

extended from his own kingdom north and west to the far side of the
Grecian peninsula; none are known in Italy or in North Africa.

Two religious buildings stand out. (1) Herod went cap in hand to
Rhodes in 31 B.C.E. to meet the victorious Octavian—later Augustus—
before Octavian punished him for supporting Mark Antony. Probably
soon thereafter he restored the city, provided a subsidy for its ailing
shipyards, and rebuilt the Pythian Temple of Apollo. (2) The games at
Olympia had gone downhill, mainly because of the Roman victory
over the Achaian League in 146 B.C.E. and later because of the civil
wars. Herod was named life president of the games at the 192nd
Olympiad in 12 B.C.E., an action without precedent in the previous 768
years (*Ant.* 16.149). Herod provided an endowment so large that the
games were restored to their normal stature. He was likely involved in
the restoration of the Temple to Zeus at Olympia, for it was during just
this period that the Temple of Zeus and the other decaying buildings
of Olympia were restored. While we have no epigraphic or literary evidence of Herod's direct involvement in these projects, it is a reasonable
conjecture that his role as patron of the games was connected with a
significant building project. Herod's role at Olympia seems extraordi-
nary. The fact that he was the client king of a minor Jewish state, albeit
the protégé of Augustus, makes it more significant.

We get a mixed picture of Herod's architecture. In his own private
villas, in the temple, and in most other structures in Judea for which we
have evidence, he obeyed the second commandment and did nothing
to offend family and citizens. He built structures dedicated to Augustus
and Roma in Caesarea Maritima, Sebaste, and Panias, with statues in
each. In Si'a he may have been partly responsible for a Temple to Ba'al
Shamim, and he or someone else included a statue of himself. In more
distant regions, even when—as in the case of Rhodes—there was a
Jewish community nearby, he restored temples to Greek gods.
Incomplete as the literary and archaeological evidence is, questions are
posed about Herod's religious views. Was he completely unprincipled?
Or was there an integrated view behind this?

THE SECOND COMMANDMENT

The second commandment (Exod 20:4) puts two prohibitions side by
side: "you shall not make yourself a graven image, or any likeness of

anything that is in the heaven above, in the earth beneath, or in the water under the earth." The prohibition against idolatry in the first clause and the prohibition against figurative representations from the natural world in the second are logically and practically different; to some extent they are treated differently. It is surprising, however, at first sight how much attention focused on the former of these two prohibitions (idolatry), and how little attention was paid to the latter (images). When the "image" rather than the "idol" was the subject, it was usually because the image was an object of worship. Missing from literature contemporary with Herod's buildings are discussions of figurative representations and architectural decoration.

Philo's discussions are very limited (*Decal.* 66–81; *Spec.* 1.21–31) and shed little light. In the *Mishnah*, the main thrust of tractate '*Abodah Zarah* deals with what is forbidden because of associations with idolatry. The most general statement on images is relatively late, attributed to Rabbi Meir: "All images are forbidden because they are worshipped once a year." Beside this are two other opinions: "the Sages say: Only that is forbidden which bears in the hand a staff or a bird or a sphere [symbols of rule]; Rabban Simeon ben Gamaliel says: That which bears ought in its hand" ('*Abod. Zar.* 3.1). Only the latest opinion was a general prohibition, while earlier ones were less general. In the earlier opinions the reason for the prohibition against imagery had to do with rulers and perhaps ruler-worship. The general danger was the possibility of idolatry. There are two other relevant *halakoth* in the *Mishnah*, the first of which is attributed to Rabban Gamaliel, a near contemporary of Herod's:

> Proklos, the son of Philosophus [or Proklos the Philosopher] asked Rabban Gamaliel in Acre [Ptolemais] while he was bathing in the Bath of Aphrodite, and said to him, "It is written in your Law "And there shall cleave nought of the devoted thing to their hand." Why [then] dost thou bathe in the Bath of Aphrodite?" He answered "One may not make answer in the bath." And when he came out he said, "I came not within her limits: she came within mine! They do not say, 'Let us make a bath for Aphrodite,' but 'Let us make an Aphrodite as an adornment for the bath.' Moreover, if they would give thee much money thou wouldest not enter in before thy goddess naked or after suffering pollution, nor wouldest thou make water before her! Yet this goddess stands at the mouth of the gutter and all the people make water before her." It is written, "Their gods" only; thus what is treated as a god is forbidden, but what is not treated as a god is permitted. (*m.* '*Abod. Zar.* 3:4)

> If a garden or a bathhouse belonged to an idol, they may be used if
> there is no need to offer thanks, but not if there is need to offer thanks.
> If they belonged both to the idol and to others, they may be used
> whether there is need to offer thanks or no need. (*m. ʿAbod. Zar.* 4:3)

Surprise at finding Gamaliel in the Bath of Aphrodite in Ptolemais
(where Herod, incidentally, built a gymnasium) is hardly mitigated by
Gamaliel's argument that the bath was for people's use, not for
Aphrodite's. He claims her presence there was incidental; from this the
Mishnah draws the practical general principle if a thing is treated as a
god it is forbidden, if not it is permitted. The second saying expands
on and is consistent with it: gardens or bathhouses are permitted if
there is no need to give thanks to the god, and if a thing belongs both
to the god and to others it is irrelevant whether thanks is required. Both
halakoth are surprisingly lenient.

In the same chapter, an unattributed *halakah* says that an idol whose
worshipers have abandoned it in time of peace was permitted (though
not in time of war), and idol-pedestals set up in honor of kings were
always permitted, since it was only when kings pass by they set up
images on them (*m. ʿAbod. Zar.* 4:6). Regardless of whether this last statement could have applied to Herod's temples to Augustus or even to the
temple at Siʿa, the *Mishnah*'s leniency is remarkable. The next *halakah* (*m.
ʿAbod. Zar.* 4:7) refers to the Elders' visit to Rome (ca. 97 C.E.) and is similarly lenient. God does not destroy idols such as the sun, moon, stars,
and planets, because it would be necessary to destroy the thing worshiped, and humans need the sun, moon, stars, and planets. So why not
save those and destroy the rest? Because then everyone would say of the
things left, "See, they are real gods!" These two *halakoth* follow on a discussion of how one desecrates an idol; the general view seems to be that
an Israelite cannot desecrate a gentile idol (*m. ʿAbod. Zar.* 4:4–5).

With reference to buildings themselves, the closest we come in the
Mishnah to a general statement is this: "none may help them to build a
basilica, scaffold, stadium, or judges' tribunal;[12] but one may help them
to build public baths or bathhouses; yet when they have reached the
vaulting where they set up the idol it is forbidden [to help them] to
build" (*m. ʿAbod. Zar.* 1:7). Again, there is little explicit help in dating the
halakah, but it reflects a situation (perhaps pre-135 C.E.) in which Jewish
collaboration in pagan buildings was common; a general practical prohibition legislated against the building of a part of the structure that
held an idol.

Even as Judaism was regulating itself in a Roman context, where the need to preserve the worshiping community from association with idolatry was strong, the *Mishnah* was relatively lenient. Its concerns focused on idolatry, the more challenging aspect of the second commandment, and even then it did not prohibit all contact with idols. On the less extreme aspect of the second commandment, imagery, it had little to say except to prohibit images having to do with the exercise of power, especially legal power. This helps to explain the incident of the eagle that is treated at considerable length by Josephus (*War* 1.648–55; *Ant.* 17.146–67, 206–9). In rebuilding the temple a golden eagle had been placed over the great gate. Judas and Matthias, on learning Herod was near to death, counseled young followers to tear down all "those structures that had been erected in defiance of their fathers' laws. It was, in fact," says Josephus, "unlawful to place in the temple either images or busts or any representation whatsoever of a living creature." The students hacked the eagle down as a major violation, whether because it was nearest to hand or because it was in the temple, or both. Herod was still alive; retribution fell swiftly.

Three things stand out from this account. First, Josephus claims that it was illegal to put an image *in the temple*, though the first temple and possibly the second temple had select images such as cherubim. Second, Jews had used the temple with the eagle over the great gate—whichever gate that was—for some time, without the temple being considered defiled and prohibited (except perhaps by the Qumran community). And third, the discussion in the *Mishnah* may provide the precise reason for this symbol in particular being held to be offensive. The eagle was a symbol of Roman power and Imperial rule. The *halakah* that prohibits images of birds may come from just such a *Sitz im Leben*. We can also infer from Josephus's account that Jews did not find many other occasions for offence in Herod's structures.

Josephus reinforces this impression elsewhere when he says that he himself, as a general in the revolutionary forces, pressed for the demolition of a palace in Galilee built by Herod's son (Antipas the Tetrarch) because it contained representations of animals (*Life* 65). This may in fact be the same palace, also built by Antipas, to which Josephus objects because it was built on a gravesite (*Ant.* 18.39). Josephus criticized Herod infrequently for his buildings; most of his criticism was reserved for Herod's appallingly bad relationships with family members. Josephus's descriptions of his palaces do not contain references to illegal ornamentation. In the confusion and near anarchy following Herod's death, several of his palaces were burned by local mob uprisings (Jericho, Sepphoris, and Betharamphtha), but for different reasons (Chapter 2). The eagle was the one major decorative element to which exception was taken.

Josephus claims that Herod was forced to depart from Jewish customs and regulations because of his attention to Caesar and the Romans, so he erected temples outside Jewish territory, for then Jews would not have to put up with statues and sculpture (*Ant.* 15.328–30).[13] Josephus uses an example inside Jerusalem to illustrate how Herod departed from the customs and corrupted the ancient way of life (*Ant.* 15.267). Herod put inscriptions and trophies around the walls of the Jerusalem theater, thought to be images surrounded by weapons. Either there was some misunderstanding of the artifacts or Herod altered the trophies, for the anger of most Jews was soon dissipated. Only a small core of die-hards continued the opposition.

Josephus knew the second commandment well. He summarizes, "the second commands us to make no image of any living creature for adoration" (*Ant.* 3.91; see also *Apion* 1.199; 2.12, 73–79). He knew, however, that there were violations of this command in Herod's buildings: Herod abode by the regulations in Judea, but he violated it in several temples to Augustus outside Judea. Why were these not more of a difficulty to his fellow Jews? Josephus may provide a partial explanation of this when he uses the phrase "for adoration" (*proskynein*) to limit the second commandment's intention. The application of the second commandment was much wider than simply buildings, of course. Herod's sensitivity to images is shown in his coins. Unlike his grandson, Philip the Tetrarch (4 B.C.E.–34 C.E.), but like his Hasmonean predecessors, Herod never used human figures on his coins (though he did use familiar imagery such as the double cornucopia and anchor). He sometimes used gentile imagery such as the caduceus, the tripod, and the *thymiatêrion*. One coin bore the image of an eagle, which may be related to the massive project to rebuild the temple. None of his coins portrayed any of his buildings, but a coin of Philip represents the facade of Herod's Temple to Roma and Augustus at Panias.[14] The picture of Herod's coinage is not inconsistent either with the impression created by his buildings or by Josephus's portrait: he did not directly contravene the second commandment but he weakened its application.

Surprisingly, there were extensive deviations from the second commandment in later synagogues and synagogue decoration. Decorative motifs that would be considered offensive were also found in upper-class houses in Jerusalem in the Second Temple period. Sensitivity to a strict interpretation of torah was diminished in contemporaneous and later structures. Hellenism could be accommodated to the second commandment. Herod was an important representative example of a process of accommodation, but he was neither a primary instance of the weakening of the second commandment in Judaism, nor was he responsible for the subsequent deviations.

HEROD'S PIETY

Were Herod's reticence with respect to the second commandment and his enthusiasm for the rebuilding of the temple to be understood merely as politically motivated attitudes, or were they a reflection of piety and respect for the Torah? Josephus provides evaluations of Herod's piety; I begin with one of the places where Josephus specifically emphasizes the far-ranging extent of Herod's building activities (*War* 1.400–28). The transition from a discussion of Herod's relationship with Octavian to a discussion of his buildings is made in this way: "Because of his favored position he advanced to the utmost prosperity; his noble spirit rose to greater heights, and his lofty ambition was mainly directed to works of piety" (*War* 1.400). The list begins with a strong "therefore" (*goun*). He categorizes structures according to the kind of piety shown; the pattern of the list is important.

- First, Jewish piety was shown by the temple restoration at incalculable cost;
- Then his patrons were commemorated:
  (a) The fortress was restored and named in honor of Antony.
  (b) The palace's two parts were named the Caesareum and the Agrippeum.
  (c) A whole city was rebuilt and renamed Sebaste in honor of Caesar.
  (d) A new temple at Panias was dedicated to Augustus.
  (e) New buildings at Jericho were named after Augustus and Agrippa. "In short," says Josephus, "one can mention no suitable spot within his realm, which he left destitute of some mark of homage to Caesar. And then he let his esteem overflow to the provinces."

(f) Thus, he rebuilt at Strato's Tower a new city named Caesarea Maritima in honor of Augustus; its tallest tower was named Drusion after Caesar's stepson.

(g) He rebuilt another harbor town, Anthedon, and renamed it Agrippias.

- Then Josephus notes Herod's filial devotion and lists these memorials:

  (a) Herod founded a new city named Antipatris after his father;

  (b) He dedicated the fortress Cypros above Jericho to his mother;

  (c) He called a tower in Jerusalem by his brother Phasael's name;

  (d) He built a whole city north of Jericho, also dedicated to Phasael.

- Then he named things after himself, such as a fortress and also a fortress-villa, both named Herodium;

- Then Josephus describes the buildings outside Herod's realm and these, to our slight surprise, are not in a single case described as memorials or as acts of piety, but are described briefly and functionally. Olympia gets special attention because the whole world benefited from Herod's generosity.

The long list is followed by a panegyric to Herod which leads to a treatment of his domestic troubles, towards the end of which is a long speech containing a pious sentiment Josephus attributes to Herod: "I have served the deity so faithfully that I may hope for the longest term of life" (*War* 1.462). Josephus, not always an enthusiastic admirer of Herod, deliberately constructs the section to balance positive and negative features of Herod: on the one hand the terrible litany of family woes, and on the other hand the vast list of building projects.[15] Two claims to piety, one by Josephus and one by Herod, bracket the whole. Herod's constructive side is described in terms of his orthodox piety shown in the temple, his piety towards his patron Augustus and Augustus's family and friends, his filial piety towards his own family, his self-aggrandizement, and his wider acts of charity not described as piety at all.

Josephus expands on the more orthodox side of Herod's piety in *Antiquities* 15.380–87, where he creates a speech for Herod on the occasion of the decision to reconstruct the temple in Jerusalem. He praises his own achievements in raising the prestige of Judaism: "I think I have, by the will of God, brought the Jewish nation to such a state of prosperity as it has never known before." Josephus attests Herod's perception of his own piety several times, nowhere more clearly than when he is quoted as saying (*War* 1:462), "I have served the deity so faithfully that I hope for long life." He refers to his building projects, and then claims, "the enterprise which I now propose to undertake is the most pious and beautiful one of our time. Since, by the will of God, I am now ruler and there continues to be a long period of peace and an abundance of wealth and great revenues, and—what is of most importance—the Romans are my loyal friends, I will by this act of piety make full return to God for the gift of this kingdom." Such a self-serving speech need not reflect either Herod's words or a genuine act of piety. But its presence, and the following evaluation of him (*Ant.* 15.388–425) may suggest widespread support for Herod's rebuilding of the temple, a structure that at the time Josephus wrote had been totally demolished by Josephus's patron. Josephus could simply have pinned Judaism's troubles on Herod; he could have seen (as later Christian writers did) the destruction of the temple as the result of the sins of Judeans or merely of Herod. Josephus does not. Instead, he paints a favorable picture of a person who had been stereotyped as a "bad thing."[16]

Josephus's evaluation (*Ant.* 16.150–59) ties together the two sides of Herod. "Herod loved honors and he was led to display generosity wherever there was reason to hope for future remembrance or present reputation, but since he was involved in expenses greater than his means, he was compelled to be harsh towards his subjects." Josephus argues that Herod flattered his superiors because he wanted to be honored by his own subjects; but it was against the law to do for himself what he did for others: "to flatter him with statues or temples or such tokens."

This perceptive evaluation of Herod suggests his actions were not motivated by selfless piety. Nevertheless, there is room for attributing a part of his motivation to piety, and Josephus indirectly affirms this in the next section (*Ant.* 16.160–78) that stresses Herod's support for the Jews of the Diaspora. He cites a number of Imperial edicts to demonstrate Rome's special treatment of Diaspora Jews (Chapter 7). There is no record of Herod providing buildings such as synagogues for Jews in the Diaspora parallel to his building of the Jerusalem temple. All his Diaspora buildings were for civic purposes, with the result that he helped Diaspora Jews attain a secure and prosperous position. His civic projects in the Diaspora (and the list includes those known from inscriptions, as in Athens), though not considered acts of piety by Josephus, were evidence of a broad concern for Jews beyond the borders of his kingdom. They too, I argue, were acts of piety.

In assessing Herod's view of torah and constraints imposed by the second commandment we need to put him in a broader context in three respects: (1) Herod was not a fully torah-observant Jew; we should avoid, however, going too far in the opposite direction by claiming he was without principles or scruples concerning torah. He had obligations to God, to Emperor, and to family, which he expressed in ways that seemed to him and others "pious"; (2) his various acts of piety ameliorated the conditions religiously, politically, and economically of Jews in the Diaspora and in Judea. He attempted to be genuinely constructive and beneficent towards his people; and (3) the criticism of Herod during his lifetime and after his death had little to do with torah; it focused on his persistence in ridding himself of all who showed the slightest degree of *lèse majesté*.[17] He was incapable of tolerating opposition, especially opposition from within the family or that came from the conservative segment of Judaism with a more restrictive view of torah. In the Judaism of Herod's day, opinions frequently conflicted, as the *Mishnah* demonstrates clearly for subsequent periods. Many Jews shared Herod's liberal views, as the *Mishnah* also shows.

CONCLUSION

Herod lived in a time of rapid social change. The attractions of Hellenism together with the effects of Roman rule created potential for conflict among pious Jews. Nevertheless, Herod was not an agent for the speedy inroads of Hellenism or Romanization. During his time, in fact, there was probably little advance on this front. In the Maccabean period and earlier, Hellenism had already made considerable inroads, and would continue to do so. Torah observance was not more difficult during Herod's reign than before. Thus, I have argued in this chapter:

- Adherence to the second commandment was debated in Herod's period; views were varied, but there was more tolerance—even of idols and statues—than is usually supposed.

- A conservative group, perhaps a strict group of Pharisees, objected to some aspects of Herod's building activities, specifically the eagle and the trophies. In the first case concern about the image must have been suppressed for some time, in the second there was a misunderstanding.

- Herod maintained the second commandment within Judea (with the exceptions noted), though not all parts of Jewish society were as scrupulous. Outside Judea Herod permitted figurative representations in his buildings, and he repaired—or perhaps even built, as in Ba'al Shamim's Temple in Si'a—temples to pagan deities.

• His building program reflected his piety: to the God of Israel, to his patron Augustus, to his family, and—through his civic projects in the Diaspora—to the well-being of far-flung Jewish communities.

These data make sense if Herod's actions and attitudes are interpreted in the light of a prevailing notion of accommodation. Herod observed some degree of piety towards Olympian gods in Olympia, Rhodes, Athens, and Cos. He may have adopted the piety of the Hauran towards Ba'al Shamim at Si'a. In a Roman setting he was one of the first to express his devotion to Augustus in the temples he erected to Roma and Augustus and in the naming of cities and towns and towers and parts of palaces. Herod accommodated his behavior in the same way that Hillel and later Paul (both "lenient" Pharisees) argued for an accommodatory stance. In Herod's case, the accommodation went farther than Hillel's, but perhaps in its own way no deeper than Paul's: "To the Jews I became a Jew in order to win Jews" (1 Cor 9:20). In Hillel's case the issue was put in terms of gaining proselytes. In Paul's case the goal was stated, "to win some" in the Diaspora for Jesus Christ.[18] Herod's goal was slightly similar, I argue: to keep Diaspora communities on a solid footing and in close touch with the homeland. There were clearly other goals in Herod's mind as well, foremost among them simply to buttress his own position as King of the Jews through enormously costly projects inside and outside Israel. He may have been attempting, as Jacob Neusner has argued, to set the stage for the acquisition of a much larger kingdom.[19] Despite the more narrowly political goals that undoubtedly concerned Herod, he voluntarily maintained a concern for torah. This was not mere dissembling on his part but the outworking of a real piety.

CHAPTER FOURTEEN

WHY TURN THE TABLES? JESUS' PROTEST
IN THE TEMPLE PRECINCTS

INTRODUCTION[1]

On 12 March, 4 B.C.E., Herod had Matthias and Judas and some of their students burned alive for removing an eagle from a gate in the temple.[2] Matthias had urged the students to undertake this action, since Herod was facing imminent death. The law of Israel, they said, forbade images and likenesses of living things; "it was erected in defiance of their fathers' laws. It was in fact unlawful to place in the temple either images or busts or any representation whatsoever of a living creature" (*War* 1.649–50). Even if death should follow from their actions, the students would acquire virtue, fame, and honor (*War* 1.648–55; *Ant.* 17.149–67), so the students did the deed bravely, while people strolled in the temple precincts. Herod had placed the eagle above the "great gate," says Josephus, so the students were in clear view of guards and people. They got up on the roof—no doubt the roof of a *stoa* around the *temenos*—let themselves down with ropes and hacked off the golden eagle, probably a low relief stone sculpture covered with gold leaf. The crowds fled, but the temple captain and a band of soldiers seized Judas and Matthias and 40 students. They were taken before Herod and defended their actions on the basis of torah; they accepted punishment for their "piety." Herod sent them to Jericho, where the main perpetrators were burned alive, while the others were simply executed (*Ant.* 17.160).

This incident highlights how strongly some Jews felt about iconic representations (Chapter 13). Something similar was probably the main motivation for Jesus' overturning the tables of the moneychangers in the temple,[3] or so I shall argue. (1) Usual views of the temple incident rely too much on notions of "cleansing," often motivated by later Christian convictions, with too little attention to religious realities of the first century. (2) Tyrian shekels (Plate 35), in which the temple tax had to be paid, were as repugnant to some as the eagle was to Judas and Matthias.[4] (3) The payment of the half-shekel tax was odious to some, for it contravened torah's injunction that it should be paid only once in a lifetime. Either (2) or (3) would be sufficient to account for Jesus' action; either provides a better explanation of his action than notions of symbolic protest. The claim that turning the tables—a relatively weak symbol—was a symbol of the destruction of the temple is common. The incident was not so much a symbol as an angry reaction to a controversial practice.

INTERPRETATIONS OF THE TEMPLE INCIDENT

Early Interpretations

The earliest interpretation is Mark's, where the incident was sandwiched between two stages of the fig tree pericope. The Fourth Gospel locates the incident early, unlike Mark (John 1:14-22); Mark increased its drama, drew attention to Jesus' relationship to the cult, and linked it directly with a spiritualizing saying about destruction of the temple (Chapter 6).[5] Not much later, an anonymous homilist continued John's spiritualizing tendency in a different direction (*2 Clement* 14.1). He tore the incident from its historical roots by using a shortened form of the saying about the Lord's house becoming a "den of brigands" (Chapter 2) as a judgment on those who do not do the will of the Lord and so become a part of that "den of brigands," set over against the "first church, the spiritual one," who have "salvation."

Justin Martyr took a more harmful tack in the 150s, referring perhaps to the 130s. He used the incident polemically, linking Jesus' saying with the woes (Matt 23 and Luke 11) to suggest a judgment on Israel: "He appeared distasteful to you when he cried among you, 'It is written, My house is the house of prayer; but you have made it a den of thieves.' He overthrew also the tables of the moneychangers in the temple, and exclaimed, 'Woe unto you Scribes and Pharisees, hypocrites! because you pay tithe of mint and rue, but do not observe the love of God and justice.' . . . And to the Scribes, 'Woe to you, Scribes! for you have the keys and do not enter in yourselves . . .' " (*Dial.* 17). Justin connected the turning of the tables with tithing, turned the moneychangers into Scribes and Pharisees, dropped references to torah, and suggested that Scribes had the keys of "my house." He drove a wedge between Jesus and his contemporaries. And Heracleon, a follower of Valentinus (160s?) interprets John's account allegorically, anticipating later views of the motives of those selling and exchanging: "Those who are found in the holy place selling . . . are those who regard the coming of strangers to the temple as an occasion for trade and gain" (frag. 13).[6]

Modern Interpretations

Something along the lines of the synoptic account happened, when Jesus turned the tables of those exchanging unacceptable for acceptable currency. Moneychangers provided a necessary service,[7] trading local currencies for Tyrian shekels, a coinage whose relatively high silver content was tightly controlled. The temple authorities required a silver coin in payment of the annual half-shekel temple tax. The importance of Tyrian money is seen in the various hoards of Tyrian shekels from Mt. Carmel, Gamla, Silwan, and elsewhere.[8] Persons selling sacrificial victims also were providing a service; they made suitable sacrifices readily available and removed worries over their purity. Most interpreters agree on some such minimal view of the cultic situation. But there is substantial divergence on the social-historical background. What prompted him to upset the tables?

(1) One dominant view goes back to the Fourth Gospel (or even Mark) and interprets Jesus' action as prophetic symbolism; Jesus was a prophet anticipating the eschatological dénouement when the temple would be destroyed.[9]

(2) A once-popular variant argues that Jesus was concerned for "the nations"; his action was aimed at the "removal from the Court of the Gentiles of all that made prayer or worship difficult or impossible for Gentiles, in that one and only part of the temple to which they already had the privilege of access."[10] Jesus was a prophet of the promise to the nations.

(3) Jesus objected to substantial abuses and illicit trading in the temple, either because of corruption of the priests or because Jesus was following an officially approved line of action, with which

the priests agreed. In the latter case Jesus was aligned with the priestly authorities, in the former entirely opposed to them.[11]

(4) Jesus rejected the institutions of Judaism—he was not merely in conflict with them—including especially the temple. This Jesus was a political fundamentalist, opposed to all ruling institutions.[12]

(5) Jesus' action was the first blow in an armed revolution, trying to take over the temple precinct—as other earlier revolutionary movements had tried—to legitimate his movement. Jesus was a religious zealot.[13]

(6) Jesus' action was based on the difference between city and country, between the economic practices of urban Jerusalem and the Galilean agrarian poor. Jesus was a Galilean peasant motivated by concern for the dispossessed.[14]

Each view has some support, though not all have a large measure of it. The changing fashions represent changing scholarly perceptions and changing contemporary context. My concern is establishing a sound social-historical background for Jesus' action, especially turning the tables. I suggest two complementary explanations: the nature of the coinage for temple tax payments and the frequency of the tax's payment. I argue that Jesus' reservations about the half-shekel tax payment were related to strict views of torah's interpretation.

THE TEMPLE DUES

On the first day of Adar, they give warning of the shekel dues and against [the sowing of] Diverse Kinds. On the fifteenth thereof they read the *Megillah* in walled cities and repair the paths and roads and pools of water and perform all public needs and mark the graves. . . . On the fifteenth thereof the tables [of the money-changers] were set up in the provinces; and on the twenty-fifth thereof they were set up in the temple. After they were set up in the temple they began to exact pledges . . . from Levites, Israelites, proselytes, and freed slaves, but not from women, slaves, or minors . . . if [women, slaves, or minors] have paid the shekel it is accepted of them, but if a Gentile or a Samaritan paid the shekel it is not accepted of them. (*m. Shekal.* 1:1, 3, 5)

The five *selas* for the [firstborn] son should be paid in Tyrian coinage; the thirty due for the slave [that was gored by an ox] and the fifty due from the violator and the seducer, and the hundred due from him that hath brought up an evil name are all to be paid according to the value of the shekels of the sanctuary in Tyrian coinage. Aught that is be redeemed may be redeemed with silver or its value, save only the shekel-dues. (*m. Bek.* 8:7)

[A]ll the money of which the law speaks is Tyrian money. (*t. Ketub.* 12)

Shekels may be changed into [Persian] darics because of [lightening] a journey's load. (*m. Shekal.* 2:1)

R. Judah says: shekel dues have no prescribed limit, for when Israel returned from exile they used to pay the shekel in darics, then they changed and paid the shekel in shekel-pieces, and then they sought to pay the shekel in denars. (*m. Shekal.* 2:4)

There were thirteen Shofar chests in the temple, whereon was inscribed . . . "New shekel dues" . . . "Old [shekel dues]," if any had not paid his shekel in the last year he must pay it in the next year. (*m. Shekal.* 6:5)

[The laws concerning] the shekel dues and first fruits apply only such time as the temple stands. (*m. Shekal.* 8:8)

Since these prescriptions applied only while the temple stood, it is reasonable to think the *Mishnah*'s concerns predate the temple's destruction and represent conditions at the end of the Second Temple period. The official coinage for the temple tax, as for other fines and dues, was the Tyrian shekel. It had not always been so, and there was controversy over what was acceptable (*m. Shekal.* 2:4), but the dominant view favored Tyrian coinage. While some pledges could be redeemed with non-silver coinage, the shekel dues, like some other specific obligations, had to be in silver. Since the temple tax was paid in shekel pieces and not in "denars" (i.e., denarii or half-shekel pieces), one shekel paid two persons' dues. It was to be paid each year, but arrears were to be made good (*m. Shekal.* 6:5). The definition of who paid dues was relatively narrow: Jewish males over the age of 20 years, no matter where they lived; it could be paid voluntarily by women, underage males, slaves, and priests. There were disputes about the extent and acceptability of such voluntary payments, especially whether priests needed to pay it (*m. Shekal.* 1:5). The temple dues could be paid during a period of ten days in other parts of Judea and Galilee; elsewhere in the Mediterranean Jewish world the arrangements are less clear.[15] From 25 Adar to 15 Nissan moneychangers' tables were set up only in the temple, where payment was in Tyrian shekels; if one lived at a distance it seems one did not need to pay in this currency.

Two points are crucial. First, the moneychangers' tables were an essential part of the temple cult: even temple dues received in the "provinces" were transported to Jerusalem, where moneys were converted to approved coinage. Second, that coinage was the Tyrian shekel. Two other features are important. The moneychangers were not priests but persons licensed or approved to provide this service. And the purpose of the dues was not to support the priesthood but to pay temple overheads and community sacrifices.[16]

Tyrian Shekels

Coins from Tyre cannot have been a natural choice for, as Josephus indelicately puts it, "the Tyrians [along with the Egyptians] are our bitterest enemies" (*Apion* 1.170).[17] The choice may have had to do with the high silver content and the careful quality control.[18] The decision must have derived from the requirement that temple dues be paid in silver, coupled with a prohibition on local mints producing bronze and copper coins. Silver coins were minted only at Imperial mints and cities specifically given that right or holding it autonomously, such as Tyre.

The Tyrian shekel is well known; large numbers have been found, mostly a type minted 126/125 B.C.E. through to 19/18 B.C.E., and another type, distinguished by the letters *KP* on the reverse, from the year 18 B.C.E. on. The shekel uniformly has the god Melkart (Heracles) on the obverse and a Tyrian (Ptolemaic) eagle on the reverse, with the inscription "Tyre the holy and inviolable."[19] The combination of images—indeed either alone—contravened the plain meaning of the Decalogue and its prohibitions both of idolatry and of images. Was the adoption of foreign coinage necessary? Why settle on Tyrian coinage?

The straight answer is that foreign coinage was necessary. (1) Jewish authorities during the period of foreign domination were forbidden to mint silver coins, with one brief exception, when iconic silver coins modeled on Persian coins were minted under license in Jerusalem, bearing the inscription, "Judea" (note the *Mishnah*'s statements). (2) If Meshorer were correct, that Tyrian shekels were minted in Jerusalem from 18 B.C.E. to 66 C.E., the perplexity would only be moved one level deeper: why should Jerusalem authorities mint Tyrian shekels? (3) The first silver coins issued within Judaism, beautifully decorated with symbols of the temple, were minted during the First Revolt (Plate 36). A primary reason must have been to provide aniconic coins suitable for temple purposes. Given that the *Mishnah* suggests that the appropriateness of the Tyrian shekel was debated (*m. Shekal.* 2:4), the presence of both Tyrian and Jerusalem shekels in the same coin hoard is not so surprising.[20] (4) The requirement to pay a half-shekel (Exod 30:11-16; 38:25-26) or a third-shekel (Neh 10:32-33) states merely that it should be "according to the shekel of the sanctuary" (often just a standard of measurement); the phrase may imply, though it does not state, that it must be in silver. (5) Payment of temple dues in silver was probably derived in the Second Temple period by extension from the explicit requirements in other cases: fines, dues, and vows (Lev 27:3-8, 16-25; Deut 22:19, 29; Lev 5:15; Gen 20:16; 37:20). The temple authorities were in a bind: exegesis interpreted sanctuary shekels to be silver, not the equivalent in bronze, but the political authorities did not allow Jews to mint silver. Some other coinage had to be used.

Why Tyrian? Despite the animosity and the coins' imagery, Tyrian money was convenient, autonomous, high quality, and not politically charged.[21] It is arguable that Jewish authorities should have preferred coins minted at Antioch, Caesarea Maritima, Gaza, or Ascalon; from the Hasmonean period onwards Romans were, after all, Judea's allies or overlords. But all had symbols of Roman power, including the Emperor's portrait or other Roman symbols. If silver content and careful controls were factors, Antioch's silver coins, for example, show the difference, for they averaged about 80 percent silver content compared to Tyre's 90 percent.[22]

No explicit evidence suggests that Tyrian shekels were repugnant (though *y. ʿAbod. Zar.* 3:1 [42b] refers to Nahum, who "did not look at a coin all his days"), but this is hardly surprising, given the strength of the tradition that temple dues were paid this way. Still, Tyrian shekels must have offended some, based on four pieces of evidence: popular support for those who removed the eagle; exegetical concern for the symbols on foreign coinage; later speedy minting during the first year of the Revolt of new silver shekels and half-shekels for the first time in Jewish history; and differences of opinion over the appropriate coinage for temple dues.

ANNUAL OR ONCE ONLY?

A second question was the frequency of payment of temple dues. Qumran rejected annual dues: "Concerning . . . the money of valuation that a man gives as a ransom for his life, it shall be half [a shekel]. He shall give it only once in his life" (4Q159). The reference is to Exodus 30:11-16 and by implication its interpretation in Nehemiah 10:32. Its significance is that there was a current, ongoing, literalist interpretation of torah that rejected post-exilic reinterpretations of temple dues. 4Q159 shows one group's refusal to participate in a widely accepted obligation. The criticism seems predicated on frequency, not the question (also under debate) of priestly payment of temple dues. Others with strict views of biblical interpretation may have shared the resistance that characterized Qumran's views, though it is impossible to say how widely. Both innovations—payment annually and payment by Tyrian shekels—could be thought relatively recent and both equally unacceptable.

JESUS' PAYMENT OF THE TEMPLE DUES

The M-pericope in Matthew 17:24-27 coheres with the temple incident.[23] From 15 Adar the tables were set up in Capernaum; when Peter was asked if Jesus paid the dues, he confidently replied yes. But Jesus took a different line, according to Matthew. He likened the temple tax to taxation by surrounding kings; he claimed that since Roman taxes were collected from non-citizens the children of God were free not to pay; yet he paid the tax, since nonpayment would give offense, and he did so only as the result of a miracle (the coin in the fish's mouth, if a Tyrian shekel, paid both Jesus' and Peter's temple dues). Jesus paid only reluctantly.

Contrast this pericope with the account of the payment of tribute to Rome (Mark 12:13-17 pars//*Gos. Thom.* 100//P. Eger 2.3), with its polemical edge. Jesus cleverly ducked the issue by recourse to the coin's image. He did not object to the coin's symbolism, but clearly asserted a principle: imagery entails ownership, so use of Caesar's coins requires payment of Caesar's dues. The pericope's relevance is underscored by the parallel admonition in all versions except P. Eger 2: one should give God what belongs to him. The saying, if authentic, alludes to temple dues. The payment of those dues in Tyrian shekels conflicted with the requirement that payment to God should be in coinage acceptable to God (shekels of the sanctuary). The image on the Tyrian shekel was manifestly not part of God's sanctuary but part of Melkart's sanctuary at Tyre. One cannot give God coinage that refers explicitly to another deity and another authority: "Tyre the holy and inviolable." Mark has Jesus cite Jeremiah 7:11 and refer to the temple precincts as a "den of brigands" (Chapter 2). As Jeremiah put it, "This is the temple of the Lord . . ." (7:3); they "make offerings to Baal and go after other gods . . . come out and stand before me in this house, which is called by my name . . ." (7:9). The conflict in Jeremiah's day was replicated in Jesus' day when images of Melkart (the Baal of Tyre) were deposited in the temple treasury, turning the temple into a "den of brigands."[24]

"STRICT CONSTRUCTIONISM" IN JESUS?

Jesus and the Moneychangers

Payment of temple dues was flawed on two grounds: it had to be paid in Tyrian shekels and annually. These grounds shaped Jesus' attitude to the temple dues and prompted him to upset the tables of the moneychangers in Jerusalem. The social-historical factors proposed here provide a more immediate explanation for the action. But why, then, did Jesus not upset the tables in Capernaum during the ten days between 15 and 25 Adar, given his reluctance in paying the dues? (1) The explanation may be that payment was not required in Tyrian shekels outside Judea, since others took the dues to Jerusalem for those not able to go. (2) Or it may be that Capernaum was well outside the temple precincts; the action in Jerusalem was prompted by a recollection of Jeremiah's affront at acknowledging Baal in the temple of the God of Israel. (3) Or it may have to do with the fact that Peter, not Jesus, was the main participant.

Jesus and the Sellers

Sellers of sacrificial victims were as necessary as moneychangers. It seem likely for reasons that Sanders provides that pigeons were being sold in the temple *temenos*, but not oxen and sheep. Pigeons were less offensive because the premises could be protected from being fouled.[25] Strict consistency, however, might require the prohibition of the selling of pigeons, too. Mark, and only Mark, has what seems a garbled allusion to Jesus not allowing anyone to carry anything through the *hieron* (perhaps implying the precincts as a whole, though possibly the combination of Court of Women, Court of Israel, Court of Priests). Josephus refers to carrying nothing into the *naos* (the inner sanctuary or Holy Place; *Apion* 2.106). It is possible that Mark correctly reports that Jesus' view was that the whole *temenos* was holy to the Lord and that sellers should stay outside the temple precincts. His objection to sellers (the location of their activity) was not the same as his objection to the moneychangers (the nature of their coinage). In either case the issue was the holiness of the temple and its precincts.

Jesus and Strictness

For this interpretation to succeed, the overall portrait of Jesus must be coherent and consistent. How strict was his view of torah? (1) Jesus' attitude to vows was strict and unequivocal: no vows. Use only "yes" and "no." The corban vow in particular—dedicated to the temple and so unavailable to meet other obligations—excited his anger. At first sight this seems contrary to the argument of this chapter, but the case is similar in that he held it was incorrect to offer God these "dues." (2) Jesus' attitude to divorce was also strict: no divorce. Jesus argued against torah's provision for divorce by going back to principles derived from creation. (3) Jesus' views on purity were more complex. Jewish tradition preserved an allusion to a halakhic debate involving Jesus and James of Kefar Sekhanya concerning ritual defilement of the temple (*t. Hul.* 2:2–4; *b. 'Abod. Zar.* 16b–17a). The issue was a prostitute's offering and its use, specifically whether the proceeds could be used to build a toilet for the high priest. Jesus' answer was yes. Christian tradition reported another debate, involving Jesus and a chief priest named Levi, over temple purity (*P. Oxy* 840). It hinged on Jesus' failure to use a *mikveh* to obtain the same ritual purity as the priest and it occasioned a diatribe by Jesus on the inadequacy of ritual cleanness. Both traditions implied vigorous debate between Jesus and others over the temple's purity, a debate not likely to have been created ex post facto by either the Jewish or Christian community. While Jesus' views as implied in the two traditions were not "strict," he showed a concern in both cases for the temple cult. (4) Jesus leaned towards a radically negative attitude to money, appropriate to a Galilean peasant.[26] He turned away from profit, anticipated economic restructuring, and hinted at a community of goods. (5) Temple sayings, part of the stock of primitive material, suggest that Jesus expected a coming destruction and rebuilding, conceivably more a positive than negative anticipation.[27] Like the Qumran sectaries, he did not expect the temple to disappear but to be reconstituted; early Christians converted this positive view into a negative one.

Conclusion

One strain of Jesus' thinking adopted a strict approach to cultic matters, especially with respect to the temple. This part of the tradition is not easily attributed to later developments in the Jesus movement. Particularly in connection with the temple tax, Jesus had something in common with sectarian thought, not unlike that at Qumran, and with radical attitudes to the temple found among revolutionaries of 66 C.E. He looked for a renewed and reformed temple cult, linked with expectations of the destruction and restoration of the temple. He did not spiritualize the temple, he did not look forward to the alienation of Israel from her God, and he did not radically criticize temple authorities. These tendencies were the result of later controversies and events. The Jesus pictured here is part of a more complex portrait: charismatic prophet, passive revolutionary, Galilean peasant passionate for social justice, independent interpreter of torah. On the one matter at stake here, the primary reason for turning the tables derived from his hostility to the use of Tyrian shekels to pay temple dues. This action was not a visionary's symbol of the destruction of the temple but a reformer's anger at recognition of other gods.

CHAPTER FIFTEEN

JOSEPHUS, NICOLAS OF DAMASCUS, AND HEROD'S BUILDING PROGRAM

INTRODUCTION[1]

Josephus relied extensively on Nicolas of Damascus. Some have held that he depended on Nicolas in writing the long section of *Jewish War* dealing with Herod the Great, but that in the parallel section of *Antiquities* trained assistants revised *War* for stylistic reasons. The view is now unpopular, but Josephus's dependence on Nicolas of Damascus, especially in *War*, is still important, though the study of Josephus has moved beyond such source-related questions.

H. St. J. Thackeray developed his influential views in a series of lectures, which were soon put in written form.[2] Thackeray believed he could detect separate assistants' hands in two of the relevant sections of *Antiquities*, though he confessed that he could not distinguish separate hands in *War*. There were problems with Thackeray's views, two of which are important here. First, Josephus tells us he used assistants in *War*, but he does not say he used them in *Antiquities*. To argue for the detection of an assistant's identifying traces in *Antiquities*, where Josephus is silent about them, and not to detect them in *War*, where he says he used them, is awkward.[3] Second, Josephus explicitly tells us he used Nicolas of Damascus as a source in *Antiquities*, but he does not say the same thing in *War*,[4] so it is awkward to argue that *Antiquities* is a primarily stylistic rewriting of *War*. A third problem in these views can be added as a question. Is the degree of criticism of or distance from Herod an adequate indication of the degree of dependence on Nicolas?[5] The argument is this: Nicolas was Herod's court historian; Nicolas would not have been critical of Herod; Josephus used Nicolas; Josephus was less critical of Herod in *War* than in *Antiquities*; therefore Josephus was more dependent on Nicolas in *War* than in *Antiquities*. To this conclusion is sometimes added a purported additional motive built

on a hypothesized second edition of *Antiquities*: more criticism of
Herod was possible after Agrippa II's death in the 90s C.E.[6]

My interest in these issues arises not from such source questions,
which have become passé, but from a study of Herod's buildings. I
have been interested in Josephus's literary descriptions in both *War* and
Antiquities, and in his context in the early Roman Empire, especially
texts dealing with architecture. I have also been interested in archaeological excavations of Herod's buildings and other late Hellenistic and
Roman buildings of the same period. Archaeological reports do not
always solve difficulties in understanding what the buildings were like.
Sometimes the combination of literary descriptions and archaeological
investigations intersect in helpful and creative ways, permitting a fuller
understanding of the buildings than is otherwise possible.

It would be helpful to know which of Josephus's accounts was architecturally more reliable and which was secondary for reconstructive
purposes. If Thackeray's arguments were adopted, *War*'s descriptions
might be thought more reliable because they were based on Nicolas.
Descriptions in *Antiquities* were secondary, on this view, because an
assistant had rewritten them. I am uncomfortable with that view of
Josephus's dependence on Nicolas in *War*, for reasons I shall provide. I
conclude that in *War* Josephus based his descriptions in part, perhaps
largely, on personal observation, what an observer of the mid-first century C.E. might have seen first hand. The differences between *War* and
Antiquities probably derived from *Antiquities*' use of an earlier written
source, possibly a source going back to Nicolas, though that specific
claim is not essential. I do not argue that this is true of the whole section of *War* dealing with Herod the Great, only that this hypothesis is
consistent with Josephus's own comments about his use of eyewitness
observation and sources.[7] This chapter moves in the same direction as
the recent tendency to think that Josephus relied more fully on Nicolas
in *Antiquities*.

The hypothesis emerges from material evidence from archaeological excavations and comparisons of the two literary sources.
Knowledge of Herod's building projects can be used to good effect in
assessing the accuracy of the literary descriptions. Most of the examples are sites that have been excavated in sufficient detail that it is possible to evaluate the accuracies and inaccuracies of Josephus's
descriptions: which account has fewer factual errors, which is more
detailed and specific, or which introduces new data that cohere with

the archaeological evidence. These do not permit full consideration of the relationship between the accounts of *War* and *Antiquities*. That question depends on much more than simple questions of accuracy of his descriptions of buildings. These also do not indicate which account is historically more accurate in scope and detail. But these comparisons may provide additional evidence for those who consider the larger literary issues that emerge from a study of Josephus's writings, especially *War* and *Antiquities*, written about two decades apart. The approach has the added advantage of being based on descriptions in which unknown editorial bias was not likely to have caused changes. Josephus had little at stake in different descriptions of Herod's buildings in *War* and *Antiquities*.

I compare Josephus's descriptions of select buildings in *War* and *Antiquities*, comment on the errors and differences, assess which of Josephus's descriptions conforms better to the available archaeological information, and surmise the sources of errors or the reasons for alterations from the earlier to the later work, considering editorial or authorial intention when relevant. The selection of buildings is dictated by expediency. I have chosen (with one exception) buildings where there are two literary accounts, where excavations have been carried out, and where enough remains or where enough of the excavation reports have been published to allow effective conclusions. My examples are Herodium, Caesarea Maritima, and the temple's retaining walls. I add the account of Masada, and four brief notes of foreign benefactions.

EVIDENCE

Masada

The description of Masada in *War* 7.285–303 has no parallel in *Antiquities*, merely allusions to events that took place there. The description in *War* is moderately but not entirely accurate: the enclosure around the summit is about the right length; the number of towers is 50 percent high; the Northern Palace (Plate 37) is located on the western slope, but "inclining" to the north; but the features of that palace and its "sunken way" to the top of the hill create about the right impression. There is nothing in the description of Masada in *War* that goes beyond the picture an observer might draw, other than Herod's motive in rebuilding Masada. There are some exaggerations, but as Yigael Yadin points out[8] these are the kind an observer might make: heights of the four towers of the Northern Palace (60 cubits high; ca. 90 feet or 28 m) and of the casemate walls (12 cubits high by 8 cubits broad; ca. 18 feet high or 5.5 m; the width is about right) are two simple examples.

Two statements are obviously in error. Josephus says that "the columns [of the Northern Palace] were everywhere of monoliths" (*koinon men hapantachou monolithôn; War* 7.290). Herod used monolithic columns when he could, as in two columns of a colonnaded street found in situ along the western wall in Jerusalem. At Masada, however, as in several of Herod's other construction projects where large building stone was not readily available, columns were made from drums, half-drums, or even small quarter-drums. The Masada columns were more like brickwork than massive stone. The impression of beautiful carved monolithic columns resulted from careful plastering, with fluting, of the brick shafts. The description of these columns as monoliths was thus an accurate account of what could be seen, not an accurate description deriving from inside knowledge contemporary with the building itself.

A second error is similar. Josephus describes the casemate walls as made of "white stone" (*leukou lithou; War* 7.286). In fact the stone was dolomite, quarried on the site, a hard, almost yellow ochre-colored stone. Even the most casual visitor to Masada is impressed with the way the buildings grow right out of the site, because of the simplicity of the locally available materials. Yadin reported, however, that the excavators discovered that "the wall was covered with a white plaster, fragments of which we found in many places."[9] Small sections of this white plaster remain, with two impressive sections in the entrances to the Western Palace and the Northern Palace (Plate 38). The plaster in both was scored to replicate ashlar masonry with borders around each of the imaginary ashlars, giving an effect not unlike the monumental ashlars of the base of the temple in Jerusalem. Other examples, presumably of simpler design, can apparently be found on the exterior of the casemate walls, but they are inaccessible. This is similar to the previous case. An observer reported what he thought he saw, without access to correct information. There is no comparison passage in *Antiquities* to lay alongside the description in *War*, so no certain conclusions can be drawn from *War*'s account of Masada. The most we can say is that his description of Masada was in some degree based on first-hand observation, though it is not possible to say whether his accounts depended on his own eyewitness reportage or another's.

Herodium

The accounts of Herodium are parallel (*War* 1.419–21; *Ant.* 15.323–25), though each plays a different role and occurs at a different point in its narrative context. While the accounts are similar in many respects, the variations are significant and might indicate different sources. I consider three aspects: the overall description, including the hill; the lower level; and the palace-fortress or the acropolis (as Josephus refers to it) in *Antiquities*.

In *War* 1.419 Josephus describes Herodium (curiously subordinated to his description of a fortress, also named Herodium, on the Arabian frontier) as situated "on a rounded hill made by hand and shaped like a breast" (*ton de mastoeidê kolônon onta cheiropoiêton*). A few lines later he says it was "a high hill and entirely man-made" (*ên gar de to gêlophon epieikôs hypsêlon kai pan cheiropoiêton*; 1.420). The description in *Antiquities* on this point is both subtler and vaguer: "for there is reasonably near a rounded hill, raised to a height by hand, so that the rounding of it is shaped like a breast" (*esti gar engus epieikôs kolônos, eis hypsos aniôn cheiropoiêton, hôs einai mastoeidê tên periphoran*; *Ant.* 15.324). The most important difference between these two accounts, which share similar language, is that *War* explicitly says the hill was entirely man-made (*pan cheiropoiêton*) while *Antiquities* implies—though it does not say so precisely—that an existing hill was raised artificially. Both repeat the graphic and apt description of the resulting hill with its circular fortress and towers. It was shaped like a breast.

War's description is best explained as the result of observation, uncomplicated by reliable information. The Upper Palace was constructed to a height of seven stories above a vaulted sub-structure that sat above an existing hill. The lower levels of the construction work were then masked with fill, neatly smoothed off and merged with the existing hill so that the whole hill ended up looking artificial: everything seemed "made by hand." *Antiquities*' account, however, is subtler and more accurate; the existing hill is acknowledged—even if it could not be clearly detected by eye—and the raising of the hill is described as being by

hand. The rounding off (*periphoran*) of the hill was what made the hill
look like a breast (another element making it breast-like, a round tower
higher than the others that must have looked nipple-like, is ignored).
The difference between the two accounts can be accounted for on the
basis that *War* was based on direct observation; the author described
what he saw or understood from another eyewitness. *Antiquities* has
information based less on direct observation than on a more accurate
source closer to the original construction.

Ehud Netzer has intensely investigated Herodium's lower level. The
excavations include Byzantine churches, a monumental building, garden, pool with surrounding colonnade, bath, racecourse or other sta-
dium-like structure, intermediate palace, *exedrae*, and other related
areas. Josephus provides a rather general description of this area:
"around the base he built other palaces to accommodate his baggage
and friends" (*kateskeuasen de kai peri tas rhizas alla basileia ten te aposkeuen kai
tous philous dexasthai dynamena*; *War* 1.421). He also says, "this defence
seemed to be a town, in its outline a palace" (*hôste tôi men panta echein
polin einai dokein to eryma têi perigraphêi de basileion*). The parallel description (*Ant.* 15.325) emphasizes other features of the lower level: "around
the base (*basis*, "step, foot, pedestal," when *War* uses *rhiza* or "root") of
the hill, places of amusement have been built that are worth seeing,
because of the bringing in of water (missing in this place) from a distance and at great expense. The plain was built around as a city second
to none, the hill serving as an acropolis for the other buildings."

Comparison of these two accounts leads in the direction noted earlier. The word *basis* in *Antiquities* suggests Josephus thought of the hill as
a foot or pedestal for the new construction above, while *rhiza* in *War*
may imply that he thought the whole was a new construction. In *War*
Josephus stresses accommodations for Herod's friends and their "baggage," and he suggests that the lower level, which resembled a "town,"
acted as a fence or defense for the upper level. In *Antiquities* Josephus
describes the lower level as a city (*polis*) and only the upper level as a
defensible *akropolis*. Josephus replaces *War*'s earlier, incorrect, description of the lower level as defensive with *Antiquities*' revised description
of that part of the complex as a place of amusement with lots of water
that had been utilized effectively. The excavations of the huge pool,
with its central gazebo, gardens, adjacent complex bathhouse, and
racecourse, underline its recreational character. The main function of
the lower level was as a *paradeisos*, the exotic "paradise" that originated

in Mesopotamia, especially during Persian rule. Since no defensive role for the lower buildings has emerged from the archaeology, the later description in *Antiquities* is an improvement in accuracy.

War is exaggerated at best and wrong at worst in viewing the lower area as a fence around the Upper Ppalace, though a casual viewer could have had this impression when approaching the extensive complex. *Antiquities* avoids this incorrect understanding of the lower level as defensive, correctly stresses the lower level's main purpose as recreational and living, and sees only the upper palace as capable of defense, an acropolis for the rest. While these features could have been based on observation, since no insider's or contemporary knowledge was necessary, the later date of *Antiquities* presupposes that these changes were based not on Josephus's subsequent personal observations—by the time of *Antiquities* the palace had long since been destroyed—but on fuller or better information from other sources than he utilized earlier. *Antiquities* was not merely a stylistic revision of *War* but a more correct description.

Why was the description in *War*, which seems to have been written on the basis of personal observation, in error on the recreational and non-defensive character of the lower level? It is plausible that, as I have just suggested, the explanation is that the whole complex seemed to have defensive features. There is another possible explanation. If Josephus saw it while it was being used as a stronghold during the Great Revolt and prior to its destruction, his own observations may be the source of his misleading description. Lower Herodium could no longer have filled a recreational role then; the gardens would have been in disarray and the pool empty. During that brief period in the late 60s and early 70s, after Josephus had surrendered at Yodefat and before he went to Rome, he may have seen Herodium himself (or had other firsthand accounts), when the lower areas were likely used as a first line of defense by its defenders.

In Josephus's descriptions of the Upper Palace, neither *War* nor *Antiquities* is precise and accurate about the towers, the eastern one of which was round and the other three half-round. Neither account is precise about interior arrangements, though both refer to them in lavish terms. Both exaggerate by referring to the structure having "palaces," overlooking that there was only one palace (*basileioi* could mean "royal apartments" but more naturally means "palaces"). One minor comparison is revealing: *War* 1.420 describes steps to the upper palace as "the purest white marble" (*leukotates marmarou*), an exaggeration that might derive from a visit to the lower level without opportunity to examine the upper building closely; *Antiquities* has a more restrained "hewn stone." Remains of this stairway have been found, though not the steps. Netzer reports that they were likely of hewn stone.[10] In other words, Josephus's description in *War* was based on observation—his or someone else's—and it reported approximately the effect; his later account in *Antiquities* provided a more sober and accurate account.

Caesarea Maritima

Josephus provides two lengthy descriptions of Caesarea Maritima and its impressive harbor Sebastos (*War* 1.408–16; *Ant.* 15.331–41); there is a third description in *Antiquities* 16.136–41. The extent and duration of the archaeological excavations make it impossible to provide a full treatment, so I comment only on a few features of the descriptions that bear on the relative likelihood of the descriptions being personal observation or sources going back to a more nearly contemporary period.

Josephus's description of the harbor, Sebastos, is unusually detailed; the accounts are closely parallel, patterned in much the same way and with literary dependence of one on the other. There are, however, differences of detail and effect. Since there is detailed archaeological information on the substructure of the moles, it is appropriate to begin there. Josephus reports that the size of the stones (*lithoi*) let down into the water is 50x9x10 feet (presumably Roman feet) some being even larger (*War* 1.411). He gives their size as 50x18x9 feet, some being larger and some smaller, in *Ant.* 15.334. The marine archaeologists have shown that these details are incorrect.[11] The base for the moles was not made from large stones let down into the water but from poured concrete that set underwater, then a relatively recent innovation. Vitruvius provides information on this process (*de Architectura* 5.12.2–6), written about the same time as Caesarea Maritima was being built. If Josephus knew this technical innovation he did not mention it. The archaeologists graphically portray how large forms were floated into place and then sunk, before underwater concrete was poured into them.[12] The concrete base was discontinuous, composed of separate units joined by rock and sand fill. Though none matches exactly Josephus's reports on the size of the stones, the concrete units were probably the basis of the observed details.[13] To a nontechnical observer, the large concrete blocks viewed under water would look like large blocks of stone. This may suggest that the description in *War*, on which the description in *Antiquities* was clearly based, stemmed from observation and not technical knowledge. The report in *Antiquities* was no more correct and was not based on better information.

On one minor but valuable point, however, *Antiquities* was based on fuller and more accurate information: the materials were not local but "brought from outside at great expense" (*Ant.* 15.332). The excavation reports confirm this statement.[14] The tufa (the active ingredient in the concrete) came from Italy or Greece and wood for the forms came from Eastern Europe. Such details could not have been known by observation; they could only come from a source closer to the time of building and with insiders' knowledge. It is significant that this detail is found in *Antiquities*, and that *Antiquities*' account of Caesarea Maritima was based on *War*'s account, more closely than in the comparisons just made. Someone, Josephus or an assistant, had a source to supplement his earlier observations in *War*, as it was being revised for *Antiquities*. This point is strengthened by a minor fact, that Josephus reports the imported materials concerned the harbor, consistent with the excavation results, not the whole city.

The parallelism of Josephus's accounts of Caesarea Maritima identifies a special passage in *Antiquities* 15.340, not found in *War*. He describes passages and sewers under the city that were difficult to build. Some, he says, led to the harbor and sea at equal distances, with a diagonal one connecting the rest. He also tells how seawater flushed out the whole system. This description of a self-flushing toilet out of sight below the city is not found in *War*. Though it could have been based on personal observation, it is likelier that its insertion was prompted by a source available to him in Rome interested in technical matters.

Two small detailed additions support this impression. Josephus says that the whole task took 12 years (*Ant.* 15.341), a figure missing from *War*. He gives a precise date for the conclusion of the building operations in *Ant.* 16.136–41. These two details of the building operations would be consistent with use of written sources, since they are not likely to be based on his or a colleague's observation or memory. In the two parallel accounts, similar in structure and overlapping in language, the details in *War* rarely go beyond items readily available to personal observation. In three respects *Antiquities* implies reliable written information that was not likely to be available orally. They were not the kind of alterations that would be made by assistants whose task was the literary improvement of an existing text.

Temple

Josephus's two descriptions of the temple building activities are only partially parallel. They fill different rhetorical functions and occur at different places in the two narratives (*War* 5.184–227; *Ant.* 15.380–425). The great retaining walls of the temple are the only major portion of the building available today for analysis, so my comparisons will be limited to this structure. I begin with an observation, the significance of which will emerge, that the description of the temple in *War* 5.184–227 lacks references to Herod's role in its reconstruction. The impersonal sentences are either passive constructions or have "they" as their subject (the antecedent not made explicit); at one point Solomon is the subject. This pattern extends to *War* 5.238, where Herod's role in building the Antonia Fortress is noted. By contrast, *Ant.* 15.380 puts Herod's role in the building of the temple at the beginning of the description and Josephus stresses that the work was done at Herod's own expense. He knew, of course, of Herod's part in the rebuilding of the temple at the time he wrote *War*, for in *War* 1.401–2 he gives a brief account of its restoration and that of the Antonia Fortress, paying attention to the fact that the enormous cost of both was borne by Herod himself.

Consistent with this, and correct in its own way, is *War*'s impression of a gradual extension of the hilltop that comprises the temple mount (*War* 5.185–87). Josephus refers in passing to Solomon's role (implying, incorrectly but consistent with local nomenclature, that the east portico of the temple was built by Solomon). He refers to an extension to the north and a later enclosing of the hill on three sides. This latter observation, perhaps as easily verified in Josephus's day as in the modern period because of the "seam" at the southeast corner and the different style of masonry in the eastern wall, is essentially correct. Whether a first-century observer was likely to draw such a conclusion is a moot point, but the evidence existed. The parallel description in *Antiquities* instead proposes that Herod enlarged the precinct and raised it to a more imposing height. He had to remove the old foundations and lay

down new (*Ant.* 15.391). Josephus comments on a "great wall" (probably the south wall) and he is eloquent but unspecific about the large size
of the stones used in its construction. The description is more than circumstantial, however, for he contrasts the size of the stones "visible
along the front surface" (*Ant.* 15.399) with the invisible elements of the
retaining wall, particularly the lead and iron clamps used to hold the
stones together (15.398–99). These techniques were well known in
Greek and Roman building technology but were invisible in completed
structures. (It should be noted that the clamps were probably visible
after the temple's destruction in 70 C.E.)

This difference is similar to those noted earlier. *War* makes astute
observations and deductions based on those observations that go mar-
ginally beyond the casual. *Antiquities* knows details not normally open
to observation. Both *War* 5.189 and *Ant.* 15.399 allude to the fact, now
easily observable along the western wall, that the full depth of the
retaining walls was not visible because the Tyropoeon Valley had been
partially filled in order to smooth out the descent of adjacent streets.
War has the more accurate details, including a reference—remarkably
appropriate at this very point in the description of the western wall and
Tyropoeon Valley—to stones of 40 cubits length (ca. 60 feet; 18.3 m).
A stone north of Wilson's arch has been discovered that is 46x10x10
feet (ca. 30 cubits; or 14x3x3 m).[15]

When Josephus turns to the Antonia Fortress (*War* 5.238) he views it
as Herod's crowning work: just as the temple was over the city like a
fortress, the Antonia was over the temple. By comparison, the Antonia
plays a more subdued role and the description is flatter in *Ant.*
15.403–9. Only *Antiquities* 15.410–11 describes the gates to the temple
precinct, four on the west: the first was at the bridge, now called
Wilson's Arch; two more led to a "suburb,"[16] according to Josephus; the
last led to the Upper City and is now referred to as Robinson's Arch.
He then describes the south wall with gates in the middle (the Huldah
Gates). This leads him to the wildly exaggerated impression in *Ant.*
15.412 that the Royal Stoa was so high above the Kidron Valley that
one could not see the bottom.

Josephus's account of the temple in *Antiquities* is more detailed than
in *War*. *Antiquities* describes the temple's reconstruction where it fitted
best chronologically in Herod's reign and attributes the rebuilding
to Herod himself. *War* has its fullest description of the temple in book
5, slipped into his account of the temple's destruction. He does not

attribute its building to Herod in *War*'s main description, though earlier he attributed Herod's greatest building project properly to Herod. He attributes the reconstruction of the Antonia to Herod in *War* 5, and tacitly admits that both were by Herod (*War* 5.238), though only the Antonia was "a crowning exhibition of the innate grandeur of his genius."

His deliberate neglect of Herod at this point in *War* may have to do with two other factors. On the one hand, earlier Josephus may have been unwilling as a priest to attribute the magnificence of the temple to a commoner such as Herod; on the other, he wanted to emphasize the Antonia's grandeur and its origins in Herod's fertile activities when he emphasized the pathos of the warring parties within the temple precincts. The drama of the account may have had a stronger force when Herod's role in the one but not the other was acknowledged, or it may have rendered the account more appropriate for *War*'s original readership.

In any case, the comparisons lead in the same direction as already suggested. *Antiquities*, the fuller and more detailed account, has more reliable inside information, probably drawn from written sources. It attributes the building of the temple to Herod and provides fuller knowledge of details than would have been available from observation.

Other Benefactions

One potentially contrary piece of evidence will be assessed briefly to weigh its force. In *War* 1.422–28 and in *Ant.* 16.146–49 Josephus includes lists of Herod's generous benefactions to other cities. *War*'s list is longer than *Antiquities*', though the latter is supplemented by another list in 16.16–27, which refers to Herod's travels with Marcus Agrippa, an equally generous benefactor. *Antiquities*' main list seems an abbreviated summary of the list in *War*; it emphasizes four of Herod's greatest gifts: to Rhodes, Nicopolis, Antioch, and Olympia/Elis. They appear in the same order as in *War* with similar detail and wording, though *War*'s list is more complex. The absence of extensive archaeological remains is a problem, but since his descriptions are rather general, fuller archaeological information would not change matters much. The account in *Antiquities* is more detailed, but appears based not on better textual material but on misunderstandings or exaggerations.

- Rhodes: *Antiquities* 16.147 reduces the significance of Herod's gifts in two ways: it does not follow *War* 1.424 in saying that Herod rebuilt the Pythian temple on a grander scale, and it does not suggest that his gifts for shipbuilding were repeated.[17] The general effect, however, is the same. Herod's gifts to Rhodes went to its basic occupation, shipbuilding, and its most important religious structure, the Pythian temple.[18] The alterations and removal of a reference to the temple burning down may simply be abbreviations.

- Nicopolis: The addition of the phrase "he helped to construct the greater part of their public buildings" (*ta pleista ton demosion synkataskeuasen*; *Ant.* 16.147) is merely a vague precision—to use a deliberate oxymoron—of *War*'s lumping of Athens, Lacedemon, Nicopolis, and Pergamon together. All were laden with Herod's offerings. Josephus links Herod closely with Augustus in *Antiquities* through its use of *syn-* with *kataskeuasen* and the previous reference to Caesar.

- Antioch: *Antiquities* 16.148 altered some details about the colonnaded street from *War* 1.425, notably its length (20 furlongs, ca. 2 1/2 miles) and its previously muddy conditions. Josephus makes the account more impressive by saying Herod built colonnades on *both* sides, contributing to the convenience of the inhabitants, and that Antioch was the greatest city in Syria.

- Olympic Games: *Antiquities* 16.149 adds to the basic description in *War* 1.426–27 that Herod was made perpetual (*dienekês*) president. We cannot know if this is correct; it may well be a misreading—whether accidental or deliberate I cannot say—of the statement in *War* that his endowment was a "perpetual" (*dienekês*) memory of his term as president. There are no other sources to settle which account is correct. The excavations at Olympia suggest rebuilding and repair at about the time of Herod, but nothing connects the work with Herod or his contributions to the Games, nor is there other documentary or inscriptional evidence of his being president.

The deliberate changes in these four instances point toward misunderstandings or vagueness or abbreviation, perhaps best understood as change for change's sake. At the same time, they underscore that Josephus's other changes in *Antiquities*, when compared with *War*, contained material with more detail, greater precision, and a somewhat more elucidated understanding.

CONCLUSION

There are five types of differences between *Antiquities* and *War*: (1) errors in *War* corrected in *Antiquities*; (2) errors in *War* left uncorrected;

(3) new information in *Antiquities*, based on sources; (4) new information in *Antiquities*, perhaps common knowledge; (5) shared information, with little differentiation. Three of these five differences point in the same direction, and the other two may also point in that direction, though less clearly.

(1) Josephus made several errors in *War*'s descriptions of Herodian buildings that were corrected, presumably deliberately, in *Antiquities*. I noted four instances: the hill on which the upper palace at Herodium was built was entirely man-made; the steps at Herodium were white marble; the lower level areas were for defense; Herod's place in the rebuilding of the temple was ignored. In the first two cases the error was based on personal observation; in the defense of Herodium the error arose from inadequate observation or exaggeration; in the case of the temple it probably derived from personal motives. The errors were corrected in *Antiquities*, probably because a better source was available. In three of the cases that better source was likely to be earlier, with information contemporary, or nearly so, with the buildings. The authorial statements about the Antonia being a crowning work of Herod, linked with the absence of any reference to Herod in the temple account, may point in the same direction.

(2) Josephus left uncorrected errors in *War*. I noted four: the columns at Masada were monolithic; Masada's defensive walls were white stone; there were multiple palaces within the upper palace at Herodium; huge stones formed the substructure of the harbor at Caesarea Maritima. In the first two cases there was no parallel account in *Antiquities*; in the other two, referring to Herodium and Caesarea, the parallel account retained the errors, presumably because no better or more accurate information was available. In three of the four cases the source of the error may have been personal observation. The errors could only have been corrected with inside information; one case would have required precise technological information about pouring underwater concrete. The error about palaces at Herodium's upper level may simply mean that Josephus had not visited the palace himself or that he used the word *basileioi* loosely.

(3) The most persuasive category of differentiation between *War* and *Antiquities* was the new information contained in the later work. *Antiquities* added that materials used in Sebastos, the harbor at Caesarea, were imported from a distance and that Caesarea had a sophisticated underground drainage system, a statement missing from *War*. *Antiquities* stated that Caesarea and Sebastos took 12 years to build, being finished in 10 B.C.E., that the temple's retaining walls required the removal of the old foundations and the building of new ones, and that lead and iron clamps were used in the retaining walls. None appeared in *War*. The new information had to have come from written sources available at the time of the writing of *Antiquities*. It could not have been known from personal observation—which Josephus was unlikely to have made in the 80s and 90s—but could have been based on sources available in Rome. These minor features are the kind of information he could have gotten from sources more nearly contemporaneous with the buildings, possibly from a writer connected with Herod the Great.

(4) Josephus's account of the gates in the western wall of the temple *peribolos* contains new information that does not clearly support the above conclusion, but it is not inconsistent with it. Josephus may have been in a position to make such observations in the 90s since they were readily observable or he may have derived it from a source. When he dealt with the southern wall and the height of the Royal Basilica above the Kidron Valley he exaggerated wildly. Of the two changes, one was seemingly accurate and one rhetorically grotesque.

(5) Different information was found in *War* and *Antiquities*, but there was no persuasive way to evaluate it. Four of the five instances were foreign benefactions:

- the streets of Jerusalem were well above the bottom of the Tyropoeon Valley, with a reference in *War* to the size of the building stones;

- Herod restored the Pythian temple in Rhodes and supported shipbuilding, but the scale of the one is unclear and the number of the other in dispute;

- Herod was very generous to Nicopolis, but the accounts do not agree whether he worked with Augustus and if he built the majority of the public buildings;

- Herod built a colonnaded street in Antioch, but whether it was 20 stades long and whether he built colonnades on both sides was not agreed;

- Herod was elected president of the Olympic games, but it is unsure if it was for one set of games or as permanent president.

The last four cannot be evaluated against archaeological data, so it is impossible to say which account is better rooted in *realia*. In those cases Josephus may have altered his later work without the assistance of other source material. The alterations seem mistaken or exaggerated or generalized, with no clear pattern. In the fifth case, the Tyropoeon Valley, the sizes of the stones given in *War* were slightly exaggerated but roughly correct. Possibly this becomes a new category, good information in *War* that was overlooked in *Antiquities*.

At the risk of generalization and slight exaggeration, the differences between *War* and *Antiquities* in these limited sections are patient of two claims. First, these parts of *War* presupposed little inside information of a kind that might have come from a court historian such as Nicolas of Damascus. All could be understood on the basis of personal observation at the time of Josephus. Second, the fuller and more accurate information in *Antiquities* came from a good, reliable source. That source was likely written, and by someone fairly close to Herod's building activities. A corollary is that the changes did not derive from assistants improving the style, though they could have come from assistants who had consulted available sources.

This analysis has focused on very limited sections of Josephus's descriptions that were unlikely to have been strongly influenced by his own intentions, preferences, or shifting loyalties. It leads to the hypothesis that Nicolas of Damascus was not a primary source of these pieces of information in *War*. The source may have been Josephus himself, drawing on personal observation. The fuller information in *Antiquities*, however, likely came from a source such as Nicolas, though it cannot be said whether Nicolas was himself that source. What is noteworthy about this conclusion is that it squares with what Josephus says about his sources and his own role as an eyewitness. Perhaps his authorial statements are accurate.

He claimed eyewitness status enthusiastically for *War*, not for *Antiquities*. Statements to this effect are found in *War* 1.2–3 (a similar preface in *Antiquities* 1.5–9 stresses a source for that work), in *Life*

361–62, and *Apion* 1.47–52, in each case referring to the *Jewish War*. These seem more than rhetorical flourishes. On the other hand he claimed to have used sources in *Antiquities*, specifically Nicolas of Damascus. He refers to Nicolas as a source 11 times in *Antiquities* and once in *Apion* (he is an actor in the narrative 6 times in *War* and 11 times in *Antiquities*). Josephus's use of Nicolas cannot be confirmed precisely because the relevant sections of Nicolas's long work on *World History* are almost entirely missing. It is regrettable that there are insufficient fragments of Nicolas extant to demonstrate Josephus's dependence either in matters of content or of style. We can, however, confirm in general Josephus's use of sources and, more precisely, dependence on an accurate source. Josephus's explicit statements that *War* depended on his own eyewitness information should not be dismissed. The comparisons made above between *War* and *Antiquities* suggest he relied more on sources (perhaps Nicolas) in *Antiquities*.

This preliminary investigation suggests there is little evidence for the common assumption that Josephus worked from Nicolas of Damascus in *War*. I do not suggest that Nicolas was not used as a source for *War*, only that caution must be urged in making such assumptions.

CHAPTER SIXTEEN

ORIGINS, INNOVATIONS, AND SIGNIFICANCE OF HEROD'S TEMPLE

INTRODUCTION[1]

Renewed attention to the Jerusalem temple and its reconstruction by Herod is only slowly resulting in a more clearly considered understanding of its architecture.[2] This chapter is a prolegomenon to a reassessment of the Herodian temple that emphasizes a few architectural features,[3] the main points of which are to identify Herod's innovations on the basis of the building's architectural ambiguity and to comment on their social-historical significance. I consider function as a factor in social description. It begins from two kinds of evidence, archaeological and literary.[4] I argue against utilizing idealized measurements, theoretical courtyard layouts, or hypothetical shapes, as is sometimes done. These may have a place in discussing theoretical issues, but not as a substitute for evidence and analysis. It is special pleading to claim that Herod's building program was "unfinished" because its dimensions do not fit a symmetrical scheme or that the temple was south of the present Haram al-Sharif because only thus can Jesus' oracle be fulfilled concerning "no stone on another."[5]

The temple was rebuilt by one of the most prominent patrons in the Mediterranean world during a period of great significance in the building of temples.[6] It was a period of intense building activities by Augustus and Marcus Agrippa and a small coterie of enthusiastic builders, among whom Herod was a leading practitioner. The temple was built by trained workmen, many of whom were priests, using up-to-date techniques and technology, in most respects analogous to the situation facing other temple builders of the period. Among those various projects—even including those of Augustus and Marcus Agrippa—none outshone the temple in Jerusalem in size, scope, quality, and significance.

271

Table 16.1: Comparison of Temple's

	Date	Fosse	COURTS	Stoai	Outer Court	Soreg
Jos: Ant 8.95–98 Solomon's	95 C.E.	Valleys	Temple	Stoai (double row)	Outer/2nd Precinct	Partition, 3 cu *Gison/ thrigkos*
Ezekiel 40-48	6 C. B.C.E.		Gates and guards	Walls Chambers	Outer Court Israelites	
11QT 30–46	2 C. B.C.E.	Ditch Terrace = rampart	Sanctuary	Colonnades	Third Court Daughters Strangers	
Philo Spec. Leg. 1.71–75	40s C.E.		Outermost walls Fortifica-tions	4 Double Stoai	[implied] Foreign Vis No grove of plantation	
Jos: War 5.184–237	75 C.E.	Hill with precipices	Perimeter walls on deep foun-dations	Dbl Stoai Cols 25 cu Colored pavement	Lower Courts Foreigners	Balustrade + warning, steps Terrace
Jos: Ant 15.388–425	95 C.E.	Valleys	Perimeter walls on new foun-dations	Double Stoai Spoils Royal Basilica	First Court Secret Undergroun d passage	Balustrade + warning, Few steps
Jos: Apion 2.103–7	95 C.E.				Outer Court open to all	
m. MIDD 2.1–5.4	c. 200 C.E.		Temple Mt (500x500 cubits)			Soreg + Hel Rampart Steps
m. KELIM 1.6–9	c. 200 C.E.		Temple Mt [Gentiles]			Rampart

Architectural Features

HIERON	Middle Court	Inner Court	Sacred Area	NAOS	First Room	Second Room
		All pure people	Sacred precinct Priests			
		Gates and guards	Inner Court Priests	Vestibule	Holy Place	Inner Room Holiest Place
		2nd Court Israel	Inner Court Priests	Temple/ House		Columns west
						[implied] Innermost
	Upper Courts 2nd Court Women (our nation/ visitors) partitioned	Inner Court Parapet People who were pure Parapet 1 cu Laity	Priests	Naos	Holy House	Innermost recess: holy of holies
Inner Enclosure	2nd Court Men/Wives	Sacred Court Women forbidden	3rd Court Priests	Naos		
	2nd Court Jews and Wives	3rd Court Pure Jews	4th Court Priests		Adyton	Only High Priest
	Court of Women + balcony for viewing	Court of Israel (males)	Court of Priests	Porch	Sanctuary	Holiest Place Behind Mercy
Temple Court	Court of Women	Court of Israel (males)	Court of Priests		Sanctuary	Holiest Place

Literary texts, such as Josephus, Philo, the *Mishnah*, 11QT, and Ezekiel (more remotely, Eupolemus and Hecataeus), provide important descriptions of or ideas about the temple at various periods (Table 16.1). Josephus and Philo were contemporary witnesses and generally describe what the temple was like in their day. Whether the *Mishnah* included historical details—and if so of what period—or described what was hoped for is more controversial. Ezekiel and 11QT in different ways describe what specific groups (Babylonian exiles or eschatological visionaries) wanted to see. To what extent those two visions reflected aspects of the building at their time is moot. Neither reflected the scale and general impression of the building, as they must have known it. Much of the literary evidence is neither descriptive nor primary, and should not be preferred over physical evidence or contemporary descriptions. Though this chapter is not primarily an archaeological study, it presumes that the correct way to talk about the project architecturally is with a balanced archaeological and literary summary, set in the context of first-century cities and temples.[7] Integrating literary, archaeological, and sociological data is an important challenge.[8] I begin with a brief architectural description of Herod's temple and the influences on it that will help to point towards its social significance. I aim to view the architecture as reflecting that society's needs and the patron's goals.

DESCRIPTION AND EXTERNAL RELATIONSHIPS

Architectural Description

The temple in Jerusalem was a walled religious precinct, with access and egress controlled by ten gates. In its rebuilt form, it lay on one side of the city, and its walls were the walls of the city on the east (Plates 45, 46), north and part of the west side, though in the mid-first century C.E. a new wall on the north took over this function. The temple was partly incorporated into the city's urban fabric to the south and west (Plates 39–41, 43), yet was essentially separated from the rest of the daily activities of the city by its perimeter wall and the sharp grade changes on both those sides. Though capable of being defended, its walls and gates (forming a *peribolos*) were not designed primarily with defense in mind.[9] The *temenos* (religious precinct, the large sacred area inside the *peribolos*) contained a sacred religious complex for sacrifice (*hieron*),[10] which surrounded the central shrine (*naos*), associated with Yahweh's presence. The *hieron* included several courtyards surrounded by another wall (*peribolos*). Access to the inner areas was controlled more strictly than access to the outer areas. Subordinate functions were concentrated in two main areas, in the outer colonnades and in the rooms that formed part of the inner areas.

The innermost building (*naos*) was a "a house for God" (*domus Dei*).[11] The *temenos* in which it was set, like the courtyards around most temples of this type, provided space for worshippers, but was not a "house for the congregation" (*domus ecclesiae*), since the worshipers gathered in the open air, as was the practice in most temples. A surrounding *stoa* architecturally framed the *hieron* with its *naos* in much the same way as in other late Hellenistic and Roman temples. The Jerusalem temple was set off from other temples by the complexity of the structures included within the *hieron* and *peribolos*.

Several architectural traditions influenced the design; these were only partially integrated into a coherent complex. The central *naos*, for example, was essentially a high, opaque, solid mass, with relatively little modulation. The other structures of the *hieron* that surrounded it were lower, but interrupted by a series of doors or gates. The *stoai* of the outer courtyard were in more than one style. On the south, overshadowing everything except the central *naos*, was an immense Roman basilica (the Royal Basilica), with massive Corinthian columns; along the central section of the eastern wall was an earlier *stoa* deriving from an intermediate phase of the temple's history, known—anachronistically no doubt—as Solomon's Portico.[12] New *stoai* were constructed around the west, north, and the remaining parts of the east wall in the latest Roman style. The Antonia fortress hovered over the northwest corner; it was partially integrated into the sacred structure, but again (we may surmise) in a different architectural style. Various capitals have been found in the excavations. The axis of the *hieron* was at right angles to the axis of the *temenos*, an unusual but not unparalleled arrangement.[13] The east-west axis through the *naos* coincided neither with other architectural elements (gates, towers) nor with circulation routes. That orientation preserved an earlier arrangement; it was required because east was the traditional orientation.[14]

The pavement was multicolored and much of the other architectural elaboration would also have been colored; special parts, especially of the *naos*, were picked out in gold leaf. Among the more important architectural elements were the gateways and doorways, differentiated from each other by function, placing, and decorative motifs. The *temenos* itself varied in level, rising in stages toward the area where sacrifices were carried out; at one point the original bedrock poked through, as it still does within the Dome of the Rock. There was, however, no landscaping in the huge *temenos*.

Differentiations

Herod's structure was not wholly out of character with other major temples, but it had several important features that together made it distinctive. It was included within the city—a "capital" city like Petra, Damascus, or Alexandria—and did not occupy a holy site outside the city at the end of a processional way, as at Si'a, Ephesus, or Didyma. Yet it was segregated from the daily life of the city, not unlike some other Roman-period temples, such as Bel at Palmyra. There was no adjacent *agora* or *forum*, as with Zeus at Gerasa. The temple dominated the city's urban design, yet without being totally integrated into it (contrast Roma and Augustus at Caesarea Maritima); it was not fully incorporated into the urban street pattern (as Jupiter at Damascus was). Like membership-based cults it had controlled access (Temples of Demeter and Kore), yet rather than having only one gate, its ten gates set it apart from other exclusive and carefully controlled religious sites. Though the temple was on a ridge, it was not an acropolis style structure; Mount Moriah was religiously significant, but not the highest peak in the area. Though earlier the royal palace and temple were architecturally and symbolically linked, the temple was separated from Herod's royal palace, an important consideration in the Herodian period. The huge basilica to the south, known as the Royal Basilica, and to a lesser extent the Antonia fortress to the north, evoked a royal presence in the *temenos*, perhaps deliberately. Besides providing a very large gathering space in the *temenos* for everyone, like most Greek and Roman temples, the temple limited access to the holy place itself by imposing a system of hierarchical distinctions. The *naos* proper was closed to the people.

External Influences

The building design blended several influences from Judea, Nabatea, Palmyra, Egypt, the Hellenistic world, and Rome.[15] The complex interconnections can be described in a rough way:

- *Indigenous*: The overall conception was indigenous, harking back to the first temple, Ezekiel's idealized temple and Zerubbabel's temple following the return from the exile. It also recalled distantly the still earlier tabernacle in the wilderness. The hierarchical arrangement of its courts, together with the careful balance between its functions as a *domus Dei* and a place for all the people, should be seen as an indigenous feature. The absence of a cult statue was strictly Judean (Chapters 13, 14).

- *Nabatea*: The *naos* had affinities with the Temple of Dushara at Petra and related Nabatean temples; it was built at about the same time. Narrow stairs within the thickness of the walls gave access to the roof; a holy of holies was incorporated (though differently) within the *naos*; the temple was laid out with its axis at right angles to the *temenos* axis, which in the case of Dushara was oriented north to a mountain; it was mostly or entirely aniconic.[16]

- *Palmyra*: Palmyra's Temple of Bel also had roof access, with stairs from the *naos*; the axis of the *naos* was at right angles to the axis of the *temenos*, though no right-angled turn was required, as in the Temple of Dushara and the Jerusalem temple. The arrangement of sacrificial altar to the left of the main axis and lustration basin to the right was similar.

- *Egypt*: The hierarchical sequence of spaces and courtyards was reminiscent of large Egyptian complexes (Karnak, Luxor, Deir el-Bahri), especially those of the New Kingdom, where a similar impulse to enormous size was present. The modulation of Herod's *temenos* wall with pilasters was rather like the much earlier wall of the precinct at Saqqara. The tunnel-like access through the Huldah Gates distantly recalled tunnels to the pyramids.

- *Hellenism*: The drive to immense dimensions (the *temenos*), huge volume (the Royal Basilica), and great height (the *naos*), were late Hellenistic, as was the spatial playfulness in the underground tunnels at the Huldah Gates (cf. Apollo at Didyma; Asklepieion at Pergamon), the overpasses at the two southern corners, and the ascending changes of level.

- *Rome*: The enclosure of religious spaces with *stoai* was Roman—Greek *stoai* sometimes framed but did not regularly enclose—and their design

was probably Roman as well, to judge from descriptions and column
fragments. The eclectic use of varied capitals, the decorative elements
and the raising of the *naos* well above the surrounding *temenos* were
also Roman. In conception and form the Royal Basilica was a Roman
structure.

It is neither possible nor necessary to prove there was a direct influence
from any of these sources. Herod's temple was not purely one thing or
another. To use a literary critical term being used by architects, it was
intertextual in its use of allusions that could not be easily pigeonholed.[17]

Herod's Role

This peculiar blend of architectural features reflected similar features
within Herod's background: Judean, Arabian (Nabatean and Palmyrene), Egyptian, and Hellenistic-Roman cultural connections.
Herod was not, of course, the only person with such complex influences; others might also have expressed these same intertextual elements in eastern Mediterranean buildings, and some of these same
elements may have been evident in an earlier stage of the Jerusalem
temple; Solomon's portico, for example, was a Hasmonean structure
sufficiently Hellenizing that it was retained in Herod's rebuilding.

Herod's architectural oeuvre—a coherent program of built works in
the eastern half of the Mediterranean—has begun to be systematically
examined.[18] Its innovative features and overarching characteristics were
well illustrated in his religious buildings, which demonstrated a range of
religious interests and provided a context for the temple's reconstruction:

- *Mausolea*: The circular upper palace at Herodium, one of Herod's most
  innovative residential structures, may have been designed to serve as
  Herod's own mausoleum.[19] In part it may have been a religious building.
  Earlier he had built another circular mausoleum in Jerusalem, just north
  of the Damascus Gate, though entirely different in details. Both have
  features in common with Augustus's own circular mausoleum in Rome,
  though Herod's family tomb may predate Augustus's. Though he did
  not invent the circular tomb form, as the widespread use of *tumuli* and
  other circular mausolea demonstrates, Herod's two mausolea may have
  been innovative, and not just an aping of his patron Augustus.

- *Memorials*: Two of Herod's buildings were maquettes for the beautifully
  pilastered external walls in the Jerusalem temple. Though Hebron's
  Haram al Khalil and Mamre's Haram Ramet al-Khalil are not literarily described as Herodian projects, both were unmistakably his. Both

were open-air precincts. The Hebron memorial contained the traditional tombs of the patriarchs and matriarchs (Abraham, Isaac, Jacob,
Sarah, Leah, Rebekah); the Mamre memorial, just outside Hebron, was
dedicated to Abraham. The Idumean location of both suggests Herod
aimed to incorporate patriarchal traditions—common to both
Edomites and Israelites—and so appeal to Judeans and Idumeans, who,
like his own family, had embraced Judaism.

- *Local temples*: Herod was involved with a temple to Ba'al Shamim ("Lord
  of the Heavens") at the important three-temple site at Si'a, at the end of
  a long processional way from Canatha (Qanawat). Ba'al Shamim was a
  principal god of Canaan, Nabatea, and Palmyra, among other places,
  but he also had Edomite and Israelite connections. So it may be significant that Herod participated in the Temple of Ba'al Shamim and not
  the adjacent Temple of Dushara, a Nabatean deity less easily assimila-
  ble to Jewish convictions. A statue base, found in the 1860s in the
  remains of the porch but now lost, occupied a prominent place to the
  right of the main door; its inscription implied that Herod was a patron
  in some fashion, though in what way we cannot know. Possibly his role
  as "protector" of the Nabateans from 31 B.C.E. (*Ant.* 15.159–60)
  accounted for the statue, but it is likelier that he contributed financially
  to the project. The temple's style was purely Nabatean, unlike anything
  else of Herod's.

- *Temples to Roma and Augustus*: Herod was an early supporter of the
  Imperial cult, following his confirmation as king at Rhodes (31 B.C.E.),
  building three temples to Roma and Augustus: at Caesarea Maritima,
  dominating the harbor and the city center;[20] at Sebaste (ancient
  Samaria), at the city's highest point on top of the ninth century B.C.E.
  royal palace; and at Panias, a Hellenistic city with a complex of cult
  caves dedicated to Pan.[21] Excavations show the scale of the first two;
  excavations at Panias and at nearby Omrit are clarifying the situation
  there. The absence of religious disputes over these temples indicates he
  was successful in not giving deep offence to Jews by his choice of sites—
  one in Phoenicia, one in Samaria, and one in Tyrian or Iturean lands.

- *Other temples*: Herod built temples in Tyre and Beirut, but Josephus gives
  no details (*War* 1.422) and none have emerged from excavations.
  Josephus says (*War* 1.424) that Herod restored Rhodes' Temple of
  Pythian Apollo and that he was active at Olympia. At Rhodes there are
  substantial remains of Apollo's temple on the acropolis, but no inscription referring to Herod's role. Inscriptions have been found, however, on
  the acropolis in Athens that allude to Herodian benefactions, possibly
  related to the circular Temple of Roma and Augustus east of the
  Parthenon or possibly the Erechtheion.

- *Temple in Jerusalem*: Josephus remarks (*War* 1.400) that Herod's temple
  was a work of great piety. The scale of the temple was staggering for a
  small country. Its complexity required extensive organization, careful

preparations, huge quantities of materials of high quality, imagination, coordination with the existing cityscape, and continued regular worship. Herod left Judea—and Judaism at large—richer and prouder: "He who has not seen the temple has not seen a beautiful building" (*b. B. Bat.* 4a).

- *Synagogues*: The temple served Jews in Judea and adjacent regions. Synagogues served Jews elsewhere. The literary records are silent on Herod and synagogues, and it seems likely he never built one. A synagogue in Rome was dedicated to him, but he had nothing to do with its construction, and two of his palaces were modified during the Revolt (66–74 C.E.) to incorporate a synagogue, but neither had anything to do with Herod (Chapter 7).

We can infer Herod's religious convictions from this group of buildings. He was a Jew, strongly committed to the temple in Jerusalem but with little interest in synagogues. He followed torah on images and figurative representations to a close approximation (Chapter 13). He was pious towards the patriarchs and matriarchs of Israel, to deceased members of his family, and to Augustus, as is clear from temples inside his kingdom honoring his patron. These were all highly valued in his society. He also supported "pagan" cults, through participation in structures to Ba'al Shamim, Pythian Apollo, unspecified deities in Tyre and Sidon, and buildings in Athens and Olympia.

Herod's creative role in his architectural projects is uncertain, since no claim is made by him or on his behalf either in the literature or inscriptionally. Usually major patrons in the classical period—among whom Augustus, Marcus Agrippa, and Herod were leaders in their generation—played more important roles than modern patrons. No architect is mentioned for any of Herod's projects, so the field is open for speculation. His highly personal buildings—the northern villa at Masada, upper palace at Herodium, promontory palace at Caesarea Maritima, and the Winter Palace at Jericho—show a single mind at work, pressing beyond the architectural conventions of the day. These same buildings, plus the temple in Jerusalem and the harbor installations at Caesarea Maritima, show a marked ability to turn awkward site difficulties to advantage. His mausolea were in the forefront of a developing movement and show a degree of innovation, especially obvious in the case of Herodium, where he may have lived in his own mausoleum. His buildings used up-to-date Roman building technology—such as underwater concrete, continuous and linked barrel vaults, circular vaults with pendentives, *opus reticulatum*, and *opus sectile*—though there was little sense of a continuous process of experimentation.

His projects could derive from a single brilliant mind, a leading architect who had the same range of experiences as Herod, was interested in drawing on the same range of influences, and had visited the same places Herod had. This is not impossible, but it seems a little unlikely. No such person's name has survived in the literary record, so I lean to the view that Herod was himself largely responsible for his projects. While I would not discount the involvement of other architects—and technical help, of course—it seems preferable to imagine that Herod was extensively involved in the architecture of his projects, including the Jerusalem temple.

RELATIONSHIPS WITHIN THE TRADITION

Relation to the Temples of Zerubbabel and the Hasmoneans

Some traditional features of the temple's design could be altered more freely than others.[22] Herod could not have altered radically the location or orientation of the *naos*, but he was freer to alter the configuration of the *hieron*'s service facilities; he could enlarge the *temenos* and its *stoai*; he was free to develop new functional appurtenances outside or adjacent to the *temenos*, such as bridges and stairs. Some of the gates had liturgical associations; ritual provisions, such as the Red Heifer ceremony, may have been relatively sensitive. Generally speaking, the farther from the *naos* and the altar the more latitude there was for architectural innovation. Herod worked with the form of the temple as it had been developed under Zerubbabel and expanded by the Hasmoneans.[23]

In his reconstruction plans he extended the *temenos* northwards across a Hasmonean fosse or defensive trench; he cut away a large amount of bedrock north of that trench and filled a small transverse valley on the northeast. Above the northern scarp he built the Antonia fortress where the al-Omariyyah School is now found; its construction must have been before 31 B.C.E., the date of Marc Antony's defeat at Actium, so preparatory work must have long predated the building of the temple. He extended the platform southwards. In the southeast he built a multilevel arched and vaulted substructure on which to lay the *temenos* platform, almost like a multilevel *cryptoportico*. He constructed the Royal Basilica, along the whole south end of the *temenos*, with supports matching the locations of the columns and arches. He created tunnels and stairs underneath it connecting with the two Huldah Gates, whose general location may have predated his work, and constructed *mikvaoth* outside these gates on the platform.[24] On the west, he built other main entrances: the overpass at Robinson's Arch; the upper-level bridge and aqueduct at Wilson's Arch;[25] the street level entries at Barclay's Gate and another gate towards the middle of the western wall. He retained the earlier Hasmonean wall on the east, extending it north and south. He also built the so-called Beautiful Gate. Herod built the *stoai* inside the wall surrounding the *temenos*, except for part of the eastern one, Solomon's Portico. The *temenos* gates retained traditional names and locations in most cases, except for one named after his friend Marcus Agrippa, which was probably decorated with an eagle (*War* 1.416). It was likely the gate at the end of the bridge joining the temple mount with the western hill, and the eagle probably faced west, so that worshipers could ignore it, while those who were making a ceremonial visit from the palace would have noticed it as a symbol of Roman power.[26]

Herod was responsible for some of the water installations associated with the temple, though it is uncertain which were initiated by him and which were improved by him.[27] He built the structures that surrounded the base of the temple: shops, platforms, stairs, *mikvaoth*, and the connections between these and the rest of the city to the west and south. A bridge connected with the Red Heifer ceremony is described in *m. Parah* 3.6, with two levels of arches, which crossed the Kidron Valley to the Mount of Olives; according to *m. Shekal* 4.2 (citing Abba Saul) it was built by a high priest. (It is unclear if it was part of the Herodian complex, since this bridge does not appear in other descriptions of the temple; it may be legendary or non-Herodian.)

Nineteenth-century explorers investigated and mapped rock-cut installations below grade. Many clearly predated Herod's structures. Some were earlier cisterns, one large one possibly connected with an earlier palace or a fortress. Some, by contrast, have architectural features that imply they were part of various phases in the building of the temple, including Herod's phase. Those at the north edge of the inner platform may well have corresponded with features of the *hieron* and *naos*, and one diagonal tunnel seems to have led to the Tadi Gate. The Herodian temple differed substantially from its predecessors, especially the Hasmonean temple, in size, complexity, grandeur, decoration, and architectural sophistication.

Relationship to Ezekiel, 11QT, and Mishnah

The literary descriptions in Ezekiel (sixth century B.C.E.), 11QT (second century B.C.E.) and the *Mishnah* (early third century C.E.) differ sharply from Josephus's descriptions in literary form. All three were imaginative visionary texts portraying different ideals at different times. The three texts are relevant in different ways to architectural questions about Herod, but the relevance is more modest than is sometimes claimed, since their main concerns are communal ideologies, theologies, and social concerns at the time of writing. In the case of the *Mishnah*, they contain some recollections of what the Second Temple was like. They are important for a longitudinal history of the temple spread over almost eight centuries, but their importance for the first-century temple is limited. Each of the texts is sometimes cited in support of one or another solution to the architectural problems of the Herodian temple, but their visionary character makes it impossible to use them to settle questions about Herod's design.

Ezekiel and 11QT, the two earliest, vary in the number of courts they describe and their identification.[28] Ezekiel, reflecting the first temple and anticipating a new building after the return from exile, says it has two courts. The outer court was at a lower level, paved, with 30 rooms around it. The inner court was up eight steps, with rooms for preparing sacrifices and rooms for priests (Ezek 40:17-47). By contrast, 11QT emphasizes three courts: an inner court of the priests (11QT 37.8); a middle court for the sons of Israel (38.12); and an outer court for women, children, and proselytes (40.5). The number and details of the courts imply that such questions were actively discussed at the time and were controversial.[29] The proposals of 11QT reinterpretated the Persian period and Hasmonean temple, but to what extent its three-court arrangement was an innovation is not apparent from the text itself.

This process of interpretation and differentiation was carried on into the *Mishnah*, which varies from 11QT in important respects. While both had an obvious and understandable interest in the temple's holiness, the *Mishnah*'s more complex degrees of holiness reinterprets recollections of Herod's temple and refines them. The *Mishnah* refers specifically to a Court of Gentiles, rampart, court of women, court of Israel, court of priests and so on, features reflected in but different from 11QT's triple-court arrangement. Each, that is to say, reinterpreted the most recent form of the temple prior to the time of writing. These reinterpretative features were aimed at meeting current ideological needs; each of the three texts, however, should be understood as subordinate to historically based texts.

ARCHAEOLOGICAL AND LITERARY REFLECTIONS

A correct understanding of the several courtyards in Herod's temple derives partly from an architectural reading of the temple's remains and partly from literary evidence in Josephus's accounts in *War* 5.184–237 and *Ant.* 15.380–425. Archaeological work at Yodefat, Gamla, and other places show how accurately Josephus wrote about architectural and urban matters (Part 1). Josephus's shortest and clearest account is in *Contra Apionem*:

> All who ever saw our temple are aware of the general design of the building, and the inviolable barriers, which preserved its sanctity. It had four surrounding courts, each with its special statutory restrictions. The outer court was open to all, foreigners included; women during their impurity were alone refused admission. To the second court all Jews were admitted and, when uncontaminated by any defilement, their wives; to the third male Jews, if clean and purified; to the fourth the priests robed in their priestly vestments. (*Apion* 2.103–7)

Sequence of Courtyards

The huge *temenos* was broken up by several vertical and horizontal spatial separations that together defined a sequence of spaces, some of which coincided with "zones of holiness," as defined later in the *Mishnah*, some of which did not. These zones, however, did not in all cases coincide with major architectural separations; sometimes one zone leaked into another and this led to ambiguity in the architectural design.

The *temenos* was defined by an exterior perimeter wall (*peribolos*), which was integrated with *stoai* of several widths and heights, the southern side being occupied by the Royal Basilica. The *temenos* formed a single huge space, broken visually by the structures of the *hieron*. The largest and most amorphous part of the *temenos* was the outer court

(Court of Gentiles) that was accessible to non-Jews and uncircumcised peoples, to all except those ritually impure. The area included everything within the *peribolos* walls up to the "barricade" or *soreg* (3 cu. high or ca. 1.5 m), with twelve gates whose inscriptions warned trespassers of the death penalty. Architecturally and visually, however, the outer court included the rampart beyond the *soreg*, for the *soreg* was a minor architectural feature in this vast area. The outer court comprised four unequal units: the area between the *hieron* and the *peribolos* on the west was very small; the space on the east side was next in size (and may have housed *spolia* from military victories; *Ant.* 15.402); the north portion of the court was next in size; the largest portion was the southern area between the *hieron* and the Royal Basilica, probably used for royal addresses and meetings of the people as a whole.

The "rampart" was an odd transitional space between the *soreg* and the *hieron* walls, entered through its twelve gates. The narrow space had a flight of 14 steps, and a small platform before the Court of Women (most clearly in *War* 5.193–97). This transitional space was a separate but minor element in the sequence of spaces; ritually, however, it was not treated as a separate court or zone of holiness (though note the better developed role of the rampart in *m. Kelim* 1:6). Functionally it was part of the second court, a preliminary to the Court of Women, but architecturally it was part of the first or outer court.

Through gates in the walls at the top of the rampart was the Court of Women, the second court.[30] The name is a misleading, for males also used this court to proceed on their way from the eastern entrance. Exactly how these two functions were accommodated is unclear. A high wall (25 cubits; ca. 12 m) enclosed the courtyard, a cruciform space with flat roofed chambers in the corners that overlooked the court and the inner areas.

On the west side of the Court of Women 12 steps (a rise of another few meters) led through a major partition wall with a massive gateway to the Court of Israel, the "sacred court." It was a shallow, broad space, bounded on the west by a low balustrade. Ritually pure adult males were admitted to this area to hand over sacrificial victims to the priests on duty.[31] Despite its fundamentally important ritual function, it did not have its own spatial identity. It is odd that this space, though ritually distinct, was architecturally and visually part of the inner court. This architectural ambiguity is similar to the ambiguity of the rampart. The Court of Israel was visually a part of the next space in the sequence, but ritually part of the previous space; the rampart was visually part of the previous space but ritually part of the next in the sequence.

The Court of Priests or inner court, which *Apion* calls the fourth court and *Antiquities* calls the third court, was an amorphous space that lay between a balustrade, which defined the Court of Israel, and the *naos*. It was an extremely busy space for slaughtering animals, hanging and butchering them, dividing portions, making sacrifices at the altar, offering incense, and making ablutions. The massive *naos* dominated the court, a backdrop to and focus for the activity. In addition to various surrounding rooms and other installations (minor architecturally but important ritually) the Court of Priests was punctuated by two major structures, a large altar on the left approached by a ramp from the south and a ritual laver or ablution basin on the right.

The *naos* itself comprised two chambers; the holy place was the outer chamber and the holy of holies the inner chamber. Though they had different degrees of ritual holiness, from the exterior they were architecturally and visually undifferentiated and shared a common structure. Wings on the holy place's porch gave visual breadth to the narrow, unusually tall building.[32] It rose high above the walls of the surrounding structures, so it could be seen from everywhere in the *temenos*. The internal division into two spaces would have been common knowledge but was unimportant architecturally. None but priests could see the division.

The architecture of this sequence of structures and spaces gave a different impression than the literary descriptions convey, for the literature focuses on ritual and function. The tension between architecture and ritual is important: when questions of ritual purity are fundamental, the architecture might be expected to cohere with and embody the zones of purity. The tension between architectural expression and ritual requirements created ambiguities that call for explanation. There were three main points of tension between architecture and ritual: at the transition from the Court of Gentiles, to the *soreg*, rampart, and Court of Women; functionally within the Court of Women between male and female use; and at the transition between the Court of Women, the Court of Israel, and the Court of Priests. Such tensions, I suggest, presuppose changes, either new developments or altered relationships among the parts. Table 16.1 shows that descriptions of the temple differ most in two main respects: the courtyards and their relationships, and their accuracy in describing inaccessible or priestly areas (sacrificial areas and beyond). This is not surprising, because differences in the outer areas were changed most as the temple evolved and because the inner areas were less familiar and of less interest.[33]

Court of the Gentiles

No account of the first temple, of Ezekiel's vision, of Zerubbabel's temple, or of the Hasmonean alterations referred explicitly to a court for Gentiles or foreigners. There probably was no such provision. Pre-Herodian accounts generally referred to two courts, one associated with the holy place, intended for priests, and one for the congregation of Israel. A more complex sequence of courtyards appeared for the first time in the second century B.C.E. In the *Temple Scroll* (11QT), however, the outer court is not for Gentiles; the almost half-a-mile-square space is for daughters and strangers (proselytes) and children,[34] its huge court being suited to the vast city plan in the New Jerusalem traditions.[35] 11QT excluded those not a part of Israel (along with those ritually impure) from the temple. The barrier (*soreg*) and rampart, which delimited the Gentile area in the Herodian temple, were located, according to 11QT, outside the complex altogether. The whole temple mount had a narrow terrace or rampart with steps up to it, beyond which only "the children of Israel shall ascend to enter my sanctuary."

There were two main differences between Herod's temple and the Temple Scroll's temple: non-Israelites were left outside the temple precincts in 11QT, whereas Herod's temple brought them in; and Israelites who could not participate fully in the sacrificial ritual (women, children, proselytes) were lumped together in the outer court in 11QT, whereas the Herodian temple brought women one courtyard farther inside, while proselytes (and children) had no specific places. How the two schemes speak of two social-historical realities will be considered later; for now the primary point is that important developments in the courtyards' design were promoted in the second and first centuries B.C.E. They help to explain the architectural ambiguities identified earlier.

Were there discussions and disputes about these developments? There are only minor hints of difficulties with these innovations. An aside in 1 Maccabees 9:54–57 refers to Alcimus, the high priest and leader of "the renegades and godless," who may have felt ritual difficulties, for he began to tear down the "wall [*teichos*] of the inner sanctuary." Schürer's suggestion that Alcimus intended to remove the barrier between Gentiles and the holy place is highly unlikely, since the *teichos* of the inner sanctuary more naturally refers to a wall within the *naos*, not a barrier outside it, and since there is no evidence for a Court of Gentiles at the period.[36] Tearing down a wall implies reducing the number of courts, not increasing them. Along the same lines, *m. Middoth* 2:3 refers to an event that created "thirteen breaches [in the *soreg*] that the Grecian kings had made," which were later "fenced up again." This may be a dim recollection of the same incident concerning "the wall of the inner sanctuary," and it may have been Jonathan who later rebuilt whatever Alcimus tore down (1 Macc 10:10-11, 44-45; 14:15).[37]

Two other *mishnaic* traditions refer to disputes: one refers to the competency of various legal bodies, "they may not add to the City or the Courts of the temple save by the decision of the court of one and seventy" (*m. Sanh.* 1:5); another alludes to the same question of competency, "It is all one whether a man enters into the temple court or into any space that has been added to the temple court, since they may not add to the [Holy] City or to the Courts of the temple save by the decision of a king, a prophet, Urim and Thummim and a Sanhedrin of one and twenty [judges]" (*m. Shebu.* 2:2).[38] Both traditions likely refer to spatial additions, not changes in the number of courts. They are relevant, however, since Herod enlarged the spaces and increased the number. The *Mishnah* implies that alterations to the courts were debated, though in what period is unclear. Either the Hasmoneans or Herod may have required approval for alterations, though *m. Shebuoth* grants "a king" permission to decide, while *m. Sanhedrin* gives the responsibility to a Sanhedrin alone.

The earliest sources had two courts, 11QT's idealized temple had three, and Herod's temple had four. Architectural ambiguities in the way in which the Herodian-period spaces were conceived and constructed support the suggestion that important changes occurred in the first century B.C.E. Literary indications of disputes over the courts, with vague allusions to rebuilding a courtyard-related wall confirm that this was a period of change.

Court of Women

In the pre-Hasmonean period there was no Court of Women, although there must have been flexibility in permitting women occasionally into parts of the temple.[39] The Herodian Court of Women was not reserved for women (since men went through it); it represented the farthest point to which women might proceed.[40] While its reality is certain, its origins are murky. Its development was half anticipated by 11QT's huge courtyard for women, proselytes, and children, with Gentiles excluded from the *peribolos*. That description, of course, is anticipatory and does not reflect the situation at the time of writing. Nothing suggests provision for women in the Hasmonean period, though one might hypothesize, as a colleague once suggested, that the likeliest person to have originated a Court of Women was Queen Alexandra (76–67 B.C.E.), a pious and powerful woman in a period when a number of powerful women emerged.[41]

It is not hard to imagine conditions favorable to formalizing a Court of Gentiles, given the worldwide spread of Judaism and the broad interest in worship of one god. It is harder to imagine a social situation in Judea in the late first century B.C.E. favorable to the unexpected development of a Court of Women. Should we accept the implications of the sources' silence before Josephus's accounts and the implications of the literary data that imply that its origins lay in Herod's rebuilding of the temple? I offer a conjecture about a Jewish Egyptian origin for this development.

Onias III or IV founded a rival temple at Leontopolis (Tell el-Yehudiyeh) in the Nile Delta region in the mid-second century B.C.E.[42] Josephus claims that Leontopolis was modeled on the temple in Jerusalem (*Ant.* 13.63), though their sizes (and styles?) were substantially different. Perhaps he meant only that some features were similar, such as the way an adjacent fortress dominated the temple. The nineteenth-century excavators of Tell el-Yehudiyeh found a holy place with a two-part sanctuary, as at Jerusalem, with two architecturally independent courtyards.[43] Since the sanctuary probably included a barrier defining a priestly area as well, it is likely it was a three-court scheme, loosely analogous to 11QT's, and from about the same period. There is no literary or archaeological information suggesting how the courts at Leontopolis functioned. Inscriptional evidence from Leontopolis refers to a woman priest (Chapter 10), and Philo refers to women going to temple (*Spec. Laws* 3.171), both small bits of evidence that suggest more extensive participation of women in Egypt than in Judea. In additon, Philo speaks glowingly of the Therapeutae (*On the Contemplative Life*), a Jewish monastic group in Egypt in which men and women played equivalent roles. Buildings and rituals enshrined this parallelism, based on traditions about Moses and Miriam, a brother/sister pair of prophets (Chapters 9, 10). Such heightened roles for women within Egyptian Judaism cohered with Egyptian religious practices.

There were two high priests of Egyptian origin in the period before and during Herod's temple reconstruction, Jesus ben Phiabi (30?–24 B.C.E.) and Boethos from Alexandria (24–5 B.C.E.; *Ant.* 15.320). The latter was appointed because Herod wanted to raise the status of his new wife, Mariamme II, linking his family closely to the high priesthood. Jesus ben Phiabi is a mystery. He was given no clear origin in Josephus, the *Mishnah*, or *Tosefta*. The name Phiabi (*phabeis*) is known inscriptionally in only one place, Leontopolis (*CIJ* 1510; *CPJ* II, *App.* 1.1510), which implies that he likely originated there. Why should Herod appoint two persons from Egypt as high priests? I posit two reasons. Herod had attempted to draw the Babylonian Diaspora closer to the homeland of Judea by the appointment of Hananel in 37 B.C.E. and again in 35–30 B.C.E. He may likewise have wanted to draw the influential Egyptian Jewish community closer to Judea. Perhaps more important, Onias's temple at Leontopolis claimed legitimate high priests going back to Onias III, the last of the Zadokite line in Jerusalem. While there is nothing linking Phiabi directly with Onias III, and while the idea that Herod was seeking a "more legitimate" high priest is speculative, the appointment of Phiabi is suggestive. One other small piece of evidence works in the same direction. A list of high priests who prepared the ashes of the Red Heifer (*m. Parah* 3:5) refers to Hanamel [sic] as an Egyptian, followed immediately by "Ishmael son of Phiabi." Hanamel (the correct spelling) was the Babylonian high priest in the 30s; this Ishmael, a high priest appointed by Valerius Gratus (*Ant.* 18.34), was either the son or grandson of our Phiabi. I conjecture that the tradition transposed the epithet "Egyptian" from "son of Phiabi," where it belongs, to "Hanamel," where it does not belong. If this emendation were reasonable, the *mishnaic* and

Josephan evidence would be nearly in accord concerning Egyptian high priests.

From this hypothetical chain, I suppose that Herod, looking for a high priest, found a candidate in Egypt at the temple at Leontopolis.[44] Priests at Leontopolis claimed to be the proper priestly (Zadokite) line. It seems that Egyptians were high priests in Jerusalem during the period when Herod was negotiating alterations to the temple. Egyptian Judaism, however, had been influenced by Egyptian culture in which males and females played more nearly equal roles. The *Mishnah* recalls discussions of changes in the number and size of the courtyards, and the literary and architectural evidence suggests that the addition of a Court of Women took place at this time.

Preliminary Conclusion

I propose that Herod in concert with his appointees as high priests encouraged these changes in the cultic arrangements for Israel's worship in Jerusalem, specifically the Court of Women and the Court of Gentiles. The Temple Scroll (11QT) could have played a larger role than I have suggested, though Herod's and 11QT's intentions and programs were different. If we reckon with the importance of Egyptian high priests during the rebuilding, there is reason to link the innovations with Egyptian practices, especially those of Leontopolis.

Why should anyone have been concerned for women and Gentiles? Both were excluded groups (11QT makes this clear), whom the Herodian innovations drew closer to the sanctuary. The motivation was inclusion. Socially, Judaism must have been open to bringing women and Gentiles into a more positive relationship with the temple cult. If so, usual views of Judaism and temple practice need revision. It was slowly moving away from exclusion, through a courageous attempt to open up limited participation to foreigners and women. Social historical reflections on the Herodian period should reckon with this feature of Jewish life in the early Roman period.

Social and Architectural Reflections

City, Temple, and Temple City

The literary sources think of Jerusalem as a holy city, a temple city,[45] which, like other temple cities, had international significance. It was a city whose cult was so important that it attracted visitors from nearby and from an "extended network" of regions.[46] Herodian Jerusalem was a premier city of this international caliber, both because of its role in the Jewish Diaspora and because of its attraction to interested Gentiles.

The focus of the city in the First Temple period was the combination of palace and temple.[47] In the early postexilic period a small rebuilt temple was dominant. In the Herodian period, however, the city had three *foci*: the temple, the royal palace now on the higher western hill, and the adjacent Antonia Fortress north of the temple. This trifocal arrangement had already been anticipated in the Hasmonean period, with a Hasmonean palace on the Western Hill and the Baris (fortress) beside the temple in roughly the same location as the Antonia Fortress.

The temple's roles ensured it had a significant place in the urban fabric. It offered the only large-scale urban spaces for crowds in the city; whenever Herod held civic assemblies or national meetings, they were held in the temple's *temenos*, under the shadow of the Royal Basilica; the temple hierarchy was part of the social elite of the city; its religious observances attended by crowds of visitors dominated the yearly calendar of the city;[48] its institutions dominated the legal structures of Jerusalem and its people; its financial power dominated the economy of the city.

Temenos and Adjacent Structures

The temple was marked for holy use by high walls that closed it visually from the rest of the city, yet great care was taken to permit easy access to the temple mount from all points within the city. Innovative entries solved difficult circulation problems so that, while access was controlled, it conveyed a vital sense of openness and accessibility. For those who approached the temple from the City of David, the Huldah Gates created a sense of religious awe, with their dark tunnels, stairs up to the bright daylight, and the gold enhanced *naos* sparkling immediately in front (Plates 41–44). Public *mikvaoth* on the southern platform (perhaps only at this point) provided ritual facilities. The other directions of approach apparently had no religious installations to serve them. To the west, streets full of daily commercial traffic bounded the *temenos* (Plates 39–40), yet those commercial activities did not impinge much on temple activities. There was, then, a kind of religious ambiguity in the variety of approaches to Judaism's cult center: the traditional way from the City of David; from street level on the south and east; via a bridge from the Western Hill; even directly from outside the city on the north and east. This made it unlike most Greek and Roman internationally significant religious precincts that were approached by a sacred way from one direction only. It was even unlike most other late Hellenistic and Roman temples that usually had one main entrance.

Significance of the Outer Court

The Court of the Gentiles' significance is perfectly obvious from one point of view: it permitted non-Jews (all but "women in their impurity"; *Apion* 2.103) to gather inside the *temenos*. This is not surprising against a Greco-Roman background, for all might usually attend. Against the background of more exclusive cult centers and earlier Jewish practice, however, the new arrangement was powerfully symbolic. Non-Jews entered the sacred *temenos*, the space sanctified to Yahweh and to Yahweh alone; they were on holy ground. The *Mishnah* later developed an ordered pattern of ten finely graded degrees of holiness (*m. Kelim* 1:6–9), of which the outer court was merely one. This only sidestepped the ambiguity, however, as 11QT 46 decisively shows: there, the fundamental division was put at the *temenos* wall. No non-Jew could enter the sanctified space. The point can hardly be overemphasized.

Gentiles were drawn in to the worship and the activities of the sacred precinct of the Herodian temple in a new way. This development occurred, not accidentally, at the very period when large numbers of interested outsiders throughout the Diaspora joined Jews and proselytes in worship in Jerusalem. It was also a period when—for the first time—the *pax romana* allowed international travel on a broad scale, when the Empire's economy was healthy, and thus when increasingly large numbers of visitors might be expected. Whether this increased traffic was a cause or a result of the Court of Gentiles is unimportant. There was a homologous relationship between the external conditions of the Empire and the internal arrangements within Judaism's temple.

Neither Leontopolis nor 11QT, both of which hinted at extension of the courts of the temple, had a Court of Gentiles. Yet Herod's innovation was not entirely *de novo*. In enhancing the courts he gave built form for the first time to a court explicitly intended for the ritually excluded. To be sure, inclusion was not complete, but it overcame the exclusion of earlier periods. In the classic mystery cults or the increasingly popular eastern mystery cults, participation was impossible without initiation. Herod's innovation was of the highest order, since religious centers, where ritual exclusion was transcended by (partial) inclusion, were rare at this period.

Rampart

The rampart was visually part of the outer court, a fact emphasized by the *soreg*'s low balustrade and the dominant height of the walls of the middle court; yet for cultic purposes the rampart was part of the middle court, a fact insisted on by the inscriptions at the *soreg* gates prohibiting Gentile access. The rampart was a transition space functionally and architecturally, so regarded in the *Mishnah* though not in first-century accounts. The point is clarified by 11QT's arrangement, where the rampart (described in a similar way) was outside the outer court and ringed by a fosse, another massive separation. The purpose was stated explicitly:

> You shall make a platform around the outer courtyard, on the outside, 14 cubits in width [ca. 7 m], corresponding to the openings of all the gates; and for it you shall make twelve steps so that the children of Israel can climb up them in order to enter my temple. You shall make a trench around the temple, one hundred cubits in width [ca. 50 m], which separates the holy temple from the city so that they do not suddenly enter my temple and defile it. (11QT 46.5–11)

The feature that in 11QT protected against defilement of the whole sanctuary was relocated in the Herodian sanctuary to a point between the first and second courts. The courtyard allocated to proselytes, women, and children in 11QT was allocated to Gentiles in the Herodian scheme. This resulted in a gradual transition from a first court that embraced all, through the rampart with its balustrade, gates, steps and terrace, and eventually to a second court that was for women. The architectural ambiguity of this arrangement implicitly conveyed an invitation to those not a part of Israel to move to fuller participation.

Significance of the Middle Court

The second or middle court allowed women to participate partially. The Herodian temple moved women an important step closer than 11QT.[49] It is only a slight exaggeration to suggest that the middle court, since it was within the *hieron*, almost included women within the sacrificial system. Josephus says, "This court was thrown open for worship to all Jewish women alike, whether natives of country or visitors from abroad" (*War* 5.199). The single set of high walls around the *hieron* or holy place that enclosed the *naos*, the altar, the related appurtenances, as well as the Court of Women, was architecturally symbolic of women's inclusion in temple worship. It was hardly full inclusion, yet women were included within the enclosing walls of the *hieron* in an architecturally decisive way.[50] The architecture implies a revaluation of women in first-century Jewish opinions, of which we have little literary evidence. The ritual distance of women was reduced for a century (late first century B.C.E. to late first century C.E.), as they were drawn closer to temple ritual.[51] There seems to have been an ongoing reinterpretation in the first century B.C.E. of an approach begun by 11QT in the second century B.C.E.

Significance of the Court of Israel

The innermost or fourth court in front of the *naos* was for priests. A narrow space carved off from it, but visually and architecturally inside it, formed the Court of Israel, for adult, ritually clean, male Jews who had paid the half-shekel temple tax (Chapter 14; Plate 35). This narrow space contrasted with much larger spaces for Israel envisioned by 11QT and Ezekiel. Once again ambiguity characterized the way a single architectural space included provision for two ritually distinct courts. Josephus indirectly acknowledges this ambiguity in *War* 5.227 when he refers to impure males not being admitted to the "inner court," from which even priests were excluded if they were ritually impure. This ambiguity was analogous to the ambiguity at the rampart/*soreg*. Though crucially important functionally, the Court of Israel lacked the vigorous forms of the Court of Gentiles or even the Court of Women. It was architecturally unobtrusive, even unexpressive, despite its high liturgical importance. It seems odd that Israel was allocated such a small space in the sequence of courts, relative to the spaces allocated to Gentiles, women, and even priests. Male Israelites formed the largest group in the temple and needed substantial elbow room for handing over sacrificial victims to the priests as offerings to God. The wide, shallow space was 135 cubits by 11 deep (ca. 62x5 m; *m. Mid.* 2:6). It was an efficient shape for the purpose, but ludicrously small.[52]

Further Issues

Among other things attracting attention (*naos*, the holy place, the holy of holies, and other facilities), I limit myself to a few additional issues that bear on my main point. (1) It may be no coincidence that both 11QT and Herod's reconstruction gave the temple courts greater importance than the *naos*. (2) It has been suggested that Herod's temple involved Essene priests.[53] This is unlikely, since it is inconceivable that Herod made arrangements with Essene priests and that non-Essene priests subsequently winkled it away from them without a trace. (3) A perpetually unresolved issue is the rock of Mount Moriah and how its higher elevation was accommodated. There are three main suggestions: it was under the altar, under the holy of holies, or poking through a courtyard somewhere. Most arguments have been theologically driven, leaning to the first or second solution; I lean to the third possibility. The problem is not easily resolved, but solutions based on ideological considerations should be avoided.[54]

I note two examples of difficulties arising from too great a reliance on secondary considerations in place of archaeological and architectural data. (1) Johann Maier proposes a highly hypothetical "unfinished" *temenos*, proposing a line for the northern wall parallel to the southern wall. The material evidence, however, suggests that the north wall of the *temenos* was completed as intended. (a) Trapezoidal socles— for the roof beams of the *stoa*—were cut in the scarp's rock-cut face below the walls of the al Omariyah School and can still be seen. (b) A tower in the perimeter wall at the present northeast corner of the *temenos* clearly indicates the location of that corner (Plate 46).[55] Both pieces of evidence prohibit such a hypothetical reconstruction and imply that the wall ran as it does today. (2) The location and form of the Royal Basilica has been an object of speculation for a century and a half. An important but often neglected short study shows that the pattern of columns in the Islamic Museum in the southwest corner of the Haram al-Sharif, when extended across the whole width, gives exactly the number of columns in Josephus's account.[56] This means that the location and spacing of the museum's columns represent the original locations of the columns of the Royal Basilica. And this implies, in turn, that the south wall of the *temenos* was a finished product and that the southern extension was built to incorporate the Royal Basilica (Plate 45). This makes architectural sense, for the construction problems of supporting the massive Royal Basilica with its very large columns required provision from the ground up.[57] Locating it within the area of Herod's extension along the new south wall of the *temenos* was the sensible, as well as the most imaginative, solution. Both points work against the abstract mathematical calculations that some have used to fit the size and square shape of a court derived in part from 11QT (and even Ezekiel) onto the Herodian plaza. Reconstructions of Herod's rebuilding of the temple can only be done after thoroughly evaluating the archaeological data.

CONCLUSION

In discussing the urban and architectural context for the social-historical significance of Herod's temple I have emphasized the importance of archaeological and architectural data. Texts are important, even if secondary, and have to be used; texts that are rooted historically are obviously more important than ideologically driven or visionary texts, though some ideological visions such as 11QT's can be used as a foil against which to interpret the different architectural programs of Herod's temple. There is much more to say about the Herodian temple; this chapter highlights ambiguous places where the architecture and the cultic requirements did not coincide, where the design did not straightforwardly implement the cult's intentions. I have urged that the social significance of the structure can be seen best at those points of ambiguity, especially those points where there were important social and religious innovations. Why has Herod not been more frequently credited with these innovations? It is one of the great ironies of Jewish history that, despite the ways he has been demonized in both Jewish and Christian traditions, both Jews and Christians have taken his form of the temple to be so "normative" that his version of the "proper" arrangements has been read back into the earlier periods and his innovations largely overlooked.

CHAPTER SEVENTEEN

HEROD'S TEMPLE ARCHITECTURE
AND JERUSALEM'S TOMBS

The Akeldama tombs shed new light on burials and related questions in late Second Temple Judaism.[1] The tombs' importance extends to other related social-historical and architectural questions; here, I connect the tombs with the architecture of Herod's temple. Jerusalem was a temple-city—focused on a major temple—prior to its destruction in 70 C.E., but it was unlike most other such cities in having only one temple. From the time of its rebuilding under Herod the Great in the last quarter of the first century B.C.E. until its destruction about a century later, it was the largest and most striking temple of the whole Roman Empire. Jerusalem's colossal religious precinct was the most sacred site in Judaism. The city was a major fortified city of some 60,000 to 80,000 inhabitants and included the usual range of required ancillary functions—shops, public buildings, water systems, and so on. As with other cities with internationally important religious structures (the Temple of Apollo at Didyma near Miletus; the Asklepieion at Pergamon; the Temple of Apollo at Delphi; the Asklepieion at Epidauros), people traveled from great distances to visit Jerusalem. These crowds were mainly, but not exclusively (Chapter 16), pious Jews worshiping at Judaism's central cultic site out of a sense of obligation and devotion, usually on one of the year's great festival occasions.

JERUSALEM TOMBS

Visitors approaching Jerusalem from most directions passed through an extensive necropolis, the city of the dead that surrounded most ancient cities. Burials in ancient cultures ordinarily did not take place inside the city; even in small villages the usual pattern was to locate graves outside settlement areas, consistent with the view that contact with dead bodies rendered one impure. If the city were walled, graves were outside the walls, as was the case in Jerusalem.

The temple lay on a ridge between two major north-south valleys, the Kidron and Tyropoeon Valleys, just north of the Hinnom Valley, which ran north-south but then turned east-west, joining the other two valleys. The combination of valleys and ridges constituted a defensively strong position that made Jerusalem a natural capital, surrounded by walls where it was most defensible. The opposite slopes of these valleys faced the Temple Mount and the ancient City of David. They provided natural opportunities for Jerusalem's necropolis. Akeldama, on the south side of the Hinnom Valley facing north up the ridge occupied by the city of David, looked straight at the main pilgrim access to the temple through the Huldah Gates, on the south of the temple platform. The location was perfect for a major complex of tombs in the Second Temple period (Plates 47, 48, 49). It had two advantages, shared with sites on the east slope of the Kidron Valley and in nearby Silwan: its visual connection with the temple and its physical proximity to the temple on the day of resurrection (Plates 50, 51).

Three Akeldama ossuaries (bone boxes used for secondary burial of bones about a year after primary burial; Chapter 18; Plate 52) illustrate one of the tombs' important lessons. An ossuary with a bull's head on both ends has a Greek inscription: "Aza (Azariah) from Beirut has made [it]."[2] Another ossuary's Greek inscription refers to "Eiras of Seleucia."[3] A bilingual Greek and Hebrew inscription on a third ossuary reads, "Ariston of Apamea," followed by "Judah the proselyte," in Hebrew only.[4] All three refer to places outside Judea in the Roman province of Syria: Beirut on the coast, Apamea on the Orontes River, and Seleucia, Antioch's port city. The tombs show that Jews from a distance were buried in prominent locations facing the temple.[5] We cannot know whether their bodies had been brought to Jerusalem for burial, if they had moved to Jerusalem near the end of their lives, or if they had been long settled in Jerusalem. Ariston is the most interesting case (Ossuary 31). His name is clearly Greek, yet other ossuaries with Hebrew names and bilingual inscriptions also refer to him (Ossuary 28; figs. 3.15; 3.16; 3.17; possibly Ossuary 29; Ossuary 35; fig. 3.22; 3.23), possibly implying he had moved to Jerusalem and that his family members then took Hebrew names. Ariston raises two other important questions. Was he in fact "Judah the proselyte" mentioned on the same ossuary (did Ariston take the Hebrew name Judah when he converted)? Was this Ariston the same "Ariston of Apamia" mentioned later in *m. Hal.* 4:11: "Ariston brought his first-fruits from Apamia and they accepted them from him, for they said: He that owns [land] in Syria is as one that owns [land] in the outskirts of Jerusalem"?[6] Five other ossuaries from Jerusalem refer in various ways to the occupant of the ossuary being a proselyte, reinforcing the general point that proselytes wanted to be buried in Jerusalem and presupposing pagan interest in Judaism, conversion, and then burial in the city.[7]

Diaspora connections with Jerusalem were strong. Two other Jerusalem tombs amplify the general point. Jason's tomb in west Jerusalem had a boat drawn in charcoal on the wall, perhaps reflecting his involvement in pilgrim traffic to and from Jerusalem, whether as ship's captain, merchant, or naval officer, we cannot know. The drawing suggests a maritime role and is analogous to a later Crusader period graffito of a boat in the Church of the Holy Sepulcher. More important than this slight hint is the so-called Tomb of the Kings, which presumes not merely Jewish pilgrim traffic but converts to Judaism who settled in the holy city. Queen Helena of Adiabene (a minor state near the Caspian Sea) converted to Judaism with her son Izates. She moved to Jerusalem in the mid-40s C.E. (Josephus, *Ant.* 20.17–51, 92–96), using some of her wealth to alleviate a famine ravaging Judea just then (Acts 11:27-30 and also Paul's collection; Suetonius, *Claudius* 18.2; Tacitus, *Annals* 12.43). The tomb was the largest family tomb in the city, lying north of the mount in the general direction in which Helena's homeland lay. Its architectural evidence exemplified the profundity of her conversion.

This phenomenon can be linked to Herod's temple architecture sociohistorically. When Herod redesigned and rebuilt the temple he introduced two major innovations, whose importance outweighed the other significant design elements. The organizational features that set it apart from its predecessors were two courtyards, a middle one for women and an outer one for non-Jews (Chapter 16). The Court of the Gentiles lay inside the outer *temenos* wall that defined the perimeter of the religious precinct with its paved courtyards (ca. 35 acres; 14 hectares). A large percentage of the area within the holy space was for non-Jews; they could enter the holy precinct though they were not so close to the holy space that they defiled it. Protection against impurity was offered by a barricade—the *soreg*—with warnings at the gates in Greek telling non-Jews not to go any farther on pain of death: "No outsider shall enter the protective enclosure around the sanctuary. And whoever is caught will only have himself to blame for the ensuing death."

When compared with other religious precincts in the Mediterranean world this solution was unusual. Most were open, so that anyone who wished could enter even into the holy place, the *naos*. A radically different solution adopted by the less common "mystery religions" prohibited all access to nonmembers. Jerusalem's temple serving a radically exclusive monotheistic religion adopted neither approach; it allowed partial access. This is important because at exactly this period Judaism was attractive to pagans, who showed an interest in the God of Israel both in synagogues around the Mediterranean world and by visiting the temple. Herod's Court of the Gentiles reflected and provided for an increased flow of pilgrims to Jerusalem. Among the many thousands who could be crammed into the temple precinct were a significant number of non-Jews, to judge from the space allocated to them. Burial practices mirror the religious situation: pilgrim traffic of Jews from outside Judea who returned to Jerusalem for burial and converts to Judaism, such as Queen Helena, who moved to Jerusalem to be at the center of their new-found religious attachment.

The Akeldama evidence complements another major innovation of the layout of Herod's temple, the Court of Women. Akeldama's ossuaries, unlike most ossuaries and customary burial usage, mentioned substantially more women than men. The inscriptions named only five or six males as compared with fifteen women (two names are uncertain). It is difficult to know why this should be so, but it is tempting to think that for a period of time in the late first century B.C.E. and the first century C.E. women had more prominence and wider roles than is usually thought. There is a related surprise. Ossuary 18's inscription referred to "Megistês the priestess."[8] One should not quickly claim that Megistês was a priestess in the temple in Jerusalem, for *hierisês* can refer to a wife or daughter of a priest. An earlier study showed that none of the inscriptions that attributed high status or important roles to women linked the woman's description to her husband's role. In all cases, the role pertained to the woman, not to a related male.[9] On Megistês's role, and women's roles generally, more evidence is needed.

The main point is that Herod's temple architecture gave a high degree of prominence to women in the cult, a prominence they had not had before. The increased prominence of women was paralleled by increased visibility of Gentiles, a visibility they had never had before. Both features were reflected in the inscriptions on the ossuaries from the Akeldama tombs. The parallels are intriguing.

TEMPLE ARCHITECTURE

The architectural decoration of the Akeldama tombs and its ossuaries is linked with the architecture of the Jerusalem temple. Though we know more about the temple's form and layout than was known before the extensive excavations near the temple mount, many details are irrecoverable. The temple incorporated features rarely found together in other religious buildings: vast scale, rich details, dramatic approaches, ancillary structures, and so on. Herod's rebuilding altered both large-scale features and minor details. It differed substantially from the building it replaced, built after the return from exile in the sixth century B.C.E. and altered and expanded by the Hasmoneans in the second and first centuries B.C.E. So much of the temple and of the city was destroyed in 70 C.E. that only glimpses of its character can now be recovered directly from the archaeological remains. An indirect way to appreciate the sophistication of the temple's architecture is to examine carefully Jerusalem's tombs, which have often survived intact and little modified by later usage. They reflect, even if palely, the temple's character.

Ossuary Decoration

Several ossuaries had an attractively simple decorative feature, where the main motif, in some cases covering the lid as well as the sides, used incised lines mimicking the massive ashlar masonry of the temple's perimeter wall (Plate 52).[10] There are enough of these to suggest that the reflection of the temple in burial practices was deliberate. Some wished burial not only physically and visually close to the temple but also in a box reminiscent of the temple itself. These ossuaries seized on the single most dramatic and skillful feature of the whole great construction: its sophisticated masonry, regular ashlar courses, finely crafted margins, smooth bosses, and subtly inclined walls. Other ossuaries were intended to represent a single ashlar stone with a bossed central panel.[11] Still others had architectural motifs possibly reflecting details of the temple, but without the same deliberateness. Curiously, an ossuary found at Giv'at Hamivtar referring to "Simon, builder of the sanctuary," seems not intended to represent an ashlar of the temple, though Rahmani suggests it was.[12] Numerous ossuaries had architectural details as part of their decoration: façades, columns and capitals, doors, friezes, pyramidal monuments, and occasionally a full tomb or temple façade. The most common column/capital motif was Ionic, though there was a range of types. The tomb façades have been compared to Nabatean tombs, like those at Petra and elsewhere. It would be difficult though not impossible to claim that some of these fuller decorative programs reflected the temple.

Ossuary Inscriptions

The ossuary just noted refers twice to Simon, emphasizing the importance of his role in the temple's construction. The extent of Simon's involvement is not known. An ossuary found on Mount Scopus was more specific:[13] it held the "bones of [possibly of the sons of] Nicanor the Alexandrian who made the doors." He is specifically identified as an Alexandrian and may well be Nicanor mentioned in the *Mishnah*;[14] the gates may be the Corinthian gates of the Jerusalem temple—probably the eastern gates between the Court of Women and the Court of Gentiles described as beautifully constructed from Corinthian bronze—and if so Nicanor located his tomb on the Mount of Olives across from his gates.[15] The most reliable information on the gates is Josephus, *War* 5.201: one of the pairs of outer gates of the temple was made of Corinthian bronze, even more valuable than the other nine gates that were plated with gold and silver.[16] He does not give any reason for this gate to be special—no donor's name or source of the gates—other than the material used.

The earliest rabbinic tradition is *t. Yoma* 2:4, where Josephus's account is partly repeated: "All the gates . . . were changed into golden ones except for the Nicanor Gates, because a miracle was wrought through them. And others say because their bronze was a bright yellow." R. Eliezer b. Jacob says: "their bronze was Corinthian and was as beautiful as gold. . . ." Eliezer b. Jacob (first century C.E.) was, according to one tradition, the author of *m. Middoth*, the main *mishnaic* source on the temple and its measurements (*b. Yoma* 16a; *y. Yoma* 2:3). The later account in the Babylonian Talmud (*b. Yoma* 38a) deleted all the points of correspondence with Josephus from the earlier *Tosefta*, and exaggerated substantially the legendary features,[17] in contrast to the simple comments of *m. Middoth* 1:4 and 2:6 that the east gate was Nicanor's Gate.

Another inscription, not on an ossuary, alludes to participation in the building of the temple: "[In the reign of Herod the King] in the twentieth year, upon the high priest [Simon, S]paris Akeonos [a foreign resident] in Rhodes [donated the] pavement [at a cost of?] drachmas" (*SEG* 1277). Sparis was probably a Jew living in Rhodes, whose donation was a portion of the paving of the temple courts or of the platform at the Huldah Gates.[18] This rather simple inscription attests the importance associated with benefactions to the temple.

Tomb Decoration

There are suggestive connections between Jerusalem tombs and Herod's architecture. Cave 3 in the Akeldama tombs belonged to the Ariston family; the most richly decorated of the four chambers was Chamber C, which acted as an entrance passageway to Chamber D, where Ariston's ossuary was found. Chamber B was connected to Chamber C with a door (0.6x0.8 m, with surrounding frame; 0.7x1.4 m in low relief), surmounted by an arch. The details of the low relief frame of the doorway were modeled on a monumental doorway,[19] perhaps on the details of the Huldah Gates. The paneled doors were typical of many installations, no doubt, but not inconsistent with this particular model. Inside Chamber C the details were richer still, with a two-level mock Doric order in low relief on all four walls, modulated by mock panels between the pilasters. *Arcosolia* filled three sides of the chamber; the fourth side above the entrance from Chamber B had a pattern of diamonds within rectangles, with the incisions filled with dark red paint. These generic decorative details were modeled on institutional and monumental architecture, not domestic architecture.

Some other tomb complexes had richly carved, shallow-vaulted, decorative ceiling panels that would enhance any space by drawing the eye to them as one passed underneath. Almost exactly the same kind of shallow-vaulted ceiling decorations, decorated in an analogous way, were located in the Huldah Gates. They are not now accessible. These ceilings functioned in a similar way, enhancing the tunnels leading to stairs up to the temple platform, just inside the primary pilgrim gates into the temple. They lifted one's eye upwards in the long dark passage under the Royal Basilica; they were the first part of the architecture of the temple one would see after the bold masonry of the massive exterior retaining walls.

An obvious element in the temple's design was the colonnaded *stoai* or porches that surrounded the Court of the Gentiles. Nothing remains intact, though the arcades of the Haram al-Sharif (Plate 42) provide traces of their visual effect. Several capitals that might be survivals from the temple (more likely only indirectly through reuse in later buildings) were found in the Jewish quarter, though this connection is not certain. Two monolithic columns and capitals in a refined Doric order have survived in situ on a street alongside the retaining wall, at the end of the Western Wall tunnel (Plates 39, 40). These can be compared with the Doric order in Ariston's family tomb or with the Doric columns in the Bene Hezir Tomb in the Kidron Valley (Plate 51). Most of the columns in the temple were, however, Corinthian capitals; it is no accident that the majority of the capitals decorating the ossuaries and Queen Helena's tomb were also Corinthian capitals. None, however, matches the size and scale of the columns and capitals in the temple.

The tombs provide a pale reflection of the design and scale of the temple. Their builders invested them with quality and flair, though with vastly more limited resources and opportunities. One of the dominant impressions of the architecture of the tombs is that they boldly used elements from the architectural vocabularies of Greece, the Hellenistic world, Rome, Egypt, and other parts of the Middle East. This is not surprising. The tombs reflect Jerusalem's curious position in the Mediterranean world, a kind of hinge between these other regions, where there is a rather perplexing blend of eastern and western influences. There were indigenous traditions,[20] though in part the indigenous tradition was precisely this blending. Herod's temple also reflected this blend of East and West (Chapter 16), a composition that included Corinthian and Doric capitals, long *stoai*, a huge basilica, refined gateways, all characteristic of the West. It also included opaque walls, immensely high ceilings, sequential courtyards, stairs inside the walls, a flat-roofed sanctuary, characteristic of the East, and especially of the architectures of Arabia, Nabatea, and Egypt. Architecturally, then, the tombs and temple alike reflected Jerusalem's geographical location and the diverse influences upon it.

In many respects the tombs and the temple are mutually reinforcing. The temple sheds light on the tombs and the tombs on the temple. The Jerusalem tombs provide a direct and deliberate evocation of the building practices, scale, skill, and sophistication of Second Temple Judaism. Their details, contents, decoration, and architectural form enhance the understanding of first-century Jerusalem and even of the temple itself, which was so ruthlessly and totally destroyed by the Romans in 70 C.E.

CHAPTER EIGHTEEN

THE JAMES OSSUARY'S DECORATION
AND SOCIAL SETTING

THE DEBATE

The James ossuary has become notorious in a very short period of time.[1] The vitriolic debates—generated by a potential link with Jesus through an artifact connected with his brother, James the Just—require a period of calm reflection when the object itself and its implications can be assessed.[2] A new examination by the Israel Antiquities Authority (IAA) should add materially to such an assessment, but the early reports seem to add more to the confusion and controversy.[3] A recently published book, *The Brother of Jesus*, adds little to what is known about the ossuary itself; a new book on Jewish burial, *Roll Back the Stone*, has a concluding chapter on the ossuary; and a recent publication, *Jesus and the Ossuaries*, discusses this along with others.[4] This present chapter is based on an examination of the box itself before it was returned to Israel,[5] and is offered in the hope of making advances on three issues Paul Flesher noted in the conclusion of his report on the panels of the Society of Biblical Literature (SBL) and Royal Ontario Museum (ROM).[6]

The ossuary itself is significant and many have commented on its material, weathering, patina, and style of carving. The inscription is complicated further by claims to identify two different styles of writing; the analysis of the second half of the inscription has taken center stage. The relationship of the first and second parts of the inscription is a third issue needing attention. Paleographers have attributed the ossuary's style of writing to mid-first century C.E.; Kyle McCarter likened it specifically to the writing of the Copper Scroll. Even if the writing style is early, however, additional problems derive from the fact that there is no known provenance for the ossuary, since it was purchased, apparently, from an antiquities dealer in east Jerusalem after being taken illicitly from a still unidentified tomb, perhaps in Silwan. Where and when was the limestone box made? When was the inscription put on the ossuary? Was the inscription added in one or two phases? Did the inscription intend to suggest that the bones were those of James the Just? Did the box in fact hold the bones of James? Such questions cannot be answered directly, but a comparative study of other ossuaries that focuses on their artistic and inscriptional character can narrow down the range of possible answers.[7] Such an approach to the material object allows the socio-historical issues and socioreligious questions to emerge more clearly. I am neither an epigrapher nor a paleographer, so I leave aside the fundamentally important grammatical and palaeographic questions. The main options are the following.

Modern Forgery

Modern techniques can produce ancient-looking patina, with signs of age and weathering.[8] If the patina is forged, the ossuary may be lumped in with common forgeries of artifacts such as coins and lamps. Larger artifacts have been debated recently, such as the well-known "house of David" inscription from Tel Dan or the Jehoash temple tablet announced recently.[9] The tests done by the IAA should settle the forgery question, once experts have evaluated them; at present the only other close technical scrutiny of the object is that of the Israeli Geological Survey,[10] supplemented by the ROM's study.

Ancient Forgery

The ossuary could be an ancient forgery, intended to claim that it held the bones of James the Just. Christian piety may have prompted the creation of a James relic in three periods: (i) the mid- or late Roman period, when Christianity learned the benefits of claims to antiquity; (ii) the Byzantine period, when pilgrim piety fed on objects of veneration; (iii) the Medieval—especially Crusader—period, when reinvigorated pilgrim traffic had strong attachments to Jerusalem.

Ancient Alteration to the Ossuary

The ossuary may be ancient, perhaps from the Jerusalem area before 70 C.E., but it was altered in antiquity. Initially it referred only to "James the son of Joseph." "Brother of Jesus" was added afterwards, as an effort—again in the interests of Christian piety—to specify a reference to James the Just. Such an addition could have occurred in the mid- or late Roman or early Byzantine periods:[11] Either (i) an existing ossuary that referred to some James the son of Joseph was altered into an ossuary pointing specifically to James the Just by adding the reference to Jesus; or (ii) an ossuary known as James the Just's final resting place was later made more precise.

Genuine

If both the box and its inscription predated 70 C.E., (i) the inscription still need not refer to James the Just; it could refer to another James and his brother Jesus, both sons of Joseph, so the seeming association with Jesus of Nazareth would be accidental; (ii) the ossuary may have held the bones of James the Just.[12]

DEATHS AND BURIALS OF JAMES AND JESUS

Josephus describes James' execution (*Ant.* 20.197–203; 62 C.E.);[13] neither he nor other early accounts report what happened to James' body, but Eusebius quotes Hegesippus's account of James' death and burial (Eusebius, *Ecclesiastical History* 2.23, after Hegesippus, *Memoirs*, book 5). Hegesippus says James was buried where he died below the parapet of the sanctuary, and his headstone was still there in his day (ca. 110–180 C.E.). Josephus was more interested in the religious and political circumstances surrounding his death, specifically whether a Jewish council had the authority to assemble without the governor's approval.[14]

Hegesippus's account may imply inhumation, though that is not a necessary deduction from his language. Use of an ossuary implies primary burial in a tomb and later secondary burial. *Mishnah Sanhedrin* 6.5–6 discusses the case of one who was executed by the Jewish authorities: "They used not to bury him in the burying-place of his fathers, but two burying-places were kept in readiness by the court, one for them that were beheaded or strangled, and one for them that were stoned or burnt. When the flesh had wasted away they gathered together the bones and buried them in their own place." Though this

Mishnah describes primary burial in a publicly provided tomb, it also stipulates secondary burial in a family tomb in a case such as James', presumably in an ossuary. The period to which these circumstances pertained is unclear, though the intention was likely to refer to the pre-135 (perhaps pre-70) C.E. period, since it alludes to "a court," presupposes judicial responsibility, and implies use of an ossuary.

This raises indirectly the question of Jesus' death and burial. He too was executed, but his execution was Roman; often the corpse was left on the cross as a public display. In the case of Jesus, however, the body was taken down quickly and buried, not in a family tomb but in a new tomb built by Joseph of Arimathea. McCane shows how Jesus' burial in shame and dishonor explains several features of the accounts: rites of mourning were absent; the people of Israel had condemned Jesus; Joseph "dared" approach Pilate (Mark 15:43); and Jesus was buried promptly.[15] Though the degree to which Jesus' execution involved condemnation by "the people of Israel" is debatable, this was more likely the context of James' death. James (and in a different way Jesus) may have been buried in a publicly provided tomb following his execution. His death, too, was a public death in shame and dishonor. The statement concerning secondary burial in an ossuary and removal of the ossuary to another tomb (*m. Sanh.* 6:5–6) would have been consistent with reinterment of his bones in an ossuary in the pre-70 C.E. period. The deaths of Jesus and James were closely related. While it is possible—though hardly likely—that the family had acquired a tomb in Jerusalem, there is some possibility of shedding light on familial attitudes to the two deaths, if the ossuary's attribution to James the Just is correct.

FORM AND DECORATION OF THE JAMES OSSUARY

Description

The James ossuary is physically at the small end of adult ossuary sizes (approximately 57x25x29 cm at the top). It is irregular and without feet: the right end tapers towards the bottom, so the overall shape is roughly trapezoidal. The bottom is not a flat plane, for the left rear bottom corner is noticeably rounded.[16] All the surfaces are extensively pitted, corroded, and scratched. The slightly convex lid is in less good condition. A few extremely small flecks of red may be the remains of an original red paint, though this is uncertain; I saw no evidence of a general red wash. There are adhesions to the interior surfaces, including a brownish residue on the inner bottom and sides (the lower 6–8 cm) of the ossuary. When purchased, it contained small bone fragments—the largest about an inch, now in a Tupperware container. There are no signs that the ossuary was ever venerated: it was not rubbed smooth from touching by pilgrims and there are no pilgrim crosses on its surfaces, as there are for example on the container of James' relics below the altar in the Armenian Cathedral of St. James.[17]

Frames

All four sides and the lid have a simple "frame," a shallowly incised line about 1.7 cm. from the edges. A second fainter parallel line, not described in any of the published reports, is less clearly visible nearer the edges;[18] all visible surfaces thus had minimal decoration, similar to some other ossuaries.[19] The double frame line has been eroded, but is still reasonably obvious.

Rosettes

Ed Keall, the ROM curator who oversaw the ossuary's display, first reported the rosettes on the "rear" of the ossuary. The right rosette is more obvious than the left, though the central compass points for both are easily identified. Three concentric circles mark the boundaries of the rosettes, and some petals can be seen. Rosette decorations were the most typical motif on ossuaries, ranging from extremely simple to highly embellished. In many cases lavish rosettes were the most significant element in the decoration, deeply incised and enhanced by beautiful variations. The James' rosettes are utterly simple line drawings. Their present almost illegible character could be the result of erosion, but I am convinced they were never finished, despite the general erosion of the ossuary, since the line frames are more deeply incised than the rosettes.[20] Ossuaries were made as stock items for open purchase, and the rosettes may have been merely sketched prior to purchase. A few ossuaries in Rahmani's catalogue share aspects of the James ossuary's simplicity, mostly from the Jericho region, including one with shallowly incised rosettes inside a double frame on front, left, and right ends (No. 763; pl. 109).

One or Two Stages of Use

Some have proposed that the ossuary had two stages of use: the rosettes reflect the original stage and the inscription a later phase. Two factors favor such a view: the differences between the inscription and the rest of the decoration and the curious relationship between the inscription and the dimly visible rosettes. Working against this conclusion is the absence of an accompanying inscription suiting the frames and rosettes, fitting in with their location and character. Two stages of use would alter the presumed history of the box, but would not alter the debate about the ossuary itself significantly. I think one period of use is likelier.

Nefesh Sketch

On the left end, as one looks at the inscription, there is a freehand sketch, which I reported during the ROM panel. The sketch is like other freehand sketches on ossuaries and small objects. A beige-colored patina covers the lines and the adjacent surfaces. My preliminary assessment suggests that it represents a *nefesh*, not uncommon on ossuaries, though closer scientific analysis is needed.[21] Occasionally a *nefesh* appears on other objects; an evocative example was found at Yodefat (Jotapata) in the Lower Galilee, made famous by Josephus's description of its siege and his surrender to the Roman general Vespasian in 67 C.E. (Chapters 2, 3). A pottery shard was inscribed with a drawing of a tomb/*nefesh* on one side and a crab on the other; Mordechai Aviam, Yodefat's excavator, interpreted the sketches as last words from one of Yodefat's defenders: "I die in July."[22]

The ossuary sketch has four parallel diagonal lines running down to the left and six or seven parallel diagonal lines running down to the right, with horizontal lines as a "base." There are four radiating lines from the upper frame line with one or more partial arcs of circles around the point of radiation. The sketch is rougher than the Yodefat sketch, more abstract and less formal than the *nefesh* representations in

Rahmani's catalogue. It is not certain that it is a pyramidal tomb monument, but its likeliest intention was to represent a tomb or, more abstractly, the soul or *nefesh* of the deceased. (Rahmani's proposal—based on an oil lamp from the area with a similar motif, dated between 70 and 135 C.E.—that his examples originated in the Hebron Hills is hardly secure;[23] the lamp is an inadequate basis for establishing provenance.) More significant than the lamp or the Yodefat shard is the architecture of pyramid-topped tombs rooted firmly in Jerusalem and its environs: the Tomb of Zechariah in the Kidron Valley (early first century B.C.E.; Plate 51; the Tomb of Jason in West Jerusalem (first century C.E.); Queen Helena of Adiabene's tomb (mid-first century C.E.);[24] the so-called Tomb of Herod's family, whose associated monument was likely a pyramidal *nefesh* (late first century B.C.E.);[25] the literary account of the Hasmonean family tombs at Modi'in (according to 1 Macc 13:25–30; approximately 140 B.C.E.); and the Tomb of Pharaoh's Daughter in Silwan (possibly as early as the eighth century B.C.E.). These archaeological and literary examples demonstrate securely the wide popularity in Jerusalem and environs of the pyramid as a burial monument that symbolized the living "spirit" of the deceased. They provide a satisfactory geographical and socioreligious background for the sketch.

Relation of Decoration and Inscription

The decoration is primary and the inscription secondary in the great majority of ossuaries. The James ossuary reverses the relationship, for the depth of incision, the care in layout, and the style of the inscription are prominent. By contrast, the decoration of the rosettes, the *nefesh*, and the frames are informal, not primary motifs. There are two possible explanations: the rosettes were primary and the inscription was added later, or the rosettes were not finished and the ossuary was meant to be viewed with the inscription facing out, not from the side with the rosettes. If the rosettes were never finished, it is likelier that the ossuary was not used for another earlier burial and then later reused for James. If so, the *nefesh* was associated with James' interment, making the *nefesh* an important additional key element for the understanding the ossuary's socioreligious setting.

Ossuary Inscription

Location

The inscription, *Ya'akov bar Yosef ahui diYeshua* ("James, son of Joseph, brother of Jesus"), was the ossuary's main decorative motif and signaled its "front." The care in incision, placement on one long side, and formal style are consistent with this conclusion, though Rahmani's catalogue has few parallels to the placement, care, and style. There are carefully incised inscriptions, inscriptions carefully placed on the front, and inscriptions constituting the main decorative motif. There are no ossuaries that combine these three features. I limit the following discussion to ossuaries with Hebrew/Aramaic inscriptions,[26] since their social-historical setting is likely to be more similar to the James ossuary.

Frontal Inscriptions

Several ossuaries have a main frontal inscription intended to be the main decorative element; those with known provenance were almost all from the Jerusalem area and thus pre-70 C.E. One of the most interesting of the frontally inscribed ossuaries is the ossuary of "Simon, the builder of the sanctuary," from a tomb in Giv'at Hamivtar,[27] a footed ossuary with a sliding lid (like the James ossuary). Its deeply incised inscription is in roughly the same location as the James ossuary, together with a similar—though larger and less regular—version of the same inscription on the right end (Chapter 17). It has a simple double line border on all four sides, more deeply and more neatly carved than the border on the James ossuary, but with the same general effect. Simon's and James' ossuaries have a common character.

Another ossuary of special interest, also from Giv'at Hamivtar, contained the heel bone of a crucified man, "Yehohanan, son of Hezqil."[28] This must have been secondary burial after public (and Roman) execution and so probably fell under the general provisions of *m. Sanhedrin* 6:5–6, noted earlier. The name is faintly incised and the ossuary is rather plain. Other comparative examples include a relatively plain ossuary with a deeply incised double line on all four sides with an ashlar wall on three sides (Chapter 17); its inscriptions contain only one word, *shalom* ("peace"), repeated six times, three on the front, twice on the back and once on the lid.[29] Ten undecorated ossuaries from a double-chambered tomb in Talbiyeh have relatively careful inscriptions on the lid, or on the lid and front.[30] While undecorated ossuaries may have a main or frontal inscription, it is uncommon for the inscription to be incised with the same care as the James ossuary. Most ossuaries with main inscription and limited decoration have relatively informal writing. This is surprising, for one might expect inscriptions that were the dominant decoration to have their importance emphasized by careful incision. This was rarely the case.

Status and Carefully Incised Inscriptions

One might also expect social status to be related to decoration and inscriptional quality.[31] In fact, they are imperfectly correlated. Some ossuaries—it is debatable how many should be included—were carefully incised, like the James ossuary.[32] Some seem obviously high status and others not. All the ossuaries with carefully incised Hebrew or Aramaic inscriptions came from the Jerusalem area (Mount Scopus, Kidron Valley, Talbiyeh, Giv'at Hamivtar, and Abu Tor). Several Talbiyeh ossuaries were deeply incised.[33] An inscription referring to "Yehuda, son of Illma" probably alluded to Joseph son of Ellemos who was high priest for a day under Herod the Great (*Ant.* 17.166); the inscription was carefully placed frontally, on a plain ossuary, and the main decorative element.[34] A beautifully ornamented ossuary, with bold relief on three sides and centered inscription to "Yehosef son of Hananyah the scribe," shows that even high-class inscriptions were far from uniform and consistent.[35] The depth, size, location, and care alter significantly from beginning to end, with one change taking place between the first two words (just before "son") and another alteration occurring between the last two letters of "Hananyah." The ossuary looks expensive, the scribe's status was relatively high, and the inscription's center was marked by two guidelines, yet the variations were amateurish.

The inscription "Shim'on of Boethos" ("of Boethos" also appears on the back of the ossuary) likely refers to Simon, son of Boethos of Alexandria, High Priest and father-in-law of Herod the Great.[36] It had a finely finished front, with deeply incised vertical grooves—in the second of which was an altar—forming a columned porch.[37] Neither the inscription nor the sketch of the altar was careful. The inscriptions on

ossuaries from the family tomb of Caiaphas the High Priest were careless, as were inscriptions in the Akeldama tombs, whose high social status seems assured from the decorative features of the tomb itself
(Chapter 17).[38] The ossuary of "Simon the builder of the Sanctuary"
had deeply incised lettering but the lettering was irregular in spacing
and size and ran uphill relative to the frame. Other beautifully decorated and carefully finished ossuaries, whose implied status cannot
be decided so readily, had similarly careless inscriptions. The very
beautiful ornamentation on the ossuary of "Shappira, daughter of
Yehohanan, son of Revikh," with whirling rosettes and ivy leaves inside
a carefully executed border, did not match the shallowly incised
inscription on the back.[39]

There was little consistency between social status and form of script,
between character of ornamentation and incision, between the inscription's decorative role and its quality. A partial explanation is that ornamentation was professionally done while family members provided
inscriptions at the time of secondary burial. So the inscription's quality reflects family literacy (indirectly related to status, of course), while
the decoration's quality reflects the family's wealth (more directly
related to status). The relationship of status and incision affects interpretation of the James ossuary, though there are few formal parallels to
its combination of elements, with unfinished rosettes, sketch, and
frontal inscription that is the main decorative element.

One or Two Hands

The differences between the first and second halves of the inscription
have been extensively discussed. Did one or two hands incise it? Some
preliminary comments provide a context. There is no sharp break in
the style of the inscription; the change in character occurs gradually,
within the words "brother of" (*ahui de*); some of the letters in *ahui*, especially the *heth* with its wedges (ears or serifs), have more in common
with the first part of the inscription. All the forms of the various letters,
whether cursive or formal, can be paralleled at relatively early dates.
Some of the letters are damaged. My examination of the inscription
under a magnifying glass clarifies, I believe, the true situation. On the
one hand, it seems certain that someone has touched up the inscription, presumably in the modern period, to make it sharper and more

legible.[40] On the other hand, it seems equally certain that the content of the inscription has not been altered: new letters have not been created nor old letters altered. The most recent IAA report moves in this same direction, though I am baffled by its summary of its findings.

The letter from the Geological Survey (dated 17/9/2002; published with Lemaire's BAR article) says: "The same gray patina is found also within some of the letters, although the inscription was cleaned and the patina is absent from several letters."[41] Magnification shows obvious changes in color and clarity between some letters or parts of letters and others.[42] Had the Geological Survey specified which letters had been "cleaned" and which ones still had the patina, much of the controversy over the inscription would have taken a different form. I did not have time to make a sketch of the alterations, but I observed that almost all the letters at the beginning have been sharpened up while almost no letters at the end have been.

Those who have argued for two hands have correctly noticed a difference in the character of the letters (Paul Flesher and Rochelle Altman have linked stylistic differences with linguistic differences). The explanation of the differences has not been properly stated. The best explanation is that the inscription has been touched up, perhaps with a chisel. There are traces of the original patina between two strokes of the same letter and at the ends of strokes that have been "improved." The original patina, for example, seems present in the *kaph* of "Ya'akov," where the slanted stroke has been touched up but the lower end of the same stroke is more nearly original; similar variations can be seen in *beth* in "son of." On the other hand, "Yeshua'" is almost entirely untouched. More exact and detailed analysis is needed to determine precisely which letters have been retouched, which letters have complete or partial remains of their original form and patina, and what size and kind of tool was used. The IAA results are unclearly reported and not tested.

Ironically, the second part of the inscription is nearer its original condition than the first part. "Brother of Jesus" was not a secondary addition. The first half of the inscription has been improved and is more suspect, though when and by whom is difficult to say. It was likely in the modern period, despite the owner's clear statement that he has not tampered with it.[43]

An important corollary follows from the observation that the second half was less reworked than the first part. Its original character can be seen in the final phrase. Whoever improved the inscription had little interest in the final words, for the goal was not to enhance putative Christian associations but to make the inscription more legible. Further, this part of the inscription is more nearly consistent with the character of the double line frame and the *nefesh* sketch. All came from the same stage of use. Those elements differ from the faint lines of the rosettes, suggesting that the rosettes were never finished. While the general surface condition has degraded over the last two thousand years, the depth of the incision of the first half, which contrasts with the rest of the decoration, has been improved. To summarize, the ossuary has three distinctly different qualities of lines: the rosettes that are almost invisible, the frame lines and *nefesh* sketch and second half of the inscription which are in their original and extensively degraded condition, and the first "improved" half of the inscription.

Form and Language

The letterforms are both cursive and formal. Their relative dates and whether they might coexist is a subject for paleographers, who seem to agree that the forms can be paralleled in contemporary inscriptions. The question whether the language of the inscription (especially "brother of" and the double genitive with the use of *di*) is Judean or Galilean Aramaic is a specialized topic for linguists.[44]

JAMES, JESUS, AND THE FAMILY

Jesus and James

While the oddity of referring to a "brother" has frequently been noted, the simple name "Jesus" is more remarkable. The name itself was not unusual, of course: it is the sixth most frequently used male name in the first centuries B.C.E. and C.E., occurring in nine percent of male names.[45] If the ossuary were that of James the Just, the normal phrasing, even in the late first century C.E., would have been "brother of the Lord," "brother of the Messiah," "brother of Jesus Christ," or something similar. The first two were standard ways of referring to James before the end of the first century. As early as the 40s or 50s C.E. Paul commonly used "Jesus Christ" and called James the "brother of the Lord" (Gal 1:18-19). By the 90s C.E. Josephus illustrates that it was common to refer to Jesus, "who is called the messiah" (*Ant.* 20.200–202; cf. 18.63–64).[46] The letters of Peter, John, and Jude never use the stand-alone name "Jesus," and the letter of James uses "servant of the Lord Jesus Christ" (1:1; 2:1).

A forger wanting to refer unmistakably to Jesus of Nazareth in the late Roman or early Byzantine period would hardly have written "brother of Jesus," for more pious formulations had replaced the simple name "Jesus." Since a carver would have adopted language appropriate to his own period, not historicized language appropriate to James' or Jesus' lifetime, the use of "Jesus" speaks for the inscription's provenance in the early to mid-first century C.E., and more strongly against than for a forgery. Still, nothing guarantees that the inscription was intended to refer to the James and Jesus of early church tradition. Simply on probability grounds derived from statistical calculations, the probability is at the very best even.[47]

Social Status

The plainness and informality of the *nefesh* sketch, and unfinished rosettes are consistent with a relatively low family status, though the loss of all information about the tomb's context—a much clearer marker of status—makes judgments unsure. A comparison of this ossuary with others found in the Akeldama tombs, where social status can be inferred from the tombs themselves, supports, though it does not prove, the conclusion about the family's low-status (see Chapter 17).[48] The inscription's careful carving runs against this, however, even when allowance is made for the later improvements just noted. Inscriptions on ossuaries of even high-status individuals were often scratched roughly into the finished box. The regularity of this ossuary's inscription is almost sufficient to make it an argument for inauthenticity.[49]

Religious Context

If the ossuary were genuine, it reflected a practicing Jewish family of the pre-70 C.E. period. The burial conventions were consistent with

those of other Jews of the period (use of an ossuary, Aramaic inscription,
line frames, rosettes, allusion to family lineage). The sketch of a *nefesh*, if
closer scrutiny confirms this interpretation, adds significantly to understanding the family's religious context. A *nefesh* fits the burial practices of
Jews in the Jerusalem area especially, or more widely in the Galilee, the
Shephelah, and southern Judea. The *nefesh* drew on the presence of
pyramidal tomb monuments that symbolized the "soul" of the departed
and referred symbolically to what lay behind the use of the pyramid in
monumental tombs, life beyond mortality.[50] Belief in the preexistence of
souls, entrenched among both Christian and Jewish groups,[51] may have
informed such practices. In the context of burial, however, the primary
element was likely to be afterlife. Though ossuaries have been linked with
belief in resurrection, this claim goes beyond the evidence.[52] The James
ossuary's *nefesh* sketch makes an association only between burial in
ossuaries and notions of postmortem existence.

The James Ossuary

Some of the observations made above point toward inauthenticity, but
in the end I am not persuaded of the ossuary's inauthenticity. The most
telling issue, which is difficult for an amateur to evaluate, is the
ossuary's patina and whether it is a modern fabrication. It is ironic that
the evidence of modern touching up of an older inscription speaks
more for its genuineness than fraudulence. The comparison of James'
ossuary with others—their dating, provenance, style, social status, and
religious belief—suggests that it could be an authentic first-century
artifact. The stylistic analysis points not to forgery but to a pre-70 C.E.
artifact from Jerusalem whose inscription is "genuine." But even if the
inscription were early, written at one time, and derived from Jerusalem,
there is still no certainty that the inscription referred to James the Just.
The absence of all signs that Christian pilgrims knew and handled the
ossuary makes it unlikely that it was ever venerated and works against
its identification as the ossuary of James the Just. The similarity of
names may simply have been historical accident. The evidence is fairly
well balanced and the jury is still out on the question of who the James
of the ossuary was. At this stage the most we can say is that the ossuary
could have been James the Just's, but the possibility may never become
a probability.

Conclusion

The status indications, despite the inscription's care, suggest a literate but low-status family. Use of an ossuary and the *nefesh* on the left end both suggest a family that fitted easily into mid-first century C.E. religiously attuned Judaism. If the artifact can be associated with James the Just, it could add materially to understanding the convictions of the Jerusalem group of Christians. Equally important, if the ossuary once held the bones of James the Just, is that both James' and Jesus' burials were burials in shame and dishonor, following their deaths by execution, one by stoning and one by crucifixion. Despite this fact, both were interred during primary burial in tombs provided for them, in the case of Jesus by a wealthy admirer and in the case of James by someone unknown. In the case of James, secondary burial would have followed in the normal fashion, as the *Mishnah* describes, though in that case, since all knowledge of the provenance has been lost, we can say nothing at all about the tomb.

Finally, James' and Jesus' deaths raise substantial issues over their religious and political roles in Judea and Galilee in the mid-first century C.E. Jesus shared the fate of two *lêstai* ("brigands" or "bandits"; Chapter 2). The behaviors of council members and of Pilate at the trial suggest this was a plausible association. A council sanctioned James' death, too (so Josephus), implying that he had moved beyond the permissible range of "common Judaism." At the end, James and Jesus were united in their deaths. If it were shown that the ossuary was that of James the Just, we would have important burial evidence for James to add to the accounts of Jesus' burial, reinforcing the traditional character of the family's beliefs and practices.

Afterword: IAA Report

A summary of the IAA report (dated 20 June 2003) was released on 16 July 2003, and reprinted, with comments, in *BAR* 29/5 (September/ October 2003): 26–39, 83. Various components of the Final Report appeared on the Internet. Hershel Shanks comments, "What has become clear is that *there is no final report*—no document subscribed to by all committee members. . . . Instead, the 'final report' consists only of individual statements by committee members commenting on the inscriptions from the point of view of their expertise" (*BAR* 29 [2003]: 29). Some members of the committee were less than enthusiastic in their general support of its findings; Ronny Reich accepted the ossuary's inauthenticity only after submitting a report that argued for its authenticity.

The fundamental question has now become the question of the patina, whether it is original and how, if it is not original, it was replicated or forged. There are some indications in the reports of the same kinds of observations I have just made about the "improvement" of the first part of the inscription. In particular at least one member of the committee observed that the final letter of "Yeshua'" has patina results that fall within the normal range, consistent with my observations. What was not discussed was my general suggestion, that an ancient inscription has been "improved." It is possible to accept parts of the IAA report but to merge them with my observations: modern patina was added precisely to cover the tracks of whoever deepened the letters of the inscription. This leaves intact my suggestion that the second half of the inscription is more nearly original and that the first half that has been tampered with significantly more than the second. Until relevant experts have discussed the patina issue the situation is still muddy. For the time being, I stand by my description of the inscription, with the additional complicating factor that the patina on the inscription face may be modern. It is now clear that a feature of the inscription that needs careful attention is whether I am correct that even within the "improved" letters one can still see small signs of their original form.

PART FIVE

CONCLUSION

CHAPTER NINETEEN

BUILDING JEWISH IN THE ROMAN EAST

Material Evidence

The most obvious and widely recognized feature of Judaism was its monotheism, which tolerated no worship of other gods. Linked with its monotheism was another widely recognized feature; its one primary cult site in Jerusalem. A third feature was more complicated; it tended to think of itself as an ethnically cohesive people (*ethnê*), who originated with the ancient patriarchs. Still, it accepted, readily in some periods, new recruits to the *ethnê*. This was true both in the Diaspora and in the homeland from the late second century B.C.E. through to 70 C.E. In the Diaspora, there was sustained growth over a lengthy period, stemming from its ethical standards, communal worship, ancient book, and rejection of other gods; new adherents entered Judaism one-by-one or family-by-family. In Judea, however, conquest by the Hasmoneans or expansion under Herod resulted in larger groups joining Judaism's worship of the God of Israel. Idumeans in the south, for example, including Herod the Great's grandfather, joined collectively; Ituraeans in the northeast also were brought in.[1]

Judaism's self-understanding—one people, one God, one cult, one sacrificial site—influenced its built form. Such factors led to the central cult site in Jerusalem being enormously large, as if to compensate for the absence of other cults and cult sites. They led at the same time to small communal religious building in the pre-70 period. They may also have contributed to the material forms that developed at the level of small village organization and daily life, whether as a working out of the heightened importance of Jerusalem or as community-building activities.

The Jerusalem temple persistently expressed the people's attachment to God through thick and thin. After the temple was destroyed by Babylon in 587 B.C.E., it only gradually came back into prominence, beginning with a much smaller structure following the return from exile later the same century. At the time of the Hasmoneans, four hundred years later, the temple was still a relatively modest structure. By the end of the Hasmonean period it had been expanded and embellished. Under Herod, it was expanded much further and made the focal point of Jerusalem, with a prominence few other temple structures could match. Careful attention was given to its integration into the city and its civic amenities.

Its Herodian rebuilding expressed two important and changing features of Judaism. One of the most significant social and religious aspects of the temple was its series of courtyards, presupposing different degrees of holiness and nearness to God's presence. Two courts were innovations of Herod and the authorities, expressing important developments of the period. (1) The temple included a place for interested Gentiles to approach near, without being included in, God's people. This court gave built form to non-Jews' interest in Judaism; it arose from the increased numbers of Gentiles interested in Judaism and wishing to visit Jerusalem to see the primary cult site. (2) The reconstruction provided a Court of Women, given explicit form in a separate area. By the late first century B.C.E. women's place within the social and religious fabric may have become more significant—for example, Salome Alexandra's important role earlier in the second century—with the result that they were brought in closer to the place of sacrifice. They were at the door, so to speak, though not fully within the sacrificial cult.

The first alteration may have indirectly reflected the numbers of Gentiles joining Judaism as proselytes. The *Temple Scroll* (11QT; usually dated sometime in the second century B.C.E.) had envisioned a future rebuilding of the temple in which an outer courtyard was created, lumping together proselytes and women and children in its religious-architectural vision. The Herodian scheme separated these groups. Women were put close to the center, while the outer court was redesignated for unconverted Gentiles, with no specific provision for proselytes. This material commentary on changing values in Judaism of the second and first centuries B.C.E. was not reflected in other literature.

The most fundamental effect of these general features of Judaism outside Jerusalem was a paucity of expressly Jewish buildings. Some memorial structures were constructed, such as the enclosure at Mamre, traditionally associated with Abraham. And there were memorials to the patriarchs and matriarchs at nearby Hebron, marking their traditional burial places. Both memorials were large open-air enclosures, both built by Herod as part of his "piety." Note that, in line with the previous paragraphs, the Haram al-Khalil at Hebron gave unexpected prominence to the matriarchs: The prominence of three of Israel's great women paralleled three of Israel's founding fathers. It is not insignificant that the same patron commissioned both the Hebron memorial and the Jerusalem temple.

There were other sacrificial centers, most of which owed their existence to the specialized conditions of Egypt (Leontopolis, Elephantine) and Samaria (Mount Gerizim). Samaria's variant form of religion, despite having developed independently for hundreds of years, mirrored rather clearly the situation in Judaism, with one place of sacrifice balanced by small local synagogues. In Egypt, by contrast, though the temples at Leontopolis and earlier at Elephantine probably were rivals of Jerusalem, the majority of synagogues, if not all, were related to worship at Jerusalem's temple, not to alternative Egyptian temples.

For most Jews, one type of building, the synagogue, served for communal religious purposes; this was true in Samaria and Egypt, as well as more widely in the Diaspora. Large cities had several synagogues to satisfy the collective needs of large numbers of Jews (for example, Rome, Alexandria, Jerusalem). Smaller places had only one synagogue and little else in built form to indicate the presence of Jews. There were synagogues of different types—both Judean and Samaritan—in some places (Delos and Caesarea Maritima are good examples), but this fact did not alter the importance of synagogues as the way attachment to Judaism was expressed. In fact, it emphasized that importance. In towns and villages in Judea and in Diaspora cities the synagogue was the primary visible Jewish reality.

Synagogues in the Diaspora were the central Jewish organization. An almost necessary corollary was that synagogues served various communal needs. So synagogues had kitchens and dining rooms, for example, or associated living quarters. Jewish communities in Judea had fewer needs, since the community was more monolithic, so synagogues tended to be simpler. Religion was integrated into whole community, especially through the household. When there were ancillary spaces in addition to the main hall of the synagogue, they tended to include a *Beth ha-Midrash* or a *mikveh*, less frequently a courtyard. Only rarely was there the same variety of spaces of which we have archaeological and inscriptional evidence for the Diaspora.

Another consequence flows from this general situation. Jewish religion was expressed most regularly in the house. In archaeological excavations it is usually impossible to identify houses built for Jews by architecture alone. Yet other material remains frequently allow identification of the occupants' "ethnicity." Several criteria assist in identifying houses as Jewish, the most important being a *mikveh*. Sepphoris was an example of a growing city with an increasingly mixed population; one neighborhood was identifiable as dominantly Jewish by the prevalence of *mikvaoth* throughout most of the western portion of the site, in contrast to the eastern side, where Roman-period expansion was concentrated. Even small rural villages such as Yodefat and Cana, where most indicators suggest that the population was agrarian and impoverished, had *mikvaoth*. Whether urban or rural, the *mikveh* emphasized the importance of domestic purity concerns.

Provision for ritual washing did not have to be made house by house; a communal *mikveh* was sufficient. It was a mark of high seriousness in fulfilling religious obligations when ritual bathing pools were included in houses. *Mikvaoth* were located in larger wealthier houses as well as in smaller poorer houses. Inclusion of a *mikveh* may thus have served as a mark of social status or an indicator of social pretensions. These families could afford the space, the expense, and the demands of special water supply; or they chose to displace other needed facilities within their houses to accommodate space for a *mikveh*. By not having to attend public *mikvaoth*, they acquired real or implied status in the eyes of fellow townspeople.

Industrial purity concerns were expressed similarly. In Gamla, for example, a large industrial-sized installation with two large olive presses and an attached office included an en suite *mikveh*, no doubt to ensure that the oil was manufactured under controlled conditions of ritual purity. This same concern may have prompted inclusion of *mikvaoth* in two houses adjacent to a cave with a similarly large olive press at Yodefat. At Khirbet Qana, a house with a *mikveh* on the northern side of the village was beside what was likely a *columbarium*, possibly implying purity concerns in raising doves.

Smaller items that were the stuff of daily living also indicated ethnicity: kitchen utensils, dining ware, and menu-related items. Stoneware was particularly important and is a good diagnostic tool for ethnicity, since in Jewish law stone did not contract ritual impurity as easily as pottery. This prescription did not apply in neighboring cultures, so its presence is a near-certain indicator of Jewish practices.[2] Since stoneware was more expensive it, like *mikvaoth*, indicated real or hoped-for status. Some types of pottery that have been excavated almost exclusively in Jewish contexts have become important diagnostic tools. Kfar Hananiah ware, the most frequently noted in this connection, was mentioned in the *Mishnah*; its diagnostic value is still under discussion because it has now been shown that it was mimicked at other sites, such as Yodefat, which had a pottery production area on the southern extension.

In elite contexts, such as Herod's palaces, imports were common and showed features in common with upper class life elsewhere in the Empire. On Masada, for example, inscribed wine jugs, "For King Herod the Jew," contained wine imported from southern Italy. The inscription makes an important statement about Herod's ethnicity, as well as about his tastes, though wine jugs from Greek areas were a widespread phenomenon from the late Hellenistic period onwards. Similarly, the distribution of faunal bones is diagnostically relevant as an ethnic marker. Absence of pig bones and shellfish, especially when found in conjunction with other indicators just noted, may point to kosher observance in Jewish neighborhoods. Coin profiles may also indicate inhabitants' attitudes, especially resistance to the dominant Roman culture (Chapter 2); they are more difficult to use in diagnosing ethnicity.

Burial structures were religiously charged expressions of belief and practice in ancient cultures. Buildings for death were as carefully circumscribed as buildings for life, whether along the Kidron or Hinnom Valleys in Jerusalem, on hillsides around Galilean villages, or in major burial areas such as Beth She'arim.[3] Some of the most stunning structures in Jerusalem were tombs. The largest were royal tombs, such as Queen Helena's and Herod's family tombs, both north of the Damascus Gate. Hezekiah's Tomb, the Tomb of Absalom, and the Tomb of the Bene Hezir, on the east slope of the Kidron Valley, were smaller but highly visible because of their location. The Akeldama Tombs, the Tomb of Jason, and one identified as Herod's Family Tomb in West Jerusalem were also significant. Their three most noteworthy features were their architectural variety, the range of motifs borrowed from elsewhere (pyramid roofs from Egypt, circular multistoried tombs from Rome), and the public display of wealth and social prominence, while using traditional burial techniques within. The same traditional forms of burial dominate the rural repertoire of tombs in Judea and

Galilee, where similar *loculi* reflect Jerusalem styles. At Beth She'arim, a later burial site associated with leading rabbis, there is a surprising mixture of traditionally Jewish and imported forms of expression.

Ossuaries, a specialized form of stoneware, have provided important insights into Jewish customs and concerns.[4] They demonstrate developments in customs of secondary burials in the late Second Temple period, as well as shedding light on language use, proselyte issues, Holy Land burials, familial relationships, and status. There is no study of ossuaries' architectural motifs, which are fairly commonly found, but it is thinkable that the architectural repertoire—masonry walls, temple facades, pyramid motifs, columns and capitals, for example—could offer new insights into attitudes to death and burial. Burial inscriptions were prevalent on, though not limited to, ossuaries; the information mined from such inscriptions can sometimes be coordinated with literary allusions to persons, events, and social fabric.

The built and material environment of early Roman Judaism reshapes discussions of its character and its main features, which have traditionally been founded on the literary evidence alone.[5] Nowhere is this more dramatic than in the examination of small village sites in the Galilee, the Golan, Samaria, and Judea. The exponential increase in our knowledge of village life has transformed our sense of the rural, agrarian, and peasant nature of the countryside.

DIACHRONIC TRANSFORMATIONS

Judaism was never thoroughly aniconic. Literary descriptions of the First Temple period show the use of two- and three-dimensional figures in the temple: three-dimensional objects, such as *cherubim* over the ark, four sets of oxen supporting the large basin, and lions or oxen or *cherubim* decorating smaller basins; two-dimensional objects, such as *cherubim*, flowers, and palm trees decorating doors and probably the curtain to the Holy Place. Trees and flowers were always unobjectionable, but the development of more rigorous attitudes to representations of living beings, whether mythical beings or animals or persons, is more puzzling. It is unclear what figurative representations continued into the Second Temple period, since the literary evidence is imprecise. It is likely that at the very least *cherubim* were retained as "a resting place, or throne, for God's invisible presence or glory."[6]

Fascination with other peoples' images probably continued within first-century Judaism. Neighboring societies used figurative objects in religious, public, and domestic contexts, though the evidence is unevenly distributed. Iron-age archaeological excavations in Israel have turned up enough small objects of various "pagan" types that we can suppose they were found in society at large, despite "official" prohibition of images (e.g., Exod 20:4-5a, repeated several times later): gods, animals, and other cult objects were problems in the First Temple period and possibly in the Second Temple period, though there may have been a shift after the exile.[7] The practice of surrounding cultures also varied. In Petra, for example, there was a tendency towards minimalist figurative representation during the late Hellenistic and early Roman periods; Nabatea was not aniconic, but the use of semi-abstract "god-blocks" dominated early representations of deities—especially Dushara—and gave way to figurative images only in the first century C.E.

Still, the use of images within Judea and Galilee must have been restrained during the Second Temple period, whether privately or publicly. There were important exceptions to this general rule, however. A monumental instance was the Tobiad Palace at Araq al-Emir on the Wadi Sir in Jordan. One of the Tobiads—a priestly Jewish landowning family in the Transjordan—built an innovative structure (about 180 B.C.E.), a kind of "floating palace" set in a large reflecting pool, whose corners were decorated with sixteen massive lions at the second-story level, and two leopards on the lower level serving as fountains.[8] The customary understanding of Jewish convictions was provocatively contradicted in its prominent images of living animals. A minor instance of the use of images was discovered on Jerusalem's western hill, where frescoes with birds were found in elite, and perhaps priestly, houses. By contrast, none of the Herodian and Hasmonean palaces excavated in Judea or Samaria or the Transjordan had images. The decorative motifs on Herod's mosaic floors, for example, were geometric; the frescoes were either geometric (Pompeian first style) or imitations of high-quality materials such as marble. Early synagogues that have been excavated also lacked images. The slender evidence from Araq al-Emir and Jerusalem prompts a question whether priestly attitudes were more tolerant—perhaps drawing on traditional First Temple practices—than those of an increasingly conservative rank and file, reflecting common Judaism.

An important instance of artistic, though not figurative, motifs was the Hasmonean tomb at Modi'in, described in 1 Maccabees 13.25–30 (ca. 140 B.C.E.). The literary description refers to seven pyramids (undoubtedly the family's *nefeshot*) and carvings of ships and suits of armor. These were inoffensive enough, but suits of armor also were controversial in Herod's theater in Jerusalem. Josephus's account (*Ant.* 15.276) focuses on the controversy: Herod defused the argument over whether they were "images" by unveiling them. Was this, perhaps, a sign of increasing artistic conservatism?

A special use of iconic currency was the adoption of the Tyrian shekel, with its images of Melkart and an eagle on its obverse and reverse, as the unit of currency for payment of the temple tax. The custom was discussed in the *Mishnah*, though not in great detail. It may be that there were some controversies over its use, as Jesus' turning of the moneychangers' tables in the temple suggests and as Qumran's resistance to temple practices may also suggest. But surprisingly the practice seems to have been quietly accepted by most. Not only did these images offend prima facie against the Decalogue, they brought a sense of attachment to a foreign god and a foreign city right into the holiest place in Judaism.

When synagogues began to be built the prohibition against images was probably quite strong. Pre-70 C.E. synagogues with surviving remains, such as Gamla, Masada, Herodium, Jericho, Delos, and Ostia, have no artistic embellishments. In the next couple of centuries this changed. The most important transformation following the destruction of the temple was the gradual adoption of symbols associated with the temple. It is likely that the earliest was the adoption of the menorah, the seven- or five- or nine-branched candelabra, as a symbol. A menorah was already found scratched in plaster in a fine house on the western hill of Jerusalem (early first century C.E.); it was also on a coin of Mattathias Antigonus (ca. 40 B.C.E.), so its adoption may have seemed natural. Before long, however, the use of temple symbols increased substantially to include representations of the façade (already on coins of the Second Jewish Revolt; 132–135 C.E.), the altar, the table of showbread, sacrifices, the *lulav*, and the *ethrog*. These images made an important point when they were used. As long as the temple was standing such images derogated from the sanctity of the holy place; two or three hundred years later, when the temple no longer stood and expectations for its rebuilding were remote at best, the application of temple motifs to synagogues was appropriate and fitting, and added to their sanctity.

When, however, Jews in Dura Europos, on the banks of the Euphrates in eastern Syria, decorated their synagogue with frescoes in the early third century, the artistic program included people: Moses, Aaron, Ezekiel, and others. This may have represented a special case of inspiration from the surrounding culture, for other religious buildings in Dura had similar frescoes. Yet Jews in Palestine in later periods followed suit in still more surprising ways. Mosaic floors were decorated with images of persons and animals: Abraham and Isaac and Moses, once with the ram and even the hand of God (at Beth Alpha); hunting scenes, lions, cattle, sheep, eagles, birds, fish, and horses; scenes from Noah's ark (at Gerasa); scenes of daily life, including men trampling grapes (at Chorazin). Pagan images were also used. The most extensively discussed have been the zodiac figures: Helios as sun god, figures representing months and seasons (Hammat Tiberias, Beth Alpha, Sepphoris, among others). There were figures of Medusa and the rape of Ganymede (Chorazin), and the diverse repertoire could be lengthened. It is difficult to imagine an interpretation that would reduce the contrast between these later "icons" and the earlier situation when a suit of armor was thought controversial.

This development was paralleled, incidentally, in early Christianity, where similar motifs were used. The parallelism was seen in Dura's church, synagogue, and Mithraeum, or in Beth Shean's church and synagogue. Eventually the use of images was challenged from outside by the rise of Islam, and from inside by aniconic movements that developed in both Jewish and Christian circles. It is still possible to observe the vigorous removal of images in Jewish and Christian buildings, particularly their iconic mosaic floors.

It is important to underscore that Judaism's attitudes were not static. Although most of these developments took place towards the end of the period considered here, their roots were earlier. The prohibition against images was hardly strict; it was not honored in practice at all periods and in all places (it would be better to say it was interpreted in different ways at different times and in different places, under various influences). There was general restraint in the use of images, especially during the late Second Temple period when that restraint included many, but not all, Jews within Judea and the Galilee. The urge to adopt symbolic links between the temple in Jerusalem and synagogues led

eventually to an extensive repertoire of images, including Moses and
Aaron, priests, sacrifice, the Aqedah of Isaac, and so on. The inclusion
of other more clearly pagan religious symbols is harder to explain, and
inclusion of minor domestic scenes, as at Chorazin, is even harder to
explain.

Having said that, the *Mishnah*'s views on these matters were not as
absolute and prohibitive as might be expected. It presupposed debates
in the second century C.E. (and in the first century C.E.?) over how far
Jews could go, especially in Roman pagan structures such as baths,
towards an accommodation with "idolatry." The debates included
questions about festivals, idols, things that might be confused with
idols, wild animals, jewelry, and so on (*m. 'Abodah Zarah*). One debate
considered Jewish workmen being involved as a part of their daily
activity in constructing buildings where offensive images were to be
installed. Perhaps such circumstances and the debates about them soft-
ened attitudes and contributed eventually to the inclusion of decorative
art in Jewish contexts.

The Jewishness of Jewish Architecture

Judaism was a complex phenomenon, with substantial numbers of
adherents—as many as one-seventh of the population of the Roman
Empire by some estimates—and a recognized place in the wider society
of Imperial Rome. Its practices were widely known if not always understood and respected, and even after the Revolts it continued to exercise
a magnetic attraction for some Romans. Its temple in Jerusalem was its
single best-known structure, a result of the combination of its size, its
patron's importance, its distinctive features, and its historic setting. But
Jewish communal buildings were distributed around the Mediterranean
in considerable numbers, including five or six in Rome before the close
of the Julio-Claudian period. They gradually accommodated artistic
decoration and other material embellishments.

The distinctiveness of its architecture, however, was a complicated
mixture of its own specific requirements and the common conventions
of Rome and the Near East. An assessment of its architecture has to
reckon with Judaism's location in the Levant, on the eastern seaboard
of the Mediterranean, where it was directly influenced not only by late
Hellenistic traditions and Roman building conventions, but also by

those of its near neighbors, such as Phoenicia, Syria, Nabatea, Arabia, and Egypt, not to mention other more distant influences such as Parthia and Persia. The distinctiveness of Jewish architecture lay more in its way of mixing diverse influences than in anything inherent in Judaism's own architectural traditions.

Jewish villages and towns did not have exactly the same combination of buildings as similarly sized towns in Greek or Roman lands, or in the Levant adjacent to Judea, though this may have changed over time. They tended not to have *nymphaea* or other publicly visible water distribution facilities. There were fewer public baths for the use of the population at large, in part because traditions about water collection and water management had more in common with Arabian practices. This meant that only major cities such as Jerusalem, Caesarea Maritima, Sebaste, Sepphoris, and Tiberias had permanent water supply by aqueduct, a prerequisite for public baths.[9] There was less emphasis on an agora or marketplace, but the most visible difference was the limited number of temples in major towns and cities. Yet some "pagan" building types were found in Jewish cities: theaters and stadia were the most obvious, reflecting the mixed population.

The general claim that Judaism's architecture was not inherently distinctive is rather obvious, I suppose, with respect to domestic traditions, but less obvious in religious traditions. I will summarize each briefly. The situation is clearest with respect to synagogues, especially those in the Diaspora where synagogues first developed. The most helpful examples were in Italy, Greece, the Aegean, and Ionian coastal areas, though the earliest were in fact in Egypt. Their development in these areas was modeled on voluntary associations, as the examples at Delos (second century B.C.E.), Ostia (late first century C.E.), and Priene (third century C.E.) show. Comparison between synagogues and other association buildings from similar periods demonstrate striking resemblances, and show how much synagogues shared in design theory and practice with associations.

Since both literary and archaeological evidence suggest that synagogues in the Holy Land were a later development, it is likely that Judean synagogues were a spin-off from Diaspora practices. The building type was modified for use in the homeland, of course, so that Judean and Galilean synagogues were somewhat less like voluntary associations than those in the Diaspora. Those modifications were mainly simplifications. Because of their location in essentially Jewish areas, they had a different list of requirements: a *Beth ha-Midrash* was more frequent; *mikvaoth* might sometimes be found; occasionally (Jerusalem's Theodotos synagogue is the one sure example) facilities for visitors were included; but contrariwise, dining facilities and kitchens were less common. In both regions, the communal space was similarly simple in the earliest periods, usually a meeting space with columns supporting a simple gabled roof. Because of the customary lack of embellishment on the exterior, a synagogue would not be immediately identifiable by a passing pedestrian, unless, like Corinth's synagogue, it happened to have an inscription over the door. To the casual observer, the structures looked and functioned like associations.

The temple in Jerusalem, which was so remarkable in size, complexity, facilities, decoration, materials, and supporting clerical staff, drew extensively on its earlier precursors: Solomon's temple, Zerubbabel's temple, and the Hasmonean temple. These in turn drew some at least of their inspiration from neighboring temples. Even in details of Herod's reconstructed temple, contemporary similarities can be found in other Near Eastern examples. In overall design, analogies can be found in Near Eastern, Hellenistic, and Roman structures: its *naos* or holy place was indebted to near eastern religious structures, its surrounding courtyards along with the Royal Basilica were self-consciously Roman, its overall formal qualities and ambition to overawe the worshiper were late Hellenistic. But it also had a number of innovative features relating to its setting in its urban context: its multiple gates, impressive bridges and overpasses, shops and streets. The combination of external influences, indigenous qualities, and innovative details can be attributed to an innovative patron, Herod the Great.

The Near Eastern analogies can be noted briefly. The Temple of Dushara at Petra and the Temple of Bel at Palmyra closely parallel the unusual arrangement with the axis of the *naos* and related structures being at right angles to the axis of the courtyard. The crow step decoration at the eave of the temple is likewise found in Palmyrene and Nabatean cultures, indeed in Arabian architecture more widely distributed. The stairs in the wall-width leading up to a flat roof, which was used for religious purposes, was found at Petra and Palmyra. It may be, though this is less clear, that the Jerusalem temple's division between a holy place and a holy of holies was analogous—though by no means similar—to the arrangements at both the Temple of Dushara and the Temple of Bel. Having a large square altar in front was not unusual, but the combination of an altar and a laver, one to the left the other to the right of the main axis, was uncommon; the Jerusalem temple shared this feature with Palmyra's Temple of Bel. The point is that the *naos* in Jerusalem was not *sui generis*. It shared much with nearby major temples; the two nearest analogies, Petra's Temple of Dushara and Palmyra's Temple of Bel, were both major shrines in their respective cities.[10]

A further significant similarity between Jerusalem's temple and the Temple of Bel was the design approach in which a Roman-style colon-naded courtyard surrounded a typically eastern religious building. Had the courtyard come much later, this might have been less noteworthy. In the case of Jerusalem, however, the whole complex was a single inte-grated complex from the late first century B.C.E., conceived by one patron. Palmyra's overall planning is slightly less clear, but its main developments were almost precisely contemporaneous with the temple in Jerusalem. In both cases, there seemed a conscious decision to adopt a mixed architectural idiom, with ancillary spaces being indebted to a Roman model and the central religious space being local—that is, Near Eastern—in character, form, and decoration. It is likely that the same holds true of the Temple of Dushara in Petra, but the evidence is less easily determined.

This is not surprising. Cultural and religious contacts in the east had been strong for more than a millennium, so that a shared vocabulary of design elements and overall approaches was a natural consequence. It is a little more surprising that after two centuries of Greek and Roman influences their design influences were limited largely to the surrounding colonnades. Their influences on the *naos* were very restricted. Judaism's version of this combination of indigenous tradi-tions, wider Near Eastern traditions, and more recent influences from Greece and Rome was not substantially different in overall balance from the versions adopted by Nabatea, Palmyra, Syria, and to a lesser extent Egypt.

Mundane housing typical of rural and peasant areas followed the same pattern. Jewish housing in the Holy Land was much like housing in adjacent regions where conditions were the same. Even today pat-terns of housing in these regions and others with the same conditions, such as rural Morocco, follow a similar canon of architectural ele-ments: rough stone walls, usually undressed and only sometimes plas-tered with either mud plaster or lime plaster; packed dirt floors, occasionally paved, especially in exterior courtyards; floors and roofs that utilize whatever is available in the way of beams, with a dense combination of small branches and mud constituting the horizontal surfaces; small windows, limited in number, and even fewer doors. In design, the main distinguishing feature was a courtyard. Many houses did not have one, especially when the villages were built on the side of a hill where "terrace housing" tended to be the norm. In these cases houses were grouped into multiple units sharing common walls, and wresting some outdoor living space out of this arrangement by using the roof of an adjacent house for outdoor activities. Somewhat better classes of houses had a side courtyard used for the daily needs of the household, especially cooking. In some cases the courtyards were large enough to hold the family's animals. Still larger houses, a minority, were organized around a central courtyard, though in the majority of even these cases the rooms around the courtyard were more informally organized than in Greek or Roman houses with central courtyards.

In cities the range of sizes and design variations was greater. Some Jewish urban houses may have been modeled on Roman types, but probably there were not a great number of these. Decoration was more frequently influenced by Rome: a house in Jerusalem had a peristyle courtyard similar to what might have been found in Rome or Pompeii, and one house in Yodefat in the Galilee even had a frescoed wall and floor that were similar to Roman examples. The housing type that was most nearly similar to houses in Italy or other Roman provincial settings was the villa. In Judea, these were frequently royal structures; in the majority of cases of those that have been excavated, Herod was the patron and owner. Some of Herod's palaces were built on an earlier Hasmonean phase, suggesting a degree of Hellenization and Romanization within this priestly family. The structures are well known, though it bears noting that while the details of the Herodian phases of these structures were firmly Roman, their design concepts frequently transcended known Roman models. This detailed similarity and conceptual innovation is best understood not as something distinctively Jewish but instead characteristically Herodian.

INNOVATION AND ADAPTATION

This book has emphasized details—sometimes almost trivial details—in pursuit of a larger goal, to understand Judaism holistically using the material and built forms it utilized. Sometimes the details have allowed us to see a degree of independence and innovation in a culture that we habitually think of as conservatively religious in its overall character. There is, of course, truth in that general characterization of Judaism as conservative, but it must be balanced against ongoing change: Judaism depended on written law, yet it regularly adapted its interpretations of that law to apply to new conditions; it was steadfastly monotheist, yet it found numerous ways to accommodate itself to foreign overlords, not least of which was Rome; it was to a considerable extent ethnocentric, yet it could readily absorb converts in its ranks and it found several ways to include interested non-converts, even in its major cult site in Jerusalem.

The dominant argument in Part 3 was that Jews used the important Greco-Roman model of the association as a model for synagogues. Associations were an important part of Roman social and economic life, drawing together like-minded or similarly employed persons into a group of defined membership, using communal facilities to express that coherence and fulfill their goals. Often associations had distinctive religious goals and sometimes they had a limited ethnic make-up. It is not surprising, then, that Jewish communities in the Diaspora drew some of their inspiration for the development of synagogues from such associations. Where we can first make formal comparisons of synagogues and other associations, at Delos or Ostia, there were striking similarities both in form and detail. It is less susceptible of proof that synagogues began first in this precise context in a Diaspora setting and only later found their way to Judea and Galilee. That seems likely, but other suggestions are also possible. In any case, the development of the synagogue was a fertile and creative innovation, one that had an enormous impact on the history of Judaism. If my claim about their origins in the Diaspora and within the context of associations is correct, it was a remarkable instance of borrowing and adaptation.

A second institutional development might be set alongside this. Judaism was a major innovator of monasteries. The two examples that have survived, that of the Therapeutae in a literary text and that at Qumran in archaeological form, exemplify two different styles of monastic association. The Therapeutae were an eremitic or quasi-eremitic group, Qumran a coenobitic or quasi-coenobitic group. It is rather remarkable that Judaism developed two independent forms of monastic life within a very short time of each, and that it did not perpetuate either of these forms in its subsequent communal life.

A similar kind of independence and innovation appeared in the reconstruction of the temple in Jerusalem, with its blending of styles and especially in its system of courts expressing various degrees of holiness and levels of purity. In this case the innovation seems to have been a mixture of the previous forms the temple had taken and the needs of the then contemporary society, particularly with respect to women and Gentiles. There may well have been a longer history to these developments than we can recover accurately now—the discovery of the *Temple Scroll* hints at some of that history—but the Herodian reconstruction of the temple is the most direct indication both of Judaism's openness to Gentiles and its revaluation of the roles of women. In neither case did the innovation survive much beyond the destruction of the temple, so that the full story of women and Gentiles within the temple cult is hard to recover. Nevertheless, as a built expression of a social reality, the temple is a crucial piece of evidence.

There are other aspects to the built realities of this period of Jewish history that we might comment on: burial practices and tomb architecture, on the one hand, imaginative villas and palaces, on the other, for example. In such cases, the degree of innovation was more the result of the imagination of an important patron or owner, who wished to express his or her importance, values, religious beliefs, or creativity in a particularly significant "monument." This is not to denigrate them, only to say that, while still an expression of Jewish creativity and innovation, they are not so much a collective expression as the other instances just noted.

JUDAISM IN ITS NEAR EASTERN AND ROMAN SETTINGS

I have aimed to emphasize not so much the truly unusual or novel aspect of Jewish building activity and material culture but rather the unique combination of features, consistent with its specific historic position. Its geographic location on the eastern seaboard of the Mediterranean gave it a particular cultural role, due to the way it was surrounded by a number of more influential and—through most periods, at least—more powerful neighbors. This role took a specific historic guise in the first century B.C.E. and the first half of the first century C.E., when it had an especially close relationship to Rome and played an intriguing role in Rome's political machinations of the time. The economic developments in the early Imperial period, in which Judea shared and which Herod exploited though such major developments as Caesarea Maritima, created opportunities for self-expression that flourished for much of those two centuries. All these were combined with the religious self-confidence of the Jewish people, a confidence born in their convictions about monotheism and its attractiveness to some within the Roman world. In the end, there was an unusual symbiosis between Jewish understanding of religion and material expression of that religious set of convictions, a symbiosis that was epitomized in the Jerusalem temple. In numerous smaller ways, the symbiosis was also expressed in other aspects of material culture: housing, ritual purity concerns, death and burial, to name just a few prominent issues. There will be more to say as excavations unveil more of the gritty details of Jewish life in this period that has been so influential for understanding the religious rivalries of the modern period.

JUDAISM, JESUS, AND EARLY CHRISTIANITY

Occasionally this book has aimed to integrate into its concern for Judaism's material remains features of Christianity's remains. The primary reason for the concern is obvious: Jesus and all his earliest followers were Jewish and followed—albeit in their own ways—the customs and practices of Judaism. In matters of eating, purity, burial, ritual washings, torah observance, and so on, Jesus and his followers were largely indistinguishable from fellow Jews. Jesus' attitudes to social protest and his concerns for the dispossessed, who often made up the ranks of those "brigands" who protested, were not significantly different from others' attitudes. He was distinctive in a number of ways, but his distinctiveness lay more in the combination of beliefs and attitudes than in the specific details of any particular belief or practice. So while his turning of the tables was especially noteworthy, it was founded on attitudes to iconic representations and on attitudes to annual payment shared with others.

As the early Christian movement developed a distinctive identity with features that differentiated itself clearly, sometimes aggressively, from its Jewish sibling, it is striking that its architectural practices were at first barely indistinguishable from Judaism's. The use of house-churches and house-synagogues was nearly identical. The gradual alterations were almost identical as a patron's house was adapted to meet the new needs and developing liturgy within the two communities. Whereas Christianity's rhetoric increasingly distinguished between itself and neighboring Jews, Christianity seems to have been strongly tied to the model of the synagogue for indications of how it should develop artistically and functionally. The impact of synagogues on early Christian church buildings has been obscured by the lack of extensive evidence in the crucial period of the late first through late third centuries. In addition to Jews and Christians using similar strategies in the early stages of the development of communal structures— especially the strategy of using houses as the basis for their meetings— it is apparent that both developed in somewhat similar ways in their use of the basilica model as their most common long-term solution. This makes it likely that both followed similar patterns in the processes by which they moved from one to the other. But if this scenario is correct, there is little doubt in my mind that such similarities as there were derived from Christian borrowing from Jewish synagogues, not the other way around.

A parallel phenomenon, though it is harder to describe accurately, occurred with monasteries. While Judaism was an innovator in developing the earliest traceable institutions that might reasonably be labeled "monastery," it is noteworthy that it was Christianity that picked up the notion of monasteries and developed them into a major institutional form. But it seems to have done so without direct dependence on the earlier Jewish model, and at best there is a century-long gap between the latest evidence of a Jewish monastery and the earliest evidence of a Christian monastery. I am convinced there must have been a connection between Judaism's innovation and the later Christian practice, but I know of no evidence that makes that connection explicit other than the incorrect use by Eusebius of a description of the Therapeutae in describing early Christian practices. This only poses the problem; it does not solve it.

In general, it is clearer than it used to be that relationships between Christianity and Judasim continued for a fairly long period. I am reluctant to suggest dates, but I would now look to the material evidence to try to find ways of establishing parameters for contact and relationships. I briefly alluded to Capernaum and Khirbet Qana as possible sites where built evidence may imply more extended neighborly relationships, presupposing continued vigorous Jewish communal life. I have also argued elsewhere that the material evidence permits a similar observation at Corinth.[11] In this period, when Judaism and Christianity began to go their separate ways, when a growing rivalry and mistrust led to polemic and separation, it may have been that the conditions varied from place to place. It is possible that we will accumulate sufficient information in sites such as Capernaum and Khirbet Qana and Corinth that we can reformulate older reconstructions of the nature of the relationship between church and synagogue. We may find that the sense of rivalry was in some places more muted—at least in urban and architectural terms—than we previously thought. The old formulation—of intense and almost implacable polemic between the sibling communities—was constructed, of course, on the basis of literary evidence. It is the overriding conviction of this book that we must listen just as carefully to the material evidence as we do to the literary evidence. If that material evidence points towards a revision of the older consensus, it will have been worth all the effort in finding the material evidence and listening carefully to it.

NOTES

Chapter One

1. This background is reflected in *Text and Artifact*.
2. *City and Sanctuary*, especially ch.1.
3. *City and Sanctuary*, chs. 2–6.
4. *Herod*, passim.
5. In the Galilee, the doyen of this approach has been Eric Meyers, along with his colleagues, most notably Carol Meyers and James Strange. Their work at Meiron has been a model.
6. Lee I. Levine, *The Ancient Synagogue: The First Thousand Years* (New Haven: Yale University Press, 2000), chs. 1–4; Birger Olsson and Magnus Zetterholm, eds., *The Ancient Synagogue from Its Origins until 200 C.E.: Papers Presented at an International Conference at Lund University October 14–17, 2001* (ConBNT 39; Stockholm: Almqvist and Wiksell, 2003).
7. White's seminal work, *Social Origins*, particularly his emphasis on associations, has influenced me. See also *Voluntary Associations*; Richard N. Longenecker, ed., *Community Formation in the Early Church and in the Church Today* (Peabody: Hendrickson, 2002).
8. Donfried & Richardson, *Rome*, exemplifies both sides of the equation.
9. Macrobius, *Saturnalia* 2.4.11.

Chapter Two

1. I am grateful to Douglas Edwards, coauthor of this chapter, for permission to republish it from *Handbook of Early Christianity: Social Science Approaches* (ed. Anthony J. Blasi, Jean Duhaime, and Paul-André Turcotte; Walnut Creek, CA: Altamira, 2002), 247–66.
2. Richard A. Horsley, *Archaeology, History and Society in Galilee: The Social Context of Jesus and the Rabbis* (Valley Forge: Trinity Press International, 1996), 119, 123.
3. Peter S. Wells, *The Barbarians Speak: How the Conquered Peoples Shaped Roman Europe* (Princeton: Princeton University Press, 1999); James C. Scott, *Weapons of the Weak: Everyday Forms of Peasant Resistance* (New Haven: Yale University Press, 1985); James C. Scott, *Domination and the Arts of Resistance: Hidden Transcripts* (New Haven: Yale University Press, 1990); Edward Said, *Culture and Imperialism* (New York: Knopf, 1993).
4. Wells, *Barbarians*; Scott, *Weapons*; Paul Stoller, *Embodying Colonial Memories: Spirit Possession, Power, and the Hauka in West Africa* (New York: Routledge, 1995).
5. After Vespasian's ascension to the Imperial throne, Josephus settled in Rome where he wrote four major works: *Jewish War* (about 75 C.E.), *Antiquities of the Jews*, *Life*, and *Against Apion* (all in the 90s C.E.). All were in one sense or another apologetic works presenting Judaism positively.

6. Andrea Berlin, now published as "Romanization and Anti-Romanization in Pre-Revolt Galilee," in *The First Jewish Revolt: Archaeology, History, and Ideology* (ed. Andrea Berlin and J. Andrew Overman; London: Routledge, 2002), 57–73.

7. Douglas R. Edwards, "The Social, Religious, and Political Aspects of Costume in Josephus," in *The World of Roman Costume* (ed. Judith Sebesta and Larissa Bonfante; Madison: University of Wisconsin Press, 1994), 153–59.

8. Douglas R. Edwards, "Religion, Power, and Politics: Jewish Defeats by the Romans in Iconography and Josephus," in *Diaspora Jews and Judaism: Essays in Honor of, and in Dialogue with, A. Thomas Kraabel* (ed. J. Andrew Overman and Robert S. MacLennan; South Florida Studies in the History of Judaism 41; Atlanta: Scholars Press, 1992), 293–310.

9. Mordechai Aviam, "Galilee," *NEAEHL* 2:454; *Herod*, 68–72, 109–13.

10. Mordechai Aviam, "A Second-First Century B.C.E. Fortress and Siege Complex in Eastern Upper Galilee," in *Archaeology and the Galilee: Texts and Contexts in the Graeco-Roman and Byzantine Periods* (ed. Douglas R. Edwards and C. Thomas McCollough; South Florida Studies in the History of Judaism 143; Atlanta: Scholars Press, 1997), 97–105.

11. *Herod*, 33–38.

12. Ehud Netzer, "Jericho," *NEAEHL* 2:690.

13. Aviam, "Galilee," *NEAEHL* 2:454.

14. Douglas R. Edwards, *Religion and Power: Pagans, Jews, and Christians in the Greek East* (New York: Oxford University Press, 1996).

15. Shimon Dar, "Samaria: Region, the Survey of Western Samaria," *NEAEHL* 4:1313–1316.

16. Contrast Benjamin Isaac, *The Limits of Empire: The Roman Army in the East* (Oxford: Clarendon, 1990), 107, 428–29.

17. David A. Fiensy, *The Social History of Palestine in the Herodian Period: The Land is Mine* (Lewiston, N.Y.: Edwin Mellen, 1991); Horsley, *Archaeology*, passim.

18. J. D. Crossan, "The Relationship between Galilean Archaeology and Historical Jesus Research" (paper presented at the Society of Biblical Literature Annual Meeting; Nashville, 2000).

19. Rami Arav and Richard Freund, eds., *Bethsaida: A City by the North Seashore of the Sea of Galilee* (Kirksville: Thomas Jefferson University Press, 1995), passim.

20. Jonathan L. Reed, *Archaeology and the Galilean Jesus: A Re-examination of the Evidence* (Harrisburg: Trinity Press International, 2000), ch. 3.

21. Yizhar Hirschfeld, *The Palestinian Dwelling in the Roman-Byzantine Period* (Jerusalem: Franciscan Printing Press, 1995); Santiago Guijarro, "The Family in First-Century Galilee," in *Constructing Early Christian Families* (ed. Halvor Moxnes; London: Routledge, 1997), 42–65.

22. See *m. Ber.* 1:3; *m. Pe'ah* 2:7; *m. Šabb.* 2:5; *m. Pesah.* 3:7; Bernard S. Jackson, *Theft in Early Jewish Law* (Oxford: Clarendon, 1972), 20–40; Benjamin Isaac, "Bandits in Judaea and Arabia," *HSCP* 88 (1984): 183, n. 68.

23. Philip Harland, "Banditry in the Roman Empire and Herod the Great" (unpublished paper, 1993).

24. Isaac, *Limits*, 78.

25. Doron Mendels, *The Rise and Fall of Jewish Nationalism* (New York: Doubleday, 1992).

26. *Herod*, 119–30.

27. There are three minor exceptions to this: in *Ant.* 14.142 Josephus uses *lêsteia* of Aristobulus and Alexander; in *Ant.* 8.204 he uses *lêsteuô* and *lêstrikos* of Rezon, at the time of Solomon; and at *Ant.* 9.183 he uses *lêstês* of robbers at the time of Elisha. These are minor in comparison to the regularity of use of the terms from Herod onwards, as he indicates in the introduction in *War* 1.11, using *lêstrikos*.

28. Harland, "Banditry."

29. *Herod*, 79, 108–13, 250–52.

30. J. D. Crossan, *The Historical Jesus* (New York: Harper, 1991), 175–76.

31. *Herod*, 70, 109.

32. *Herod*, 155–58.

33. *Herod*, 139–42, 232.

34. Schürer 1:565–66 for the coin evidence: "Zenodorus, tetrarch and high priest."

35. *Herod*, ch. 1.

36. Terence L. Donaldson, "Rural Bandits, City Mobs and the Zealots," *JSJ* 21 (1990): 19–40.

37. Richard A. Horsley with John S. Hanson, *Bandits, Prophets, and Messiahs: Popular Movements in the Time of Jesus* (Harrisburg: Trinity Press International, 1999).

38. Donaldson, "Rural Bandits."

39. Richard Fenn, *The Death of Herod: An Essay in the Sociology of Religion* (Cambridge: Cambridge University Press, 1992); Martin Goodman, *The Ruling Class of Judaea: The Origins of the Jewish Revolt against Rome A.D. 66–70* (Cambridge: Cambridge University Press, 1987), 38–42, 139–40.

40. David Catchpole, *The Trial of Jesus: A Study in the Gospels and Jewish Historiography from 1770 to the Present Day* (StPB 18; Leiden: Brill, 1971).

41. Sanders, *Judaism*, part II.

42. John S. Kloppenborg Verbin, "Isaiah 5:1-7, the Parable of the Tenants and Vineyard Leases on Papyrus," in *Text and Artifact*, 111–34.

Chapter Three

1. I am grateful to Charles Hixon and Ann Spurling, coauthors of this publication, for permission to republish it from *Virtual Reality in Archaeology* (ed. Juan Barceló, Maurizio Forte, and Donald H. Sanders; BAR International Series 843; Oxford: Archaeopress, 2000), 195–204.

2. David Adan-Bayewitz and Mordechai Aviam, "Jotapata, Josephus, and the Siege of 67: Preliminary Report on the 1992–94 Seasons," *Journal of Roman Archaeology* 10 (1997): 131–65.

Chapter Four

1. An expansion of a lecture given in Jerusalem in 2001, to appear in *Jesus and Archaeology* (ed. James Charlesworth; Grand Rapids: Wm. B. Eerdmans, forthcoming).

2. Excavations under the direction of Douglas Edwards, University of Puget Sound, and Jack Olive, Pacific Lutheran University, in association with the IAA.

3. Julián Herrojo, *Cana de Galilea y su localización* (CahRB 45; Paris: Gabalda, 1999), 115–20.

4. Edward Robinson, *Biblical Researches in Palestine: Mount Sinai and Arabia Petraea*, vol. 3 (Boston: Crocker and Brewster, 1841), 204–5.

5. Halvor Moxnes, "Placing Jesus of Nazareth: Toward a Theory of Place in the Study of the Historical Jesus," in *Text and Artifact*, 158–75.

6. Aviam & Richardson, "Galilee," 177–209.

7. Eric M. Meyers, et al., *The Excavations at Ancient Meiron, Upper Galilee, Israel, 1971–72, 1974–75, 1977* (Cambridge, Mass.: American Schools of Oriental Research, 1981).

8. Adan-Bayewitz and Aviam, "Jotapata," 131–65.

9. James F. Strange, "First-Century Galilee from Archaeology and from the Texts," in *Archaeology and the Galilee: Texts and Contexts in the Greco-Roman and Byzantine Periods* (ed. Douglas R. Edwards and C. Thomas McCollough; South Florida Studies in the History of Judaism 143; Atlanta: Scholars Press, 1997), 39–48.

10. Aviam & Richardson, "Galilee."

11. Aviam & Richardson, "Galilee."

12. See Dominic Perring, "Spatial Organization and Social Change in Roman Towns," in *City and Country in the Ancient World* (ed. John Rich and Andrew Wallace-Hadrill; London: Routledge, 1991), 273–93.

13. Ze'ev Herzog, "Fortifications (Levant)," *ABD* 2:844–52; Ze'ev Herzog, "Cities in the Levant," *ABD* 1:1032–42.

14. Boaz Zissu, "Two Herodian Dovecotes: Horvat Abu Haf and Horvat 'Aleq," *Journal of Roman Archaeology, Supplementary Series* 14 (1995): 56–69.

15. See the contrasting essays: William E. Arnal, "The Parable of the Tenants and the Class Consciousness of the Peasantry," *Text and Artifact*, 135–57; Kloppenborg Verbin, "Isaiah 5:1-7, the Parable of the Tenants and Vineyard: Leases on Papyrus," *Text and Artifact*, 111–34.

16. For different typologies see: Yizhar Hirschfeld, *The Palestinian Dwelling in the Roman-Byzantine Period* (Jerusalem: Franciscan Printing Press/Israel Exploration Society, 1995); Santiago Guijarro, "The Family in First-Century Galilee," in *Constructing Early Christian Families* (ed. Halvor Moxnes; London: Routledge, 1997), 42–65; Santiago Guijarro Oporto, *Fidelidades en Conflicto: La Ruptura con la Familia por Causa del Discipulado y de la Mission en la Tradición Sinóptica* (Plenitudo Temporis 4; Salamanca: Pulicaciones Universidad Pontificia, 1998).

17. John S. Kloppenborg Verbin, "Dating Theodotus (*CIJ* II 1404)," *JJS* 51.2 (2000): 243–80.

18. Sanders, *Judaism*, part II.

Chapter Five

1. This was first published in *Christology, Controversy and Community: New Testament Essays in Honour of David Catchpole* (ed. David G. Horrell and Christopher M. Tuckett; Leiden: Brill, 2000), 63–83.

2. David R. Catchpole, "Tradition and Temple," ch. 9 in *The Quest for Q* (Edinburgh: T&T Clark, 1993,) 256–79, originally published in W. Horbury, ed., *Templum Amicitiae: Essays on the Second Temple presented to Ernst Bammel* (JSNTSup 48; Sheffield: JSOT Press, 1991) 305–29; here 256–57.

3. Catchpole, *Quest*, 276, 277, 279.

4. C. M. Tuckett, "Q (Gospel Source)," *ABD* 5:570.

5. Sanders, *Judaism*, part II.

6. Peter Richardson, "Enduring Concerns: Desiderata for Future Historical-Jesus Research," in *Whose Historical Jesus?* (ed. William E. Arnal and Michel Desjardins; Etudes sur le christianisme et le judaïsme 7; Waterloo: Wilfrid Laurier University Press, 1997), 296–307.

7. Jonathan L. Reed, "Galileans, 'Israelite Village Communities,' and the Saying Gospel Q," in *Galilee through the Centuries* (ed. Eric M. Meyers; Duke Judaic Studies Series 1; Winona Lake, Ind.: Eisenbrauns, 1999), 87–108. I agree with his criticism of Richard Horsley, *Galilee: History, Politics, People* (Valley Forge: Trinity Press International, 1995) and idem, *Archaeology*. Specifically, I emphasize the similarity of Galilean traditions to Judean practices.

8. See Wayne Meeks, *The First Urban Christians* (New Haven: Yale University Press, 1983).

9. Urman & Flesher, *Synagogues*; Levine, *Synagogue*.

10. White, *Social Origins*, passim.

11. *Voluntary Associations*, especially chs. 1–2.

12. Helmut Koester, ed., *Ephesos: Metropolis of Asia* (HTS 41; Minneapolis: Trinity Press International, 1991); Helmut Koester, ed., *Pergamon, Citadel of the Gods* (HTS 46; Minneapolis: Trinity Press International, 1998); Donfried & Richardson, *Rome*, especially chs. 1–3.

13. For an important alternative, see Robert Jewett, "Tenement Churches and Communal Meals in the Early Church: The Implications of a Form-Critical Analysis of 2 Thessalonians 3:10," *BR* 38 (1993): 23–43.

14. Hirschfeld, *Palestinian Dwelling*, mixes times and places in its broad chronological sweep. Santiago Guijarro, "The Family in First-Century Galilee," in *Constructing Early Christian Families* (ed. Halvor Moxnes; London: Routledge, 1997), 42–65, focuses on four types of houses: simple, courtyard, big mansion (*domus*), and farmhouse; see also Guijarro Oporto, *Fidelidades en Conflicto*, chs. 11–12.

15. Reed, "Galileans," 97, 100.

16. Shemaryahu Gutman, "Gamala," *NEAEHL* 2:459–63.

17. Hirschfeld, *Palestinian Dwelling*, 24–44.

18. I am grateful for assistance to William E. Arnal, Willi Braun, and Alan Kirk; all deeply familiar with Q.

19. William E. Arnal, *Jesus and the Village Scribes: Galilean Conflicts and the Setting of Q* (Minneapolis: Fortress, 2001), 159–64; John S. Kloppenborg, *The Formation of Q: Trajectories in Ancient Wisdom Collections* (Philadelphia: Fortress, 1987).

20. Kloppenborg, *Formation*, passim.

21. Alan Kirk, *The Composition of the Sayings Source: Genre, Synchrony, and Wisdom Redaction in Q* (NovTSup 91; Leiden: Brill, 1998); cf. Kloppenborg, *Formation*, 323–24.

22. Leif Vaage, *Galilean Upstarts: Jesus' First Followers According to Q* (Valley Forge: Trinity Press International, 1994).

23. Burton L. Mack, *The Lost Gospel: The Book of Q and Christian Origins* (San Francisco: Harper Collins, 1993), chs. 4, 11.

24. John S. Kloppenborg Verbin, *Excavating Q: The History and Setting of the Sayings Gospel* (Minneapolis: Fortress, 2000), chs. 4–5, for more detail.

25. See K. C. Hanson and Douglas E. Oakman, *Palestine in the Time of Jesus: Social Structures and Social Conflicts* (Minneapolis: Fortress, 1998), chs. 2 and 4, for other social aspects.

26. Reed, "Galileans," 103–8, criticizes Horsley's "Northern Israelite" traditions in Q; see Horsley, *Galilee*; and idem, *Archaeology*. Also see Halvor Moxnes, "The Historical Context of Jesus Studies," *BTB* (1998): 1–15.

27. Kirk, *Composition*, 399, his italics.

28. Hirschfeld, *Palestinian Dwelling*, s.v. "Upper-level" and "Living-Rooms."

Chapter Six

1. Delivered as a main paper at the Society of New Testament Studies meeting in Montreal (2001), and published in *NTS* 48 (2002): 314–31.

2. Eric M. Meyers, ed., *Galilee Through the Centuries: Confluence of Cultures* (Winona Lake, Ind.: Eisenbrauns, 1999); Reed, *Archaeology and the Galilean Jesus*; Mordechai Aviam, *Jews, Christians and Pagans in the Galilee: 25 Years of Archaeological Excavations and Surveys Hellenistic to Byzantine Periods* (Land of Galilee 1; Rochester: University of

Rochester Press, forthcoming); Douglas R. Edwards and C. Thomas McCullough, *Archaeology and the Galilee: Texts and Contexts in the Graeco-Roman and Byzantine Periods* (Atlanta: Scholars Press, 1997); Lee I. Levine, ed., *The Galilee in Late Antiquity* (New York: Jewish Theological Seminary, 1992); Horsley, *Galilee*; Horsley, *Archaeology*; Sean Freyne, *Galilee, Jesus and the Gospels: Literary Approaches and Historical Investigations* (Dublin: Gill and Macmillan, 1988); Halvor Moxnes, "The Construction of Galilee as a Place for the Historical Jesus—Part I," *BTB* 31 (2001): 26–37; and Part II, *BTB* 31 (2001): 64–77; Moxnes, "Placing Jesus of Nazareth," in *Text and Artifact*, 158–75.

3. Robert C. Gregg and Dan Urman, *Jews, Pagans, and Christians in the Golan Heights* (South Florida Studies in the History of Judaism 140; Atlanta: Scholars Press, 1996); Shimon Dar, *Settlements and Cult Sites on Mount Hermon, Israel: Ituraean Culture in the Hellenistic and Roman Periods* (Oxford: Tempus Reparatum, 1993). On Et-Tell, possibly ancient Bethsaida, see Rami Arav and Richard A. Freund, *Bethsaida: A City by the North Shore of the Sea of Galilee* (Kirksville, Mo.: Thomas Jefferson University Press, 1995).

4. The title of Emily Dickinson Townsend Vermeule's presidential address to the American Philological Association; Sarah Morris and Cynthia W. Shelmerdine, "Emily Dickinson Townsend Vermeule, 1928–2001," *AJA* 105/3 (2001): 513–15.

5. Aviam & Richardson, "Galilee," 177–209.

6. K. L. Schmidt, *Der Rahmen der Geschichte Jesu* (Berlin: Trowitzsch, 1919; repr. Darmstadt: Wissenschaftliche Buchgesellschaft, 1969), criticized by David R. Hall, *The Gospel Framework: Fiction or Fact: A Critical Evaluation of Der Rahmen der Geschichte Jesu by Karl Ludwig Schmidt* (Carlisle: Paternoster, 1998); Ernst Lohmeyer, *Galiläa und Jerusalem* (FRLANT NF 34; Göttingen: Vandenhoeck und Ruprecht, 1936); R. H. Lightfoot, *Locality and Doctrine in the Gospels* (London: Hodder and Stoughton, 1938). K. Kundsin, *Topologische Überlieferungsstoffe im Johannes-Evangelium: Eine Untersuchung* (FRLANT NF 22; Göttingen: Vandenhoeck und Ruprecht, 1925), 10.

7. Virgilio Corbo, *The House of St. Peter at Capharnaum: A Preliminary Report of the First Two Campaigns of Excavations: April 16–June 19, Sept. 12–Nov. 26, 1968* (Jerusalem: Franciscan Printing Press, 1969); Virgilio Corbo, *Cafarnao*, vol. 1, *Gli edifici della città* (Studium Biblicum Franciscanum 19; Jerusalem, 1975); S. Loffreda, *Cafarnao*, vol. 2, *La ceramica* (Studium Biblicum Franciscanum 19; Jerusalem, 1974); A. Spijkerman, *Cafarnao*, vol. 3, *Catalogo delle monete della città* (Studium Biblicum Franciscanum 19; Jerusalem, 1975); Emmanuele Testa, *Cafarnao*, vol. 4, *I graffiti della casa di S. Pietro* (Studium Biblicum Franciscanum 19; Jerusalem, 1972). See Joan Taylor, *Christians and the Holy Places: The Myth of Jewish-Christian Origins* (Oxford: Clarendon, 1993), esp. 268–94; White, *Social Origins*, 2:152–59, for critiques of the Bagatti-Testa hypothesis.

8. J. C. Iwe, *Jesus in the Synagogue of Capernaum* (Rome: Editrice Pontificia Università Gregoriana, 1999), not available to me.

9. Kundsin, *Topologische Überlieferungsstoffe*, 8–9.

10. Lightfoot, *Locality*, 133.

11. Paula Fredriksen, *Jesus of Nazareth, King of the Jews: A Jewish Life and the Emergence of Christianity* (New York: Knopf, 1999), 197–214, 28–34.

12. C. H. Dodd, *Historical Tradition in the Fourth Gospel* (Cambridge: Cambridge University Press, 1963); John A. T. Robinson, *The Priority of John* (London: SCM, 1985), explicitly rejecting a Signs Gospel as only "a pale shadow of John's theology" (p. 20).

13. Robinson, *Priority*, 159.

14. John A. T. Robinson, *Redating the New Testament* (London: SCM, 1976) argues for an early date.

15. Dodd, *Historical Tradition*, 188–95, 223–28, 312.

16. Robert T. Fortna, *The Gospel of Signs: A Reconstruction of the Narrative Source Underlying the Fourth Gospel* (Cambridge: Cambridge University Press, 1970); Robert T. Fortna, *The Fourth Gospel and its Predecessor* (Philadelphia: Fortress, 1988); John Painter, *The Quest for the Messiah: The History, Literature, and Theology of the Johannine Community* (Edinburgh: T&T Clark, 1991), 73–93, rejects Fortna's views. See also Urban C. von

Wahlde, *The Earliest Version of John's Gospel: Recovering the Gospel of Signs* (Wilmington: Michael Glazier, 1989); Gilbert van Belle, *The Signs Source in the Fourth Gospel: Historical Survey and Critical Evaluation of the Semeia Hypothesis* (BETL 116; Louvain: Leuven University Press, 1994). All studies depend on Rudolf Bultmann, *Die Geschichte der synoptischen Tradition* (FRLANT NF 29; Göttingen: Vandenhoeck und Ruprecht, 1931); Rudolph Bultmann, *Das Evangelium des Johannes* (KEK 22; Göttingen, 1941).

17. Anthony J. Blasi, *A Social History of Johannine Christianity* (Lewiston: Edwin Mellen, 1996), 316, n. 1; contrary Raymond E. Brown, *Gospel According to John* (2 vols.; Garden City: Doubleday, 1970), 2:1068.

18. Fortna, *Gospel of Signs*, 39, 102.

19. Dwight Moody Smith, *The Composition and Order of the Fourth Gospel: Bultmann's Literary Theory* (New Haven: Yale University Press, 1965), 111, argues for preservation of the source's order; Jürgen Becker, *Das Evangelium nach Johannes* (Gütersloh: Gütersloher Verlagshaus Mohn/Würzburg: Echter-Verlag, 1979), thinks only 5:1-18 is out of order, and includes no passion narrative. Mark W. G. Stibbe, *John as Storyteller: Narrative Criticism and the Fourth Gospel* (Cambridge: Cambridge University Press, 1992), 82–84, dismisses a Signs Gospel and argues for a collection of Galilean signs/miracles with a Jerusalem-centered Gospel of Lazarus. See also van Belle, *Signs Source*, ch. 5.

20. Kundsin, *Topologische Überlieferungsstoffe*, table on 11–12; D. Mollat, "Remarques sur le vocabulaire spatial du quatrième évangile," in *Studia Evangelica: The Four Gospels in 1957* (ed. Kurt Aland; TU 73; Berlin: Akademie Verlag, 1959), 321–28; R. D. Potter, "Topography and Archaeology in the Fourth Gospel," in *Studia Evangelica: The Four Gospels in 1957* (ed. Kurt Aland; TU 73; Berlin: Akademie Verlag, 1959), 329–37; Robert T. Fortna, "Theological Use of Locale in the Fourth Gospel," in *Gospel Studies in Honor of Sherman Elbridge Johnson* (ed. M. H. Shepherd, Jr. and Edward C. Hobbs; *ATR Supplementary Series* 3, 1974), 58–95; C. H. H. Scobie, "Johannine Geography," *SR* 11.1 (1982): 77–84.

21. Fortna, *Gospel of Signs*, 36, 99.

22. So Scobie, "Johannine Geography."

23. Sjef van Tilborg, *Reading John in Ephesus* (Leiden: Brill, 1996), 3–4 and 59–63, on "interference."

24. Schmidt, *Rahmen*, 17 (translation from Hall, *Gospel Framework*, viii).

25. Kundsin, *Topologische Überlieferungsstoffe*, 52, 69–71; "How is it explained that the starting point of the new itinerary in Galilee is no longer Capernaum but Cana? The answer is 2.1–12; 4.6ff." (my translation).

26. James F. Strange, "Cana of Galilee," *ABD* 1:827, prefers Khirbet Qana but puts the shift to Kefr Kenna earlier than I would. Details of pilgrim accounts in Herrojo, *Cana de Galilea*.

27. 'Ain Qana (near Reina, about 1.5 km north of Nazareth) was first suggested as the site of Cana in the nineteenth century because it has a spring; it is not seriously considered today. James Charlesworth has drawn my attention to Youssef El Hourani, *Cana of Galilee in South Lebanon* (Lebanon Ministry of Tourism, 1995), which locates Cana east of Tyre.

28. John Wilkinson, *Jerusalem Pilgrims before the Crusades* (Warminster: Aris and Phillips, 1977).

29. Finegan, *Archeology*, 123.

30. Reinhold Roehricht, "Karten und Pläne zur Palästinakunde . . .," *ZDPV* 14 (1891) and *ZDPV* 15 (1895); so Richard M. Mackowski, "Scholars' Qanah: A Reexamination of the Evidence in Favor of Khirbet Qanah," *BZ* NF 23 (1979): 278–84, esp. 282, and n. 6.

31. Text in Mackowski, "Scholars' Qanah."

32. Edward Robinson, *Biblical Researches in Palestine: Mount Sinai and Arabia Petraea*, vol. 3 (Boston: Crocker and Brewster, 1841), 204–6.

33. See S. Klein, *Beiträge zur Geographie und Geschichte Galiläas* (Leipzig, 1909), 93.

34. Bellarmino Bagatti, "Antichità di Kh. Qana e Kefr Kenna," *LASBF* 15 (1965): 251–92, esp. 256–58, 291; B. Bagatti, *Antichi Villagi Cristiani di Galilea* (Jerusalem: Franciscan Publications, 1971), 121–22.

35. Piacenza Pilgrim, Willibald, Commemoratorium, possibly Nasir-I Khusrau, Saewulf, Burchard, Sanutus. The church must have been destroyed between 1321 C.E. (Sanutus) and the early 1600s (Quaresmius).

36. The class paper of a student, Lawrence Morey, prompted my skepticism.

Chapter Seven

1. This chapter combines two publications, one from Donfried & Richardson, *Rome*, 17–29, the other from *Voluntary Associations*, 90–109.

2. S. L. Guterman, *Religious Toleration and Persecution in Ancient Rome* (London: Aiglon, 1951), 150.

3. Mary E. Smallwood, *The Jews under Roman Rule* (Leiden: Brill, 1976), 133–43.

4. Urman & Flesher, *Synagogues*.

5. Methodological issues: What constituted a synagogue? Were there other public buildings with which a synagogue could be confused? What role should the presence or absence of "defining" elements play (e.g., niche, bema, reading desk, *mikveh*, gallery, orientation, symbolism, benches, architectural decoration)? Should an inscription or its absence settle the issue?

6. He includes Magdala (Migdal), which I exclude; he excludes Capernaum and Chorazin.

7. See also Andrew R. Seager, "The Recent Historiography of Ancient Synagogues," in Rachel Hachlili, *Ancient Synagogues in Israel, 3–7 Century C.E. BAR International Series* 499 (1989): 85–90; Joseph Gutmann, ed., *Ancient Synagogues: The State of the Research* (Chico: Scholars Press, 1981), especially the articles by Seager, Kraabel, Marilyn J. Chiat, and Eric Myers.

8. Wendy Cotter, "*Collegia* and Roman Law: State Restrictions on Voluntary Associations, 64 BCE–200 CE," *Voluntary Associations*, 74–89; Smallwood, *Jews under Roman Rule*, 133–43.

9. *Senatus consulto collegia sublata sunt, quae adversus rem publicam videbantur esse;* Cotter, "Collegia," 76. Note the later coin of Nerva: *Fisci iudaici calumnia sublata*.

10. Smallwood argues that Caesar's favorable view of Judaism depended upon Antipater's help, Hyrcanus II's friendly relations, and the fact that Caesar's enemy was Pompey, who desecrated the temple.

11. Philo, *Legat.* 156–58; cf. 311–17.

12. Schürer 2:425–26, n. 5. I have adjusted the translations of *CIJ* in a more literal direction. The dates are from Everett Ferguson, *Backgrounds of Early Christianity* (Grand Rapids: Wm. B. Eerdmans, 1993), 15–17.

13. *CPJ* I.138, a fragmentary papyrus (provenance unknown), dating from the second half of the first century B.C.E.: *epi tês genêtheisês synagôgês en têi proseuchêi* ("at the gathering which was held in the prayerhouse").

14. An inscription from Berenice in Cyrenaica (42 C.E.) uses *synagôgê* twice, two lines apart, first for the community and then for the building: "Year two of Nero Claudius Caesar Drusus Germanicus Autokrator, 6th day of Choiach. It seemed good to the gathering (*synagôgê*) of the Jews in Berenice to inscribe the names of the contributors to the repair of the synagogue (*synagôgê*). . . ." B. Lifshitz, *Donateurs et fondateurs dans les synagogues juives* (Paris: Gabalda, 1967), 81. I take the name to be a mistaken form of Tiberius Claudius Drusus Nero Germanicus.

15. Three inscriptions (*CIJ* 1435, 1436, 1437) refer to "the holy place," possibly a synagogue but more likely a temple, either in Jerusalem or at Leontopolis.

16. *Legat.* 132, 134, 137, 138, 148, 152, 165, 191; *Flacc.* 41, 45, 47–49, 53, 122.

17. H. R. Moehring, "The *Acta pro Judaeis* in the *Antiquities* of Flavius Josephus. A Study in Hellenistic and Modern Apologetic Historiography," in *Christianity, Judaism and other Greco-Roman Cults*, vol. 3 (ed. Jacob Neusner; Leiden: Brill, 1975), 124–58, doubts their authenticity. See also Christiane Saulnier, "Lois romaines sur les juifs selon Flavius Josèphe," *RB* 88 (1981): 161–95.

18. Hyrcanus II (High Priest 76–67) may have been Regent or King during the latter part of his mother's reign. He was reappointed High Priest and Ethnarch by Pompey in 64, and held this position almost continuously until 40 B.C.E. Josephus's comment that he was weak and ineffective needs reassessment.

19. Other topics included Hyrcanus's loyalty and bravery, his right to sit among senators at the gladiatorial games, and his right to enter the Senate; Jews as "allies and friends," refortification of Jerusalem, reduction of tribute in Sabbatical years, prohibitions on quartering Roman troops among Jews.

20. Tithes in kind were likely unusual, except from areas close to Judea (Tyre and Sidon).

21. Harry J. Leon, *The Jews of Ancient Rome* (Philadelphia: Jewish Publication Society, 1960 [1995]), 135–66.

22. Synagogue of Hebrews: *CIJ* 291, 317, 510, 535; Synagogue of Vernaculars: *CIJ* 318, 383, 398, 494.

23. *CIJ* 284, 301, 338, 368, 416, 496; all are funeral inscriptions, alluding to a synagogue only incidentally. The inscriptions themselves are later, but their dates have relatively little bearing on the date of the origin of the institution, which could have been much earlier.

24. *CIJ* 365, 425, 503.

25. *CIJ* 343, 402, 417: "Volumnesians"; *CIJ* 523, *Bolumni* (in Latin).

26. Volumnius is a hazy figure. He appears in Josephus, *War* 1.535–42 and *Ant.* 16.277–83; 344–69. It is not clear if Josephus thought there was only one Volumnius or two. He was likely a military tribune who acted in association with the governor of Syria to agree to Herod's expedition against Syllaeus. He later carried a letter concerning Herod's two sons to Augustus and was present at their trial in Berytus, urging a "pitiless sentence."

27. J.-B. Frey, *CIJ*, lxxii, 124–26; A. Momigliano, "I nomi delle prime 'synagoghe' romane e la condizione giuridica delle communità in Roma sotto Augusto," *Rassegna Mensile di Israel* 6 (1931–32): 283–92; S. Kraus, *Synagogale Altertümer* (Berlin and Vienna: Verlag Benjamin Harz 1922), 247–59; G. La Piana, "Foreign Groups in Rome during the First Centuries of the Empire," *HTR* 20 (1927): 183–403, especially 341–71. H. J. Leon, *Jews of Ancient Rome*, 159–62; also idem, "The Synagogue of the Herodians," *JAOS* 49 (1929): 318–21; *JQR* 20 (1930): 305–6. Smallwood, *Jews under Roman Rule*, 137–38, inclines to Herod.

28. David Noy, *Jewish Inscriptions of Western Europe*, vol. 2 (Cambridge: Cambridge University Press, 1995), 252–54.

29. Frey, in *CIJ*; Joan Goodnick Westenholz, *The Jewish Presence in Ancient Rome* (Jerusalem: Bible Lands Museum, 1995), 24.

30. Schürer, 3.1:73–81, 97–98.

31. Highlighted names intentionally occupying the first line: *CIJ* 222, 229, 252, 269, 298, 460; decorated ends of first lines: *CIJ* 213, 283, 299, 340, 354 (generally decoration occurs at the bottom).

32. Inscriptions sometimes begin with a name in the dative. No inscription in *CIJ* has this exact combination proposed here.

33. Note the space available for the first line relative to the right side and bottom.

34. The genitive of *synagôgê* requires a word such as *archôn* before it, which establishes the line length.

35. I have not seen the inscription itself, but examination of the photograph and comparison of the vertical stroke and serifs with the other two *iotas* and the other *êta* suggests the missing letter is likelier *êta*.

36. Leon, "Synagogue," 318–21.

37. A. Reifenberg, *Ancient Jewish Coins* (3d ed., Jerusalem: Rubin Mass, 1963), #70 (47) and plate V.

38. Menorah on the lower left: *CIJ* 396 especially; cf. 97, 111, 150, 161, 193, and less clearly 50, 51, 89.

39. Similar lettering: *CIJ* 155, 196, 365, 440, among others; cf. also 417.

40. *CIJ* 1440 from Scheidia, near Alexandria (246–221 B.C.E.) is the earliest: "In honour of King Ptolemy and Queen Berenice, his sister and wife, and their children, the Jews built this house of prayer." In the light of the point just made about Augustus, Agrippa, and Herod it is important to note that the dedication was to the royal family. Another, *CIJ* 1432 (37 B.C.E.), was dedicated to Cleopatra and Caesarion (Caesar's son by Cleopatra).

41. Paul-Eugène Dion, "Synagogues et temples dans l'Egypte hellénistique," *SCES* 29 (1977): 45–75.

42. Kraabel says a first-century B.C.E. synagogue underlies a fourth-century synagogue on Delos (perhaps the earliest yet excavated). It was simple, "the sort one would expect from this early period: a converted residence, little more than an assembly hall, with no permanent Torah shrine and no Jewish symbols." A. T. Kraabel, "The Diaspora Synagogue. Archeological and Epigraphic Evidence since Sukenik," *ANRW* II.19.1 (1979): 477–510, esp. 493. The distinguishing Jewish marks are epigraphic references to a *proseuchê* and to *theos hypsistos* (*CIJ* 725, 726, 769).

43. B. D. Mazur, *Studies in Jewry in Greece*, vol. 1 (Athens: Hestia, 1935); Kraabel, "Diaspora Synagogue."

44. A lintel from Corinth read*s* *SYNAGÔG HEBRAIÔN*, dated to the second century.

45. Kraabel is unsure if the earlier building was a synagogue; "Diaspora Synagogue," 497–500.

46. James F. Strange, "Archeology and the Religion of Judaism in Palestine," *ANRW* II.19.1 (1979): 646–85.

47. Final reports have now appeared: Joseph Aviram, Gideon Foerster, and Ehud Netzer, eds, *Masada I–V: The Yigael Yadin Excavations 1963–1965 Final Reports* (Jerusalem: Israel Exploration Society, 1989–95).

48. I now doubt the earliest phase was a synagogue, though it deserves more debate.

49. Yigael Yadin, *Masada* (London: Weidenfeld and Nicolson, 1966), 184.

50. A pre-70 date is implied in the reference to "needy travellers from abroad," presupposing pilgrims fulfilling temple obligations, impossible after 70 C.E.

51. A somewhat similar inscription (*CIJ* 694) comes from Stobi in Macedonia (Chapter 12).

52. I now conclude Magdala was not a synagogue and I am doubtful of Capernaum.

53. John Wilkinson, "Orientation, Jewish and Christian," *PEQ* (1984): 16–30, emphasizes variety in orientation but he tends to interpret wide-ranging archaeological data in the light of later literary evidence.

54. Summary in Strange, "Archeology," 656–61.

55. Solomon Zeitlin, "The Origin of the Synagogue," *PAAJR* 2 (1930–31): 69–81.

56. Harold W. Turner, *From Temple to Meeting House. The Phenomenology and Theology of Places of Worship* (RelSoc 16: The Hague: Mouton, 1979), has a helpful theoretical analysis.

57. On developing a Temple-imagery, see Helen Rosenau, *Visions of the Temple. The Image of the Temple of Jerusalem in Judaism and Christianity* (London: Oresko, 1979).

Chapter Eight

1. First published in *Common Life in the Early Church: Essays in Honor of Graydon F. Snyder* (ed. by Julian V. Hills, et al.; Valley Forge: Trinity Press International, 1998), 373–89.

2. Graydon F. Snyder, *Ante Pacem: Archaeological Evidence of Church Life before Constantine* (Macon: Mercer University Press, 1985), 67, my emphasis.

3. J. B. Ward-Perkins, "Constantine and the Origins of the Christian Basilica," *Papers of the British School in Rome* 22 (1954), 80, 121–22; R. Krautheimer, *Early Christian and Byzantine Architecture* (Baltimore: Penguin, 1979).

4. Snyder, *Ante Pacem*, 67–117.

5. Snyder, *Ante Pacem*, 34–35, 74–7, 581–82.

6. Snyder, *Ante Pacem*, 77–80; Robert Jewett, "Tenement Churches and Communal Meals in the Early Church: The Implications of 2 Thess. 3:10," *BR* 38 (1993): 23–43.

7. Snyder, *Ante Pacem*, 159, 163.

8. White, *Social Origins*.

9. Volume 2 is the most complete collection of data presently available on early Christian architecture.

10. Bibliographies in Urman & Flesher, *Synagogues*; Donald D. Binder, *Into the Temple Courts: The Place of the Synagogue in the Second Temple Period* (SBLDS 169; Atlanta: Society of Biblical Literature, 1999).

11. White, *Social Origins*, vol. 1, ch. 4; L. Michael White, "Synagogue and Society in Imperial Ostia: Archaeological and Epigraphic Evidence," in Donfried & Richardson, *Rome*, 30–63. On Delos, B. Hudson McLean, "The Place of Cult in Voluntary Associations and Christian Churches on Delos," in *Voluntary Associations*, 186–225.

12. Bradley Blue, "Acts and the House Church," in *The Book of Acts in its Graeco-Roman Setting* (vol. 2 of *The Book of Acts in its First Century Setting*; ed. David. W. J. Gill and Conrad Gempf; Grand Rapids: Wm. B. Eerdmans/Carlisle: Paternoster, 1994), 119–222.

13. On Caesarea Maritima, *Herod*, 91–94; on the synagogue, Michael Avi-Yonah, "Synagogues," *NEAEHL* 1:278–80.

14. *Herod* 183–86, on Netzer's views.

15. White, *Social Origins*, 2:135–52.

16. William L. MacDonald, *Early Christian & Byzantine Architecture* (New York: Braziller, 1962), 23.

17. We lack Jewish texts on this topic: *m. Ned.* 9.2 reflects a dispute between R. Eliezer and the Sages whether a vow to turn a house into a synagogue was binding; *m. Meg.* 3.1–3, on selling a synagogue.

18. Robert Milburn, *Early Christian Art and Architecture* (Berkeley: University of California Press, 1988), 83: "the pagan basilica was, by the second or third century A.D., being readily adapted to the religious uses of the Hebrews . . . the synagogue may be said to have cleansed the basilica of its pagan associations and helped to prepare for the free use of the basilican style in Christian churches, but the influences run both ways." Contrary, G. Foerster, "Dating Synagogues with a 'Basilical' Plan and an Apse," in Urman & Flesher, *Ancient Synagogues*, 1:87–94.

19. Lee I. Levine, "Synagogues," *NEAEHL* 4:1421–1424; here 1423.

20. Vitruvius, *De architectura* 5.1.4–9: "Basilicas should be constructed on a site adjoining the forum and in the warmest possible quarter, so that in winter business men may gather in them. . . . It is thought that the columns of basilicas ought to be as high as the side-aisles are broad; an aisle should be limited to one third of the breadth which the open space in the middle is to have. . . . But basilicas of the greatest dignity and beauty may also be constructed in the style of that one which I erected [at Fano]. . . . The two middle columns on [one] side are omitted, in order not to obstruct the view of the pronaos of the temple of Augustus . . . and also the tribunal which is . . . shaped as a

hemicycle . . . so that those who are standing before the magistrates may not be in the way of the business men in the basilica. . . ." Vitruvius's description stresses the multi-use character of basilicas.

21. Basilica of Porcia in Rome, 189 B.C.E.; Basilica of Sempronius, 180 B.C.E.; Aemilian Basilica, 179 B.C.E.; Basilica of Pompeii, 130 B.C.E. or a little later.

22. Trajan's Basilica Ulpia is the best-known example of double apses, but note Corinth (Basilica A and Basilica B), Augustica Raurica, Aspendos, and Cosa.

23. There are few "true" basilicas in Judaism. Sardis's monumental synagogue is monumental, though it was not modeled on a basilica but was a renovation of a gymnasium.

24. The list is not complete; it includes synagogues whose essential plan and features can be known reasonably well. A later, more complete, version of the table is in Chapter 12.

25. Details of most in *NEAEHL*. See also Dennis Groh, "The Stratigraphic Chronology of the Galilean Synagogue from the Early Roman Period through the Byzantine Period (ca. 420 C.E.)," in Urman & Flesher, *Synagogues*, 1:51–69.

26. Ehud Netzer reported a synagogue at the Hasmonean Winter Palace complex in Jericho (dated 70–50 B.C.E.), with *mikveh*, benches, a small niche, courtyard, outbuildings, and columns on all four sides of the hall. See Abraham Rabinovich, *Jerusalem Post* (30 March 1998): 1.

27. Abraham Rabinovich, *Jerusalem Post* (8 April 1991): 1.

28. Gerasa had a church that took over an earlier synagogue, while reversing its orientation.

29. Perhaps *m. 'Abod. Zar.* 3.7 is relevant to Sardis: "if a house was built from the first for idolatry it is forbidden; if it was plastered and bedecked for idolatry . . . one need only remove what was done to it anew; but if a gentile did but bring in an idol and take it out again, such a house is permitted." See also 1.7 (on basilicas) and *m. Teharot* 6.8.

30. Rachel Hachlili and Ann Killebrew, "Qazyon" (paper read at the ASOR 1997 Annual Meeting), think it likelier that Qazyon was a pagan temple. The inscription, however, has much in common with synagogue inscriptions from Egypt and Rome: "For the salvation of the Roman Caesars / Lucius Septimus Severus Pius / Pertinax Augustus and Marcus / Aurelius Antonius and Lucius / Septimius Geta, their sons, by a / vow of the Jews"; within a wreath, "and Julia Domna Augusta" (dated 197 C.E.).

31. Two churches at Herodium had perimeter seating on benches. See Ehud Netzer, "The Churches of Herodium," in *Ancient Churches Revealed* (ed. Yoram Tsafrir; Jerusalem: Israel Exploration Society/Washington: Biblical Archaeology Society, 1993), 219–32.

32. A balcony over the aisle may have been used (third century?) as a "women's gallery"; since there was no separation in earlier synagogues, it may have come only after adopting a building form that permitted it.

33. White refers to these as "true" basilican churches, though I see no need to insist on such splendor as essential. He avoids the term basilican in other cases; see *Social Origins* 2.124, 192, 242 n. 189, among others. Milburn, *Early Christian Art*, 86, says "basilica" need not be used technically.

34. Constantine's mother, Helena, dedicated the first three (ca. 329); Constantine also built in Rome (St. John Lateran, St. Costanza, St. Peters), Constantinople, and Trier.

35. From the earlier edition of Eusebius. White suggests several times that "erected from the foundations" may mean major renovations, not necessarily new structures.

36. In the Constantinian and post-Constantinian periods, the other important architectural form to appear was a centrally focused space: memorials were octagonal or round; some churches utilized square or cruciform plans, topped by concrete domes.

37. B. Bagatti, "Nazareth," *NEAEHL* 3:1103–5, argues for third century. This is too early.

38. Vassilios Tzaferis, "Early Christian Churches at Magen," in Tsafrir, *Ancient Churches*, 283–85.

39. There was nothing inevitable about these developments. Mithraism began with similar architectural solutions as Judaism and Christianity but did not move on to basilicas. Roger Beck has confirmed to me verbally that a couple of instances of basilican Mithraea do not undercut this general evaluation.

40. There is unmistakable crosscultural borrowing of forms and decoration between a Temple of Apollo at Kedesh and the nearby Baram synagogue, pointed out to me by Mordechai Aviam.

Chapter Nine

1. First published in *Origins and Method: New Understandings of Judaism and Early Christianity. Essays in Honour of John C. Hurd, Jr.* (ed. Bradley McLean; Sheffield: Sheffield Academic Press, 1993), 334–59.

2. G. Vermes, "Essenes and Therapeutae," *Post-Biblical Jewish Studies* (Leiden: Brill 1975), 30–31; Schürer, 2:591–97; P. Géoltrain, "La contemplation à Qumran et chez les Thérapeutes," *Semitica* 9 (1959): 49–57.

3. T. D. Barnes, *Constantine and Eusebius* (Cambridge. Mass.: Harvard University Press, 1980), 195–96.

4. Eusebius and Philo before him use *hyper*, whose natural meaning when used of relative geographical position is not "above" but "beyond" or "farther inland."

5. Eusebius thinks Philo had listened to expositions of the Therapeutae; he thought the writings they studied were "the gospels, the apostolic writings and in all probability passages interpreting the old prophets, such as are contained in the Epistle to the Hebrews and several others of Paul's epistles" (*CH* 2.17).

6. On Eusebius's sources, R. Grant, *Eusebius as Church Historian* (Oxford: Clarendon Press, 1980), 52, 73–75; M. Gödecke, *Geschichte als Mythos: Eusebs* "Kirchegeschichte" (Frankfurt: Peter Lang, 1987).

7. Barnes, *Constantine and Eusebius*, 130; R. L. Wilken, *The Myth of Christian Beginnings* (Notre Dame: University of Notre Dame Press, 1980), 73.

8. Eusebius's comments may advance the pace of development a little; it is strange that D. J. Chitty, *The Desert a City: An Introduction to the Study of Egyptian and Palestinian Monasticism under the Christian Empire* (Oxford: Basil Blackwell, 1966), and A. Guillaumont, *Aux origines du monachisme chrétien* (Spiritualité orientale, 30; Bégrolles-en-Mauges: Abbaye de Bellefontaine, 1979), make little use of Eusebius.

9. R. Kasser, *Kellia 1965: Topographie générale, mensurations at fouilles aux Qouçoûr* (Geneva: Georg, 1967); F. Daumas and A. Guillaumont, *Kellia 1, Kom 219: Fouilles exécuté au 1964 et 1965* (2 vols.; Cairo: L'lnstitut français d'archéologie orientale, 1969); R. Kasser, *Kellia: Topographie* (Geneva: Georg, 1972); idem, *Survey archéologique des Kellia (Basse-Égypte) Rapport de la campagne 1981* (2 vols.; Leuven: Peeters, 1983); Yvette Mottier and Nathalie Bosson, eds. *Les Kellia, ermitages coptes en Basse-Egypte* (Geneva: Editions de Tricorne, 1989).

10. P. Bridel, "La dialectique de l'isolement et de l'ouverture dans les monastères kelliotes: Espaces reservés espaces d'acceuil," in *Le site monastique copte des Kellia: sources historiques et explorations archéologiques: actes du Colloque de Genève 13 au 15 août 1984* (Geneva: Mission Suisse d'archéologie copte de l'Université de Genève, 1986), 145–61.

11. Kasser, *Survey*, 56, identifying pre-500 C.E. features.

12. See the colloquium on Kellia, *Le site monastique*, especially contributions by Weidmann, Grossman, Krause, Thierry, Al-Tawab.

13. D. Weidmann, "La construction des plans des monastères," in *Le site monastique*, 257–60; R.-G. Coquin, "Evolution de l'habitat et évolution de la vue érémitique au Kellia," 261–72.

14. Kasser, *Les Kellia*, figs. 12–15; Coquin, "Evolution de l'habitat," figs. 1 and 2, p. 252.

15. Guillaumont, *Origines*, chs. 8, 9, 11; Kasser, *Les Kellia*, figs. 19–29; P. Corboud, "L'oratoire et les niches-oratoires: Les dieux de la prière," in *Le site monastique*, 85–92.

16. Daumas and Guillaumont, *Kellia 1*; D. Weidmann, "Dispersion et concentration," in Daumas et Guillaumont, *Kellia 1*.

17. Daumas and Guillaumont, *Kellia 1*, chs. 3, 7; G. Descoeudres, "L'architecture des ermitages et des sanctuaries," in *Les Kellia*, 47–55.

18. Guillaumont, *Origines*, ch. 10.

19. Antony may have been a disciple of Paul of Thebes, who fled to the desert ca. 249–51 C.E. (Jerome, *Vita Pauli*). The name anchorite, referring to a life of solitary seclusion, derives from the Greek *anachorein*, "flee to the country." P. Miquel, *Lexique du désert: Etude de quelques mot-clés du vocabulaire monastique grec ancien* (Spiritualité orientale, 44; Bégrolles-en-Mauges: Abbaye de Bellefontaine, 1986), 67–72.

20. Pachomius was associated with Nag Hammadi, where a Coptic gnostic library was found. "Cenobite" refers to life in a communal setting; it derives from the Greek word "common" (*koinon*).

21. A similar development occurred in Palestine, also associated with three persons: Chariton (founded the first monastery ca. 330 C.E.), Euthymius (376–473 C.E.), and Sabas (439–532 C.E.).

22. He later moved near the Red Sea; J. Doresse, "Les monastères de Saint-Paul et de Saint-Antoine au désert de la Mer Rouge," in *La site monastique*, 163–72.

23. Guillaumont, *Origines*, chs. 6, 10; F. Daumas, "Essai d'interpretation du couvent," in *Kellia 1*, 135–45.

24. P. Géoltrain, "La Traité de la vie contemplative de Philon d'Alexandrie," *Semitica* 10 (1960): 1–61, esp. 25–26; F. Daumas and P. Miquel, *De Vita Comtemplativa* (Les Oeuvres de Philon d'Alexandrie 29; Paris: Cerf, 1963), 32–34.

25. Daumas locates the community 2 km west of Dikhela, between Mex and Agame: Daumas and Miquel, *De Vita Comtemplativa*, 39–46 (with map); F. Daumas, "La 'solitude' des Thérapeutes et les antécédents égyptiens du monachisme Chrétien," in the colloquium *Philon d'Alexandrie (Lyon, 11–15 September 1966)* (Paris: CNRS, 1967), 347–59. F. C. Conybeare, ed., *About the Contemplative Life, or, The Fourth Book of the Treatise concerning Virtues* (New York: Garland, 1987), 294–97, argues for a location northeast of Alexandria, a little beyond Nicopolis. If Philo's use of *hyper* implies "farther inland," as I think, it was on the other side of the lake close to Nitria.

26. Strabo, *Geographica* 17.1.7, 10, 14, 22 for descriptions of the lake, using two different names for the lake: "Mareia" and "Mareotis." The lake extended farther east and south in antiquity, almost to Nitria. A canal joined the lake to the Nile at Naukratis. Strabo refers (17.1.22) to a village named "Gynaecopolis" (city of women) south of Schedia; is this a jesting reference to the Therapeutrides?

27. Qumran's buildings were communal, but the caves may have been like Philo's houses.

28. *Contempl.* 20 and 23 are similarly ambiguous: 23 speaks of "farm buildings" or "country house," suggesting they form "villages," but 20 says that they lived "in gardens or solitary fields."

29. Translated by F. H. Colson: "outside door" (Philo [Loeb Classical Library; vol. 9; Cambridge, Mass.: Harvard University Press, 1951]); it is preferable to translate "courtyard," as the root suggests.

30. B. Brooten, *Women Leaders in the Ancient Synagogues* (Chico: Scholars Press ,1982).

31. Sanders, *Judaism*, 57, 61–62; E. P. Sanders, *Jewish Law from Jesus to the Mishnah* (London: SCM Press, 1990), 104–5.

32. My reconstruction is analogous to large dining rooms in the Greco-Roman world; for a Jewish parallel, see "The New Jerusalem" (5Q15), col. 2, describing space for 22 couches in a room 19x12 cubits (roughly 9x5.5 m).

33. Sarapeia and Asklepieia often had facilities for participants, sometimes in withdrawn locations; but in neither was the community closed, nor was the primary function contemplation.

34. The temple barrier (*soreg*) was between Jews and non-Jews, not males and females.

35. *Barn.* 4:10 hints at an early form of Christian seclusion, though not monasticism. On an early date for Barnabas (late 90s) see P. Richardson and M. B. Shukster, "Barnabas, Nerva and Yavnean Rabbis," *JTS* 34 (1983): 31–55; M. B. Shukster and P. Richardson, "A Temple and *Beth ha-Midrash* in the Epistle of Barnabas," in *Anti-Judaism in Early Christianity*, vol. 2 (ed. S. G. Wilson; Etudes sur le christianisme et le judaïsme 2; Waterloo:Wilfrid Laurier University Press, 1986), 17–31.

36. Guillaumont, *Origines*, chs. 1, 2, 4, 13, emphasizes the importance of 1 Cor 7:32-40 for monasticism.

37. Summary in Jerome Murphy-O'Connor, *The Ecole Biblique and the New Testament* (Freiburg: Universitätsverlag, 1991), 55–56, citing Pierre Benoit, "Colossiens (Epitre aux)," *Dictionnaire de la Bible* (Paris: Letouzey and Ané, 1961), 7:157–70, esp. 159–63; Grant, *Eusebius*, 75, also hints at such a connection.

38. Peter Richardson, "The Thunderbolt in Q and the Wise Man in Corinth," in *From Jesus to Paul* (ed. Peter Richardson and John C. Hurd; Waterloo: Wilfrid Laurier University Press, 1984), 91–111; idem, "On the Absence of Anti-Judaism in I Corinthians," in *Anti-Judaism in Early Christianity*, vol. 1 (ed. Peter Richardson; Waterloo: Wilfrid Laurier University Press, 1986), 59–74.

Chapter Ten

1. I am grateful to Valerie Heuchan, the coauthor of this chapter, for permission to republish it from *Voluntary Associations*, 226–51.

2. "Egypt is accustomed to put up with a queen and to make no distinction of sex": Lucan, *Civil War*, 10.91–92.

3. V. Tcherikover, ed., *Corpus Papyrorum Judaicarum*, vol. 2 (Cambridge: Magnes Press, 1957), 1514.

4. *Apion* 2.49 confirms that Ptolemy and Cleopatra placed their whole army under the control of two Jewish generals, Onias and Dositheus.

5. The site had a long history of settlement back at least to the Twelfth Dynasty. In the Nineteenth Dynasty Ramses II built a temple west of Onias's temple, and Ramses III fortified the town and built a "beautiful little pavilion" near it: F. L. Griffith and E. Naville, *The Mound of the Jew and the City of Onias* (London: Kegan Paul, Trench and Trübner, 1890), 38. There was a temple on the site of Ramses's town in the Twenty-Sixth Dynasty and again in Ptolemaic times: W. M. Flinders Petrie, *Hyksos and Israelite Cities*; with chapters by J. Garrow Duncan (London: School of Archaeology, 1906), 2, 8.

6. The site was originally excavated in the late nineteenth century. New excavations were undertaken in the 1990s, but did not reveal a great deal. There is little new information about the buildings that were once on the site.

7. Petrie, *Hyksos and Israelite Cities*, 20–25.

8. The dimensions show that Josephus exaggerates grossly in saying the dimensions were like Jerusalem's.

9. Petrie, *Hyksos and Israelite Cities*, 22–26.

10. Petrie, *Hyksos and Israelite Cities*, 25–26.

11. Petrie, *Hyksos and Israelite Cities*, 22.

12. V. Tcherikover, *Hellenistic Civilization and the Jews* (Philadelphia: Jewish Publication Society of America, 1959), 281.

13. The affair was the result of complex political circumstances in the area. The community supported the Ptolemies officially, but the Ptolemies had pro- and anti-Roman factions. The Jews, even if they were on the anti-Roman side, would have felt some motivation to support Antipater, since he was an Idumean Jew.

14. Petrie, *Hyksos and Israelite Cities*, 22.

15. Griffith and Naville, *Mound of the Jews*, 13. The underground chamber, with more than 80 inscriptions, had horizontal niches for the bodies. Most of the niches were empty; the corpses that remained were neither mummified nor ornamented and had a burnt brick under the head as a pillow.

16. *CPJ* 2.145. None of the inscriptions makes any military references, surprising if it was a military colony. Perhaps the troops who served the Ptolemies had been disbanded in the Roman period: Aryeh Kasher, *The Jews in Hellenistic and Roman Egypt* (Tübingen: J. C. B. Mohr, 1985), 126.

17. Kasher, *Jews in Hellenistic and Roman Egypt*, 123.

18. Kasher, *Jews in Hellenistic and Roman Egypt*, 125.

19. Kasher, *Jews in Hellenistic and Roman Egypt*, 127.

20. Peder Borgen, "Judaism (Egypt)," *ABD* 3:1063.

21. There is a slim possibility that Marin was not Jewish, but this is unlikely given the Jewish setting of her grave and the Jewish character of her name, Marin; cf. *SEG* 16.887; 28.1476; 33.1372, 1499.

22. B. Brooten, *Women Leaders in the Ancient Synagogue* (BJS 36; Chico: Scholars Press, 1982), 78–83.

23. Brooten, *Women Leaders*, 99.

24. F. Dunand, "Le statut des hiereiai en Egypte Romaine," in *Hommages à Maarten J. Vermaseren*, vol. 1 (Leiden: Brill, 1978), 354–55.

25. Brooten, *Women Leaders*, 96–97.

26. I. J. Peritz, "Women in the Ancient Hebrew Cult," *JBL* 17 (1898): 145–46.

27. Brooten, *Women Leaders*, 86.

28. Peritz, "Hebrew Cult," 143–44.

29. A. M. Blackman, "On the Position of Women in the Ancient Egyptian Hierarchy," *JEA* 7 (1921): 8.

30. Blackman, "Position of Women," 14.

31. Blackman, "Position of Women," 9–10.

32. Gay Robins, *Women in Ancient Egypt* (London: British Musuem Press, 1993), 145.

33. Robins, *Women in Ancient Egypt*, 148–49.

34. Dunand, "Le statut des hiereiai," 353–54.

35. Blackman, "Position of Women," 25–26.

36. Dunand, "Le statut des hiereiai," 372; Blackman, "Position of Women," 27.

37. Blackman, "Position of Women," 12.

38. Robins, *Women in Ancient Egypt*, 151–52.

39. S. B. Pomeroy, *Women in Hellenistic Egypt* (New York: Schocken Books, 1984), 55–57.

40. Dunand, "Le statut des hiereiai," 361–62.

41. Blackman, "Position of Women," 22.

42. Dunand, "Le statut des hiereiai," 373–74 (our translation).

43. L. H. Feldman, "The Orthodoxy of the Jews in Hellenistic Egypt," *Jewish Social Studies* 22 (1960): 232–34.

44. Colson, *Philo* 9.103–69. For a brief introduction to the group, Ross S. Kraemer, *Her Share of the Blessings* (New York: Oxford University Press, 1992), 113–17, 126–27.

45. *Proairesis* is found in 2, 17, 29, 32, 67, 79; for the various meanings see LSJ; for translation problems see Colson, *Philo*, 9.518–19, arguing for a broad sense.

46. A "house of prayer" at Nitria, in the same area as the Therapeutae, had a dedicatory inscription to King Ptolemy and Queen Cleopatra (dated 143–114 B.C.E.) as "their benefactors" (*CIJ* 1442).

47. A term used in Nehemiah 13:30 and Luke 1:5 to refer to priests and Levites serving in the temple.

48. Philo makes a connection with Essenes in the first paragraph; it is not clear if he intends readers to imagine the Therapeutae are an Egyptian variant on a group in the Holy Land.

49. Dorothy Sly, *Philo's Perception of Women* (Atlanta: Scholars Press, 1990).

50. Isis is a near analogy, with its male and female priests, seen in a wall painting from Herculaneum.

51. Geza Vermes, "Essenes and Therapeutae," in *Post Biblical Jewish Studies* (Leiden: Brill, 1975), 30–31.

52. Musonius asks if women should study philosophy: Cora Lutz, *Musonius Rufus "The Roman Socrates"* (YCS 10; New Haven: Yale University Press, 1947), 39–43: "women as well as men have received from the gods the gift of reason. . . . Likewise the female has the same senses as the male . . . both have the same parts of the body . . . not men alone, but women too, have a natural inclination toward virtue . . . and it is the nature of women no less than men to be pleased by good and just acts." William Klassen, "Musonius Rufus, Jesus, and Paul: Three First Century Feminists," in *From Jesus to Paul. Studies in Honour of Francis Wright Beare* (ed. Peter Richardson and John C. Hurd; Waterloo: Wilfrid Laurier University Press, 1984), 185–206.

53. Colson's translation misleadingly refers to women making "part of the audience," as if they were passive; more correctly, "for women also habitually listen together with the same zeal . . ." (Philo [Loeb Classical Library; vol. 9; Cambridge, Mass.: Harvard University Press, 1951]).

54. Philo refers to leaders as if male: *hoi ephemêreutoi* (66), *hoi presbyteroi* (67), and *ho proedros* (75).

55. This is the natural meaning of *tote gar exêchousi pantes te kai pasai* (80); since Philo has just described exposition and singing, when "all the others" take turns "in the proper order," he includes women taking part.

56. A fresco of the Isis cult from Herculaneum (before 79 C.E.) shows a comparable scene. In the center a stair ascends to the façade of a small temple; a male priest stands in the middle, with a male and female priest on either side. An altar is located near the bottom of the stair, with two matched choirs flanking it.

57. Philo describes Moses and Miriam leading choirs in *Agr.* 80–82 (cf. *Leg.* 2.66, 3.103).

58. *Symphonian* is better translated "agreement," "common mind." Singing together created unity (88).

59. R. A. Baer, *Philo's Use of the Categories Male and Female* (Leiden: Brill, 1970), 48, 100–101, suggests the Therapeutrides were women in name only, since all had left their sexuality behind for a unity of the Spirit.

60. The text does not say "prophet *like* Moses"; there is no indication in *On the Contemplative Life* that eschatology is a factor (cf. Deut 18:15, 18-19; Acts 3:22-23; 7: 37; 4QTest 5–8; 1QS 9.11). But if Moses was eschatologically charged, was Miriam also? On prophetic celibacy associated with Moses, see *b. Šabb.* 87a; *Sifre Numbers* 12.1 (99); Philo, *Mos.* 2.68–69; G. Vermes, "Essenes and Therapeutae," *RevQ* 3 (1962): 495–502.

61. Both mirror the custom of Pharaoh marrying his sister, a brother-sister relationship noted in synagogue dedications (Chapter 7): the earliest was *CIJ* 1440, "In honor of King Ptolemy and Queen Berenice, his sister and wife, and their children, the Jews built this house of prayer" (Schedia, 246–221 B.C.E.).

62. Pierre Géoltrain, "La traité de la Vie Contemplative de Philon d'Alexandrie," *Semitica* 10 (1960): 1–61, suggests women wrote *Testament of Job, Wisdom of Solomon, Joseph and Aseneth, Testament of Abraham.*

63. Tran Tam Tinh, *Le culte des divinités orientales à Herculaneum* (Leiden: Brill, 1971), 85–86, #59, plate 41; Theodore H. Feder, *Great Treasures of Pompeii and Herculaneum* (New York: Abbevillle, 1978), 128–29.

64. J. A. S. Evans, *Life in an Egyptian Temple in the Graeco-Roman Period* (New Haven: Yale University Press, 1961), 3. The Isis buildings at Pompeii, for example, included cells for resident priests.

65. See S. K. Heyob, *The Cult of Isis Among Women in the Graeco-Roman World* (Leiden: Brill, 1975), 87, 100; in 200 of 1089 inscriptions women are mentioned as priestesses or members of Isis associations. Delos inscriptions (third to second century B.C.E.) refer to worshipers as Therapeutae; 82–83, 104–5.

66. Miriam is not mentioned by name here, though Josephus mentions her in *Ant.* 2.221.

67. Josephus, *Ant.* 4.78, says she was buried at Sin; Jerome's tradition says near Petra.

68. Jospehus, *Ant.* 3.54, refers to Miriam's husband Hur, who helped hold up Moses' arms during the battle with the Amalekites; Exod 17:8-13 does not refer to Miriam.

69. Pomeroy, *Women in Hellenistic Egypt*, xvii–xviii.

Chapter Eleven

1. First published in *Models of Ministry: Community Formation in the New Testament, the Ante-Nicene Fathers, and the Church Today* (ed. R. N. Longenecker. Peabody: Hendrickson, 2002), 36–56.

2. Philip A. Harland, "Honouring the Emperor or Assailing the Beast: Participation in Civic Life among Associations (Jewish, Christian and Other) in Asia Minor and the Apocalypse of John," *JSNT* 77 (2000): 99–121.

3. Roger Beck, "The Mysteries of Mithras," in *Voluntary Associations*, 176–77.

4. White, *Social Origins*, passim.

5. John S. Kloppenborg, "*Collegia* and *Thiasoi*: Issues in Function, Taxonomy and Membership," in *Voluntary Associations*, 16–30; here 25.

6. White, *Social Origins*, 2:325–32.

7. White, *Social Origins*, 2:343–56.

8. Philip A. Harland, "Claiming a Place in *Polis* and Empire" (Ph.D. diss., University of Toronto, 1999), now published as *Associations, Synagogues, and Congregations: Claiming a Place in Ancient Mediterranean Society* (Minneapolis: Fortress, 2003), 108–12.

9. Philip A. Harland, "Association and Empire: A Social-Historical Study of Associations in Ephesus (I–II C.E.)" (unpublished paper, University of Toronto, 1995; appendixes 1, 2).

10. G. H. R. Horsley, "A Fishing Cartel in First-Century Ephesus," in *New Documents Illustrating Early Christianity*, vol. 5 (North Ryde, N.S.W.: Ancient History Documentary Research Centre, Macquarie University, 1989), 95–100.

11. B. Hudson McLean, "The Place of Cults in Voluntary Associations and Christian Churches on Delos," in *Voluntary Associations*, 186–225.

12. White, *Social Origins*, 1:64–67.

13. For the long inscription describing the building and patrons, see McLean, "Place of Cults," 197–200.

14. White, *Social Origins*, 1:32–40.

15. Helmut Koester, ed., *Pergamon, Citadel of the Gods: Archaeological Record, Literary Description, and Religious Development* (HTS 46; Harrisburg: Trinity Press International, 1998).

16. L. Richardson, jr, *Pompeii, An Architectural History* (Baltimore: Johns Hopkins University Press, 1988), 218–20.

17. Richardson, *Pompeii*, 281–85.

18. Richardson, *Pompeii*, 290–98.

19. Russell Meiggs, *Roman Ostia* (Oxford: Clarendon, 1960), 312, for the former point. Gustav Hermansen, *Ostia, Aspects of Roman City Life* (Edmonton: University of Alberta Press, 1982), 56–59, 239–41, for total.

20. Meiggs, *Roman Ostia*, 325–26.

21. Meiggs, *Roman Ostia*, 354–66

22. Meiggs *Roman Ostia*, 370–76.

23. L. Michael White, "Synagogues and Society in Imperial Ostia: Archaeological and Epigraphic Evidence," in Donfried & Richardson, *Rome*, 30–68.

24. The Lund project has since argued that the structure was purpose built.

25. White, *Social Origins*, 1:40–44.

26. Robert Jewett, "Tenement Churches and Communal Meals in the Early Church: The Implications of 2 Thess. 3:10," *BR* 38 (1993): 23–43.

Chapter Twelve

1. First published in *The Ancient Synagogue From Its Origins until 200 C.E.: Papers Presented at an International Conference at Lund University October 14–17, 2001* (ed. Birger Olsson and Magnus Zetterholm; Coniectanea Biblica NT series 39; Stockholm: Almqvist and Wiksell, 2003), ch. 5.

2. Much of what follows is in dialogue with Levine, *Synagogue*; Lee I. Levine, "The First-Century Synagogue: New Perspectives." *STK* 77 (2001): 22–30. See Anders Runesson, *The Origins of the Synagogue: A Socio-historical Study* (Stockholm: Almqvist and Wiksell, 2001), on history of research.

3. Levine, *Synagogue*, 33: "the emergence of the Judean synagogue was not the outcome of any specific event or crisis, but rather a gradual development. . . ."

4. Sometimes Jewish temples were referred to as *proseuchai*; Runesson, *Origins*, 409–22; 429–36.

5. Lester L. Grabbe, "Synagogues in Pre-70 Palestine," in Urman & Flesher, *Synagogues*, 17–26.

6. Six of Josephus's decrees (*Ant.* 14.188–264; *Ant.* 16.162–73) plausibly presuppose buildings: Sardis (three times), Delos, Ephesus, and Halicarnassus. Other allusions suggest the presence of a building, such as performing sacred rites at Alexandria, Laodicea, Tralles (twice), and Miletus. Allusions to Jewish "superstitions" (Delos, Sardis, Ephesus [twice], Alexandria) may likewise presuppose cultic buildings.

7. Khirbet Qana may add another first/second century C.E. synagogue; Chapter 4.

8. White, *Social Origins*, vol. 1, chs. 2 and 5; Bradley Blue, "Acts and the House Church," in *Graeco-Roman Setting* (ed. David W. J. Gill and Conrad Gempf; vol. 2 of *The Book of Acts in its First Century Setting*, ed. Bruce W. Winter; Grand Rapids: Wm. B. Eerdmans, 1994), 119–222.

9. Table in Runesson, *Origins*, 171–73.

10. An inscription from Berenice in Cyrenaica (G. Lüderitz, *Corpus Jüdischer Zeugnisse aus der Cyrenaike* [Wiesbaden: Reichert, 1983], 72; 55 C.E.) uses *synagôgê* twice, in line three of the community and in line five of the building. In the Bosporan Kingdom, *proseuchê* tends to be used of the building and *synagôgê* of the community: Irena Levinskaya, *Diaspora Setting* (vol. 5 of *The Book of Acts in its First Century Setting*, ed. Bruce W. Winter; Grand Rapids: Wm. B. Eerdmans, 1996), 105–16, appendix 3.

11. John S. Kloppenborg Verbin, "Dating Theodotos (*CIJ* ii.1404)," *JJS* 51 (2000): 243–80: it "attests a synagogue building in Jerusalem, probably constructed in the early first century C.E. . . . It confirms that *synagôgê* was used of buildings not only in Egypt and Cyrenaica but also in Roman Palestine . . ." (277).

12. Meiggs, *Roman Ostia*, 382, fig. 27, shows cult distribution.

13. Birger Olsson, Dieter Mitternacht, and Olof Brandt, eds., *The Synagogue of Ancient Ostia and the Jews of Rome* (Stokholm: Paul Åstrom, 2003); Donald D. Binder, *Into the Temple Courts: The Place of the Synagogues in the Second Temple Period* (Atlanta: Society of Biblical Literature, 1999), 322–26.

14. Anders Runesson, "The Oldest Original Synagogue Building in the Diaspora: A Response to L. Michael White." *HTR* 92 (1999): 409–33, supporting Maria Squarciapino.

15. White began a five-year project in 2001 to answer such questions.

16. Meiggs, *Roman Ostia*, 547 (cf. 543, 140), dated by the brick stamps.

17. Meiggs, *Roman Ostia*, 244. Plans in Gustav Hermansen, *Ostia: Aspects of Roman City Life* (Edmonton: University of Alberta Press, 1982), fig 12; Meiggs, *Roman Ostia*, fig. 8.

18. Hermansen, *Ostia*, 75, suggests the *triclinia* were added later and that banquets earlier took place in the colonnade.

19. Meiggs, *Roman Ostia*, 551 and plate IXb.

20. Hermansen, *Ostia*, 64 and fig 33.

21. Excavations began in 1873; H. Holleaux excavated significant areas in 1904–1914.

22. B. Hudson McLean, "The Place of Cult in Voluntary Associations and Christian Churches on Delos," in *Voluntary Associations*, 186–225, especially 186–90.

23. Excavated 1912–1913; André Plassart, "La synagogue juive de Délos," in *Mélanges Holleaux: Receuil de mémoires concernant l'antiquité grecque offert à Maurice Holleaux* (Paris: Auguste Picard), 201–15.

24. McLean, "Place of Cult," 189. Four inscriptions refer to "God most high" (*theos hypsistos*), none refers to Jews or Judeans, and the fifth (naming Lysimachos, who appears on one other) refers to the *proseuchê*.

25. An inscription (*OGIS* 417) found in front of the Temple of Apollo honored Herod Antipas or Herod Philip: "the Athenian people and those living on the island" (Delos). Three fragments of an inscription—found on Syros but probably originating on Delos—referred to "King Herod"; the inscription was likely associated with the *xystos* near the synagogue finds. *Herod*, 205–6, 209.

26. Philippe Bruneau, "'Les Israélites de Délos' et la Juiverie délienne," *BCH* 106 (1982): 465–504; one inscription has *proseuchê*, both have *Israêlitai* and *Argarizein* ("Mount Gerizim"); texts and translations conveniently in L. Michael White, "The Delos Synagogue Revisited: Recent Fieldwork in the Graeco-Roman Diaspora." *HTR* 80/2 (1987): 33–60, esp. 139–41.

27. S. R. Llewelyn, "An Association of Samaritans in Delos," in *New Documents Illustrating Early Christianity* (ed. S. R. Llewelyn; Grand Rapids: Wm. B. Eerdmans, 1998), 8:148–51.

28. McLean, "Place of Cult."

29. White, *Social Origins*, 2:335 n. 81, "another building."

30. White, "Delos Synagogue Revisited," 147–52; McLean, "Place of Cult," 191–96.

31. Runesson, *Origins*, 187, n. 79I, notes the similarity between its form and my schematic drawing of the Therapeutae's assembly room, which I had not noticed.

32. White, *Social Origins*, 2.332–39; idem, "Delos Synagogue Revisited," 147–51.

33. Binder, *Temple Courts*, 299–316; Runesson, *Origins*, 185–87.

34. Belle D. Mazur, *Studies on Jewry in Greece* (Athens: Hestia, 1935), 15–24, denies it was a synagogue.

35. Excavations began in 1895 under Karl Humann's direction; Theodor Wiegand, and Hans Schrader, *Priene: Ergebnisse der Ausgrabungen und Untersuchungen in den Jahren 1895–1898* (Berlin: Georg Reimer, 1904).

36. White, *Social Origins*, 325–32; see also Michele Murray, "Was There Religious Coexistence or Competition in Ancient Priene?" in *Religious Rivalries and the Struggle for Success in Sardis and Smyrna* (ed. Richard Ascough; ESCJ; Waterloo: Wilfrid Laurier University Press, forthcoming).

37. Wiegand and Schrader, *Priene*, 172–73.

38. Martin Schede, *Die Ruinen von Priene* (Berlin: de Gruyter, 1964 [1934]), 101.

39. Wiegand and Schrader, *Priene*, 480, call it a Hauskirche of the fourth to fifth centuries C.E. It has been redated to the second to third centuries C.E. and identified as a synagogue (White, *Social Origins*, 2:329–30).

40. Details in Murray, "Religious Coexistence."

41. Another menorah relief was found in a Byzantine church theatre, sometimes incorrectly associated with the synagogue; P. R. Trebilco, *Jewish Communities in Asia Minor* (SNTSMS 69; Cambridge: Cambridge University Press, 1991), 55.

42. Levine, "First-Century Synagogue."

43. J. G. Griffiths, "Egypt and the Rise of the Synagogue," in Urman & Flesher, *Synagogues*, 3–16.

44. *Herod*, 264–70.

45. Jean-Baptiste Humbert and Alain Chambon, *Les Fouilles de Khirbet Qumran et de Aïn Feshkha* (Göttingen: Vandenhoeck und Ruprecht, 1994).

46. *City and Sanctuary*, ch. 5.

47. R. Pummer, "Samaritan Synagogues and Jewish Synagogues: Similarities and Differences," in *Jews, Christians, and Polytheists in the Ancient Synagogue* (ed. Steven Fine; London: Routledge, 1999), 118–60.

48. Runesson, *Origins*, holds a variant on this view.

Chapter Thirteen

1. This chapter combines parts of two of my studies, "Law and Piety in Herod's Architecture," *SR* 15.3 (1986): 347–60; "Religion and Architecture: A Study of Herod's Piety, Power, Pomp and Pleasure," *Bulletin of the Canadian Society of Biblical Studies* 45 (1985): 3–29.

2. Shimon Appelbaum, "Herod," *EncJud* 8:382.

3. *EJ* 8:383–84.

4. Since drafting the essays that lie behind this chapter, considerable work has been done on Herod's buildings. See Chapters 15–18.

5. W. B. Dinsmoor, *The Architecture of Ancient Greece* (London: Batsford, 1902; repr., 1975), 266, sees Hellenistic architecture as a decadent phase.

6. A. W. Laurence, *Greek Architecture, Pelican History of Art* (rev. ed; Harmondsworth: Penguin Books, 1962), 224, refers to "the work of Hellenized monarchs such as Juba or Herod the Great."

7. C. G. Starr, *Civilization and the Caesars* (New York: Norton, 1965), 11; Frank E. Brown, *Roman Architecture* (New York: Brazillier, 1961), 9–30.

8. For the relationship of Herod's Northern Villa at Masada to Augustus's and Tiberius's villas on Capri, see A. G. Mackay, *Houses, Villas and Palaces in the Roman World* (London: Thames and Hudson, 1975), 218–19.

9. N. Yalouris and O. Szymiczek, *The Olympic Games in Ancient Greece* (Athens: Athenon, 1976), 61.

10. J. Ringel, *Césarée de Palestine* (Paris: Editions Ophrys, n.d.), 42–43.

11. Lee I. Levine, *Caesarea Under Roman Rule* (Leiden: E. J. Brill, 1975), 14, argues for a large and powerful Jewish community in Caesarea from its founding by Herod.

12. The prohibitions all refer to structures associated with legal activities and judgment. Permitted activities include public services.

13. Leviticus 26:1—among the various explanations of the second commandment (Exod 20:3-4; 20:23; 34:17; Lev 19:4; Deut 4:15-19; 27:15)—limits the prohibition to "your land."

14. Y. Meshorer, *Jewish Coins of the Second Temple Period* (Tel Aviv: Am Hassefer, 1967), plate xi; A. Reifenberg, *Israel's History in Coins* (London: East and West Library 1953), plate 24.

15. Much of Josephus's material originates with Nicolas, an admirer of Herod, so it is not always possible to know when Josephus is giving his own views and when they are Nicolas's (Chapter 15).

16. He does this in other places also: *Ant.* 14.482–86; 15.388–90; 15.425 (repeated in the Talmud); 16.220–27; 17.23–26; 1.27–65; 15.315–16; 15.365.

17. *Assumption of Moses* 6:2–6: "And an insolent king shall succeed them, who will not be of the race of priests, a man bold and shameless, and he shall judge them as they deserve. And he shall cut off their chief men with the sword, and shall destroy them in secret places, so that none shall know where their bodies are. He shall slay the old and the young, and he shall not spare. Then the fear of him shall be bitter unto them in their land. And he shall execute judgments on them as the Egyptians executed upon them, during thirty and four years, and he shall punish them."

18, On accommodation, Peter Richardson, "Pauline Inconsistency: 1 Cor. 9:19-23 and Gal. 2:11-14," *NTS* 26 (1980): 347–46; Peter Richardson, *Paul's Ethic of Freedom* (Philadelphia: Westminster, 1979).

19. Jacob Neusner, *History of the Jews in Babylon*, vol. 1 (Leiden: Brill, 1965), 33.

Chapter Fourteen

1. First published in *SBL Seminar Papers*, 1992 (Atlanta: Scholars Press, 1992): 507–23.

2. The moon's eclipse occurred on 13 March (*Ant.* 17.167); for the year see Schürer 1:326–28.

3. *Mishnah 'Abodah Zarah* distinguishes between images that were and were not forbidden (e.g., 3:1, 3, 4; 4:4–5). In practice attention was given to coin representations, architectural decoration, and the plastic arts.

4. Scholars often overlook the actual situation; for example, Marcus Borg, *Jesus. A New Vision* (San Francisco: Harper, 1987), 174–77: "the image-bearing coins of pilgrims were exchanged for 'holy' coins without images."

5. R. E. Brown, *The Gospel According to John I–XII* (Garden City: Doubleday, 1960), 114–25; J. A. T. Robinson, *The Priority of John* (London: SCM, 1985), 127–31; C. H. Dodd, *Historical Tradition in the Fourth Gospel* (Cambridge: Cambridge University Press, 1953), 300–303.

6. Translation of R. M. Grant, *Gnosticism* (London: Collins, 1961), 195–208.

7. E. P. Sanders, *Jesus and Judaism* (Philadelphia: Fortress, 1983), 61–76.

8. L. Kadman, "Temple Dues and Currency in Ancient Palestine in the Light of Recently Discovered Coin-Hoards," *Israel Numismatic Bulletin* 1 (1962): 9–11 (not available to me).

9. For example, Sanders, *Jesus and Judaism*, 61–71; William Horbury, "The Temple Tax," in *Jesus and the Politics of His Day* (ed. Ernst Bammel and C. F. D. Moule;

Cambridge: Cambridge University Press, 1984), 265–86; Paula Fredriksen, "Jesus and the Temple, Mark and the War," *SBL Seminar Papers*, 1990.

10. R. H. Lightfoot, *The Gospel Message of Mark* (Oxford: Oxford University Press, 1950), 60–65; Joachim Jeremias, *Jesus' Promise to the Nations* (Philadelphia: Fortress Press, 1982 [1958]); T. W. Manson, *Only to the House of Israel?* (Philadelphia: Fortress Press, 1964 [1955]).

11. Contrast Haim Cohn, *The Trial and Death of Jesus* (New York: Harper, 1971), 54–59, with Craig Evans, "Jesus' Action in the Temple and Evidence of Corruption in the First-Century Temple," *SBL Seminar Papers*, 1989: 522–39.

12. Richard A. Horsley, *Jesus and the Spiral of Violence* (San Francisco: Harper, 1987), 130–32, 285–300.

13. S. G. F. Brandon, *Jesus and the Zealots* (New York: Scribners, 1967), 322–58; also in his *The Trial of Jesus of Nazareth* (London: Granada, 1968) 97–127; Joel Carmichael, *The Death of Jesus* (New York: Dell, 1962), 112–34.

14. Gerd Theissen, *The First Followers of Jesus* (London: SCM, 1978), 47–48.

15. Sanders, *Jewish Law*, 283–308.

16. Sanders, *Judaism*, 84–87.

17. Yaakov Meshorer, "One Hundred Ninety Years of Tyrian Shekels," in *Festschrift für/Studies in Honor of Leo Mildenberg* (ed. Arthur Houghton et al.; Wetteren, Belgium: Editions NR, 1984), 171–91.

18. Arye Ben-David, *Jerusalem und Tyros. Ein Beitrag zur palästinensichen Münz- und Wirtschaftsgeschichte (126 a.C.–57 p.C.)* (Basel: Kyklos Verlag/Tübingen: Mohr, 1969), gives details and analysis of silver content. Ben-David exaggerates the degree to which Tyrian coinage was used as a standard. Michael H. Crawford, *Roman Republican Coin Hoards* (London: Royal Numismatic Society, 1969), inventories 567 hoards and lists Tyrian coins in only one (from Russia, dated 44–27 B.C.E.). Other studies show that hoards are mixed: Margaret Thompson, Otto Morkholm and Colin M. Kraay, eds., *An Inventory of Greek Coin Hoards* (New York: American Numismatic Society, 1973), especially items 1616–1631; H. Seyrig, *Trésor du Levant anciens et nouveaux* (Paris: Paul Geuthner, 1973), 113–20; R. S. Hanson, *Tyrian Influence in the Upper Galilee* (Cambridge, Mass.: ASOR, 1980), 52–53.

19. Meshorer, "Tyrian Shekels," argues that the latter type was minted in Jerusalem; per contra, Jacob Maltiel-Gerstenfeld, *260 Years of Ancient Jewish Coinage* (Tel Aviv: Kol, 1982), 28–29.

20. A. Reifenberg, *Ancient Jewish Coins* (Jerusalem: Rubin Mass, 1963), 29–33.

21. Biblical references to Tyre stress two contradictory factors: Hiram, King of Tyre, was friendly with David and Solomon, and helped build the temple, but Tyre was the object of violent prophetic oracles.

22. Y. Meshorer, *Ancient Jewish Coinage* (New York: Amphora, 1982), 2.7–9; Frederic W. Madden, *History of Jewish Coinage and of Money in the Old and New Testaments* (New York: KTAV, 1967), 4.

23. Horsley, *Spiral of Violence*, 279–84; David Daube, "Temple Tax," in *Jesus, the Gospels and the Church* (ed. E. P. Sanders; Macon: Mercer University Press, 1987), 121–34; Hugh Montefiore, "Jesus and the Temple Tax," *NTS* 10 (1964–65): 60–71.

24. George W. Buchanan, "Mark 11:15-19: Brigands in the Temple," *HUCA* 30 (1959), 169–77.

25. Sanders, *Judaism*, 85–92, citing Philo's statement, *Spec. Laws* 1.74–75.

26. Douglas E. Oakman, *Jesus and the Economic Questions of his Day* (Lewiston, N.Y.: Mellen, 1986), ch. 4 and conclusion.

27. Fredriksen, "Jesus and the Temple."

Chapter Fifteen

1. A paper given at the SNTS meeting in Cambridge, England, August 11, 1988.

2. H. St. John Thackeray, *Josephus, the Man and the Historian* (New York: Jewish Institute of Religion Press, 1929). See also Richard Laqueur, *Der Jüdische Historiker Flavius Josephus* (Giessen: Münchow, 1920), 136.

3. Tessa Rajak, *Josephus. The Historian and His Society* (Philadelphia: Fortress Press, 1984), 233–36.

4. Ralph Marcus in the Loeb edition of Josephus is sympathetic to Otto's and Schürer's views at *Ant.* 15.266 and 299 and open to an anti-Herodian source in 15.267–98. Otto believed Josephus did not use Nicolas directly in either *War* or *Antiquities* but used two anonymous historians: Schürer rejected the idea of anonymous sources.

5. Thackeray, *Josephus*, 66–67, 100–20, believes an assistant recast *War* for *Antiquities* after checking Nicolas and other authorities such as Herod's memoirs.

6. B. Z. Wacholder, *Nicolaus of Damascus* (Berkeley: University of California Press, 1962), ch. 5, analyzes such issues. Wacholder argues Josephus must have used Nicolas in *Antiquities* even more than in *War* (64).

7. Shaye J. D. Cohen, *Josephus in Galilee and Rome* (Columbia Studies in the Classical Tradition 8; Leiden: Brill, 1979), argues similarly; he holds (24–67) that *Antiquities* 13–14, 15–17 in different ways rework a common source, but with greater dependence on that source (and with fresh consultation of it) than *War*.

8. Yadin, *Masada*, 141.

9. Yadin, *Masada*, 141.

10. Ehud Netzer, "Searching for Herod's Tomb," *BAR* 9 (1983): 30–51.

11. Kenneth Holum, Robert L. Hohlfelder, et al., *King Herod's Dream: Caesarea on the Sea* (New York: W. W. Norton, 1988).

12. See especially John Peter Oleson, et al., "The Caesarea Ancient Harbour Excavation Project . . . 1980–83 Seasons," *Journal of Field Archaeology* 11 (1984): 281–305; John Peter Oleson, "Herod and Vitruvius . . .," in *Harbour Archaeology* (ed. A. Raban; Haifa, 1985): 155–72.

13. Oleson, "Caesarea Ancient Harbour Project," 288, reports that the southern breakwater had concrete blocks "as large as 100 or 125 cubic metres." The blocks of stone described in *War* (50x9x10 feet; 15.3x2.7x3.0 m), by a curious coincidence, would be 124 cubic meters. Several concrete blocks were 4.3x3.2x1.5 m (21 cubic), and one was about 4x7x8 m (225 cubic m, which is the same volume as Josephus's description in *Antiquities* (50x18x10 feet = 225 cubic m). The largest concrete block was 11.5x15x2.0 m (345 cubic m).

14. Oleson, "Herod and Vitruvius," 168; see also Vitruvius, *De architectura* 2.6.

15. This stone is about the size Josephus reports to have been let down as the substructure of the moles at Caesarea Maritima. See Murray Stein, "How Herod Moved Gigantic Blocks," *BAR* 7/3 (1981): 42–46; Michael Zimmerman, "A Tunnel Exposes New Areas," *BAR* 7/3 (1983): 34–41.

16. The notes in the Loeb edition are not entirely correct. Josephus describes only the gates in the west wall, none of which led to Bezetha, the most obvious "suburb." The two additional gates on the west were at street level, one at the south end of the modern plaza, the other half way up the tunnel to the north. It is unclear what suburb he means.

17. D. Blackman, "Rhodes: Survey of Ancient Shipsheds," *Archaiologikon Delfion* 27 (1972): 686–87, says some excavated shipsheds were not in use in the Roman period.

18. The Pythian Temple at Rhodes was probably destroyed when Cassius attacked Rhodes in the civil wars after Caesar's death, so a rebuilding involving Herod is not improbable.

Chapter Sixteen

1. This is an expanded form of a paper given at the Annual Meeting of the Society of Biblical Literature, Chicago, 21 November 1994.

2. Some relevant studies on archaeological investigations of Jerusalem and areas around the Temple Mount: Brian Lalor, "The Temple Mount of Herod the Great at Jerusalem: Recent Excavations and Literary Sources," in *Archaeology & Biblical Interpretation* (ed. John R. Bartlett; London: Routledge, 1997), 95–116; Benjamin Mazar, *The Mountain of the Lord* (Garden City: Doubleday, 1975), part III; Meir Ben-Dov, *In the Shadow of the Temple: The Discovery of Ancient Jerusalem* (Jerusalem: Keter, 1982); Leen Ritmeyer and Kathleen Ritmeyer, "Reconstructing Herod's Temple Mount in Jerusalem," *BAR* 15/6 (1989): 23–42; Leen Ritmeyer, "Locating the Original Temple Mount," *BAR* 18/2 (1992): 24–45, 64–65; W. Harold Mare, *The Archaeology of the Jerusalem Area* (Grand Rapids: Baker, 1987), ch. 7; Lee I. Levine, *Jerusalem: Portrait of the City in the Second Temple Period (538 B.C.E.–70 C.E.)* (Philadelphia: Jewish Publication Society, 2002); idem, ed., *Jerusalem: Its Sanctity and Centrality to Judaism, Christianity, Islam* (New York: Continuum, 1999); Ronny Reich, Gideon Avni, and Tamar Winter, *Jerusalem Archaeological Park* (Jerusalem: IAA, 1999); Hillel Geva, ed., *Ancient Jerusalem Revealed* (Jerusalem: Israel Exploration Society, 1994); John Wilkinson, *Jerusalem as Jesus Knew it: Archaeology as Evidence* (London: Thames and Hudson, 1978). On Herod as king and patron: *Herod*; Achim Lichtenberger, *Die Baupolitik Herodes des Grossen* (Wiesbaden: Harrassowitz, 1999); Duane W. Roller, *The Building Program of Herod the Great* (Berkeley: University of California Press, 1998); Abraham Schalit, *Koenig Herodes: Der Mann und sein Werk* (Berlin: de Gruyter, 1969); Ehud Netzer, *The Palaces of the Hasmoneans and Herod the Great* (Jerusalem: Israel Excavation Society, 2001). On Josephus as a source of information about the period and about the temple: Steve Mason, *Flavius Josephus on the Pharisees: A Composition-critical Study* (Leiden: Brill, 1991), chs. 5 and 11; Steve Mason, *Josephus and the New Testament* (Peabody: Hendrickson, 1992). On the *Temple Scroll* (11QT): Yigael Yadin, *The Temple Scroll* (3 vols. in 4; Jerusalem: Israel Exploration Society, 1977–1983); Yigael Yadin, *The Temple Scroll* (New York: Random House, 1985), part 4; Ben Zion Wacholder, *The Dawn of Qumran: The Sectarian Torah and the Teacher of Righteousness* (Cincinnati: Hebrew Union College Press, 1983); Michael O. Wise, *A Critical Study of the Temple Scroll from Qumran Cave 11* (Chicago: University of Chicago Press, 1990); George J. Brooke, ed., *Temple Scroll Studies* (JSPSup 7; Sheffield: JSOT Press, 1989). On symbolic, architectural, art-historical, urban, theological views: Stanley Tigerman, *The Architecture of Exile* (New York: Rizzoli, 1988), 89–122; Helen Rosenau, *Vision of the Temple: The Image of the Temple of Jerusalem in Judaism and Christianity* (London: Oresko, 1979); Francis E. Peters, *Jerusalem and Mecca: The Typology of the Holy City in the Near East* (New York: New York University Press, 1986); Margaret Barker, *The Gate of Heaven. The History and Symbolism of the Temple of Jerusalem* (London: SPCK, 1991); Leibel Reznick, *The Holy Temple Revisited* (Northvale: Aronson, 1990); Yisrael Ariel, *The Odyssey of the Third Temple* (Jerusalem: Temple Institute, 1993); Ernest L. Martin, *The Temples that Jerusalem Forgot* (Portland: Ask, 2000); Vincent Scully, *Architecture: The Natural and the Manmade* (New York: St. Martin's Press, 1991), ch. 2; Christian Norberg-Schulz, *Genius Loci: Towards a Phenomenology of Architecture* (New York: Rizzoli, 1980); Mark C. Taylor, *Disfiguring: Art, Architecture, Religion* (Chicago: University of Chicago Press, 1992).

3. This chapter responds in part to Johann Meier, "The Architectural History of the Temple in Jerusalem in the Light of the Temple Scroll," and Mathias Delcor, "Is the Temple Scroll a Source of the Herodian Temple?," both in Brooke, *Temple Scroll*, 23–62; 67–90; Yadin, *Temple Scroll* (1983); Yadin, *Temple Scroll* (1985).

4. Ritmeyer, "Reconstructing"; Ritmeyer, "Locating"; Levine, *Jerusalem*, ch. 6.

5. Maier, "Architectural History," 23–62; Martin, *Temples*, ch. 11 and passim.

6. The first century B.C.E./first century C.E. was a period of substantial projects: for example, Bel and Ba'al Shamim at Palmyra; Dushara, the Great Temple and the Winged Lions at Petra; the Three Temples complex to Ba'al Shamim, Dushara, and a still unknown deity at Si'a; Zeus, Dionysus, and Artemis at Gerasa; the Great Temple at Baalbek; Mars Ultor, Venus Genatrix, and Julius Caesar at Rome; the Maison Carré at Nîmes (Nemausus); Temple of Claudius at Colchester (Camulodunum); Temples of Roma and Augustus at Caesarea Maritima, Sebaste and Panias; the Temple of Domitian at Ephesus; the Sebasteion at Aphrodisias.

7. Ideally other ancient material evidence should be included, such as numismatic evidence (e.g., Bar Kokhba coins), mosaic representations (e.g., Beth Shean, Beth Alpha, Susiya), gilt glass (Rome), wall paintings (Dura), architectural decoration (Capernaum) and even manuscript illuminations (Ashburnham Pentateuch); even though these are later—often much later—they are representations of the architecture of the temple.

8. Philip R. Davies, "Sociology and the Second Temple," and Richard A. Horsley, "Empire, Temple and Community—But No Bourgeoisie! A Response to Blenkinsopp and Petersen," both in *Second Temple Studies 1. Persian Period* (ed. Philip R. Davies; JSOTSup 117; Sheffield: JSOT, 1991), 11–19; 163–74.

9. Lalor, "Temple Mount," has useful sketches; cf. also Maier, "Architectural History," 29.

10. Sometimes *hieron* is used of everything inside the surrounding walls, but I will use *temenos* as the general term and *hieron* for the central complex, including the *naos* proper, and Courts of Priests, Israel, and Women.

11. Turner, *Temple to Meeting House*, 41–42.

12. Acts 3:11 provides the name; it implies that first-century observers thought this section of the *stoa* was old. In fact, it could not have had anything to do with Solomon.

13. The commonest arrangement in the Roman world was axes in the same direction, most typically with the *naos* and *temenos* on the very same axis. This was by no means invariable, and different arrangements can be found. Late Hellenistic practice was more sophisticated, but rarely with axes at right angles.

14. The rising sun was symbolically important; the red heifer was brought in to be slaughtered through the Shushan Gate in the east wall, which was directed towards Susa, one of the capitals of Darius I.

15. *City and Sanctuary*, chs. 2, 3, and 6.

16. Strabo, *Geographica* 16.4.26, says (following Athenodorus, who lived at Petra for a while in the second half of the first century B.C.E.): "Embossed works, paintings, and moulded works are not produced in [Nabatean] country." Nabatean art tended to be aniconic, though it is surprising that Strabo does not mention Jewish conventions, as well. *City and Sanctuary*, ch. 2; Joseph Patrich, *The Formation of Nabatean Art: Prohibition of a Graven Image among the Nabateans* (Jerusalem: Magnes/Leiden: Brill, 1990), 36.

17. Taylor, *Disfiguring*, passim.

18. *Herod*, ch. 8; Roller, *Building Program*, chs. 7 and 8; Lichtenberger, *Baupolitik*, chs. 1, 3.

19. This is uncertain, since his tomb has not been found; it may have been on the lower level.

20. *City and Sanctuary*, ch. 5.

21. Aviam & Richardson "Galilee," 177–217; A. M. Berlin, "The Archaeology of Ritual: The Sanctuary of Pan at Banias/Caesarea Philippi," *BASOR* 315 (1999): 27–45.

22. Josephus's account of the rebuilding should be preferred, especially *War* 5.184–237; see also *Ant.* 15.380–425.

23. Ritmeyer, "Reconstructing."

24. Reich, et al., *Jerusalem*, 12–13, 34–41, 146; on the duality, Lalor, "Temple

Mount," 104–5.

25. A bridge may have existed as early as 63 B.C.E. When Pompey besieged Jerusalem, it was destroyed by Jewish forces camped within the *temenos* (*Ant*. 14.58). Dan Bahat, *The Illustrated Atlas of Jerusalem* (New York: Simon and Schuster, 1990), 38.

26. *Herod*, 16–18.

27. This includes some or all of the Pool of Israel, the Bethesda Pools, the Mamillah Pool, Hezekiah's Pool, Sultan's Pool, the Struthion Pool, and Solomon's Pools (one begun by the Hasmoneans and one probably by Pilate).

28. Yadin, *Temple Scroll* (1985), 163–69; Yadin, *Temple Scroll* (1983), 2:188–90.

29. Yadin, *Temple Scroll* (1985), 119, 139, 145, 150, 163; per contra, Sanders, *Jewish Law*, 104–5.

30. Sanders, *Judaism*, 57.

31. Women offering sacrifice after childbirth might have entered: *t. 'Arak*. 2:1; *m. Mid*. 2:6.

32. The mass of the *naos* was immense, larger than comparable *naoi* in the ancient world, such as Bel in Palmyra, Jupiter in Damascus, Artemis in Ephesus, or similar complexes.

33. The *Mishnah* and Ezekiel were most interested in the latter areas; *m. Kelim* 1:9 refers to a dispute in the name of R. Jose over the relation of the Sanctuary to the area between Porch and Altar.

34. Yadin, *Temple Scroll* (1983), vol. 2: col. 40; vol. 1:190–92; Wacholder, *Dawn of Qumran*, 13–16.

35. Wise, *Temple Scroll*, 83.

36. Schürer 1:175, n. 6.

37. Jonathan A. Goldstein, *1 Maccabees* (AB; Garden City New York, Doubleday, 1976), 391–94.

38. Formal Sanhedrin arrangements are later, so the references are anachronistic.

39. Sanders, *Judaism*, 57; Th. A. Busink, *Der Tempel von Jerusalem, von Salomo bis Herodes; eine archäologisch-historische Studie unter Berücksichtigung des westsemitischen Tempelbaus* (Leiden: Brill, 1970), 2:1073–1079.

40. Levine, *Jerusalem*, 240.

41. In general, Tal Ilan, *Integrating Women into Second Temple History* (Tübingen: Mohr Siebeck, 1999), 21–23; Ellen Case, "Salome Alexandra: A Study in Achievement, Power and Survival" (unpublished thesis, York University, 1997), passim.

42. On Egypt, Runesson, *Origins of the Synagogue*, 409–14; 436–59.

43. Petrie, *Hyksos and Israelite Cities*, ch. 4; Griffith and Naville, *Mound of the Jews*, 18–21, 51–53.

44. The *Mishnah* thought Leontopolis priests met the qualifications, at least partly (Chapter 11).

45. On the "new Jerusalem" and 11QT, Wise, *Temple Scroll*, 64–84.

46. Peters, *Jerusalem and Mecca*, 3 and passim.

47. On conflict between sanctuary and palace, Johann Maier, *The Temple Scroll: An Introduction, Translation & Commentary* (JSOT Sup 34; Sheffield: JSOT Press, 1985), 28–33.

48. Sanders, *Judaism*, chs. 7, 8.

49. Maier, *Temple Scroll*, 110.

50. Herod was a third-generation proselyte, and thus eligible to participate as these matters were usually understood within Judaism generally, outside the stricter requirements of 11QT.

51. Things changed by the mid-second century C.E.; Peter Richardson, "From Apostles to Virgins: Romans 16 and the Roles of Women in the Early Church," *TJT* 2/2 (1986): 232–61.

52. 11QT solves the space problem but provides no solution to the practical prob-

lem of handing over victims; the very large middle court is for Israelites but there are only four gates that communicate between the middle and inner courts. Herod's solution was more practical, even if very small.

53. Maier, *Temple Scroll*, 84.

54. Underground features may point to a location, but in part the answer depends on which location works best in terms of layout and plan. Its location in precursor temples is unclear.

55. Ritmeyer "Locating," 42.

56. R. Grafman, " Herod's Foot and Robinson's Arch," *IEJ* 20 (1970): 60–66.

57. Lalor, "Temple Mount," 100–109.

Chapter Seventeen

1. Delivered as a memorial lecture—in conjunction with the traveling exhibition, "From the Diaspora to Jerusalem"—honoring Ben Meyer, at McMaster University in Hamilton, Ontario, 25 September 1996.

2. Gideon Avni and Zvi Greenhut, *The Akeldama Tombs: Three Burial Caves in the Kidron Valley, Jerusalem* (Jerusalem: Israel Antiquities Authority, 1996), Ossuary 17, and figs. 2.12, 3.7, 3.8: *pepoiêken aza beroutos/erôtas*; see also discussion by Ilan, 60–61.

3. Avni and Greenhut, *Akeldama Tombs*, Ossuary 11; figs. 2.7, 3.3: *eiratos sel(e)uk(idos)*; discussion by Ilan, 59.

4. Avni and Greenhut, *Akeldama Tombs*, Ossuary 31; figs. 2.25, 3.19: *aristôn* [in Greek]; *ariston apamê/yehudah ha-gêr* [in Hebrew]; discussion by Ilan, 66.

5. One was a Jew with a Hebrew name (or at least the Greek form of a Hebrew name); another was a person with a Greek name linked with a Jewish name; a third was a clearly Greek name, known elsewhere as a Jewish name only at Leontopolis. See Ilan in Avni and Greenhut, *Akeldama Tombs*, 59; on Leontopolis, see Chapter 10.

6. Terence L. Donaldson, "Jerusalem Ossuary Inscriptions and the Status of Jewish Proselytes," in *Text and Artifact*, 372–88; here 377–78.

7. Donaldson, "Jerusalem Ossuary Inscriptions": "Maria the fervent [?] proselyte"; "Judah of Laganion, proselyte"; "Salome the proselyte"; "Judah the proselyte"; "Diogenes the proselyte [of?] Zena."

8. Avni and Greenhut, *Akeldama Tombs*, Ossuary 18; figs 2.13, 3.9: *megistês hierisês*.

9. Brooten, *Women Leaders*, ch. 10, concerning a Jewish "priestess" at Leontopolis. Ilan in Avni and Greenhut, *Akeldama Tombs*, 61–62, leans away from a priestly interpretation, though she notes a similar inscription at Beth She'arim.

10. Rahmani, *Catalogue*: No. 34, plate 5; 217, plate 31; 353, plate 50; 407, plate 58; 420. plate 61; 455, plate 66; 481, plate 71; 487, plate 73; 668, plate 95.

11. Rahmani, *Catalogue*, No. 14, plate 3; 294, plate 42, on front and back; perhaps 460, plate 67.

12. Rahmani, *Catalogue*, No. 200; plate 27: *shimôn banah hêkalah*, in Aramaic.

13. William Horbury and David Noy, *Jewish Inscriptions of Graeco-Roman Egypt* (Cambridge: Cambridge University Press, 1992), 243–45 (#153), for text, translation and summary. The inscription (found in 1902) was bilingual: *osta/tôn/tou/neikanoros/alexandeôs/poiêsantos/ta/thyas* (Greek); *nknr 'lk'* (Hebrew).

14. Some have argued this was not the Nicanor of the *Mishnah* and *Tosefta*, others the doors were merely the doors of Nicanor's tomb; the latter view was anticipated and refuted by C. Clermont-Ganneau, PEFQS 35 (1903): 125–31.

15. Finegan, *Archeology*, 357–59.

16. A. Buechler, "The Nicanor Gate and the Brass Gate," *JQR* 11 (1898–99): 46–63, claimed the gate was between the Court of the Women and the Court of Israel,

but between the Court of Women and the rampart is likelier.

17. One of the doors was thrown into the sea to lighten the load and miraculously followed the ship; when the ship reached shore the gate was bobbing along beside (*t. Yoma* 2:4; *b. Yoma* 38a).

18. *Herod*, 205.

19. Avni and Greenhut, *Akeldama Tombs*, 25–30; plans 1.9–13 and figs. 1.37–59 and color plates.

20. *City and Sanctuary*, passim.

Chapter Eighteen

1. This chapter was written for submission to a journal in March/April 2003. When events continued to move speedily, I withdrew it, anticipating the IAA's final report on the ossuary's authenticity. I let it stand more or less as it was then, with a short postscript on the report.

2. André Lemaire, "Burial Box of James the Brother of Jesus," *BAR* 28/6 (2002): 24–33, and subsequent articles, especially in *BAR*.

3. "Israel's Antiquities Authority began studying an ancient stone box yesterday. . . .," *Toronto Globe and Mail*, 6 March 2003. The examination has been completed and the report written, but it was still not fully accessible when the penultimate draft of this chapter was written in September 2003.

4. Hershel Shanks and Ben Witherington III, *The Brother of Jesus: The Dramatic Story & Meaning of the First Archaeological Link to Jesus & His Family* (San Francisco: Harper, 2003); Byron R. McCane, *Roll Back the Stone: Death and Burial in the World of Jesus* (Harrisburg: Trinity Press International, 2003), 27–60, contextually situates the ossuary; Craig A. Evans, *Jesus and the Ossuaries* (Waco, Texas: Baylor University Press, 2003), 112–22.

5. I examined the ossuary on 7 January 2003 with members of the ROM staff, courtesy of Ed Keall.

6. Two panels were convened at the annual meeting of the SBL in Toronto, one at the ROM (23 November 2002: Ed Keall, Oded Golan, Hershel Shanks, Peter Richardson, Kyle McCarter, and Ben Witherington); the other at the SBL (24 November 2002: André Lemaire, Steve Mason, Eric Meyers, John Painter, and Hershel Shanks, with Golan in the audience). For Paul Flesher's report, see *http://www.bibleinterp.com/articles/The_experts.htm*.

7. Rahmani, *Catalogue*, provides the primary collection of examples for comparison.

8. Discussion by John Lupia on the museums' security Web site, discussing the James ossuary http://www.museum-security.org/02/139.html#8. The IAA's study has now concluded the patina has been fabricated.

9. On the latter see Hershel Shanks, "Is It or Isn't It? King Jehoash Inscription Captivates Archaeological World," *BAR* 29 (2003): 22–23, 69. The IAA Final Report links discussion of the Jehoash tablet with the James ossuary.

10. Lemaire, "Burial Box"; Shanks and Witherington, *Brother of Jesus*, 18.

11. Rochelle I. Altman, "Final Report on the James Ossuary," arguing against genuineness: *http://web.infoave.net/~jwest/ossuary.html*. The article makes pertinent observations alongside erroneous statements. Altman dates alterations to the third or fourth century, Flesher to the second to sixth/seventh centuries.

12. The latter view could never be proved; DNA analysis of bone fragments would prove nothing.

13. John Painter, *Just James: The Brother of Jesus in History and Tradition* (Minneapolis: Fortress, 1999); Shanks and Witherington, *Brother of Jesus*, part II.

14. Russell Martin argues in a University of Toronto dissertation that Josephus's editorial addition is an attack on his opponents, "the fair-minded in Jerusalem." Cf. John W. Marshall and Russell Martin, "Government and Public Law in Galilee, Judaea, Hellenistic Cities, and the Empire," in *Handbook of Early Christianity: Social Science Approaches* (ed. Anthony J. Blasi et al.; Walnut Creek: Altamira, 2002), 409–29.

15. McCane, *Roll Back the Stone*, 93–106.

16. The dimensions given in McCane, *Roll Back the Stone*, 142, and in Shanks and Witherington, *Brother of Jesus*, 71–72, are incorrect. No two parallel dimensions are exactly the same. Its approximate dimensions in cm are Back: B = 53, L = 28.5, R = 28, T = 57; Left End: B = 24, L = 28, R = 29, T = 24; Right End: B = 26, L = 30, R = 28.5, T = 25. The right front corner sits 2.5 cm above a plane surface. The top's slides are 2.5 cm wide and .75 cm deep. Rahmani, *Catalogue*, p. 6, gives a range of sizes: 42–68 cm long, 23–28 cm.

17. The phenomenon is well known; an extreme example is the Stone of Unction in the Church of the Holy Sepulcher. In less extreme forms, it can be seen in the upper edge of the sarcophagus lid at Khirbet Qana, which forms the front of an altar holding six stone jugs; see Chapters 4–6, above.

18. Shanks and Witherington, *Brother of Jesus*, 72; McCane, *Roll Back the Stone*, 142, incorrectly.

19. Rahmani, *Catalogue*, No. 253 (plate 37) from Jerusalem, has a double frame on all sides; cf. also Nos. 625, 626 from Mt. Scopus (both plate 91), and Nos. 763 (on three sides), 764 (on one side; both plate 109), both from Jericho.

20. McCane, *Roll Back the Stone*, 142: "preliminary marks used by the carvers for creating rosettes."

21. Rahmani, *Catalogue*, pp. 31–32; see figs. 26, 27; Nos. 199, 231, 465, 473, 730, 814, 825, 837.

22. The *nefesh* represents "I die," the crab represents the month of July. Yodefat fell on 20 July 67 C.E.; a photo is at *http://www.israel.org.mfao/go.asp?MFAJ088j0*.

23. Rahmani, *Catalogue*, p. 124.

24. Steven Fine reports an ossuary in the Cincinnati Art Museum with what may be a picture of Queen Helena's three pyramids on the front face between a pair of rosettes: *http://www.uc.edu/news/fine.htm*.

25. The tomb has recently been restudied by Hebrew University's Ancient Art section. They were skeptical of the tomb's attribution to Herod, but considered the monument a *nefesh*: "architectural elements . . . found near the tomb were considered to be part of the upper section" by the nineteenth–twentieth century excavators, and "some of these architectural elements [were] tucked away in the terrace of the modern park"; see *www.hum.huji.ac.il/cja/NL13-Herod.htm*.

26. McCane, *Roll Back the Stone*, 41, says "slightly more than 40 percent" are in Greek.

27. Rahmani, *Catalogue*, No. 200; plate 27; see also Chapter 17.

28. Rahmani, *Catalogue*, No. 218.

29. Rahmani, *Catalogue*, No. 217.

30. Rahmani, *Catalogue*, Nos. 70–79.

31. Altman introduced the question of status and writing in her "Final Report," correctly emphasizing that status pertains to the survivors.

32. Shanks, *Brother of Jesus*, says "the day's wages of a skilled artisan could buy an ossuary"; he thinks 15 inscriptions "were carved with great care, in formal script" (73–74).

33. Rahmani, *Catalogue*, Nos. 70, 71, and esp. 75.

34. Rahmani, *Catalogue*, No. 117.

35. Rahmani, *Catalogue*, No. 893, plate 135.

36. *Herod*, 235, 243.

37. Rahmani, *Catalogue*, No. 41, plate 6; see also p. 85.

38. Avni and Greenhut, *Akeldama Tombs*.

39. Rahmani, *Catalogue*, No. 198.

40. Altman, "Final Report," observed the evidence of "over-carving," though she has incorrectly understood the situation, since she could not examine it first-hand. She says the first part of the inscription "was very probably written by the eldest son of a second generation, nouveau riche mercantile family . . . [with] commercial connections in both Alexandria and Jerusalem. This would also accord with the *nefesh*, or pyramids, found among the tombs in the Kidron Valley." Her instinct about the *nefesh* is interesting, because she had not seen the sketch described above. She comments that the second part of the inscription "is a poorly executed, mostly commercial cursive without any sign of wedges. . . ." Her conclusion is clear but incorrect: "The ossuary itself is undoubtedly genuine; the well-executed and formal first part of the inscription is a holographic original by a literate (and wealthy) survivor of Jacob bar Yosef, probably sometime during the Herodian period. The second part of the inscription bears the hallmarks of a fraudulent later addition probably around the third or fourth centuries, and is questionable to say the least."

41. Report of the Geological Survey of Israel, Lemaire, "Burial Box," 29.

42. Curiously, the Survey also comments that "no signs of the use of a modern tool or instrument was [sic] found. No evidence that might detract from the authenticity of the patina and the inscription was found."

43. Flesher, "The Aramaic Dialect of the James Ossuary Inscription" (draft, courtesty of the author) says, "If the 'several letters' from which the patina is missing are those of the second half of the inscription, then this would suggest a modern forgery." His correct intuition is vitiated by the fact that the alterations are mainly to the first half. Golan said (ROM panel) he had not cleaned it, though his mother may have.

44. Flesher concludes that "the dialect of the second part of the inscription . . . conforms to the . . . dialect used in Galilee from the late second to the seventh centuries." *www.bibleinterp.com/articles/James_Ossuary.htm*.

45. Shanks and Witherington, *Brother of Jesus*, 56, citing Hachlili's study.

46. Steve Mason, *Josephus and the New Testament* (Peabody: Hendrickson, 1991), 163–84.

47. Shanks and Witherington, *Brother of Jesus*, 54–63; Shanks summarizes the calculations of André Lemaire (twenty persons with 5 percent probability) and Camil Fuchs (two to four persons with 25–50 percent probability).

48. Avni and Greenhut, *Akeldama Tombs*, 33, 35; Cave 3 belonged to wealthy Syrian Jews.

49. Roman criteria do not apply, though the epigraphic habit was present. There was little interest in uniformity or regularity, conventions that were irrelevant in private burial inscriptions.

50. On individualism, Eyal Regev, "The Individualistic Meaning of Jewish Ossuaries: A Socio-Anthropological Perspective on Burial Practice," *PEQ* 133 (2001): 39–49; McCane, *Roll Back the Stone*, 14–15; 42–47.

51. S. Kent Brown, "Souls, Pre-existence of," *ABD* 6.161, noting both Jewish (Josephus, Philo, the Wisdom of Solomon, and 2 Enoch) and Christian interest (Paul and Gnosticizing elements).

52. James D. G. Dunn, "On the Relation of Text and Artifact: Some Cautionary Tales," in *Text and Artifact*, 192–206, especially 200: "Ossuaries have been particularly fruitful. The growth of the practice during the Herodian period . . . strengthens the view that hope for a physical resurrection . . . became firmly established during that period."

Chapter Nineteen

1. Josephus suggests that in the Idumean case this was forced conversion. That is less likely than a process partly the result of military conquest and partly voluntary; Aryeh Kasher, *Jews, Idumaeans and Ancient Arabs* (Tübingen: J. C. B. Mohr, 1988), especially 46–78. Some Idumean converts became its strongest supporters, as roles in the Great Revolt imply. Material evidence underscores converts' wish to be buried in Jerusalem; T. L. Donaldson, "Jerusalem Ossuary Inscriptions and the Status of Jewish Proselytes," in *Text and Artifact*, 372–88.

2. Andrea Berlin, "Romanization and anti-Romanization in pre-Revolt Galilee, in *The First Jewish Revolt: Archaeology, History, and Ideology* (ed. Anrea Berlin and J. Andrew Overman; London: Routledge, 2002), 57–73, has a perceptive discussion of relevant evidence.

3. Richard N. Longenecker, "'Good Luck on your Resurrection': Beth She'arim and Paul on Resurrection of the Dead," in *Text and Artifact*, 249–70.

4. McCane, *Roll Back the Stone*.

5. Peter Richardson, "Jewish Galilee's Hellenization, Romanization, and Commercialization," in *New Views of First-Century Jewish and Christian Self-Definition* (ed. Fabian Udoh, *Christianity and Judaism in Antiquity*; South Bend: University of Notre Dame Press, forthcoming).

6. Carol Meyers, "Cherubim," *ABD* 1:899–900, with references.

7. Edward M. Curtis, "Idol, Idolatry," *ABD* 3:376–81, for summary and discussion.

8. Ehud Netzer, "Tyros, the 'Floating Palace'," in *Text and Artifact*, 340–53.

9. On Caesarea Maritima and Jerusalem, see *City and Sanctuary*, chs. 5, 6.

10. *City and Sanctuary*, chs. 2–4, 7.

11. Peter Richardson, "Judaism and Christianity in Corinth after Paul: Texts and Material Evidence," in *Pauline Conversations in Context: Essays in Honor of Calvin J. Roetzel* (ed. Janice Cappel Anderson, Philip Sellew, and Claudia Setzer; Sheffield: Sheffield Academic Press, 2002), 42–66.

GLOSSARY

Acropolis/Akropolis. Citadel or fortified upper part of a city.

Adyton. Sanctuary or inner shrine, especially of a Syrian temple.

Agora. Greek public space for civic and commercial purposes (cf. *forum*).

Amphitheater. Elliptical or oval theater-like building for gladiatorial games or combat, such as the Colosseum in Rome.

Amphora/amphorae. Wine jug.

Architrave. Structural member, usually stone, spanning between columns or piers.

Arcosolium/arcosolia. Wide arched recess in wall of tomb, carved in bedrock, for laying out body.

Ashlar wall. Masonry of rectangular stones laid in regular horizontal courses.

Balk. In excavations, the one-meter strip left in place between adjacent squares (typically on a 5x5 m grid), maintaining a record of the sequence of layers (strata).

Ballista. A large military catapult for hurling stones during a siege.

Basilica. Rectangular building, usually with two rows of columns, side aisles, apse, and higher roof over the central space with clerestory windows.

Beth ha-Midrash. Literally, "house of study": a room, usually with benches, attached to a synagogue as a space for education, interpretive discussions, and the like.

Bouleutêrion. Council chamber.

Cardo maximus. Main street of Roman city, often aligned north-south.

Casemate wall. Defensive structure with two parallel walls joined at intervals by cross walls, sometimes with houses integrated into it.

Cavea. Seating area of a theater.

Cella. Holy place in a temple where the statue of the god was placed.

Circumvallation. Wall built by besieging forces around a town or city to prevent inhabitants from escaping.

Circus: *see* Hippodrome.

Clerestory. High windows above nave lighting basilica or church or synagogue.

Clivus/clivi. Latin for "slope"; hence the term for streets that climb hills (cf. *vicus*).

Colonia. A privileged form of municipal status; originally military colony.

Columbarium/colmbaria. Dovecote: a circular structure above ground or a cave below ground, with small niches for nesting doves or pigeons.

379

Cryptoportico. Literally, hidden portico; vaulted structure below ground level, usually for storage.

Decumanus. Principal cross street of city, often east-west.

Diadochoi. Collective name for Alexander's generals (Antigonus, Antipater, Seleucus, Ptolemy) who struggled for control of the Macedonian Empire after Alexander's death.

Domus dei. Literally "house of god"; a building specifically to house the god.

Domus ecclesiae. Literally "house of the community"; a structure for a group of worshipers.

Dromos. Entrance courtyard to a tomb.

Dunam. Unit of square measure: ten dunams make one hectare; approximately four dunams make an acre.

Engaged column. Column that projects from but is attached to a wall.

Entablature. Horizontal superstructure carried by a colonnade or wall.

Ethrog. Palm branch, used a a symbol, especially on synagogue mosaics.

Exedra. Semicircular or rectangular recess, often used as a seating area in a *stoa*.

Forum. Roman public space for civic and commercial purposes (cf. *agora*).

Frieze. Portion of entablature above the architrave, sometimes decorated (e.g., band of triglyphs and metopes in Doric order), sometimes plain.

Genizah. Small room off synagogue for storing discarded scrolls.

Gymnasium. Greek cultural and athletic institution, sometimes merged with bath.

Hasmonean. Family name of the Maccabees, who established a priestly ruling dynasty following a successful revolt against Syrian rule.

Hellenistic. Strictly speaking, period between 323 and 31 B.C.E. (death of Alexander to Battle of Actium); culture of that period and its continuation into Roman Imperial period.

Heroon. Building or enclosure dedicated to a hero (someone out of the ordinary, sometimes considered a demi-god).

Hippodamian plan. Plan of city with streets laid out at right angles, characteristic of Greek cities and sometimes applied to Roman cities.

Hippodrome. A long course, usually round at one end and square at the other, for horse races (Latin, *circus*).

Hypogeum. Literally, below the earth; a tomb carved out of bedrock below ground level.

Insula/ae. 1. Apartment building, usually occupying a whole block. 2. Individual city block in town planning context.

Kittim. Name by which the Romans are known in some of the Dead Sea Scrolls.

Komê. Small town or village.

Lêstai/lêsteia. Greek for "brigands/brigandage."

Levant. Old-fashioned term, still useful, for the regions along the eastern Mediterrean (roughly Syria, Lebanon, Israel, West Bank, Jordan).

Lintel. Beam over door or window carrying weight of masonry above.

Loculus/loculi. Literally, "little place": a niche for burial, usually about 2 m long, 0.5 m wide, 0.6 m high.

Lulav. Citron or lemon, used as a symbol, especially on synagogue mosaics

Maccabees: *see* Hasmonean.

Martyrium. Place to deposit relics of martyrs.

Menorah. Seven-branched candlestick, originally part of the furniture of the Court of Priests.

Merlons. Crenellation surmounting wall or entablature, in Syria often of crow-step design.

Mikveh/mikvaoth. A small immersion pool for purposes of ritual purity; some were domestic, some public.

Mishnah. Early third-century C.E. document, containing legal discussions and judgments of rabbinic authorities, originally orally transmitted.

Mithraeum. A temple for the worship of Mithra, usually designed to simulate a cave, with benches along the side walls.

Naos. Holy place or inner shrine where the god dwelled.

Necropolis. Literally, "city of the dead"; an area in which tombs are found.

Nymphaeum/nymphaea. Public fountain; literally "place for nymphs" (or water spirits).

Odeion. Small, usually roofed, theater (Latin, *odeum*) used primarily for lectures and concerts.

Oecus. Living area of a Hellenistic house.

Opus incertum. Roman wall of irregularly shaped small stones with concrete core.

Opus quadratum. Roman wall of small squared stones with concrete core.

Opus reticulatum. Roman wall of small stones laid in a diagonal pattern with concrete core.

Opus sectile. Decorative paving of geometric marble slabs, usually in several colors.

Orchestra. In a Roman theater, semicircular area (in a Greek theater, circular area) between the stage and cavea.

Ossuary. Small limestone "bone box" for secondary burial of bones after flesh decomposed.

Paradeisos. Park or pleasure ground, often in a royal palace; garden.

Pediment. Gabled end of a roof (i.e., tympanum plus raking cornice).

Peribolos. Wall encircling a temple or precinct.

Peripteral. With a continuous row of columns around perimeter.

Peristyle. A courtyard with columns on four sides; often used in domestic-scale courtyards.

Podium. Platform supporting temple or other structure.

Polis/poleis. City (in Greek), usually with a surrounding area of land to support it.

Pronaos. Area in front of *naos*; porch of temple.

Propylaea. Entrance to enclosure, often in a religious sanctuary.

Rolling Stone. Large, crudely rounded stone used by defenders to roll down onto besieging force.

Scaenae. Stage of a Roman theater (Greek, *skênê*). *Scaenae frons* was the stage's backdrop.

Soreg. Literally "barricade" in the Jerusalem temple outside the Court of Women.

Stadium. A long course, often round at one end and square at the other, for foot races.

Stele. Upright stone slab for inscriptions, reliefs, and graves.

Stoa/stoai. Long, narrow, roofed and colonnaded structure (often two-storied).

Stylos. Column; used in the form distyle (two columns), tetrastyle (four columns), hexastyle (six columns), etc. When used with anta (projecting ends of walls), as in tetrastyle-in-antis, it refers to four columns between the projecting ends of walls in a façade.

Stylobate. Foundation supporting a row of columns.

Syrian arch (arcuated lintel). Arch over central opening of a horizontal entablature in a façade.

Tablinum. Central room at back of *atrium* in a Roman house, originally the main bedroom.

Tabun. Spherical oven in domestic context for baking flat bread.

Talmud. Later compilation of Jewish law (fifth/sixth centuries C.E.), expanding on the earlier *Mishnah*.

Temenos. Piece of land dedicated to a god; precinct of a temple or sanctuary enclosing the *naos*.

Tetrapylon. Square, monumental arch at a major intersection with two intersecting passageways.

Tetrakionion. Structure with four groups of four columns marking a major intersection.

Theater. In a Roman theater the *cavea* and orchestra were semicircles, and the stage was usually as wide as the *cavea* and as high as the rear row of seats. In a Greek/Hellenistic theater the cavea was more than a semicircle, the orchestra circular and the stage relatively small.

Theatron. Often used of a informal raked seating area in a religious structure, as distinct from theater.

Triclinium/triclinia. Dining room (literally, "three benches"), with benches on three sides of a room.

Tympanum. Vertical face of pediment below the raking cornice.

Vicus/vici. Latin for "town, village, quarter"; used derivatively for streets, especially those on the level (cf. *clivus/clivi*).

Wadi. A dry river bed, usually filled with water during the winter rains.

Xystos. Covered colonnade in gymnasium; garden.

FURTHER READING

Introductory and General Matters

Ball, Warwick. *Rome in the East: The Transformation of an Empire*. London: Routledge, 2000.

Esler, Philip F., ed. *Modelling Early Christianity: Social Scientific Studies of the New Testament in its Context*. London: Routledge, 1995.

Richardson, Peter. *City and Sanctuary: Religion and Architecture in the Roman Near East*. London: SCM, 2002.

Rousseau, John J. and Rami Arav. *Jesus and his World: An Archaeological and Cultural Dictionary*. Minneapolis: Fortress, 1995.

Sanders, E. P. *Judaism: Practice and Belief: 63 B.C.E.–66 C.E.* Philadelphia: Trinity Press International, 1992.

Schürer, Emil, et al. *The History of the Jewish People in the Age of Jesus Christ (175 B.C.–A.D. 135)*. 3 vols. Edinburgh: T&T Clark, 1973–1987.

Turner, Harold W. *From Temple to Meeting House. The Phenomenology and Theology of Places of Worship*. Religion and Society 16. The Hague: Mouton, 1979.

Wilson, Stephen G. and Michel Desjardins, eds. *Text and Artifact: Essays in Honour of Peter Richardson*. Etudes sur le christianisme et le judaïsme 9; Waterloo: Wilfrid Laurier University Press, 2000.

PART I. TOWNS AND VILLAGES

Galilee and the Golan

Aviam, Mordechai and Peter Richardson. "Josephus's Galilee in Archaeological Perspective." Pages 177–209 in *Josephus, Translation and Commentary*. Edited by Steve N. Mason. Vol. 9. Appendix A. Leiden: Brill, 2000

Aviam, Mordechai. *Jews, Christians and Pagans in the Galilee: 25 Years of Archaeological Excavations and Surveys Hellenistic to Byzantine Periods*. Land of Galilee 1. Rochester: University of Rochester Press, forthcoming.

Crossan, John Dominic and Jonathan Reed. *Excavating Jesus: Beneath the Stones, Behind the Texts*. San Francisco: Harper, 2001.

Dar, Shimon. *Settlements and Cult Sites on Mount Hermon, Israel: Ituraean Culture in the Hellenistic and Roman Periods*. Oxford: Tempus Reparatum, 1993.

Edwards, Douglas R. and C. Thomas McCullough, eds. *Archaeology and the Galilee: Texts and Contexts in the Graeco-Roman and Byzantine Periods*. South Florida Studies in the History of Judaism 143. Atlanta: Scholars Press, 1997.

Freyne, Sean. *Galilee, Jesus and the Gospels: Literary Approaches and Historical Investigations*. Dublin: Gill and Macmillan, 1988.

Gregg, Robert C. and Dan Urman. *Jews, Pagans, and Christians in the Golan Heights*. South Florida Studies in the History of Judaism 140. Atlanta: Scholars Press, 1996.

Horsley, Richard A. *Archaeology, History, and Society in Galilee: The Social Context of Jesus and the Rabbis*. Valley Forge: Trinity Press International, 1996.

Horsley, Richard A. *Galilee: History, Politics, People: The Social Context of Jesus and the Rabbis*. Valley Forge: Trinity Press International, 1995.

Levine, Lee I., ed. *The Galilee in Late Antiquity*. New York: Jewish Theological Seminary, 1992.

Meyers, Eric M., ed. *Galilee through the Centuries: Confluence of Cultures*. Duke Judaic Studies Series 1. Winona Lake, Ind.: Eisenbrauns, 1999.

Reed, Jonathan L. *Archaeology and the Galilean Jesus: A Re-examination of the Evidence*. Harrisburg: Trinity Press International, 2000.

House, Family, and Village

Amiry, Suad and Vera Tamari. *The Palestinian Village Home*. London: British Museum, 1989.

Arnal, William E. *Jesus and the Village Scribes: Galilean Conflicts and the Setting of Q*. Minneapolis: Fortress Press, 2001.

Balch, David L. and Carolyn Osiek, eds. *Early Chrisitan Families in Context: An Interdisciplinary Dialogue*. Grand Rapids: Wm. B. Eerdmans, 2003.

Frankel, Rafael, Nimrod Getzov, et al. *Settlement Dynamics and Regional Diversity in Ancient Upper Galilee: Archaeological Survey of Upper Galilee*. Jerusalem: Israel Antiquities Authority, 200.

Hanson, K. C. and Douglas E. Oakman. *Palestine in the Time of Jesus: Social Structures and Social Conflicts*. Minneapolis: Fortress, 1998.

Hirschfeld, Yizhar. *The Palestinian Dwelling in the Roman-Byzantine Period*. Jerusalem: Franciscan Printing Press, 1995.

Mackay, A. G. *Houses, Villas and Palaces in the Roman World*. London: Thames and Hudson, 1975.

Moxnes, Halvor, ed. *Constructing Early Christian Families*. London: Routledge, 1997.

Oporto, Santiago Guijarro. *Fidelidades en Conflicto: La Ruptura con la Familia por Causa del Discipulado y de la Mission en la Tradición Sinóptica*. Plenitudo Temporis 4. Salamanca: Publicaciones Universidad Pontificia, 1998.

Osiek, Carolyn and David L. Balch. *Families in the New Testament World: Households and House Churches*. Louisville: Westminster John Knox, 1997.

Selected Excavations

Bethsaida: Arav, Rami and Richard Freund, eds. *Bethsaida: A City by the North Seashore of the Sea of Galilee*. Kirksville: Thomas Jefferson University Press, 1995.

Capernaum: Corbo, Virgilio. *The House of St. Peter at Capernaum: A Preliminary Report of the First Two Campaigns of Excavations: April 16–June 19, Sept. 12–Nov 26, 1968*. Jerusalem: Franciscan Printing Press, 1969; Corbo, Virgilio. *Cafarnao*, vol. 1, *Gli edifici della città*. Studium Biblicum Franciscanum 19. Jerusalem, Franciscan Printing Press, 1975; Taylor, Joan. *Christians and the Holy Places: The Myth of Jewish-Christian Origins*. Oxford: Clarendon, 1993.

Gamla: Gutman, Shemaryahu. "Gamala," *NEAEHL* 2:459–63.

Keren Naftali: Aviam, Mordechai. "A Second-First Century B.C.E. Fortress and Siege Complex in Eastern Upper Galilee," in *Archaeology and the Galilee: Texts and Contexts in the Graeco-Roman and Byzantine Periods*. Edited by Douglas R. Edwards and C. Thomas McCollough. South Florida Studies in the History of Judaism 143; Atlanta: Scholars Press, 1997.

Yodefat: Adan-Bayewitz, David and Mordechai Aviam. "Jotapata, Josephus, and the Siege of 67: Preliminary Report on the 1992–94 Seasons." *Journal of Roman Archaeology* 10 (1997): 131–65.

Meiron: Meyers, Eric M., et al. *The Excavations at Ancient Meiron, Upper Galilee, Israel, 1971–72, 1974–75, 1977*. Cambridge, Mass.: American Schools of Oriental Research, 1981.

PART II. SYNAGOGUES AND CHURCHES

Voluntary Associations

Harland, Philip A. *Associations, Synagogues, and Congregations: Claiming a Place in Ancient Mediterranean Society*. Minneapolis: Fortress, 2003.
Hermansen, Gustav. *Ostia, Aspects of Roman City Life*. Edmonton: University of Alberta Press, 1982.
Kloppenborg, John and Steven G. Wilson, eds. *Voluntary Associations in the Graeco-Roman World*. Routledge: London and New York, 1996.
Longenecker, Richard N., ed. *Community Formation in the Early Church and in the Church Today*. Peabody: Hendrickson, 2002.

Jewish Synagogues

Binder, Donald D. *Into the Temple Courts: The Place of the Synagogue in the Second Temple Period*. SBLDS 169. Atlanta: Society of Biblical Literature, 1999.
Levine, Lee I. *The Ancient Synagogue: The First Thousand Years*. New Haven: Yale University Press, 2000.
Lifshitz, B. *Donateurs et fondateurs dans les synagogues juives*. Paris: Gabalda, 1967.
Olsson, Birger and Magnus Zetterholm, eds. *The Ancient Synagogue From Its Origins until 200 C.E.: Papers Presented at an International Conference at Lund University October 14–17, 2001*. Coniectanea Biblica NT Series 39. Stockholm: Almqvist and Wiksell, 2003.
Olsson, Birger, Dieter Mitternacht, and Olof Brandt, eds. *The Synagogue of Ancient Ostia and the Jews of Rome*. Stockholm: Paul Åstrom, 2003.
Runesson, Anders. *The Origins of the Synagogue: A Socio-Historical Study*. Stockholm: Almqvist and Wiksell, 2001.
Urman, Dan and Paul V. M. Flesher, eds. *Ancient Synaogogues: Historical Analysis and Archaeological Discoveries*. StPB 47.1–2. Leiden: Brill, 1994.

Samaritan Synagogues

Dar, Shimon. "Samaria: Region, The Survey of Western Samaria." *NEAEHL* 4:1313–16.

Pummer, R. "Samaritan Synagogues and Jewish Synagogues: Similarities and Differences." Pages 118–60 in *Jews, Christians, and Polytheists in the Ancient Synagogue.* Edited by Steven Fine. London: Routledge, 1999.

Egyptian Judaism

Kasher, Aryeh. *The Jews in Hellenistic and Roman Egypt.* Tübingen: J. C. B. Mohr, 1985.

Pomeroy, S. B. *Women in Hellenistic Egypt.* New York: Schocken Books, 1984.

Robins, Gay. *Women in Ancient Egypt.* London: British Musuem Press, 1993.

Sly, Dorothy. *Philo's Perception of Women.* Atlanta: Scholars Press, 1990.

Tcherikover, V. *Hellenistic Civilization and the Jews.* Philadelphia: Jewish Publication Society of America, 1959.

Churches and Monasteries

Blue, Bradley. "Acts and the House Church." Pages 119–222 in *The Book of Acts in its Graeco-Roman Setting.* Vol. 2 of *The Book of Acts in its First Century Setting.* Edited by David. W. J. Gill and Conrad Gempf. Grand Rapids: Wm. B. Eerdmans/Carlisle: Paternoster, 1994.

Chitty, D. J. *The Desert a City: An Introduction to the Study of Egyptian and Palestinian Monasticism under the Christian Empire.* Oxford: Basil Blackwell, 1966.

Guillaumont, A. *Aux origines du monachisme chrétien.* Spiritualité orientale 30. Bégrolles-en-Mauges: Abbaye de Bellefontaine, 1979.

Krautheimer, R. *Early Christian and Byzantine Architecture.* Harmondsworth: Penguin, 1979.

Meeks, Wayne. *The First Urban Christians.* New Haven: Yale University Press, 1983.

Milburn, Robert. *Early Christian Art and Architecture.* Berkeley: University of California Press, 1988.

Snyder, Graydon F. *Ante Pacem: Archaeological Evidence of Church Life before Constantine.* Macon: Mercer University Press, 1985.

Tsafrir, Yoram, ed. *Ancient Churches Revealed.* Jerusalem: Israel Exploration Society/Washington: Biblical Archaeology Society, 1993.

White, L. Michael. *The Social Origins of Christian Architecture.* 2 vols. Valley Forge: Trinity Press International, 1996, 1997.

Selected Excavations

Ostia: White, L. Michael. "Synagogue and Society in Imperial Ostia: Archaeological and Epigraphic Evidence." Pages 30–63 in *Judaism and Christianity in First-Century Rome.* Edited by Karl P. Donfried and Peter Richardson. Grand Rapids: Wm. B. Eerdmans, 1998; Runesson, Anders. "The Oldest Original Synagogue Building in the Diaspora: A Response to L. Michael White." *HTR* 92 (1999): 409–33.

Delos: McLean, B. Hudson. "The Place of Cult in Voluntary Associations and Christian Churches on Delos." Pages 186–225 in *Voluntary Associations*. Edited by John S. Kloppenborg and Stephen G. Wilson. London: Routledge, 1996; White, Michael L. "The Delos Synagogue Revisited: Recent Fieldwork in the Graeco-Roman Diaspora." *HTR* 80/2 (1987): 33–60.

Kellia: Daumas, F. and A. Guillaumont. *Kellia 1, Kom 219: Fouilles exécuté au 1964 et 1965*. 2 vols. Cairo: L'Institut français d'archéologie orientale, 1969; Kasser, R. *Kellia 1965: Topographie générale, mensurations at fouilles aux Qouçoûr*. Geneva: Georg. 1967; Kasser, R. *Kellia: Topographie*. Geneva: Georg, 1972; Kasser, R. *Survey archéologique des Kellia (Basse-Égypte) Rapport de la campagne 1981*. 2 vols. Leuven: Peeters, 1983; Kasser, R. *Les Kellia, ermitages coptes en Basse-Egypte*. Geneva: Editions de Tricorne, 1989.

Chorazin: Yeivin, Ze'ev. *The Synagogue at Korazim: The 1962–1964, 1980–1987 Excavations*. Jerusalem: Israel Antiquities Authority, 2000.

Sepphoris: Martin Nagy, Rebecca, Carol L. Meyers, Eric M. Meyers, and Zeev Weiss, eds. *Sepphoris in Galilee: Crosscurrents of Culture*. Chapel Hill: North Carolina Museum of Art, 1996; Weiss, Ze'ev and Ehud Netzer. *Promise and Redemption: A Synagogue Mosaic from Sepphoris*. Jerusalem: Israel Museum, 1996.

PART III. JUDEA AND JERUSALEM

Judea

Eshel, Hanan and Peter Richardson. "Josephus' Judea, Samaria, and Perea: An Archaeological Perspective." in *Josephus: War 1–3*. Edited by Joseph Sievers and Steve Mason. Leiden: Brill, forthcoming.

Finegan, Jack. *Archeology of the New Testament*. 2d ed. Princeton: Princeton University Press, 1992.

Kasher, Aryeh. *Jews, Idumaeans and Ancient Arabs*. Tübingen: J. C. B. Mohr, 1988.

McLaren, James S. *Power and Politics in Palestine: The Jews and the Governing of their Land 100 BC–AD 70*. Sheffield: Sheffield Academic Press, 1991.

Smallwood, E. Mary. *The Jews Under Roman Rule*. 2d ed. Boston/Leiden: Brill, 2001.

Jerusalem and its Archaeology

Bahat, Dan. *The Illustrated Atlas of Jerusalem*. New York: Simon and Schuster, 1990.

Ben Dov, Meir. *In the Shadow of the Temple. The Discovery of Ancient Jerusalem*. Jerusalem: Keter, 1982.

Kenyon, Kathleen. *Digging up Jerusalem*. New York: Praeger, 1974.

Levine, Lee I. *Jerusalem: Portrait of the City in the Second Temple Period (538 B.C.E.–70 C.E.)*. Philadelphia: Jewish Publication Society, 2002.

Mare, W. Harold. *The Archaeology of the Jerusalem Area*. Grand Rapids: Baker, 1987.

Mazar, Benjamin. *The Mountain of the Lord*. New York: Doubleday, 1975.

Ritmeyer, Kathleeen and Leen. "Reconstructing Herod's Temple Mount in Jerusalem," *BAR* 15/6 (1989): 23–53.

Ritmeyer, Leen. "Locating the Original Temple Mount," *BAR* 18 (1992): 24–45, 64–65.

Wilkinson, John. *Jerusalem as Jesus Knew it: Archaeology as Evidence.* London: Thames and Hudson, 1978.

Herod the Great and His Buildings

Grant, Michael. *Herod the Great.* New York: American Heritage, 1971.

Kokkinos, Nikos. *The Herodian Dynasty: Origins, Role in Society and Eclipse.* Sheffield: Sheffield Academic Press, 1998.

Lichtenberger, Achim. *Die Baupolitik Herodes des Grossen.* Wiesbaden: Harrassowitz, 1999.

Richardson, Peter, *Herod, King of the Jews and Friend of the Romans.* Minneapolis: Fortress, 1999 [1996].

Roller, Duane W. *The Building Program of Herod the Great.* Berkeley: University of California Press, 1998.

Schalit, Abraham. *Koenig Herodes: Der Mann und sein Werk.* Berlin: de Gruyter, 1969.

The Jerusalem Temple

Barker, Margaret. *The Gate of Heaven: The History and Symbolism of the Temple in Jerusalem.* London: SPCK, 1991.

Brooke, George J., ed. *Temple Scroll Studies.* JSPSup 7; Sheffield: JSOT Press, 1989.

Busink, T. A. *Der Tempel von Jerusalem.* Leiden: Brill, 1970.

Reich, Ronny, Gideon Avni, and Tamar Winter. *Jerusalem Archaeological Park.* Jerusalem: Israel Antiqities Authority, 1999.

Rosenau, Helen. *Visions of the Temple. The Image of the Temple of Jerusalem in Judaism and Christianity.* London: Orseko, 1979.

Yadin, Yigael. *The Temple Scroll.* 3 vols. in 4. Jerusalem: Israel Exploration Society, 1977–1983.

Yadin, Yigael. *The Temple Scroll.* New York: Random House, 1985.

Death, Burial, and Tombs

Avni, Gideon and Zvi Greenhut. *The Akeldama Tombs: Three Burial Caves in the Kidron Valley, Jerusalem.* Jerusalem: Israel Antiquities Authority, 1996.

Bloch-Smith, Elizabeth. *Judahite Burial Practices and Beliefs about the Dead.* Sheffield: JSOT Press, 1992.

Evans, Craig A. *Jesus and the Ossuaries.* Waco, Texas: Baylor University Press, 2003.

Hachlili, Rachel. *Ancient Jewish Art and Archaeology in the Land of Israel.* Leiden: Brill, 1988.

McCane, Byron R. *Roll Back the Stone: Death and Burial in the World of Jesus.* Harrisburg: Trinity Press International, 2003.

Meyers, Eric M. *Jewish Ossuaries: Burial and Rebirth.* Rome: Biblical Institute Press, 1971.

Pearson, Mike Peter. *The Archaeology of Death and Burial*. Stroud, Gloucestershire: Sutton, 1999.

Rahmani, L. Y. *A Catalogue of Jewish Ossuaries in the Collections of the State of Israel*. Jerusalem: Israel Antiquities Authority/Israel Academy of Sciences and Humanities, 1994.

Shanks, Hershel and Ben Witherington III. *The Brother of Jesus: The Dramatic Story & Meaning of the First Archaeological Link to Jesus & His Family*. San Francisco: Harper, 2003.

Josephus

Cohen, Shaye J. D. *Josephus in Galilee and Rome*. Columbia Studies in the Classical Tradition 8. Leiden: Brill, 1979.

Mason, Steve, ed. *Understanding Josephus: Seven Perspectives*. JSPSup 32. Sheffield: Sheffield Academic Press, 1998.

Mason, Steve. *Josephus and the New Testament*. Peabody: Hendrickson, 1991.

Mason, Steve. *Josephus on the Pharisees: a Composition-Critical Study*. Leiden: Brill, 1991.

Rajak, Tessa. *Josephus. The Historian and His Society*. Philadelphia: Fortress Press, 1984.

Thackeray, H. St. John. *Josephus, the Man and the Historian*. New York: Jewish Institute of Religion Press, 1929.

Wacholder, B. Z. *Nicolaus of Damascus*. Berkeley: University of California Press, 1962.

Selected Excavations

Caesarea Maritima: Holum, Kenneth, Robert L. Hohlfelder, et al. *King Herod's Dream: Caesarea on the Sea*. New York: W. W. Norton, 1988; Raban, Avner and Kenneth G. Holum, *Caesarea Maritima: A Retrospective after Two Millennia*. Leiden: Brill, 1996.

Jericho: Netzer, Ehud. *Hasmonean and Herodian Palaces at Jericho: Final Reports of the 1973–1987 Excavations*. Jerusalem: Israel Exploration Society, 2001.

Herodium: Netzer, Ehud. *Greater Herodium*. Jerusalem: Institute of Archaeology, Hebrew University of Jerusalem, 1981.

Masada: Netzer, Ehud. *Masada: the Yigael Yadin Excavations 1963–1965, Final Reports: The Buildings, Stratigraphy and Architecture*. Vol. 3 of 6. Jerusalem: Israel Exploration Society, 1993; Yadin, Yigael. *Masada*. London: Weidenfeld and Nicolson, 1966; Nachman, Ben-Yahuda. *Sacrificing Truth: Archaeology and the Myth of Masada*. Amherst, N.Y.: Humanity Books, 2002.

INDEX OF ANCIENT SOURCES

INDEX OF MODERN AUTHORS

INDEX OF SITES AND PLACES

Plate 1. Gamla, general view to southwest. Gamla occupied one side of a very steep ridge, providing natural defenses on three sides. Josephus built the wall across the middle of the picture in the early stages of the Revolt, inserting short stretches of new walls between existing buildings. He mentions the circular tower where the wall meets the ridge. The synagogue's Beth ha-Midrash, at the lower left, was part of Josephus's wall.

Plate 2. Keren Naftali, view from the fortress to the southeast. The Huleh Valley, with its swamps is below the hill; in the distance are the Golan Heights. The Hasmoneans took the Tyrian fortress and occupied it. Later, brigands took it, but were besieged by Herod, after which it was no longer used. The remains of the fortress include walls, houses, and a huge mikveh.

Plate 3. Yodefat/Jotapata, view to north. The walled town occupied the hilltop and the southern plateau in the middle ground. The courtyard houses with mikvaoth were behind the foreground trees on the right; the terrace housing was around the right side of the hilltop. In the siege of 67 C.E. Vespasian camped on the hill in the background.

Plate 4. Khirbet Qana (Cana), view to south. Khirbet Qana visually dominated the Beth Netofa Valley with its fine agricultural land. The unwalled village occupied the hilltop and an intermediate terrace halfway down the hill on the south side (not visible). It was within sight of Nazareth Illit, on the distant hill; Sepphoris lay just off the right edge.

Plate 5. Yodefat, 3-D aerial view, view to south. The computer-generated image shows the hilltop town in the foreground with its defensive walls; the upper walls were from the Hellenistic period. The terrace housing is on the left slope; the southern plateau is in the rear. The Roman siege ramp rose up the slope on the right.
(Illustration courtesy of Bergmann Associates Visualization and Charles Hixon.)

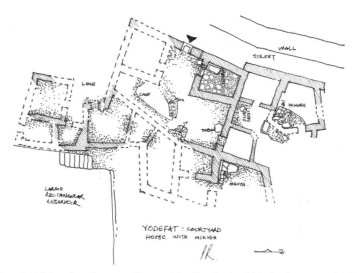

Plate 6. Yodefat, plan of courtyard house with mikveh. *A neighborhood was organized around a large rectangular pool between the hill and southern plateau. The reconstruction works partly from evidence of rock cut foundations. The collection basin for catching water from the roof is inside the door, a cistern on the other side of the wall. The house incorporated a natural cave and had a private* mikveh.

Plate 7. Yodefat, mikveh *in courtyard house, view to east. The small private ritual bathing pool had four steps down, a still visible channel for water on the lower left, and several layers of plaster in an excellent state of preservation. A column drum from a monumental building on the top had rolled down the hill into the* mikveh.

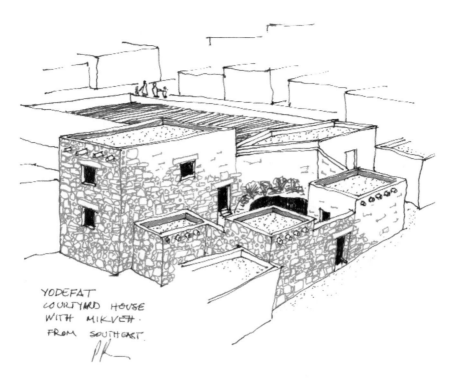

YODEFAT
COURTYARD HOUSE
WITH MIKVEH.
FROM SOUTHEAST

Plate 8. Yodefat, perspective, courtyard house with mikveh, view to northwest. The street
that gave access to the house sketched here was just inside the later town wall (not shown).
In the background is the open communal pool. Just visible as a part of the house's courtyard
is a natural cave, probably used for animals and storage.

Plate 9. Yodefat, courtyard house with mikveh, *view to southeast. On the right is the* mikveh, *on the left the room with paving and the cistern, and the courtyard in between. In the rear a second courtyard house also had a* mikveh. *Both houses open off a street just inside the wall built before the Revolt. Outside the wall was a cave with a large olive press.*

Plate 10. Yodefat, 3-D reconstruction, courtyard house with mikveh, *view to east. In the left corner of a main room was the cistern, which was fed from water collected from the roof. The roof construction used small beams with a mud-packed surface, renewed every year (Illustration courtesy of Bergmann Associates Visualization and Charles Hixon.)*

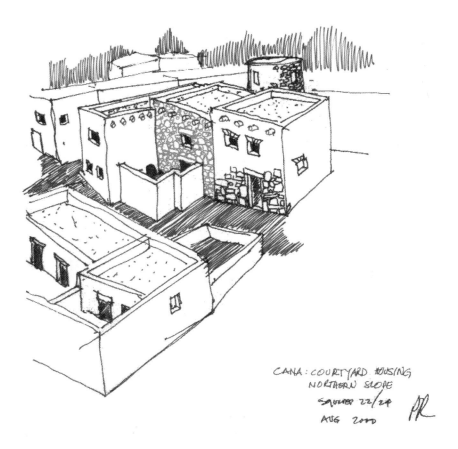

CANA: COURTYARD HOUSING
NORTHERN SLOPE
SQUARE 22/24
AUG 2000

Plate 11. Khirbet Qana, perspective, courtyard housing on north, view to northeast. The house
in the center of the sketch, with a street-level room and courtyard, is partially excavated.
The opening off the courtyard is the mikveh. A kitchen occupied the excavated parts of the room,
with bench and small hewn storage cave. In the rear is a columbarium.

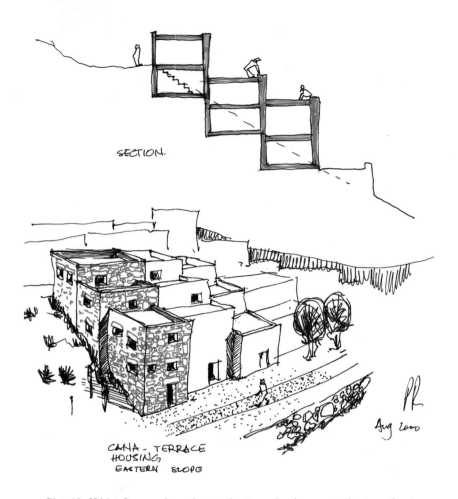

SECTION.

CANA - TERRACE
HOUSING
EASTERN SLOPE

PR
Aug 2000

Plate 12. *Khirbet Qana, section and perspective, terrace housing on east, view to northwest.
The terrace housing at Khirbet Qana, like that at Yodefat and Gamla, was densely packed,
with no courtyards. Common walls supported the beams of two adjacent houses; the roofs
became part of the living space.*

Plate 13. Khirbet Qana, east side, terrace housing, view to southwest. The wall in the foreground served two houses, supporting the floor beams of both. Notches are still evident between the top two courses. The basement of the higher-level house has survived, with early Roman walls and Byzantine period flagstone floor and steps.

Plate 14. Khirbet Qana, north side, courtyard housing, view to north. The courtyard in the left foreground had a very large bell-shaped cistern, and an early Roman mikveh (the opening left of center). The main level of the Byzantine-period house on the right, through a collapsed doorway, served as a kitchen: a bench or "counter" is visible in the middle and a storage cave on the right edge.

Plate 15. Capital, Khirbet Qana, hilltop. The capital, an unusual mock-Ionic design decorated with hanging fruit (?), belongs to a monumental building. It was found in situ, but in secondary construction, in the north wall of a rebuilt structure, and was dislodged by looters. The photo has been turned ninety degrees.

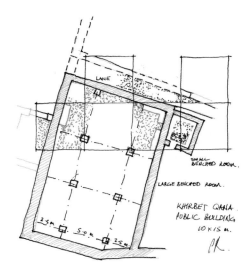

Plate 16. Khirbet Qana, plan, monumental public building. The room was 10x15 m with partial benches, and columns breaking the space into a central 5 m wide unpaved space and plastered aisles of 2.5 m. Beside its northeast corner was a small benched room, about 3x5 m. It was likely a first- or second-century C.E. synagogue and Beth ha-Midrash. The light lines indicate the excavated squares.

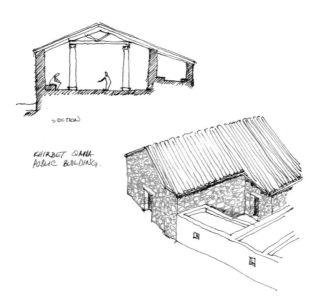

SECTION

KHIRBET QANA
PUBLIC BUILDING.

Plate 17. Khirbet Qana, section and sketch, monumental public building. The building probably
had a simple pitched roof, which may have extended to cover the adjacent benched building as well.
The roof was tiled with typical Roman tiles; the interior walls may have been frescoed,
to judge from a small fragment.

Plate 18. Khirbet Qana, small benched room, hilltop, view to east. A small, 3x5 m room,
was located higher than and east of a large monumental room with benches. The floor was carved
bedrock and the walls were plastered; a door (later blocked up) was on the south.
It may have been a Beth ha-Midrash.

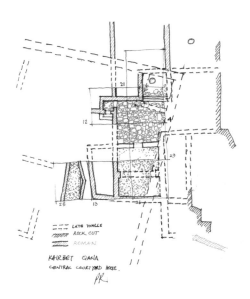

Plate 19. Khirbet Qana, plan, central courtyard house on hilltop. Seven squares were excavated to understand this building and the street pattern. To judge from the pilaster with well-executed capital, a (hypothesized) arch, and the size of the room of which it was a part, the house was larger and better finished than most. Its main entrance was from a lane on the west and its cistern in the room north of the courtyard.

Plate 20. Khirbet Qana, hilltop, capital with pilaster, view to the northwest.
A large room in a better finished courtyard house would have had an arch springing from the pilaster across the middle of the room to increase its size. A corresponding pilaster on the other side of the room has not yet been found. The room had a plastered floor, plastered walls, and opened onto a paved courtyard to the north.

Plate 21. Gamla, terrace housing below synagogue, view to northwest. The walls survive almost two full stories and show clearly the character of such houses. The projecting stones (consoles) about two meters from the floor on both side walls carried basalt beams for the construction of the second floor. The opening is a storage cupboard in the wall.

Plate 22. Gamla, terrace housing, below ridge. This section of housing was from the Hasmonean period and may not have been occupied during the Revolt. The middle wall shows the construction techniques at that period, with long "headers" bonding the wall for stability.

Plate 23. Capernaum, insula, *view to south. The houses were irregularly organized within "blocks," most having a small courtyard. The rooms were small; roofs and floors were made mainly of packed mud and sticks, on small beams. The vertical stones with beams are "window walls," characteristic of construction in much of the Golan and occasionally in the Galilee, as here and at nearby Chorazin.*

Plate 24. Capernaum, house west of synagogue, view to north. Courtyards were often paved with flagstones, as in this case, where the flagstoned area acts as an entrance to the house. The doorjambs and threshold were carefully finished, setting the occupants apart from the neighbors. The walls on either side show typical construction, with headers running across the wall.

*Plate 25. Gamla, synagogue, view to the northeast. This is the best example of an early syna-
gogue/communal building. Benches lined all four sides and wrapped around the entry
(lower left corner); there were five benches on the far wall. The floor was beaten earth; columns
(each with a differently designed capital) supported a simple pitched roof. There was a* mikveh
a few steps away.

*Plate 26. Masada, synagogue, view to northeast. Constructed during the First Revolt,
the synagogue was adapted from an existing room. The entry was taken into the main room,
a small room (on the left) was added as a* genizah, *and the columns were adjusted to suit the new
arrangement. Benches wrapped around the doorway, as they did at Gamla.*

Plate 27. Herodium, synagogue, view to east. Constructed during the First Revolt, this synagogue was inserted into Herod's triclinium in the upper palace, whose circular main tower can be seen in the background across the peristyle courtyard. The renovations included adding benches and building a new mikveh just outside the door to the left.

Plate 28. Qumran, benched room, view to southeast. This room with benches was a communal space, not unlike a synagogue. On the left is the entrance door, and beyond it a curious water installation at about waist height, presumably for ritual purity purposes. There were other communal rooms at Qumran, but this was the only benched room.

Plate 29. Jericho, synagogue, view to northeast. In the foreground is a mikveh with a large reservoir beside it, fed by a water channel (diagonally from the left crossing the main space) that entered the reservoir directly and the mikveh by a bypass. The structure was adapted from a house; perhaps the main space was originally a courtyard, since the raised platforms just outside the column bases were not typical of synagogue benches.

Plate 30. Sardis, synagogue, view to northwest. The Jewish community in Sardis adapted one wing of a bath/gymnasium/Imperial cult building for its needs. The peristyle atrium focused on a fountain; three doors led into the synagogue proper. On either side of the central door were the bema and Torah niche, whose tops still rise above the wall. A large table and an apse with tiered seating are through the door.

Plate 31. Priene, synagogue, view to east. A typical Hellenistic house near the end of West Gate Street was adapted to suit the needs of the Jewish community. The renovation included the benches in the foreground and a Torah niche in the wall across the middle, just out of the picture on the right.

Plate 32. Pergamon, Hall of Benches, upper city, view to southeast. The Dionysiac association housed in this building accommodated their needs with benches resembling two triclinia *facing each other. The benches were so high steps were needed to mount them. A white marble altar to Dionysus lies on its side in front of the doorway.*
(Photo courtesy of Steve Friesen.)

Plate 33. Pergamon, Philosophers' Association, theatral room, view to northeast.
This association is beside the Hall of Benches, directly on the processional way. A marble-panelled
entrance with inscriptions and statuary honoring the patron(s) was to the right of this unusual
theatral meeting space.

Plate 34. Ostia, synagogue, view to northwest. The view is across the entrance yard with its
wellhead to the main door, beyond which are four columns that monumentalized the approach
to the meeting hall. Beyond the two left columns was the Torah niche, a late addition.
The room in the left rear was a kitchen in later phases, but earlier it was a triclinium.

Plate 35. Siloan, hoard of Tyrian shekels. The container for the hoard is pictured, as well as a number of the shekels, with the god Melqart on one side and a Tyrian eagle on the other. A number of Tyrian coin hoards have been found in Judea, Galilee, and the Golan (e.g., in Gamla), implying their importance for paying the temple tax.

Plate 36. Jerusalem shekel, Bar Kokhba Revolt. Silver shekels and half shekels were minted during both revolts as a replacement for the use of Tyrian shekels. Some types minted during the Second Revolt, like this one, showed the temple's façade. Note the round-arched structure between the two middle columns, probably representing the ark.

Plate 37. Masada, Northern Palace, lower level. The engaged columns of the gazebo show Masada's construction techniques. The column with capital has a carefully carved capital on a less carefully built column of local stone. The columns were plastered, and the plaster was fluted and scored to look as if it was monolithic; the plaster is visible just below the capital and at the bottom of several columns.

Plate 38. Masada. Western Palace courtyard, plastered wall. The typical wall construction was randomly laid, locally available stone. In areas intended to impress, as in the palaces, the walls were plastered and scored to look like massive masonry construction, similar to the Jerusalem temple, with drafted margins and flat, raised bosses.

Plate 39. Jerusalem, colonnaded street, to east. Tunneled excavations exposed a street running parallel to the western wall of the temple. At the north end of the tunnel two finely carved Doric columns were found still in situ, providing a good impression of the quality of Jerusalem's colonnaded streets in the first century.

Plate 40. Jerusalem, Robinson's Arch, western wall area. Four first-century B.C.E. *shops filled a pier that carried the outer end of an arch at the southwest corner of the temple. The masonry was dressed like the masonry supporting the* peribolos *wall. Above the door lintels were semicircular "relieving arches" to distribute the heavy loads from above. The paving, with surface drains, was completed in the first century* C.E.

Plate 41. Jerusalem, Huldah Gates, southern wall area, view to north. Only the middle and left stones in the picture are from the Herodian building; the rest are later repairs and blocking. The vertical moldings are the left doorjamb of the eastern Huldah Gate, and show the finely carved finishes typical of the temple construction.

Plate 42. Jerusalem, Haram al-Sharif, view to north. The viewpoint is from in front of the al-Aqsa mosque, looking across what was the Court of Gentiles to the magnificent Dome of the Rock. The stairs in the foreground are in the same position as the main pilgrim route that led from the Huldah Gate tunnel up to the courtyards.

Plate 43. Jerusalem, plaza at southern wall, view to west. The plaza (reconstructed) was reached from the stairs in the background, many of which are original and were cut from the bedrock. In the foreground was a complex of mikvaoth *for ritual purity purposes. The western Huldah Gate was just behind the cluster of people.*

Plate 44. Jerusalem, Hecht Museum, architectural fragment. This piece of a low-vaulted, domed ceiling slab came from the Huldah Gates (or possibly a similar construction). The quality of the low relief work is remarkably fine, and is one of the few surviving remnants to give a sense of the artistic character of the decoration.

Plate 45. Jerusalem, eastern foundations of temple, view to west. Herod's southern extension of the temenos *is reflected in the "seam" just north of the southeast corner. On the right of the seam is Hasmonean masonry, on the left Herodian masonry. In the upper left corner the beginning of a vaulted exit from the temple is visible, matching the exit at Robinson's Arch.*

Plate 46. Jerusalem, northeast corner of peribolos *wall, view to west. Several periods of wall construction are obvious in this photograph. The join at the right marks the corner of the* temenos. *Herodian masonry is visible in the bottom four courses in the middle of the picture, establishing the original line of the north wall.*

Plate 47. Jerusalem, Akeldama tombs. This tomb chamber had three loculi in a decorated wall that may allude to the temple. Framing the middle loculus was a nicely decorated door, whose jamb was similar to the jambs at the Huldah Gates. The arched opening in the upper register, under a pedimented roof, is reminiscent of the arch in the Bar Kokhba coins.

Plate 48. Jerusalem, Akeldama tombs. The low vaulted ceiling decoration in one of the tomb chambers created an aura of opulence. It replicated the effect of the low-vaulted ceilings in the Huldah Gates, though it is not as finely carved as those panels.

Plate 49. Jerusalem, Akeldama tombs. The dromos *and main door of one of the tomb chambers sits almost underneath the modern Monastery of St. Onuphrias. The doorway is an excellent example of plain but carefully carved moldings. These tombs look directly up the City of David to the southern wall of the temple and the Huldah Gates.*

Plate 50. *Jerusalem, Absalom's Tomb, Kidron Valley. Located in one of the most exclusive parts of Jerusalem's necropolis, both Absalom's Tomb and Hezekiah's tomb looked directly up to the southeast corner of the temple. The concave, circular roof (no doubt intended as a* nefesh) *was built of masonry; the remaider was rock-cut.*

Plate 51. Jerusalem, Hezekiah's tomb, Kidron Valley. Hezekiah's tomb also looked directly up to the temple from the other side of valley. The pyramid-shaped nefesh *was entirely carved from bedrock; there are no chambers directly connected with the tomb. The rock-cut façade was the Tomb of the Sons of Hezir. Its rather fine Doric porch opened into a large set of tomb chambers.*

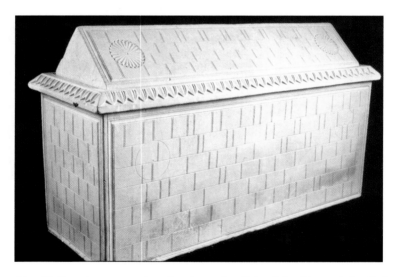

Plate 52. Jerusalem, ossuary. A number of ossuaries, all from before 70 C.E., had stylized representation of monumental masonry on some or all sides. The intention seems to be deliberately to imitate the masonry of the Herodian temple. This example has very fine moldings on the corners and around the lid; its lid has a rosette decoration.
(Rockefeller Museum collection.)